"Evangelicals have always been pe[...] [...] they have loved and tried to live [...] [...] bible. Some have done so as highly learned theological exegetes. Most have been more simple hearers and doers of the Word. But no matter their ethnicity, race, gender, or social class, they have done their best, when at their best, to honor every 'leaf, line, and letter' of the Scriptures. This all-star cast of first-rate scholars and associates of David Bebbington, one of the most important evangelical scholars of our age, has compiled the best collection of short essays ever written on the diversity of evangelical uses of the Bible. This book is a must-read for serious students of evangelicalism, their study of the Scriptures, and the historiographical legacies of Bebbington himself."

Douglas A. Sweeney, dean and professor of divinity, Beeson Divinity School, Samford University

"Those readers, whether friendly or hostile to evangelicals, who imagine that there is one standard 'evangelical' approach to the Bible will receive a salutary surprise from this volume of essays. Each piece is of high scholarly level, marking an advance in its own area; together they demonstrate that the relation of evangelicals to the Bible has always been relative to history, geography, politics, and culture, and that this contextual shaping of the evangelical mind is especially true of the new generation of evangelicals in the Global South. Yet the reader is enabled to recognize an evangelical identity in all the diversity and is left with a greater understanding of how, for evangelicals, this stems from a confidence that the biblical text has the capacity to transform human lives. The book is itself an outstanding example of a new era of evangelical scholarship and demands to be taken into account henceforth by all who presume to write about 'evangelicals,' an achievement which is due in no small measure to its skillful compilation by Timothy Larsen."

Paul S. Fiddes, professor of systematic theology, University of Oxford, and author of *A Unicorn Dies*

"In *Every Leaf, Line, and Letter*, an all-star list of contributors offers fresh insight into how evangelicals across time, space, and cultures share an emphasis on Scripture and yet interpret the Bible in a rich variety of ways. This volume is a feast that will tantalize and satisfy all sorts of readers, from the casual browser to the rigorous scholar. A welcome addition to every library of evangelical studies."

Candy Gunther Brown, professor of religious studies at Indiana University and author of *The Word in the World: Evangelical Writing, Publishing, and Reading in America, 1789-1880*

"One could hardly ask for a more interesting and comprehensive set of essays on the role of the Bible in evangelical life. It is a historical anthology that 'gets into the weeds' without getting lost—meaning each essay prompts one to think about contemporary biblical issues that evangelicals wrestle with today."

Mark Galli, former editor in chief of *Christianity Today*

"It's not exactly true that this book explores *Every Leaf, Line, and Letter* of the Bible, as if such a project were even possible in a single volume. But the dozen contributions still offer a dazzling range of acute and informative studies of evangelical uses of Scripture over the past three centuries, all rooted in exemplary scholarship. Global and transnational themes are very well covered, and the authors show admirable concern with perennial themes of race and empire, of gender and social justice. The resulting book is both valuable and provocative."

Philip Jenkins, Baylor University

Every Leaf, Line, and Letter

Evangelicals and the Bible from the 1730s to the Present

Edited by Timothy Larsen

Introduction by Thomas S. Kidd

IVP Academic

An imprint of InterVarsity Press
Downers Grove, Illinois

InterVarsity Press
P.O. Box 1400, Downers Grove, IL 60515-1426
ivpress.com
email@ivpress.com

InterVarsity Press® is the book-publishing division of InterVarsity Christian Fellowship/USA®, a movement of students and faculty active on campus at hundreds of universities, colleges, and schools of nursing in the United States of America, and a member movement of the International Fellowship of Evangelical Students. For information about local and regional activities, visit intervarsity.org.

Scripture quotations, unless otherwise noted, are from the Holy Bible, Authorized King James Version.

The publisher cannot verify the accuracy or functionality of website URLs used in this book beyond the date of publication.

Cover design and image composite: Cindy Kiple
Interior design: Jeanna Wiggins
Image: © desifoto / DigitalVision Vectors / Getty Images

ISBN 978-0-8308-4175-2 (print)
ISBN 978-0-8308-4176-9 (digital)

Printed in the United States of America ♾

InterVarsity Press is committed to ecological stewardship and to the conservation of natural resources in all our operations. This book was printed using sustainably sourced paper.

Library of Congress Cataloging-in-Publication Data
A catalog record for this book is available from the Library of Congress.

P	25	24	23	22	21	20	19	18	17	16	15	14	13	12	11	10	9	8	7	6	5	4	3	2	1
Y	39	38	37	36	35	34	33	32	31	30	29	28	27	26	25	24	23	22	21						

For *David Bebbington*

Scholar, mentor, and friend

"I was filled with a pineing desire to see Christs own words in the bible. . . .
I got along to the window where my bible was and I opened it and the first
place I saw was the 15th Chap: John—on Christs own words and they spake
to my very heart and every doubt and scruple that rose in my heart about the
truth of Gods word was took right off; and I saw the whole train of Scriptures
all in a Connection, and I believe I felt just as the Apostles felt the truth of the
word when they writ it, every leaf line and letter smiled in my face; I got the
bible up under my Chin and hugged it; it was sweet and lovely; the word was
nigh me in my hand, then I began to pray and to praise God."

THE SPIRITUAL TRAVELS OF NATHAN COLE, 1765

Contents

Introduction

Thomas S. Kidd

THERE IS SEEMINGLY NO END to definitions of the term *evangelical*. But it would be hard to imagine any sufficient definition of an evangelical Christian that did not include a reference to the Bible. In the words of the prophet Zechariah, evangelicals have always been Christians who carry "the burden of the word of the Lord." That mandate has included Bible reading, Bible preaching, and Bible distribution, among many other Bible-centered practices. As this volume shows, however, the uses that evangelicals have made of the Bible are almost as varied as evangelicals themselves.

David Bebbington crafted the best-known definition of evangelicals: the so-called Bebbington Quadrilateral. As Bebbington outlined them in his landmark book, *Evangelicalism in Modern Britain* (1989), the four defining characteristics of evangelicals are activism, biblicism, conversionism, and crucicentrism (the centrality of the cross). Bebbington undoubtedly would give each of these four characteristics equal weight, but conversionism and biblicism are arguably the most distinctive characteristics of the four. Conversion, or being born again, is the entryway into life in Christ as an evangelical, and many of the most characteristic practices of converted believers and their churches center on the Bible.[1]

We could multiply examples of the connection between conversion and the Bible for evangelicals (and in the longer Reformed and Augustinian traditions), but consider the experience of Connecticut farmer Nathan Cole, who

---

[1] David Bebbington, *Evangelicalism in Modern Britain: A History from the 1730s to the 1980s* (London: Routledge, 1989), 2-3.

went through a long conversion travail after hearing the great evangelist George Whitefield preach in the early 1740s. Cole wrote in his conversion testimony that when he broke through to assurance of salvation, his "heart was broken; my burden was fallen off my mind; I was set free." Instantly he wanted to "see Christ's own words in the Bible," and when he began to read, it was a delightful experience like he had never had before. "Every leaf, line, and letter smiled in my face," he wrote. "I got the Bible up under my chin and hugged it." He began to pray and to praise God for the new life he had in Christ, mediated by new understanding of the Bible.[2]

Instead of discussing evangelicals generally, or even all four of the Quadrilateral's characteristics, this volume focuses on *evangelicals and the Bible*. That theme allows us to emphasize that amid the vast ethnic, denominational, geographic, and cultural differences among evangelicals around the world, there are characteristics and habits that still sufficiently mark certain Protestant Christians to identify them as evangelicals. In America, the term *evangelical* has now become inextricably connected to Republican politics, to an extent that puzzles and disturbs many scholars as well as some evangelicals, including many outside the United States. Although White American evangelical voters' attachment to the Republican Party is an important story, in global and historical perspective there is much more to say about what has made an evangelical an evangelical than politics. There's no better place to start with evangelical identity than examining the uses that evangelicals— including men and women of many nations and ethnicities, but increasingly those of the Global South—have made of the Bible.

Befitting the broader chronological and geographic trajectory of the evangelical movement, this volume begins with the Bible and Anglo-American evangelicals of the eighteenth century, but moves out to consider the experiences of African American evangelicals, and then (especially in the case of the chapters written by Brian Stanley and John Maiden) to offer broad perspectives regarding biblicism and global evangelical development in the twentieth and even twenty-first century. As always in such discussions, pastors and published writers receive a lot of attention here, but the contributors also balance the experiences of men and women, the famous and the obscure, in

---

[2]Thomas S. Kidd, ed., *The Great Awakening: A Brief History with Documents* (Boston: Bedford/ St. Martin's, 2007), 63-64.

order to get a deeper sounding of what difference the Bible has made in evangelicals' beliefs, experiences, and religion as they actually lived it.

The scholars writing for this volume assume, with Bebbington, that whatever precedents there were for evangelical piety in the older Protestant and Augustinian traditions, evangelical faith represented a significantly new development in the era of the Great Awakening (beginning in the 1730s). Bible reading and interpretation was inescapably central to that development, but evangelical biblicism was also immediately contested. Bruce Hindmarsh's chapter shows that while evangelicals are often characterized by scholars and journalists as taking a "literal" or "commonsense" reading of Scripture, they also could employ a "figurative" reading when text, disposition, or circumstance warranted it. This figurative reading was the practice of evangelicals from little-known English Methodist women to Jonathan Edwards, whose grand typological readings of Scripture represented a response to aspects of the Enlightenment that seemed to be marginalizing God in the world. As Jonathan Yeager shows, however, Edwards's interpretations of Scripture did not yield universal affirmation, even from some of his most admiring correspondents, such as the Reverend John Erskine of Edinburgh. Common devotion to the Bible, even among people from such common intellectual and cultural circles as Edwards and Erskine, did not necessarily produce agreement on such fundamental questions as the nature of salvation. Kristina Benham illustrates the dizzying variety of uses that evangelical writers could make of a single biblical narrative such as the exodus. When the politics and struggles of the American Revolutionary era intruded, evangelicals spun a host of creative and sometimes contradictory uses of such biblical narratives, and conflicting ideas about their contemporary applications.

Moving into the nineteenth century, Elise Leal's chapter shows that evangelical leaders desperately wanted children and teenagers to become familiar with the Bible and to create a "children's Bible culture." Adult sponsors of the American Sunday school movement labored to achieve transmission of Scripture across the generational divide (a perennial challenge for each generation of evangelicals), but they were never quite certain how much to view or empower Sunday school pupils and young teachers as religious agents in their own right. Mark Noll's examination of the near-simultaneous emergence of anti- and pro-slavery biblical arguments during America's antebellum era extends the point that biblicism did not always lead to agreement among evangelicals, especially evangelicals of differing regional identities and economic interests. Noll also suggests just how much historical circumstances—such as the crises over the admission of Missouri to the Union and the alleged Denmark Vesey slave revolt in Charleston in the 1820s—could affect Bible interpretation.

Mary Riso focuses our attention on the piety of one evangelical Bible reader—Josephine Butler, a prominent English women's rights reformer of the late 1800s. Butler encapsulated the individualistic, quasi-mystical, and enormously powerful engine that was evangelical biblicism. The life of evangelical faith undergirded Butler's energetic career as a writer and political activist. David Bebbington's contribution to this book illustrates, in classic Bebbington fashion, the enduring mandate to defend the "divine authority, truth, and integrity of the whole Bible," which drew on a striking range of British evangelicals and fundamentalists in the 1920s. Bebbington shows that the evangelical campaign to defend the Bible against the perceived assaults of modernist thought was hardly limited to American denominations and seminaries in the era of the fundamentalist-modernist conflict. It was a cause taken up throughout the Anglophone world. England's Bible League united a remarkable cohort of British churches and parachurch organizations, including ministries for soldiers and policemen, Protestant (anti-Catholic) alliances, associations for premillennial theology, Jewish evangelization societies, and more. Timothy Larsen's chapter reminds us, however, that there has always been tension between the *category* of evangelical, and the *name* evangelical. He illustrates this dilemma by reference to the early twentieth century's "Liberal Evangelical" cohort in the Church of England, especially Vernon Storr, who for much of his ministry was a Canon of Westminster. Storr and his followers enthusiastically embraced the moniker "evangelical" and promoted three of the four attributes in the Quadrilateral—all of them except biblicism. The Liberal Evangelicals were thoroughly modernist in their view of Scripture, with Storr even endorsing the higher critical opinions of one of America's most forceful leaders on the modernist side in the fight with fundamentalism, Harry Emerson Fosdick.

Malcolm Foley returns to the American scene and the acute racial tensions there within the evangelical community. He focuses on the post-Reconstruction era, which is often regarded as the "nadir" of race relations in American history. Foley introduces the great African American pastor-theologian Francis Grimké, who never used "evangelical" to describe himself yet embraced all the traits of the Quadrilateral (again, we see tension between the label and the category of evangelical). Foley considers how evangelicals of different races, who agreed on evangelical essentials, reached such starkly different conclusions on social and political issues, including the widespread lynching of African Americans. For Grimké, Foley explains, "the problem with an American Christianity that allowed lynching to continue was that it was a Christianity that was not evangelical enough."

Moving closer to present day, Catherine Brekus examines an American evangelical biblicism that seems a far cry from Grimké's—the biblicism exemplified by *The American Patriot's Bible* (2009). As Brekus shows, the militarism and nationalism exemplified by this study Bible resonates with many evangelicals today, especially White American evangelicals. But it stands in demonstrably stark contrast with much of the American history it claims to defend. Even some other White American evangelicals today regard this kind of biblicism as "idolatrous" and aberrant. John Maiden introduces yet another kind of evangelical biblicism: that of the charismatic renewal movement of the late twentieth century, with focus on Britain and New Zealand. While charismatics and Pentecostals are often marginalized in discussions of evangelicalism and biblicism, Maiden contends that there was a "charismatic reanimation of Scripture" that accounted for much of the movement's appeal to believers. The effort to integrate "pneumatic experience" and biblicism is a notable example of how the ministry of the Holy Spirit has sometimes competed for status as a fifth defining element of evangelical piety, especially if one accounts for the surging prominence of charismatics and Pentecostals in the global Christian movement.

That movement is the subject of Brian Stanley's concluding chapter, which not only assesses Bebbington's historiographical legacy, but considers the fate of the Quadrilateral—including biblicism—since the Global South has become the primary locus of evangelical, Pentecostal, and Christian growth generally. In a fitting finish to the book, Stanley concludes that the local believers of the Global South have tested some limits of the Quadrilateral's undergirding assumptions, such as the mandates of literacy and printed texts in biblicism. Yet "evangelical forms of Christianity have frequently proved unwittingly responsive to the cultural environment in which they seek to discharge their mission," Stanley writes. Bebbington's defining traits of evangelicalism have often become incarnated in surprisingly flexible ways in Africa, Asia, and Latin America, but their adherents have remained recognizably evangelical nonetheless.

Part One

The Eighteenth Century

1

British Exodus, American Empire

Evangelical Preachers and the Biblicisms of Revolution

Kristina Benham

IN 1760, ON A DAY OF THANKSGIVING, David Hall, an itinerant preacher and minister of Sutton, Massachusetts, preached a sermon titled "Israel's Triumph," a response of praise and thanksgiving for God's providential victory in favor of British forces in Canada during the Seven Years' War. He took as his text the song of praise by the Israelites after the drowning of Pharaoh in the Red Sea, comparing the British colonies and empire to the people of God in opposition to their French Catholic enemies. "A vast and fertile country is now subject to the British Sovereignty. . . . And the Lord shall hasten the day when the Gospel shall run and be glorified; that it may prevail from the east to the western ocean; and from the rivers to the utmost limits of our North America."[1] Sixteen years later, on July 4, 1776, the Continental Congress set up a committee that included Benjamin Franklin, Thomas Jefferson, and John Adams to propose a seal for the brand new American nation. Though their version was never adopted, the committee later reported on a design including a depiction of the presence of God in a pillar of fire

---

[1]David Hall, *Israel's Triumph* (Boston, 1761), 6-8, 10-11, 16.

and Moses standing at the Red Sea as the waters overwhelmed the monarch Pharaoh.[2] Just months before Adams had written to his wife, Abigail, that he heard a sermon by Presbyterian minister George Duffield of Philadelphia, former assistant to Great Awakening preacher Gilbert Tennent and then chaplain to the Continental Congress. The sermon Adams heard compared the actions of King George to Pharaoh's oppression of the Israelites. Adams admitted to feeling awe at participating in what Duffield concluded was God's providential design to drive the American colonies to independence.[3] At the accomplishment of peace in 1783 and on a day of thanksgiving appointed by Congress, Duffield again made the comparison between the exodus and American deliverance. This "American Zion" was a nation that had been born at once and had "brought forth her children, more numerous than the tribes of Jacob, to possess the land, from the north to the south, and from the east to the yet unexplored, far distant west."[4]

In the years between these points, the exodus narrative became one of the most important ways that Americans applied biblical knowledge to understanding their transition from British colonies to a new nation. While reviving a deep English tradition of Hebraic nationalism, Americans set themselves up for a providential interpretation of deliverance from British rule. In the exodus they at first sought a principled, nonrebellious defense of resistance, but they tapped into a ready revolutionary potential that was unleashed with the opening of war and the Declaration of Independence. Providential applications, however, could take multiple forms, and the years of resistance and revolution provoked competing national providential ap-plications of the exodus narrative. Before independence, uses of the exodus to explain oppression and warn both rulers and subjects of God's judgment appealed to a timeless principle of judicial providence. This interpretation could be used to criticize British rulers and hope for God's intervention, but it could also be used to turn criticism on American society itself, especially to address chattel slavery. While these interpretations continued to hold

---

[2]"IV. Report of the Committee," *The Papers of Thomas Jefferson Digital Edition*, ed. James P. McClure and J. Jefferson Looney (Charlottesville: University of Virginia Press, 2008–2017), https://rotunda. upress.virginia.edu/founders/TSJN-01-01-02-0206-0004.

[3]John Adams to Abigail Adams, May 17, 1776, in *The Book of Abigail and John: Selected Letters of the Adams Family, 1762-1784*, L. H. Butterfield, Marc Friedlaender, and Mary-Jo Kline, eds. (Cambridge, MA: Harvard University Press, 1975), 129-30.

[4]George Duffield, *A Sermon Preached in the Third Presbyterian Church* (Philadelphia, 1784), 5-6.

broad appeal, the experience of civil war and the declaration and peaceful settlement of independence led Americans to the application of a historical providence in God's deliverance of his particular people and divine purpose for their new nation.[5] This chapter makes three claims. (1) The exodus was a particularly important biblical narrative for the process of revolution and independence. (2) The ways Americans used the exodus in their revolutionary context changed significantly over a very short span of time. (3) There were distinct, and sometimes competing, categories of religious-political inter-pretation, or biblicism, involved in the American Revolution and the exodus narrative: biblically identifying political oppression, warnings, and lessons about God's judgment (against Americans and British alike), hoping in or claiming providential victory, and identifying the new American nation as the people of God.

In late-colonial American history, identifying evangelicalism based on biblicism is far from straightforward. American culture from colonial begin-nings through the American Civil War was suffused with biblical principles, references, and arguments. Mark Noll's synthesis of American Protestantism throughout these periods is closely tied to evangelical reliance on the Bible alone for religious authority.[6] More specifically, in *American Zion*, Eran Shalev examines the distinct version of Hebraic Biblicism developed in America in the late-eighteenth and nineteenth centuries, through other lessons and par-allels applied to public life from several major points in Hebrew history.[7] Historians who have studied, more specifically, the Bible during the American Revolution find that a diverse range of people among the founding generation— from evangelical chaplains to theologically liberal ministers to deist political thinkers—turned to biblical allusions, warnings, parallels, and principles on a regular basis.[8] For example, James P. Byrd's analysis of the most commonly used passages of Scripture during the Revolution emphasizes the military

---

[5]For discussion of the different kinds of providence described here see Nicholas Guyatt, *Providence and the Invention of the United States, 1607-1876* (New York: Cambridge University Press, 2007).

[6]Mark Noll, *America's God: from Jonathan Edwards to Abraham Lincoln* (New York: Oxford University Press, 2002), 11-12.

[7]Eran Shalev, *American Zion: The Old Testament as a Political Text from the Revolution to the Civil War* (New Haven: Yale University Press, 2013).

[8]James P. Byrd, *Sacred Scripture, Sacred War: The Bible and the American Revolution* (New York: Oxford University Press, 2013); Daniel L. Dreisbach, *Reading the Bible with the Founding Fathers* (New York: Oxford University Press, 2016).

applications of biblical history and New Testament justifications. It is significant to the argument here to note that Byrd found the exodus to be the second most cited biblical passage of the era, and he concludes that "no biblical narrative surpassed the exodus in identifying the major themes, plots, characters, and subplots of the Revolution."[9] This chapter, a close study of the exodus narrative as it was used during the era of the American Revolution, echoes these findings. The types of sources used range widely, including especially newspapers and sermons, but also letters, diaries, poems, and Congressional proclamations and proposals. Evangelical preachers relied on the exodus narrative as a biblical pairing with arguments from natural rights and British constitutional tradition. David Avery, the military chaplain who held his arms aloft in prayer over the Battle of Bunker Hill like Moses over the Israelite battle with Amalek, was one such example.[10] But others who were far from evangelicalism also picked up the parallel as relevant to the nation. Charles Chauncy, a Unitarian Congregationalist from Boston, testified to the widespread cry during the Stamp Act crisis, "We shall be made to serve as bond-servants; our lives will be bitter with hard bondage," which he compared to the plight of the Jews in Egypt before God delivered them.[11] Decades later, with the Revolution settled and the new nation surviving constitutional upheaval, the exodus and America as the new Israel lived on. In 1805, in his second inaugural address, Thomas Jefferson appealed to the help of God, whom he described thus: "in whose hands we are, who led our forefathers, as Israel of old, from their native land, and planted them in a country flowing with all the necessaries and comforts of life; who has covered our infancy with his providence, and our riper years with his wisdom and power."[12]

Evangelical preaching, however, had a distinct prominence in these uses of the exodus. Nearly every sermon in this chapter comes from an evangelical preacher (with the possible exception of Phillips Payson, for whom there is little immediate information, and two others who are likely, but not guaranteed, evangelicals: Stephen Johnson and Elijah Fitch). Newspaper sources

---

[9]Byrd, *Sacred Scripture, Sacred War,* 47; see table of biblical passages on 170.

[10]Thomas S. Kidd, *God of Liberty: A Religious History of the American Revolution* (New York: Basic Books, 2010), 1-2.

[11]Charles Chauncy, "Good News from a Far Country," in *The Pulpit of the American Revolution* (Boston: Gould and Lincoln, 1860), 129.

[12]Thomas Jefferson, "Second Inaugural Address," The Avalon Project, Inaugural Addresses of the Presidents of the United States, http://avalon.law.yale.edu/19th_century/jefinau2.asp.

are much harder to identify, since common practice was to publish controversial issues anonymously and often even to mask the real author as a very different character. Though touching on other specific concerns, newspapers using the exodus followed many of the same arguments as these sermons. Therefore, by following the transition in uses of the exodus during the American Revolution, these sources reveal that biblicism could mean quite different things, especially when applied to national purposes. Admonitions for repentance in the face of national judgment, hope in God's providential purposes through suffering and victory, and claims to divine national identity are quite different types of interpretation. This is, of course, leaving out entirely the variety of interpretations of the exodus that evangelicals such as Jonathan Edwards or Hannah Heaton or Sarah Osborne used, which were almost entirely focused on personal sanctification, prayers for the spiritual transformation of the people within the nation, typologies of redemption in Christ, or prophecies of the final glorification of the church.[13]

The story of the exodus of Israel from Egypt as Americans used it in the Revolutionary era can be divided into four major interpretations: oppression, divine judgment, providential victory, and the emergence of the people of God. And these interpretations connect directly to the ways that uses of the exodus narrative changed. Americans, at first unwillingly on the road to political independence, increasingly adopted this biblical story as a parallel to their own situation in all of these four ways. In earlier uses of the story during the Stamp Act crisis and the years immediately following, colonists explained what seemed like an inexplicable change in imperial policy with principles of political oppression and navigated the dangerous ideological waters of disobedience to authority with justifications for biblical resistance. They also perceived what seemed like intentional attacks on their rights and resources and the havoc of war as suffering that confirmed the justness of

---

[13]A survey of the works of Jonathan Edwards by search terms shows that Edwards emphasized especially the example and sinful qualities of Pharaoh and also the typology of redemption in Christ. See the Jonathan Edwards Center at Yale University online: http://edwards.yale.edu/. Barbara E. Lacey, ed., *The World of Hannah Heaton: The Diary of an Eighteenth-Century Farm Woman* (DeKalb, IL: Northern Illinois University Press, 2003). Hannah used the exodus to pray for comfort for those in Separate churches and as a comfort to herself that Jesus would lead her, diary page 35 (31-32) and 346 (214). Sarah Osborn did address the exodus to the Seven Years' War and the American Revolution in her written prayers for her country. Catherine A. Brekus, ed., *Sarah Osborn's Collected Writings* (New Haven: Yale University Press, 2017), 141, 320.

their cause and indicated the judgments of God against them for sins. Suffering, however, was also a tool in God's hands to bring about his plan for his people, whether repentance, expansion, or independence. Warnings of judgment, however, came most easily for wicked and hard-hearted rulers, whose apparent reckless pride destined them for ruin. And in this judgment colonists encouraged each other to trust in God's eventual deliverance from oppression. God's miraculous victory over their enemies became more relevant as the newly independent states fought what started as a civil war against a superior force with no powerful allies. With each step toward victory—independence, the flight of the British from Boston, the alliance with France, and peace on terms of two independent nations—Americans perceived the hand of God. Finally, looking back on what appeared to be stunning victories and the sudden change in form of government and national identity, Americans thought of themselves religiously and politically as like the people of God. The narrative of miraculous intervention and national blessing and expansion which once applied to the British Empire, or regionally to Puritan forebears, now applied to the stunning event of a nation redeemed by God and born in a day.

By the end of the Seven Years' War, British Americans had already learned through several rounds of European colonial wars some of the national applications of the exodus story that would become central in the Revolutionary era. Ministers often applied the exodus to debates about the justness of war or in celebrations of God's apparent providential intervention in history. In 1747, Gilbert Tennent, Presbyterian minister of Philadelphia and Great Awakening evangelist, used the song of Moses at the Red Sea to assert God's approval of just wars. The exodus claim that "the Lord is a Man of War" settled the principle question, since something by which God was named could not contradict his character. Still, Tennent's argument indicates the conflict over religious and political meanings attached to British imperial goals, and he sought to outline how the approval of God could be identified by those who feared God as opposed to their enemies under the sway of the Antichrist. Just war decidedly excluded wars of ambition and glory for monarchs.[14] Likewise, though David Hall's 1760 thanksgiving sermon used the

---

[14]Gilbert Tennent, *The Late Association for Defence, Encourag'd, or The Lawfulness of a Defensive War* (Philadelphia, 1748).

song in Exodus as a celebration of complete victory in North America, Hall warned his audience against falling into the trap of sinful pride in their victory and not giving glory to God for his deliverance.[15] Before the Revolution, uses of the exodus fell more clearly along imperial lines. When these lines began to break apart under new imperial policy and the contradiction of the language of political slavery, Americans began to find many more meanings in the exodus.

The Stamp Act instigated the first major effort for political resistance before the Revolution, and colonists turned to the exodus story to argue through principles of political oppression why resistance was necessary and biblical. Colonists took practical and spiritual cues from this story. The draining of colonial money in a time of great debt left them in a worse position than the Israelites punished by Pharaoh with the task of making bricks without straw provided to them. They argued that at least the Israelites could go out and gather their own straw.[16] Throughout resistance and the war, Pharaoh's taskmasters and making bricks without straw became phrases synonymous with unreasonable and cruel impositions in response to humble petitions by loyal subjects.[17] Demonstrating the injustice of British policies and comparing them to the actions of Pharaoh, whose heart was hard against God in his plots to destroy the Israelites, made resistance righteous to colonists. Hebrew history revealed that God favored the people in the face of oppression, and the exodus was a prime example.

Americans used the exodus to understand increasing and unreasonable political burdens as evidence for political oppression and biblical sanction for resistance. In December of 1765, Connecticut held a day of fasting in response to the Parliamentary tax on paper goods in the colonies, which had not yet been repealed. Stephen Johnson, a Congregational minister of Lyme, preached a sermon for the occasion taken from the example of the Israelites in bondage in Egypt. From the story of the exodus, he drew four main points: that enslaving the people of God was a great sin, that Pharaoh's gradual

---

[15]David Hall, *Israel's Triumph*, 17.

[16]Anglo-Americanus, "To the Printer of the Virginia Gazette," *The Boston Post-Boy & Advertiser*, July 29, 1765.

[17]"To the King's Most Excellent Majesty," *The New-Hampshire Gazette, and Historical Chronicle*, December 8, 1769. "[Oppressions; Tears; Comforter; Judgment; Higher; Highest; Regardeth; King Solomon]," *The Connecticut Courant, and Hartford Weekly Intelligencer*, December 16, 1776. Sylvanus Conant, *An Anniversary Sermon Preached at Plymouth* (Boston, 1777), 26.

method of oppression was typical of tyrants, that God instructed the Israelites through their suffering, and that God finally delivered them from oppression.[18] The thrust of his argument was in coupling submission and dependence on God with justification for resisting rulers, traditionally assumed to be appointed by God. In this story, God clearly took the side of those under cruel and oppressive measures. Johnson drew a parallel between British policies and Pharaoh's attempt to stop the growth of the Israelite people. Parliamentary encroachments on rights and false accusations that the colonists schemed for independence were like Pharaoh fearing and attacking the growing strength of his subjects by setting taskmasters over them and having Israelite male infants murdered.[19] Clearly, Johnson argued, there were cases where civil authority must be resisted in order to obey God. Throughout the Revolution colonists praised the Hebrew midwives in Egypt who resisted the command to carry out the execution because they feared God.[20]

Colonists also carefully backed up their righteous resistance with new explanations of New Testament injunctions to obey civil authorities. Here more evangelical-leaning preachers used direct biblical precedents in conjunction with other ministers' revision of New Testament passages through Lockean theory. Johnson objected to the "doctrine of passive obedience and non-resistance to arbitrary, enslaving edicts," often endorsed through several New Testament passages. "Render to Caesar the things which are Caesar's," he countered, could not mean forfeiting what God had given in natural rights, nor could it mean the kind of obedience that was due only to God.[21] Therefore, any laws that contradicted God's revealed moral laws could not be rightly obeyed. He took a similar approach even to the more direct command: "Let every soul be subject to the higher powers . . . [for] The powers that be, are ordained of God, [and] Whosoever resisteth the power, resisteth the ordinance of God."[22] The higher powers, he insisted meant civil government and the rule of law, at least laws that were just. The key to understanding this assertion was the explanation in this New Testament passage that rulers were ordained

---

[18]Stephen Johnson, *Some Important Observations* (Newport, RI, 1766), 5.

[19]Johnson, *Some Important Observations*, 14, 50.

[20]David Jones, *Defensive War in a Just Cause Sinless* (Philadelphia, 1775), 14. Conant, *An Anniversary Sermon*, 11-12. Integer, "To the Printer," *The New-York Gazette; and the Weekly Mercury*, March 3, 1777.

[21]Johnson's quotation of Matthew 22:21.

[22]Johnson's quotation of Romans 13:1-2.

"for good," which Johnson and others understood to mean the common good found in the social compact to protect rights.[23] David Jones—who held a variety of pastoral positions in New Jersey and Pennsylvania as well as work as a Baptist missionary to Native Americans and chaplain in the American Revolution—preached a sermon on a fast day declared by the Continental Congress in 1775. In it he made similar points about obedience to authority. The "higher powers," he argued, meant constitutional laws and civil government as a means to "secure the property and promote the happiness of the whole community" and applied to both subjects and rulers. The Hebrew midwives who disobeyed Pharaoh and feared God were a perfect example of the principle that only laws that reflected the just nature of God could be considered God's ordinance. Jones even went so far as to assert that only the people can rightly judge that the laws are just.[24]

The exodus story held more explanatory power than could be found in principles of government and obedience alone. The example of Pharaoh's increasingly hard-hearted resistance to Israelite deliverance was important to understanding what seemed like unprovoked, secret plots against the colonies. Colonists often quoted Pharaoh plotting with his advisors, "Behold, the people of the children of Israel are more and mightier than we. Come, let us deal wisely with them; least they multiply, and it come to pass, that when there falleth out any war, they join also unto our enemies, and fight against us, and so get them up out of the land."[25] In contrast to parallels with the deliverance from Egypt in past sermons on British victories over Catholic enemies, Americans now saw a deeper betrayal than even the Israelites experienced, since this war was between Protestants and fellow subjects. Jealousy and false suspicions seemed the only explanation for such a falling out.[26] As the war progressed, Americans focused more on the unrighteous attributes of Pharaoh, as seen in particular rulers, beginning with local appointed officials and

---

[23]Johnson, *Some Important Observations*, 24-25. Byrd, *Sacred Scripture, Sacred War*, 123-27. Byrd explains that these New Testament passages were among the most quoted of the era, and that the argument that rulers were ordained of God "for good" was a key defense for resistance.

[24]Jones, *Defensive War in a Just Cause Sinless*, 12-14.

[25]Johnson, *Some Important Observations*, 14. Johnson's quotation of Exodus 1:9-10. Israel Evans, *A Discourse, Delivered, on the 18th Day of December, 1777* (Lancaster, PA, 1778), 7. Israel Evans, *A Discourse, Delivered in New-York* (New York, 1784), 10.

[26]Conant, *An Anniversary Sermon*, 24. George Duffield, *A Sermon Preached in the Third Presbyterian Church*, 4.

generals like Thomas Gage, and eventually denouncing the king himself as a wicked, murdering Pharaoh. The Egyptian tyrant was most commonly remembered as hard-hearted against just petitions and prideful in resisting God's ordered law and gift of natural rights. In the end, years of warfare could best be described, in American minds, as being executed by a ruler so against God and his people that he rushed madly to his own destruction in the Red Sea.[27]

Preachers and other Americans saw in the exodus not just the evil oppression of Pharaohs in their own time but the threat of judgment on tyrannical rulers. A subscriber to the *New-London Gazette* in 1771 expounded on the nature of plagues, asserting that the causes of them are "tyranny, oppression, and cruelty."[28] In the same year, "A Field Labourer" argued in the *Essex Gazette* that a good king keeps his Bible close to his heart and meditates on his duty and the fate of bad kings, that "Pharaoh was drowned in the Red Sea for oppressing the Israelites."[29] Sometimes God's judgment meant simply enforcing reciprocity, as when a fast day sermon in the *Connecticut Courant* claimed that God drowned Pharaoh for commanding the drowning of Hebrew children.[30] A series of widely reprinted newspaper reports about General Gage's occupation of Boston in 1775 called the British military leader a perfect example of Pharaoh and hoped he would meet the same judgment as that biblical tyrant.[31] Colonists occasionally continued to emphasize the threat of judgment against bad rulers even after independence and military success. In 1783, "Lucullus" responded to the king's speech before Parliament on the event of peace negotiations: "O,

---

[27]On changes in including the king in parallels to the exodus see the difference between "To the King's Most Excellent Majesty," *The New-Hampshire Gazette, and Historical Chronicle*, December 8, 1769 and Lucullus, "[No Headline]—A Few Reflections on Reading the King's Most Gracious Speech to His Parliament," *The Freeman's Journal: Or, the North-American Intelligencer*, March 5, 1783. Israel Holly, *God Brings about His Holy and Wise Purpose or Decree* (Hartford, CT, 1774), 14. "Extract of Another Letter from the Same Person, Dated April 10, 1775," *Dunlap's Pennsylvania Packet Or, the General Advertiser*, June 12, 1775. "Worcester, September 6," *The New-York Journal; Or, the General Advertiser*, September 14, 1775. "Philadelphia, Sept. 25," *SUPPLEMENT Connecticut Journal*, October 4, 1775. Cato, "To the People of Pennsylvania. Letter III," *The Pennsylvania Ledger: Or the Virginia, Maryland, Pennsylvania, & New-Jersey Weekly Advertiser*, March 23, 1776. "Hartford, July 17," *The Connecticut Courant, and Hartford Weekly Intelligencer*, July 17, 1775.
[28]"To the Printer. Plague," *The New-London Gazette*, January 11, 1771.
[29]A Field Labourer, "A Complaint," *The Essex Gazette*, November 19, 1771.
[30]"Fast Sermon, Concluded from Our Last," *The Connecticut Courant, and Hartford Weekly Intelligencer*, November 28, 1774.
[31]"Hartford, July 17," *The Connecticut Courant, and Hartford Weekly Intelligencer*, July 17, 1775. This was reprinted in at least four other newspapers. "Worcester, September 6," *The New-York Journal; Or, the General Advertiser*, September 14, 1775.

Pharaoh! How is it possible you can ever hope . . . [for reconciliation] with America; when after being so long called upon, by the good and wisest part of your nation, to let the people go, and your hard heart would not consent to it, continuing maliciously and wantonly to spill their blood . . . Repent! repent! and humble yourself immediately in the dust, murderer, if you wish to obtain mercy; and make all the restitution in your power, whilst you continue to exist."[32]

Oppression and war also led Americans to believe that God's judgment applied to themselves. The idea of plagues and other general calamities falling on an entire people had long suggested the need for general repentance. In the midst of his Exodus reading of British oppression in 1765, Stephen Johnson concluded, "We must piously and dutifully acknowledge the correction of God. . . . It is a great judgment of God upon a nation, when suffered to fall into very hurtful measures, which impoverish and tend to the slavery and ruin of a free people."[33] The writer on plagues in the *New-London Gazette* in 1771 also reminded his readers that the Israelites fell to plagues after leaving Egypt for their disobedience to God.[34] "J. P. Juvenus" appealed to young people in the *New-London Gazette* in 1771, arguing that British tyranny should concern them even more than their parents, since "as Pharaoh increased the burden of the Israelites, by degrees, so all other tyrants, add to the weight of their galling yoak." He encouraged youths to support the patriot cause by avoiding vice—including vanity, swearing, keeping bad company, Sabbath-breaking, and ridiculing religion, which were the cause of God's judgments—and to "humble ourselves for our sins, pursue the path of virtue, and exert ourselves . . . for the glorious cause of liberty."[35] And a deacon's letter from 1775 in the *Essex Journal* urged readers not to rejoice too soon and to re-member God's judgment to "a stubborn incorrigible people." In this letter, the typical use of the exodus was turned upside down, and Americans were the hard-hearted sinners. "Did the Almighty bring ten dreadful plagues upon Egypt before Pharaoh would let his slaves go? witness the consequence."[36]

---

[32]Lucullus, "[No Headline] A Few Reflections on Reading the King's Most Gracious Speech to His Parliament," *The Freeman's Journal: Or, the North-American Intelligencer*, March 5, 1783.

[33]Johnson, *Some Important Observations*, 36.

[34]"To the Printer. Plague," *The New-London Gazette*, January 11, 1771.

[35]"Mr. Green," [Mr. Green; Paper; Readers . . .], *The New-London Gazette*, August 9, 1771.

[36]Benjamin Colman, "The Following Letter, from Deacon Benjamin Colman, Is Inserted by Desire of Some, of Newbury Sept. 16, 1775," *Supplement to the Essex Journal and New-Hampshire Packet*, March 8, 1776.

The deacon's letter was more controversial than simply turning judgment on Americans, though. The reason that Americans were like hard-hearted Pharaoh was that they held actual slaves. The central theme of slavery and deliverance in the exodus story was useful for Americans who portrayed British policies as enslaving them but tricky when it came to facing their own slaveholding or complicity in it. In 1773 a writer to the *New-London Gazette* reminded his readers that Pharaoh's enslavement of the Israelites was "very provoking to God" and that "God's demand on Pharaoh was to let them go, and his refusing was the cause of God's controversy with him." The result was plagues and a final over-throw in the Red Sea. He continued, "May we not conclude that God has a controversy with us, and his demand on us is to let the Africans so long enslaved go free?" Surely, he concluded, this was the cause of God allowing their enemies in government to oppress them.[37] In a 1774 fictional letter in the *Connecticut Journal*, another writer used the same comparison. Writing as if from Pharaoh from beyond the grave, the subscriber addressed "Philemon," another contributor who had submitted a four-part series containing a biblical argument for slavery. Pharaoh praised his worthy friend in the land of the living for taking up the "glorious cause" of slavery, inverting Americans' common phrase "the glorious cause of liberty." Pharaoh recounted his own misunderstood position, calling Moses a cunning magician and using all the arguments for slavery common to American slaveholders. Instead of getting into difficult biblical passages and debates on slavery, the writer simply skewered his opponent's lengthy and detailed approach by comparing him to the wicked and hard-hearted Pharaoh, who oppressed the people of God and refused to acknowledge God himself.[38] Other Americans took a more seriously applied approach to the comparison, such as when Virginia Quakers petitioned the state legislature in 1782 against the re-enslavement of their former slaves. Since they had endured God's judgment in the war, "we earnestly desire to improve the present Prospect of Tranquility, and that it may not have the same effect upon us, as the respite of the Plagues had upon Pharaoh, who refused to let Israel go from under his Bondage."[39]

---

[37] A hearty friend to all the northern colonies, "To the Printer," *The New-London Gazette*, September 10, 1773. This article also cited excessive litigation as a cause for judgment. It is worth noting that the use of the exodus story against slavery in newspapers appeared almost exclusively in the northern and middle colonies, though newspaper printing in general was more prevalent there.

[38] "Pharaoh's Compliments to Philemon," *Supplement to the Connecticut Journal*, September 16, 1774.

[39] "Quakers: Petition," May 29, 1782, Virginia Memory: Legislative Petitions Digital Collection, Library of Virginia, www.virginiamemory.com/collections/petitions.

Many Americans held more complicated views of slavery and the exodus story, Christianity, and the patriot cause. In 1775 a contributor to the *Providence Gazette* addressed the General Assembly with an argument against slavery, like others, using the example of Pharaoh, but his plea was also a sharp rebuke for hypocritical patriots. The writer responded to the declaration of a fast day by addressing a biblical passage often cited along with the exodus, frequently shortened to "let the oppressed go free." Taken from Isaiah, the full passage criticized fasting that was a pretense of repentance simultaneous with oppression. How much more joyous would deliverance be, the contributor argued, were slaves freed to join and thank God for liberty? Then he challenged his readers to consider all of the arguments for their own liberty, first taking natural rights, and arguing that no one, from the one capturing slaves to the buyer several transactions removed from Africa, had any ground to stand on. Next he responded to the argument that it would not be good for slaves to be freed. Here he turned to the exodus, imagining that Pharaoh might have very wisely claimed that suddenly freeing all of the Israelites and sending them with no experience of government into a desert would be disastrous for them. But many of his contemporaries, he continued, would make this exact argument about Africans and then urge their fellow patriots to risk any consequences and trust God for the result in the cause of their own freedom. To the argument that their cause was too important to risk disunity over slavery, he continued the comparison with Pharaoh. "The present, I aver with certain knowledge, is the only time to do well; that neglected, we are not sure we will have it in our hearts to do so tomorrow. It is a most dangerous procrastination, and may, as on Egypt of old, bring down judgment after judgment upon our heads, accompanied with the hardness of Pharaoh's heart." Finally, he finished with a mock prayer of such double-minded lovers of liberty, pleading for God's intervention in their own fight against oppression while explaining why they could not possibly obey him yet in freeing their slaves. "What solemn mockery," he declared, "must have been the fastings, humiliations and prayer of men of such principles?"[40]

Still others coupled pitying dehumanization of African Americans with mockery of the whole patriot cause, using the exodus as an analogy. One writer in New York penned a sarcastic rebuke of a declaration by the state

---

[40]"Mr. Carter," *The Providence Gazette; and Country Journal*, September 2, 1775.

legislature in 1777. In response to the American claim to enslavement, he declared, "All of us know, what Wretches, what Israelites in Bondage, we have hitherto been, till our good Representatives above mentioned undertook our Deliverance." He continued that everyone knew that no one could hold any possessions, or live in peace and security, or say he held life and property "before we were under the direction of our Congress, Conventions, and watchful Committees." Then he turned the contradiction of chattel slavery on these supposed patriotic "poor Jews in Egypt under [Britain's] arbitrary domination." It must also be clear, he concluded, that the argument that all men are created free and able to set up their own government applied to African slaves. "We may therefore justly expect to have, in a little time, a black Assembly, a black Council, a black Governor, and a black Common Wealth . . . Such a Constitution would shine like my shoe."[41]

African Americans would also apply the exodus story to their own deliverance, especially by the second decade of the nineteenth century with leading examples among the Revolutionary generation like Lemuel Haynes. During the era of the Revolution itself, however, Phillis Wheatley is considered the first African American to put the parallel in writing.[42] In her "Letter to Samson Occum" of February 1774, Wheatley used the exodus to argue for both American liberty and freedom for slaves. After explaining the essential unity of religious and civil liberty in general with the Israelite example of liberation, she argued that "in every human Breast, God has implanted a Principle, which we call Love of Freedom; it is impatient of Oppression, and pants for Deliverance; and by the Leave of our Modern Egyptians [American slaveholders] I will assert, that the same Principle lives in us." Wheatley turned to more open criticism of the colonists' hypocrisy, pointing out "the strange Absurdity of their Conduct whose Words and Actions are so diametrically opposite." She was responding to Occum's assertion that natural rights applied to Africans and concluded, "How well the Cry for Liberty, and the reverse Disposition for the Exercise of oppressive Power over others agree,—I humbly think it does not require the Penetration of a Philosopher to determine."[43]

---

[41]Integer, "To the Printer," *The New-York Gazette; and the Weekly Mercury*, March 3, 1777.

[42]Rhondda Robinson Thomas, *Claiming Exodus: A Cultural History of Afro-Atlantic Identity, 1774–1903* (Waco, TX: Baylor University Press, 2013), 4.

[43]Phillis Wheatley, *The Collected Works of Phillis Wheatley*, John C. Shields, ed., *The Schomburg Library of Nineteenth-Century Black Women Writers* (New York: Oxford University Press, 1988), 176-77.

The crucial moment for this message of providential suffering and victory, though, came with independence, proof to many Americans that God's purpose was more than just repentance and redress of political grievances. Through the tumultuous years of resistance, Americans who interpreted British tyranny as oppression at God's hand, believed that his purposes involved political results, including unity, defending their liberties, and eventually independence. When the mother country turned to outright military action in April of 1775, the number of uses of the exodus expanded significantly.[44] Thomas Paine's timely argument against monarchy in *Common Sense* tapped into the broader Hebraic republican ideal, a period of Hebrew history Americans saw as being inaugurated with the exodus. Paine argued that the Israelite demand that God give them a king was sin and remembered the battles of Lexington and Concord as the point when he finally rejected "the hardened, sullen tempered Pharaoh of England" in favor of independence.[45] As early as 1765, Johnson addressed all of these political purposes. For his point on God's eventual deliverance of the Israelites, he drew a parallel to the "remarkable and almost unparalleled spirit of unanimity, unity, and public zeal for their important rights and privileges, which now happily reigns in the American colonies." This zeal for their rights came through the day of trial as God's means of making them aware of their oppression and ready to resist it. Like the Israelites, who suffered increasing tyranny because of Egyptian suspicions of them, refusal to recognize their loyalty and legitimate claims could lead to what Pharaoh feared most: their entire deliverance and independence.[46] Elijah Fitch, who preached his sermon only months before independence (though it may have been printed after), argued that, though it looked at first like God was against the Israelites, "in truth it was only to make way for their freedom from bondage and slavery, to let the oppressed go free." Pharaoh's "grievous impositions," he argued, "made them all with one heart and mind resolve to be free." From this he concluded,

---

[44]In the sources that I found in colonial newspapers and sermons that used the exodus, though I do not claim to have an exhaustive list, references to the exodus tripled from 1774 to 1775 and was also twice the references I found in 1776, though the attachment of the exodus to independence lived long after 1776.

[45]Thomas Paine, *Common Sense* (Philadelphia, 1776), 47.

[46]Johnson, *Some Important Observations*, 14-15, 19-20.

Perhaps our God, by these commotions, contentions, disturbances [etc.], is about to lay a firm foundation for the lasting future peace, tranquility and liberty of these American Colonies. . . . The means, that our unnatural enemies have made use of . . . are much the same which Pharaoh, Egypt's haughty Monarch used, and they have as yet had the same effect: Their schemes to oppress, divide, and then subjugate these Colonies, have served to unite our hearts, as one man, to cast off the burthens they have been imposing upon us.[47]

As the difficulties of war dragged on, Americans turned to the exodus more to demonstrate God's miraculous military victory for his people, though war itself could lead to either justification or doubts about the cause. Some continued to qualify victory with repentance. Sylvanus Conant was a Congregational minister from Middleboro, Massachusetts, who gained his pastorate from the revival party of a church split during the Great Awakening. In December of 1776 Conant preached an anniversary sermon at Plymouth in celebration of the landing of the Pilgrims, but he used the occasion to expound on a threefold comparison of the Israelites in Egypt, the New England forefathers, and the patriot cause. He reminded his audience that their victory was sure if they avoided sin. God used the war to increase their military strength and skill and could do the same for their Christian virtue. With those assurances, they could be certain that "tho never so great an host comes against our country, it will live through the war—we shall rise superior to the powers that combine against us, and finally triumph over all the enemies of our salvation." Remembering how the Israelites increased and succeeded under bondage, like their forefathers under persecution, it was clear how easy victory could be to God.[48] Many more, along with Conant, focused more on the need to give credit to God's intervention for their victories. On a day appointed by the Continental Congress for thanksgiving in 1777, Israel Evans, an evangelical preacher and a trusted military chaplain of George Washington, urged his fellow soldiers to praise God for their victories. First, he reminded them, "that many years past the language of Britain corresponded with the language of Pharaoh and his cruel task-masters, who said, 'come let us deal wisely with them, lest they multiply.'" Since God granted them success in

---

[47]Elijah Fitch, *A Discourse, the Substance of Which Was Delivered at Hopkinton, on the Lord's-Day, March 24th, 1776, Being the next Sabbath Following the Precipitate Flight of the British Troops from Boston.* (Boston: Printed by John Boyle, in Marlborough-Street, 1776), 16-17.

[48]Conant, *An Anniversary Sermon*, 23-26.

escaping these snares, he continued, the British government brought against them the formidable enemies of "the arms of the King of England," his "invincible navy," the "veterans of Britain," and the mercenaries of Germany. And yet they found themselves free, a good cause for thanksgiving.[49]

Though fear of divinely ordained defeat continued through the war, by the end Americans using the exodus story exalted in a reenactment of miraculous victory of the people of God. In 1779 Congress issued a proclamation in preparation for a day of fasting that reflected the earlier mix of apprehension of judgment and hope for nearly miraculous victory. The reason for the need of national prayer, they explained, was the apparent judgment of God on Americans in the calamity of war. Congress declared that because too few Americans had come to realize their sin and turn from it, that "the malevolence of our disappointed enemies, like the incredulity of Pharaoh, may be used as the scourge of Omnipotence to vindicate his slighted Majesty, there is reason to fear that he may permit much of our land to become the prey of the spoiler, our borders to be ravaged, and our habitations destroyed." Yet Congress also declared that "divine Providence hath hitherto in a wonderful manner conducted us, so that we might acknowledge that the race is not to the swift, nor the battle to the strong."[50] This belief in God's help to the weak and oppressed encouraged Americans to hope for God's intervention. And many others used this hopeful passage in connection to the exodus.[51]

By the 1780s Americans using the exodus story began focusing more exclusively on the Israelites entering the Promised Land and enjoying a series of miraculous victories from God. In 1781 Robert Smith, a Presbyterian in the Log College network of theological schools, preached a sermon in response to a national day of thanksgiving with special notice of "the Various Interpositions of His Providence in Their Favor, during Their Contest with Great Britain, Particularly . . . the Capture of Lord Cornwallis with His Whole Army . . ." Smith reminded them that God chose Moses out of his brush with death in a watery grave to confound the great court

---

[49]Evans, *A Discourse Delivered on the 18th Day of December*, 6-7.

[50]"Philadelphia Proclamation," *The Pennsylvania Packet or the General Advertiser*, March 27, 1779. The proclamation was reprinted in newspapers throughout the colonies over the following weeks.

[51]"Philadelphia Proclamation," *The Pennsylvania Packet or the General Advertiser*, March 27, 1779. "From the Edinburgh Gazette, of April 14th, 1780," *The Pennsylvania Packet or the General Advertiser*, October 24, 1780.

of Pharaoh, but he also encouraged them with the lesson that God would fight for them as he did for the Israelites at Jericho.[52] In 1782 Phillips Payson preached a sermon on the anniversary of the battles of Lexington and Concord on "Some Signal Interpositions of Providence in the American Revolution." He took his text from Exodus 12, a passage on the feast of the Passover for the Israelites he described as a memorial of God's deliverance. Payson told his audience that "The finger of God has indeed been so conspicuous in every stage of our glorious struggle, that it seems as if the wonders and miracles performed for Israel of old, were repeated over and anew for the American Israel, in our day." After recounting the comparison of the British king and his government as possessing the same hardheartedness and madness of Pharaoh, he compared the miraculous victories of the Israelites taking the land of Canaan as a parallel to the American victories in the Revolution.[53] In 1783 Israel Evans, this time preaching on a day of thanksgiving for peace and American independence, addressed his audience with a text from the song of Moses after the defeat of the Egyptians in the Red Sea. Though he hesitated to make more detailed comparisons to the Israelites, he still rewrote the song of Moses as a prayer of praise to God for his intervention in the American war. He confidently declared to his audience that their victories would be remembered, or doubted, as much as the miracles of the Israelite deliverance.[54]

With peace accomplished, or at least in sight, American independence attained a new significance in connection to the exodus. Uses of Israelite deliverance now supported direct assertions of Americans as the people of God, as providentially brought into nationhood, and as promised a future expansion of their land and ideals. Phillips Payson also included in his 1782 sermon another passage commonly used in recounting God's deliverance: "The time, it seems, was come . . . appointed by the councils of Heaven, in the course of nature, when a new Empire should arise in the world, and a nation be born in a day . . ."[55] Americans frequently used the idea of a "nation born in a day" as a response to the question in the book of Isaiah, "Shall the earth

---

[52]Robert Smith, *The Obligations of the Confederate States of North America to Praise God* (Baltimore, MD, 1783), 14, 28.

[53]Phillips Payson, *A Memorial of Lexington Battle* (Boston, 1782), 5, 8-9.

[54]Evans, *A Discourse Delivered in New-York*, 3-4, 6, 10.

[55]Payson, *A Memorial of Lexington Battle*, 10.

be made to bring forth in one day, or shall a nation be born at once?"[56] Since independence Americans had begun to answer this question in the affirmative with their own sudden emergence as a nation. Sylvanus Conant, whose 1776 sermon emphasized the fulfillment of prophecy, claimed that, taken in a literal sense, American independence was the first such occurrence in Christian history, and he reminded his audience that, though independent, they must acknowledge their dependence on God's providence.[57] In 1782 Payson used this supposed fulfillment of Scripture to argue that God, who inspired Americans with a zeal for liberty and united them in the cause, formed them into an empire that might grow in strength greater than any before them and spread across all of North America. Though peace had not yet been settled, the perceived works of God in their favor so far led him to conclude "we cannot but entertain raised hopes that our deliverance is just at hand, and the blessings of peace will soon be restored, and our independence secured; when this kind of liberty will become a quiet habitation; the wilderness blossom like a rose; commerce and agriculture flourish; the arts and sciences be cultivated; and generations yet unborn shall rejoice in the happy purchases of our treasure and blood."[58]

On the day of thanksgiving for peace and independence in 1783, George Duffield's sermon addressed the nation being born in a day: "Who hath heard such a thing? who hath seen such things? Shall the earth be made to bring forth in one day, or shall a nation be born at once? For as soon as Zion travailed, she brought forth her children!" He compared these pains of birth to the Israelite and American deliverances, but he argued that the American exodus was even more sudden. The Israelites, after all, had to wander in the desert, but "almost as soon as our American Zion began to travail . . . she brought forth her children, more numerous than the tribes of Jacob, to possess the land, from the north to the south, and from the east to the yet unexplored, far distant west . . ." Duffield recognized that the British government seemed to model the policies of Pharaoh, especially in his jealousy of potential independence, but Duffield argued that the American case was even more grievous. The Israelites and Egyptians were at least different peoples, but Americans, whose "religion and manners" were the same as their rulers, were truly

---

[56]This is the version of the passage in Conant, *An Anniversary Sermon*, 24-25.
[57]Conant, *An Anniversary Sermon*, 24-25.
[58]Payson, *A Memorial of Lexington Battle*, 10, 12, 17.

betrayed through false suspicions. The "American Zion" had once been part of the British imperial people of God, in opposition to their outside (Catholic) enemies, but after years of resisting their own unjust rulers, to many, God had confirmed their separate purpose.[59]

Through the process of internal conflict, both with their rulers at a distance and with their rulers and neighbors close by, Americans reapplied the exodus narrative of an empire with divine favor. What began as confirmation of oppression and justification of resistance transformed through the experience of war and victory into a new American Zion. Internal conflict over the meanings of the exodus would continue, especially when connected to real slavery. Where the British imperial picture of deliverance from Pharaoh was composed of more clear-cut lines between Catholic enemies and the Protestant succession, Americans applying it to their own dramatically changing situation pictured a vague divine empire of new and old ideals, of the gospel and a new kind of civil society. The influence of evangelical preachers, or their participation in developing a national divine purpose was not straightforward, just as national biblicism came in many forms of interpretation and produced conflicting political conclusions. Nevertheless, a triumphant narrative of a new American Zion emerged through the application of the exodus to the process of revolution.

BIBLIOGRAPHY

Primary

Avery, David. *The Lord Is to Be Praised for the Triumphs of His Power. A Sermon, Preached at Greenwich, in Connecticut, on the 18th of December 1777. Being a General Thanksgiving through the United American States. By David Avery, V.D.M. Chaplain to Col. Sherburne's Regiment. [One Line from Psalms]*. Norwich, CT: Printed by Green & Spooner, 1778. America's Historical Imprints, Evans Collection, 1639–1800.

Conant, Sylvanus. *An Anniversary Sermon Preached at Plymouth, December 23, 1776. In Grateful Memory of the First Landing of Our Worthy Ancestors in That Place, An. Dom. 1620. By Sylvanus Conant, Pastor of the First Church in Middleborough. [Two Lines from Samson's Riddle]*. Boston: Printed by Thomas and John Fleet, 1777. America's Historical Imprints, Evans Collection, 1639–1800.

Duffield, George. *A Sermon, Preached in the Third Presbyterian Church, in the City of Philadelphia, on Thursday, December 11, 1783. The day appointed by the United States*

---

[59]George Duffield, *A Sermon Preached in the Third Presbyterian Church*, 5-6.

in Congress assembled, to be observed as a day of thanksgiving, for the restoration of peace; and establishment of our independence, in the enjoyment of our rights and privileges. By George Duffield, A.M. Pastor of the said church. Published at the request of the committee of the said congregation. [Five lines of Scripture quotations]. Philadelphia: Printed by F. Bailey, 1784. America's Historical Imprints, Evans Collection, 1639–1800.

Evans, Israel. *A Discourse, Delivered in New-York, before a Brigade of Continental Troops, and a Number of Citizens, Assembled in St. George's Chapel, on the 11th December, 1783. The Day Set Apart by the Recommendation of the United States in Congress, as a Day of Public Thanksgiving for the Blessings of Independence, Liberty and Peace, by the Rev. Israel Evans, A.M. Chaplain in the American Army.* New York, NY: Published, and sold by John Holt.

———. *A Discourse, Delivered, on the 18th Day of December, 1777, the Day of Public Thanksgiving, Appointed by the Honourable Continental Congress, by the Reverend Israel Evans, A.M. Chaplain to General Poor's Brigade. And Now Published at the Request of the General and Officers of the Said Brigade, to Be Distributed among the Soldiers, Gratis.* Lancaster, PA: Printed by Francis Bailey, 1778. America's Historical Imprints, Evans Collection, 1639–1800.

Fitch, Elijah. *A Discourse, the Substance of Which Was Delivered at Hopkinton, on the Lord's-Day, March 24th, 1776, Being the next Sabbath Following the Precipitate Flight of the British Troops from Boston. By Elijah Fitch, A.M. Published at the Request of the Hearers. [Two Lines from Solomon].* Boston: Printed by John Boyle, in Marlborough-Street, 1776. America's Historical Imprints, Evans Collection, 1639–1800.

Fletcher, John. *The Bible and the Sword: Or, the Appointment of the General Fast Vindicated: In an Address to the Common People, Concerning the Propriety of Repressing Obstinate Licentiousness with the Sword, and of Fasting When the Sword Is Drawn for That Purpose.* London, 1776.

Hall, David. *Israel's Triumph. It Concerns the People of God to Celebrate the Divine Praises, according to All His Wonderful Works. A Sermon Preached at Sutton on a Publick Thanksgiving, October 9th. 1760. For the Entire Reduction of Canada. Also, Delivered Afterwards, with Some Alteration, at Hollis, in New-Hampshire, on a Private Thanksgiving, Observed There November the 20th Following, upon the Same Occasion. And Now Published at the Repeated Desire of Many of the Hearers. By David Hall, A.M. Pastor of the First Church in Sutton. [Six Lines from Psalms].* Boston: Printed and Sold by J. Draper, 1761. America's Historical Imprints, Evans Collection, 1639–1800.

Holly, Israel. *God Brings about His Holy and Wise Purpose or Decree, Concerning Many Particular Events, by Using and Improving the Wicked Dispositions of Mankind in Order Thereto; and Often Improves the Present Corruptions of Sinners, as the Means to Chastise and Punish Them for Former Wickedness; Briefly Illustrated in a Sermon,*

Preached at Suffield, December 27, 1773, the next Sabbath after the Report Arrived, That the People at Boston Had Destroyed a Large Quantity of Tea, Belonging to the East-India Company, rather than to Submit to Parliament-Acts, Which They Looked upon Unconstitutional, Tyrannical, and Tending to Enslave America. Published with Some Enlargements. By Israel Holly, Preacher of the Gospel in Suffield. [One Line of Scripture Text]. Hartford, CT: Printed by Ebenezer Watson, 1774. America's Historical Imprints, Evans Collection, 1639–1800.

Johnson, Stephen. *Some Important Observations, Occasioned By, and Adapted To, the Publick Fast, Ordered by Authority, December 18th, A.D. 1765.* Newport, RI: Printed and sold by Samuel Hall, 1766. America's Historical Imprints, Evans Collection, 1639–1800.

Jones, David. *Defensive War in a Just Cause Sinless. A Sermon, Preached on the Day of the Continental Fast, at Tredyffryn, in Chester County, by the Revd. David Jones, A.M. Published by Request. [One Line from Daniel].* Philadelphia: Printed by Henry Miller, 1775. America's Historical Imprints, Evans Collection, 1639–1800.

Paine, Thomas. *Common Sense; Addressed to the Inhabitants of America, on the Following Interesting Subjects. I. Of the Origin and Design of Government in General, with Concise Remarks on the English Constitution. II. Of Monarchy and Hereditary Succession. III. Thoughts on the Present State of American Affairs. IV. Of the Present Ability of America, with Some Miscellaneous Reflections. [Two Lines from Thomson].* Philadelphia, PA: Printed and sold by R. Bell, 1776. America's Historical Imprints, Evans Collection, 1639–1800.

Payson, Phillips. *A Memorial of Lexington Battle, and of Some Signal Interpositions of Providence in the American Revolution. A Sermon Preached at Lexington, on the Nineteenth of April, 1782. The Anniversary of the Commencement of the War between Great-Britain and America, Which Opened in a Most Tragical Scene, in That Town, on the Nineteenth of April, 1775. By Phillips Payson, A.M. Pastor of the Church in Chelsea. [Two Lines in Latin from Virgil].* Boston: Printed by Benjamin Edes & Sons, 1782. America's Historical Imprints, Evans Collection, 1639–1800.

Smith, Robert. *The Obligations of the Confederate States of North America to Praise God. Two Sermons. Preached at Pequea, December 13, 1781, the Day Recommended by the Honourable Congress to the Several States, to Be Observed as a Day of Thanksgiving to God, for the Various Interpositions of His Providence in Their Favour, during Their Contest with Great Britain, Particularly Those of the Present Year, Crowned by the Capture of Lord Cornwallis with His Whole Army. By Robert Smith, A.M. Minister of the Gospel at Pequea.* Philadelphia, PA: Printed by Francis Bailey, 1782. America's Historical Imprints, Evans Collection, 1639–1800.

Tennent, Gilbert. *The Late Association for Defense, Encourag'd, or The Lawfulness of a Defensive War. Represented in a Sermon Preach'd at Philadelphia December 24. 1747. By Gilbert Tennent, A.M. [Twelve Lines of Quotations] Published at the Request of the*

Hearers. Philadelphia, PA: Printed by William Bradford, 1748. America's Historical Imprints, Evans Collection, 1639–1800.

Secondary

Byrd, James P. *Sacred Scripture, Sacred War: The Bible and the American Revolution*. New York: Oxford University Press, 2013.

Coffey, John. *Exodus and Liberation: Deliverance Politics from John Calvin to Martin Luther King Jr*. New York: Oxford University Press, 2014.

Dreisbach, Daniel L. *Reading the Bible with the Founding Fathers*. New York: Oxford University Press, 2016.

Glaude, Eddie S., Jr. *Exodus!: Religion, Race, and Nation in Early Nineteenth-Century Black America*. Chicago: University of Chicago Press, 2000.

Guyatt, Nicholas. *Providence and the Invention of the United States, 1607–1876*. New York: Cambridge University Press, 2007.

Hatch, Nathan O., and Mark A. Noll, eds. *The Bible in America: Essays in Cultural History*. New York: Oxford University Press, 1982.

Saillant, John. *Black Puritan, Black Republican: The Life and Thought of Lemuel Haynes, 1753-1833*. Religion in America Series. New York: Oxford University Press, 2003.

Shalev, Eran. *American Zion: The Old Testament as a Political Text from the Revolution to the Civil War*. New Haven, CT: Yale University Press, 2013.

Thomas, Rhondda Robinson. *Claiming Exodus: A Cultural History of Afro-Atlantic Identity, 1774–1903*. Waco, TX: Baylor University Press, 2013.

2

Lectio Evangelica

Figural Interpretation and
Early Evangelical Bible Reading

Bruce Hindmarsh

DAVID BEBBINGTON GAVE A SET OF THREE LECTURES at Regent College in 1989 when I was a graduate student contemplating PhD work. Based on his book *Evangelicalism in Modern Britain,* which came out the same year, he offered an overview of the relationship of evangelicalism and culture in three episodes: eighteenth-century Enlightenment, nineteenth-century Romanticism, and twentieth-century Modernism. It was a lucid and compelling analysis. As a young scholar, I had been reading Richard Niebuhr's *Christ and Culture*, and I had been learning from George Marsden to think about fundamentalism in terms of American culture, so what Bebbington offered seemed like exactly the right approach to understanding evangelicalism. I did not realize at the time that this heuristic of "evangelicalism and culture" would shape my own research in my doctoral work at Oxford and well beyond.

Later, when my wife, our three-week-old daughter, and I arrived in Oxford, Bebbington visited and stayed with us. I was about to submit my first essay to my supervisor, and he kindly consented to have a look over it the night before. He pulled out his fountain pen and read. I wish I had kept his notes, since, as those who have studied with him know, his feedback was characteristically detailed and precise, and returned to me in a closely written page of his meticulous round-hand. This is only one example of many acts of scholarly generosity I have experienced from Bebbington over the years.

So now, many years later, it is my purpose here to reflect on that first lecture Bebbington gave at Regent College, titled "Evangelical Christianity and the Enlightenment." In that lecture Bebbington set out what was then a bold and revisionary argument that evangelicalism was not to be contrasted with the Enlightenment as a religion of mere feeling. Rather, it was something "actually started by the Enlightenment."[1] Again, "The Enlightenment and Evangelicalism were aligned with each other," and "the Enlightenment actually gave rise to Evangelical Christianity with its sense of mission. The two were *entirely* compatible with each other."[2] Or, as he concluded the corresponding chapter in his book: "The Evangelical version of Protestantism was created by the Enlightenment."[3] Bebbington's central argument was that Enlightenment sensationalist epistemology (of the sort set out by John Locke) transformed the received doctrine of assurance for the early evangelicals, such that it produced tremendous confidence in proclamation and mission. Moreover, evangelicals embraced the Enlightenment's scientific method and its optimism, moderation, ethical concern, pragmatism, taste, and reforming ideals. All this contrasted significantly with seventeenth-century Protestant piety.

Now, just as Bebbington pulled out his A4 pad and made his notes on my first paper at Oxford, so now it is my turn to raise a few questions for him to consider. He had one evening; I have had thirty years to prepare my response.

In my own work I have located evangelical religious thought and experience as something not so much *created by* the Enlightenment as poised *between* it and earlier forms of traditional Christianity. Evangelical Christianity appeared in a transitional space, on the trailing edge of Christendom and the leading edge of modernity, or, in eighteenth-century terms, in the midst of the "Quarrel of the Ancients and the Moderns." John Wesley was familiar with the "Quarrel." He wrote, "Alas! how little new has been discovered, even by . . . Mr. *Locke*, or Sir *Isaac Newton*? How plain is it, that in Philosophy, as well as the course of human affairs, *there is nothing new under*

---

[1] David Bebbington, "Evangelical Christianity and the Enlightenment," *Crux* 25, no. 4 (December 1989): 32.
[2] Bebbington, "Evangelical Christianity and the Enlightenment," 36 (italics added).
[3] David Bebbington, *Evangelicalism in Modern Britain: A History from the 1730s to the 1980s* (London: Unwin Hyman, 1989), 74.

the sun.[4] Clues such as this have led me to look again at some of Bebbington's themes: assurance of salvation, the reception of science, attitudes to contemporary ethics, and so on. For the most part, I see a more equivocal relationship to Enlightenment thought. I would not say that evangelicalism was "entirely compatible" with the Enlightenment. In some important ways, evangelicals stood opposed to Enlightenment thought, especially where there seemed to be a loss of transcendence in the new scientific outlook. For euphony, I would say that evangelicals were as Augustinian as they were Augustan.

In this chapter, I would like therefore to explore the hybrid nature of evangelicalism (both ancient and modern) in terms of one of the defining characteristics of evangelical Christianity identified by Bebbington, namely, its emphasis upon Scripture. Evangelicals continued to read the Bible in traditional ways, with devotional intent, in the age of science. I will focus in particular on the contested practice of figural reading. After describing the so-called eclipse of this pattern of reading in the early Enlightenment, I will show how evangelicals continued to read the Bible figurally, and especially how they used this traditional form of reading to incorporate their own lives robustly into the world of Scripture. There was a *lectio evangelica* that stood in continuity with *lectio divina*. Finally, my closing case study will be Jonathan Edwards, who, among all his peers, pushed back against Enlightenment trends most emphatically by expanding the range of figuration to include the whole of nature.

TRADITIONAL FIGURATION

What is figural reading? At one level, figuration is simply the practice of treating something (a word, an event, an object) as somehow symbolic of something else. As Augustine wrote in *De doctrina*, setting out a basic semiotic theory for reading the Bible, human beings have to do with things and signs, signs themselves being really just a special category of things that point to other things. Ciphers on a page or sounds produced by mouth are real things, but for human beings they can "signify" and thereby become words. A proper sign for Augustine was like using the word *ox* to signify the animal; a metaphorical sign would be like using the word *ox* to signify not only the animal but also the evangelist Luke, as in the traditional iconography of the Gospel

---

[4]John Wesley, *Survey of the Wisdom of God in the Creation*, 3rd ed., vol. 5 (London, 1777), 169.

writers.[5] Very early in the history of Christianity, believers came to regard many of the "things" contained in the Old Testament as "signs" that pointed to other "things" having to do with Christ and the church. Crucially, it was this pattern of figuration that unified the Old and New Testaments.

Over time there was a spectrum of Christian figural reading ranging from the minimal to the maximal, the chaste to the lush. From Origen to Joachim of Fiore, there were many fecund instances of figural reading in which the spiritual meaning of the text of Scripture was extended, seemingly without restraint. Traditionally, however, all Christians have maintained some level of figuration based on the precedents in the New Testament itself, so that David is seen as prefiguring Jesus as Messiah (as in Peter's sermon in Acts 2), and Melchizedek is seen as prefiguring the priestly work of Christ (as in the fifth chapter of Hebrews), and so on. Minimalists have sometimes reserved the word *typology* for only such figuration as was explicitly authorized by New Testament usage, wanting to distinguish this sharply from allegory, tropology, anagogue, or other levels of figurative meaning. Reacting against medieval excesses, the Reformers famously returned to a more literal interpretation of Scripture, limiting the scope for typology and rejecting fanciful spiritual interpretation.[6] But, as Erich Auerbach has argued, all figuration, even the most restrained, plucks a person, thing, or event from its historical embeddedness in the particular, limited chronological sequence of immediate antecedents and consequences, and places it a new *non-temporal* relation to something else.

Auerbach (1892–1957) was an influential German philologist writing in the early twentieth century, and he analyzed this kind of figuration extensively and remarked perceptively on the different mode it represents from strictly historical analysis. In the figural interpretation of events, "the connection between occurrences is not regarded as primarily a chronological or causal development but as a oneness within the divine plan, of which all occurrences are parts and reflections. Their direct earthly connection is of secondary importance." The perception of the figural connection of events is therefore a special act of reading or interpretation. Both events are, he said, "contained

---

[5] Augustine, *Teaching Christianity (De doctrina christiana)*, trans. Edmund Hill (Hyde Park, NY: New City Press, 1996), 1.2; 2.1-5, 15.

[6] A classic nineteenth-century study of typology is Patrick Fairbairn, *The Typology of Scripture* (Philadelphia: Daniels & Smith, 1852).

in the flowing stream which is historical life and only the comprehension, the *intellectus spiritualis*, of the interdependence is a spiritual act."[7] This insight has been taken up and applied to great effect in recent criticism by the biblical scholar Richard Hays with his notion of "reading backwards."[8] In Auerbach's analysis, however, the critical distinction is between temporal (earthly) connections and non-temporal (spiritual) connections. No wonder that figural reading was described, at least from the time of Origen, as *spiritual* reading. It is not that event A leads to event B, as cause to effect, but that event A is perceived to figure or foreshadow event B.[9]

Auerbach was a major influence upon Hans Frei (1922–1988), who claimed that it was precisely in the eighteenth century, during the period of the Enlightenment, that figural interpretation began to break down. Famously, Frei argued that there was an "eclipse of biblical narrative" in the Enlightenment. The eclipse is fitting image for a period fascinated by astronomy, and not least by eclipses, which were regularly noted in the press.[10] In an eclipse, the sun is occluded, and its light dimmed. So also for Frei, traditional figural ways of reading the Bible were inhibited, and the Bible no longer *illuminated* the life and events of the present age.

What did Frei mean? He contended that before the rise of historical criticism, Bible reading was strongly realistic, that is, "at once literal and historical, and not only doctrinal or edifying."[11] The smaller stories in the

---

[7]Erich Auerbach, *Mimesis: The Representation of Reality in Western Literature*, trans. Willard R. Trask, repr. ed. (Princeton: Princeton University Press, 2013), 555.

[8]Hays has reprised Auerbach's definition of figuration and applied it to the practice of New Testament authors in their appreciation of the "echoes" of Old Testament events and writings in the life of Christ and the church. The focus is on the spiritual act of the later interpreter: "Figural reading is a form of intertextual interpretation that focuses on an intertextuality of *reception* rather than of *production*." Richard Hays, *Echoes of Scripture in the Gospels* (Waco, TX: Baylor University Press, 2016), 367n3; see also 2-8. In his earlier *Reading Backwards* (Waco, TX: Baylor University Press, 2014), Hays developed this idea of "retrospective reading" in terms of figuration: "Figural readings do not annihilate the earlier pole of the figural correspondence; to the contrary they affirm its reality and find in it a significance beyond that which anyone could previously have grasped" (xv).

[9]The distinction is sometimes made that whereas typology works along a temporal axis of past and future, allegory works along a vertical axis of the particular and the abstract. Thus, for example, "The typical is not properly a different or higher sense, but a different or higher application of the same sense." Fairbairn, *Typology of Scripture*, 11.

[10]"How Did 18th Century People React to Eclipses?," OpenLearn: History and the Arts, The Open University, March 6, 2015, www.open.edu/openlearn/history-the-arts/history/history-science-technology-and-medicine/history-science/how-did-18th-century-people-react-eclipses.

[11]Hans Frei, *The Eclipse of Biblical Narrative: A Study in Eighteenth and Nineteenth Century Hermeneutics* (New Haven: Yale University Press, 1974), 1.

Bible together made up a single historical sequence of events, and the real world was formed by these. The natural environment and human culture were accounted for in a narrative of the temporal world that "covered the span of ages from creation to the final consummation to come." Crucially, this biblical world was "the one and only real world," and so "it must in principle embrace the experience of any present age and reader."[12]

Figuration was key to this. The reader was duty bound to fit him- or herself into this world by *figural* interpretation and by mode of life. The events of his or her life were elements in *that* storied world. This realistic biblical narrative, argued Frei, "remained the adequate description of the common and inclusive world until the coming of modernity. As the eighteenth century went on, this mode of interpretation and the outlook it represented broke down with increasing rapidity."[13] Consequently, Frei saw a kind of reversal taking place in the eighteenth century. Instead of trying to fit events of the present into the real world of Scripture, the attempt was to fit the depicted biblical world into the seemingly *more* real extrabiblical world as we apprehend it, especially as described by science.[14] With this reversal of direction came a breakdown of figural interpretation, for such interpretation offended against both literary and historical rationality, for precisely the reason, as Auerbach said, that "the connection between occurrences is not regarded as primarily a chronological or causal development." Figural interpretation was now regarded as the opposite of the literal sense, instead of the literal sense as extended to the whole narrative or unitary canon. "The depicted biblical world and the real historical world began to be separated at once in thought and in sensibility. . . . This logical and reflective distance between narrative and reality increased steadily."[15] Whereas typology had been an important way that the Scriptures were bound together in a unitary whole, in terms of promise and fulfilment, type and antitype, now figural interpretation was regarded as the *opposite* of the literal sense.

Bible reading and the rise of science were closely linked in these developments, since another way of putting Frei's reversal is to say that the depicted biblical world now had to be fit into the world as described by science. The

---

[12]Frei, *Eclipse of Biblical Narrative*, 3.
[13]Frei, *Eclipse of Biblical Narrative*, 3-4
[14]Frei, *Eclipse of Biblical Narrative*, 5.
[15]Frei, *Eclipse of Biblical Narrative*, 5.

intellectual historian Peter Harrison (b. 1955) was a student of Hans Frei, and in his Gifford Lectures and other writings on religion and science, he has argued that premodern people, prior to the rise of science, viewed nature something like literature. As with types in Scripture, the things of nature signified, pointing beyond themselves, like words, to spiritual meanings. Meanings were read off, so to speak, natural objects. As Hugh of St. Victor wrote in the twelfth century, "The whole sensible world is like a kind of book written by the finger of God—that is, created by divine power—and each particular creature is somewhat like a figure, not invented by human decision, but instituted by the divine will to manifest the invisible things of God's wisdom."[16] However, as the modern period progressed, the language of typology and symbolism for nature was replaced by the language of mathematics and classification. In this development, Bible reading led the way. "The new conception of the order of nature was made possible," Harrison argues,

> by the collapse of the allegorical interpretation of texts, for a denial of the legitimacy of allegory is in essence a denial of the capacity of things to act as signs. The demise of allegory, in turn, was due largely to the efforts of Protestant reformers, who in their search for an unambiguous religious authority, insisted that the book of Scripture be interpreted only in its literal, historical sense.

Critically, Harrison noticed that with literalism it was now *only* words that refer; the things of nature no longer had any semiotic value. Natural objects were mute. Mathematical and taxonomic categories filled this void. "It is commonly supposed that when in the early modern period individuals began to look at the world in a different way, they could no longer believe what they read in the Bible." However, Harrison argues that the reverse is the case, that "when in the sixteenth century people began to read the Bible in a different way, they found themselves forced to jettison traditional conceptions of the world."[17]

Literal approaches to the Bible thus went hand in hand with the rise of mathematical and taxonomic accounts of nature in the early modern period. At the close of the seventeenth century, mechanical philosophy and the hegemony of Newtonian science further intensified this trend toward the

---

[16]Hugh of St. Victor, *De tribus diebus*, quoted in Peter Harrison, *The Bible, Protestantism, and the Rise of Natural Science* (Cambridge: Cambridge University Press, 1998), 1.

[17]Harrison, *The Bible, Protestantism, and the Rise of Natural Science*, 4.

nontypological reading of Scripture. Uniting terrestrial and celestial mechanics in a physics founded on particulate matter in motion, Newtonianism radically revised traditional cosmology, replacing the form principle with a doctrine of the absolute inertness of matter. In the new science there was now, literally, nothing "inside" matter and no apparent spirituality to the observable universe. Material objects were bare surfaces. As religious thinkers worked out how to think about the Bible in the light of this Newtonianism, they were forced to explain miracles and prophecy in terms of a closed, uniform world of temporal cause and effect, in which such phenomena could only be seen as radically disruptive divine interventions from outside the system. In such a world there was little room for figuration. Newton's own preoccupation with prophecy, as with his followers, was now less a matter of promise and fulfillment, type and antitype, foreshadow and reality, as it was a matter of looking for clairvoyant predictions of future temporal events. Old Testament prophecies were thought of pretty much like predicting the return of Halley's Comet.

This was, for example, the way the historian, theologian, and mathematician William Whiston (1667–1752) treated Scripture in the period just prior to the rise of evangelicalism. Whiston was one of the most important popularizers of the scientific theories of Isaac Newton in the early eighteenth century and followed Newton in the Lucasian chair of mathematics at Cambridge.[18] He thought prophecies in the Old Testament, though "peculiar and enigmatical," were "single and determinate" in their meaning and not capable of double meanings or "typical Interpretations."[19] As with science, his approach was empirical, accumulating some three hundred cases of prophecies literally fulfilled as a knock-down argument for the veracity of Scripture.[20] Where necessary, he did a little creative textual criticism to make sure everything fit.[21] His thesis was quickly dismissed by the arch nemesis of the orthodox at the time, Anthony Collins (1767–1829), and it added fuel to the fire of the ongoing Deist controversy. The debate between Collins and Whiston, which

---

[18]Stephen D. Snobelen, "Whiston, William (1667–1752), Natural Philosopher and Theologian," *Oxford Dictionary of National Biography*, October 8, 2009, https://doi.org/10.1093/ref:odnb/29217.
[19]William Whiston, *The Accomplishment of Scripture Prophecies* (Cambridge, 1708), 13.
[20]Snobelen, "Whiston, William (1667–1752)."
[21]William Whiston, *An Essay Towards Restoring the True Text of the Old Testament: And for Vindicating the Citations Made Thence in the New Testament* (London, 1722), 334-35.

revolved around predictive prophecy and eschewed typology, is for Hans Frei a good example of the eclipse of biblical narrative.[22]

It was precisely at this moment, however, in the middle third of the eighteenth century, that we find the rise of evangelicalism as a popular, modern religious movement. Evangelicals would place a special emphasis upon the Bible. They would be Bible-reading and Bible-loving people. Indeed, this would be one of their defining characteristics, as David Bebbington argues. So how does evangelical Bible reading appear against the background of the Enlightenment "eclipse of biblical narrative"?

LECTIO EVANGELICA: BIBLICAL TYPOLOGY MADE PERSONAL

Though living in the modern world, the early evangelicals approached Scripture with fervent devotional intent, and they sought to interpret their lives within its narrative, assimilating their experience to the world depicted in the Bible by means of figuration. For men like Anthony Collins and William Whiston and those scientific minds embroiled in the Deist controversy, the Bible was treated as a text like any other. For someone like Wesley, who was willing to do a little textual criticism and emend the *textus receptus* here and there, the scientific and historical questions were not wrong, but they were incomplete. Evangelical Bible reading was shaped from the outset by their vivid sense of the divine authorship of the Scriptures. The consequences for Bible reading could not be more dramatic. To read with devotional intent as the early evangelicals did was to re-enchant the scientific universe and to re-animate the Scriptures.

In a hymn entitled, "Before Reading the Scriptures," Wesley invoked God's assistance with great reverence:

> While in Thy Word we search for Thee,
> (We search with trembling Awe)
> Open our Eyes, and let us see
> The Wonders of thy Law.[23]

The Scriptures invited a "trembling awe." The desire was for God himself to open out the divine and spiritual meaning of the Bible to the reader, as the

---

[22]Frei, *Eclipse*, 66-70.
[23]John and Charles Wesley, *Hymns and Sacred Poems* (1740), 41-43.

hymn continues: "Open our eyes," "Open the Scriptures," and "Unseal the Sacred Book." This prayerful approach to reading had profound metaphysical and hermeneutical consequences. The praying reader simply does not read within a wholly "immanent frame" of metaphysical naturalism. And with this devotional earnestness and reverent attitude, evangelicals quite instinctively read the Bible as a unitary whole, making use of figural readings to include the present reader within the frame of Scripture. Israel, Christ, the church, and the believer were held within one frame. In Frei's terms, this was figural but realist reading. It was not somehow a matter of just constructing pleasing tropes, but rather of opening up the real meaning of the text as an account of the common and inclusive world.

The most important and influential expression of this way of reading the Bible came with the large body of hymnody produced by the Evangelical Revival. As a particularly apt example, we might take the hymn "Guide Me, O Thou Great Jehovah" by William Williams of Pantycelyn.[24] First published in Welsh, the hymn's title was "A Prayer for Strength to Go through the Wilderness of the World," and it is rich in symbolism and biblical typology.[25]

An Anglican minister, though only in deacon's orders, William Williams was one of the leading figures of the Evangelical Revival in Wales and one of the founders of Welsh Methodism.[26] Known to Welsh speakers as Williams Pantycelyn, he is chiefly remembered for his literary contribution to the

---

[24]The discussion that follows draws upon my article, Bruce Hindmarsh, "'End of Faith as Its Beginning': Models of Spiritual Progress in Early Evangelical Devotional Hymns," *Spiritus* 10, no. 1 (2010): 10-15.

[25]The hymn appeared in Welsh in five verses in William Williams's *Y Mor o Wydr* (Carmarthen, 1762). Various English translations appeared over the following years. There is a very rare twelve-page pamphlet published by Peter Williams, *Hymns on Various Subjects* (Carmarthen, 1771), which I have not been able to examine, but this likely includes an early English version of the hymn. A three-verse version, which includes the verses in common use today, appeared in *The Collection of Hymns Sung in the Countess of Huntingdon's Chapels* (Bath, 1773), hymn #94, p. 138, and a four-verse version was printed in the 1780 edition of the same collection (hymn #39, pp. 59-60). The English version that entered common use appears to be a text comprised of some verses translated by William Williams himself, and some by Peter Williams. See further J. R. Watson, ed., *The Annotated Anthology of Hymns* (Oxford: Oxford University Press, 2002), 228-29.

[26]Derec Llywyd Morgan, *The Great Awakening in Wales*, trans. Dyfnallt Morgan (London: Epworth, 1988); "Williams, William (1717–1791)," in *Oxford Dictionary of National Biography*, ed. H. C. G. Matthew and Brian Harrison (Oxford: Oxford University Press, 2004); *The Blackwell Dictionary of Evangelical Biography, 1730–1860*, 2 vols., ed. Donald M. Lewis (Oxford: Blackwell, 1995), s.v. "Williams, William."

revival, and he remains one of the giants of Welsh literature to this day.[27] He was the Charles Wesley, and perhaps also the Jonathan Edwards, of Wales.[28] The Welsh hymnbook in which "Guide Me, O Thou Great Jehovah" first appeared was published near the end of 1761, and it was a catalyst for a spectacular revival in mid-Wales in 1762 that centred in Llangeitho but then spread widely.[29] The revival was associated with ecstatic manifestations, including the Welsh jumpers and shouters, who would bounce up and down during meetings. Williams wrote of Martha Philopur as an archetypal convert, one of those who did "shout praise to the LORD, bless and glorify my God, leap and jump for joy."[30] Williams defended this sort of behaviour to its critics, saying it was a continuation of the dancing spoken of in the Old Testament in the city of David, which Michal, Saul's daughter, despised.[31] Even the Welsh jumpers were treated typologically.

This context of popular reception in the midst of revival is important to bear in mind as we consider Williams's text. Typology was not an academic exercise. In the hymn "Guide Me, O Thou Great Jehovah," Williams accomplishes a masterpiece of biblical typology in which episodes from the wilderness wanderings of Israel prefigure the life and work of Christ and the journey of the Christian believer through this life. Believers had long recognized that just as the exodus was the supreme salvific event in the history of Israel, so also the Gospels announced in Jesus Christ a new exodus, a new deliverer doing the mighty works of Yahweh, going through the waters and

---

[27]There are very few critical studies of Williams in English. One study that examines his poetry in terms of both Romanticism and classical Christian spirituality is J. Gwilym Jones, *William Williams Pantycelyn* (Caerdydd: Gwasg Prifysgol Cymru, 1969).

[28]He wrote epic poems, too, including one of over a thousand stanzas, titled *Theomemphus* (1764), on the soul's pilgrimage through the world. Few of his hymns are sung widely in English today, though during his lifetime he wrote more than eight hundred hymns and published two hymnbooks in English. William Williams, *Gloria in Excelsis: or, Hymns of Praise to God and the Lamb* (Carmarthen, 1772), and *Hosannah to the Son of David; or, Hymns of Praise to God for our Glorious Redemption by Christ* (Bristol, 1759). These works have been reprinted in *Songs of Praises: English Hymns and Elegies of William Williams, Pantycelyn, 1717–1791*, ed. R. Brinley Jones (Porthyrhyd, Llanwrda: Drovers, 1995).

[29]Eryn M. White, "'I Will Once More Shake the Heavens': The 1762 Revival in Wales," *Studies in Church History* 44 (2008): 154-63; R. Geraint Gruffydd, "The Revival of 1762 and William Williams of Pantycelyn," in *Revival and Its Fruit* (Bryntirion, Wales: Evangelical Library of Wales, 1981), 19-40; Geraint H. Jenkins, *The Foundations of Modern Wales: 1642–1780* (Oxford: Oxford University Press, 1993), 366.

[30]William Williams, *Llythyr Martha Philopur* [Martha Philopur's Letter] (1762), quoted in Morgan, *Great Awakening*, 25.

[31]Williams, *Llythyr Martha Philopur*, 26; cf. Gruffydd, "Revival of 1762," 27-28.

passing through the desert, giving a new law on a new mountain, and ultimately acting as the suffering servant of Isaiah who would lead his followers through his death and resurrection into a new Promised Land. In the Gospel of Matthew, this typology is set up by presenting Christ as the fulfillment of Hosea's words: "Out of Egypt have I called my son" (Hosea 11:1; cf. Matthew 2:5). At the transfiguration, Jesus talked with Elijah and Moses of his approaching death as his "exodus" (*tēn exodon autou*, Luke 9:31). The precedents of 1 Corinthians 10 ("That rock was Christ") and Hebrews 4 ("There remains a rest for the people of God") were taken up very early in the history of the church to allow Christians to interpret the experience of the believer too in terms of exodus, wilderness, and Canaan. In his homily on Numbers 33 (where the wilderness journey of Israel is summarized) the early church father Origen provided one of the first interpretations of the desert wanderings in terms of the Christian spiritual life, tracing no less than forty-two stages in the spiritual itinerary of the believer.[32] Gregory of Nyssa did something similar, and it was very soon embedded in Christian consciousness that our journey through this life is in some way prefigured by the experience of Israel.[33]

It is unlikely that William Williams was familiar with the allegorical biblical commentary of Origen and Gregory of Nyssa, though by the eighteenth century the exodus was a well-established type. However, evangelical devotional intent naturally reproduced a parallel sort of exegesis, joining the literal-historical to the literal-prophetic meaning of Scripture. This way of reading Scripture was altogether characteristic of Williams's hymns and epic poetry, which were rich in biblical symbolism.[34]

His famous hymn begins with the exodus experience already in the past and plunges the singer into the dilemma of the pilgrim in the barren

---

[32]Origen, "Homily XXVII on Numbers: Concerning the Stages of the Children of Israel (Numbers 33)," in *Origen*, trans. Rowan A. Greer, Classics of Western Spirituality (London: SPCK, 1979), 245-69.

[33]See *Gregory of Nyssa: The Life of Moses*, trans. Abraham J. Malherbe and Everett Ferguson (New York: Paulist Press, 1978).

[34]The theme of pilgrimage in "Guide Me, O Thou Great Jehovah" was in fact a predominant theme in much of his poetry. In a hymn that begins with the aspiration, "I Long to feel that blessed Rest," for example, he describes his life in terms similar to his more famous hymn: "Here I wander to and fro, / Fearful and weak where e'er I go, / A Pilgrim like, in Wilds unknown." Williams, *Gloria*, hymn # 23, p. 21. See also his epic, *Theomephus*. Eifon Evans, introduction to *Pursued by God: A Selective Translation with Notes of the Welsh Religious Classic, Theomemphus by William Williams of Pantycelyn* (Bryntirion, Wales: Evangelical Press of Wales, 1996).

wilderness of this life. The singer is on the other side of conversion, looking ahead to the journey through this life and beyond:

> Guide me, O Thou great Jehovah,
> Pilgrim thro' this barren land;
> I am weak, but Thou art Mighty,
> Hold me with Thy powerful hand:
> Bread of heaven! bread of heaven!
> Feed me now and evermore.[35]

There are three horizons that are fused here in this stanza: Israel, Christ, and the believer. The singer is figured in first person as Israel in the wilderness. For the moment, singing these words, *I* am Israel wandering in the Sinai desert. For William Williams, this allowed the singer to turn with Israel to trust God's leading in the midst of weariness. This was something Williams sought to emphasize in this hymnbook, since, as he wrote in the preface to the 1762 hymnal, he wanted to address the needs of weak believers who might not have a robust assurance of salvation.[36] A more literal translation of the Welsh of the original stanza brings this out even more clearly:

> Lord, lead through the wilderness
> me a wretched-looking pilgrim
> with no strength or life in him
> as if lying in the grave.
> Almighty is the one who will lift me up.[37]

However, for the singer whose imagination is formed by the Scriptures, the "bread of heaven" in first stanza is eucharistic (John 6:32-33), and the stanza is addressed to Christ himself. The New Testament horizon is fused with that of Israel in the desert.

In Numbers 33: 9 the Israelites encountered twelve "fountains of water" at Elim, the place of refreshing, and Williams turns this into a prayer for the Christian pilgrim too:

---

[35]I am following here the form of the hymn in *Collection of Hymns . . . Countess of Huntingdon* (1780), 59-60.

[36]White, "1762 Revival," 15.

[37]Translated by Richard Jeffrey in Marjorie Reeves and Jenyth Worsley, eds., *Favourite Hymns: 2000 Years of Magnificat* (London: Continuum, 2001), 126.

> Open now the crystal fountain
> Whence the healing streams do flow;
> Let the fiery cloudy pillar
> Lead me all my journey through:
> Strong *Deliv'rer*! Strong *Deliv'rer*!
> Be Thou still my *strength* and *shield*.

The typology is here extended from the first stanza. For the singer, there are further unmistakable New Testament allusions. The "crystal fountain" is baptismal. It further symbolizes the living water of the Holy Spirit (1 Corinthians 10:2-3). The fiery cloudy pillar invites comparisons to the Spirit who descends in tongues of fire. For the believer, Williams's imagery of water and fire turns this stanza into a prayer for more of the Holy Spirit (Luke 3:16; cf. John 1:33; 7:39).[38] Thus, though Christians may encounter the barrenness of "the wilderness state," they may also expect to experience spiritual refreshment and guidance.

Finally, having been led through the wilderness, where the means of grace sustain, the pilgrim approaches the destination. But first he or she must face death, the last and greatest test of all, before reaching heaven. The type is of crossing the River Jordan and entering the Promised Land:

> When I tread the verge of *Jordan*,
> Bid my anxious fears subside;
> Death of deaths, and hell's destruction,
> Land me safe on Canaan's side.
> Songs of praises, songs of praises,
> I will ever give to Thee.[39]

In sum, there is here no eclipse of biblical narrative or collapse in traditional patterns of figurative reading. On the contrary, traditional typology that may be traced all the way back to Origen is here taken up and made intensively personal. This personalizing of the typology is, I think, the distinctive evangelical emphasis. John Newton does exactly the same thing in his figural appropriation of the experience of King David in 1 Chronicles 16:16-17. He

---

[38]"Come, Holy Spirit, fire by night, / Pillar of cloud by day; / Lord, for I dare not take a step / Unless thou show the way." A translation of a hymn of Williams quoted in Evans, *Pursued*, 31. The same theme is in Williams, *Gloria*, hymn #4, 6, and hymn #35, 31.

[39]Cf. Williams, *Gloria*, hymn #20, 19, which begins, "Lord, when I make my passage through / Great Jordan . . ." The trial of death, under the trope of Jordan, recurs in many places in Williams's hymns.

does this in his hymn "Amazing Grace," viewing Christ as the greater son of David and figuring the singer into story in first-person language of prayer and praise. Newton made all this explicit in a sermon preached alongside the hymn when he first wrote it.[40]

Elsewhere I have explored the range of ways evangelical figuration worked to incorporate the reader or singer into the biblical narrative. For example, one may reconstruct the key moments in the entire biblical narrative from single lines of famous hymns of Charles Wesley, and in each case one is not simply narrating the biblical story but indwelling it and responding in direct address to God. When one sings, "Veiled in flesh the Godhead see! / Hail the incarnate Deity!," this is no mere account of the hypostatic union. The past and present are merged in the burning heat of devotion. The singer cannot help but be involved in the story, in personal response, in alleluias of praise, or simply by getting caught up in the rushing syntax where lines seem to pile up, crashing one after the other like waves on the seashore.

Another figural technique that appears especially in sermons is the transposition of the reader into the biblical narrative in the place of one of its characters. We may look at this from the side of the hearers. Margaret Austin was a lay woman who heard George Whitefield preach on "the Rich man of the Gospel, how he had Laid up treasures on Earth but none in heaven," and she knew on the spot, "I was that Person." She was substituted into the biblical narrative, cut and paste, as it were. As she followed the young Methodist preachers around, and listened to them preach, she found herself personally addressed in every sermon: *she* was the rich man who went empty away, *she* was the proud Pharisee, *she* was at the foot of the cross watching the soldiers pierce the bleeding side of Christ. This was a powerful experience. "The Lord Saw fit to Lett me See my Self," she said.[41] The biblical narrative presented so forcefully by Whitefield reconstructed her own biography. She was assimilated to the biblical world and its account of reality. Instead of the modern world swallowing the Bible, the Bible was swallowing her world. Instead of an eclipse of biblical narrative, there was light in her darkness.

---

[40]See further Hindmarsh, "'Amazing Grace': The History of a Hymn and a Cultural Icon," in *Sing Them Over Again to Me: Hymns and Hymnbooks in America*, ed. Mark A. Noll and Edith L. Blumhofer (Tuscaloosa, AL: University of Alabama Press, 2006), 3-19.

[41]Margaret Austin, MS letter to Charles Wesley, May 19, 1740, John Rylands Library, Manchester.

Another similar pattern was to cut and paste verbatim words or phrases, not just characters, from the Bible, and place them into one's own narrative. The result is that one's own language glowed under a borrowed sacred light. Charles Wesley's hymns were a great primer for this technique, and lay people learned therby to narrate their experience in the language of Scripture. Ann Martin appropriated the words of the Virgin Mary, saying of herself, "the power of the most highest Overshaw'd me." Mary Ramsay turned to a different analogue, writing, "With the woman of Samaria, I may say, come see a man that told me all that ever I did."[42] There was an intensification of this use of biblical language in certain cases where individuals testified to words from Scripture lighting up their experience as life-changing locutions. The phrase in many lay narratives was, "The word came home with power." Like a bunker-busting bomb, a single line from the Scriptures would penetrate the soul. The discreet biblical text, lifted from the page, was sent to do a special kind of work now in a psychological context. At his conversion at Cambuslang, George Tassie found "that word came upon my heart with power, 'My Lord, and My God,'" and thus the biblical confession of the disciple Thomas reordered the inner world of a Scottish layman near Glasgow in 1741. Janet Jackson was spinning at her wheel and in spiritual distress, and then, all of a sudden, she says, "These words came into My Mind with great sweetness & power Thou art a New Creature: upon which I was Made to believe I was no Hypocrite, But a new Creature."[43]

In such ways, the hymnody and preaching of evangelicals extended traditional biblical typology into the modern period. Typology was a means to unite the Old and New Testament into one overarching, cohesive narrative. Evangelicals were invited to read the Bible this way and were further catechized in techniques by which they could figure their own lives personally into the story. Perhaps this personal emphasis is what led Hans Frei to dismiss evangelical experience as an insufficient response to the eclipse of biblical narrative. He felt that evangelicals assimilated the biblical story into their own experience, rather than the other way around. Although Jesus is real, he became little more than

---

[42]I provide these and other examples from the lay Methodist narratives at the John Rylands Library in Bruce Hindmarsh, *The Evangelical Conversion Narrative: Spiritual Autobiography in Early Modern England* (Oxford: Oxford University Press, 2005), 149-50.

[43]William MacCulloch, "Examinations of Persons under Spiritual Concern at Cambuslang, during the Revival in 1741-42," 2 vols., bound MSS, New College, Edinburgh, 1:23, 146.

a cipher in their stories, and it remained one's *own* life, absent any wider context, that was primary. "It is not the lack of an objective savior but the location of the cumulative narrative bond which indicates how loose and tentative the hold of this profound religious movement on a context or world, temporal, eternal, or both, in which one may feel at home. The crucial and indispensable continuity or linkage in the story is the journey of the Christian person from sin through justification to sanctification or perfection."[44] W. R. Ward makes a similar case: "Wesley exemplified what came to be characteristic of Western evangelicalism, an inability to place the drama of salvation within a larger framework of thought. What Methodists were to call 'our doctrines' . . . were all about salvation and not creation. This tended to be left to Unitarians and deists."[45] Ward argued that by the nineteenth-century evangelical Christianity came to be based on a set of central doctrines without general intellectual context.[46]

JONATHAN EDWARDS AND THE EXPANSION OF TYPOLOGY

However, the evangelical who provides the best counter to this criticism is Jonathan Edwards, who expanded the range of typology to an extent seen only rarely since before the Reformation, and it was precisely with the aim of uniting the temporal and eternal world with the personal experience of salvation. As with his metaphysics and his ethics, Edwards was quite self-consciously swimming against the current of elite thought. To men like Collins and Whiston, who had tossed out typology altogether, Edwards would look just plain silly. So, as he laid out his grand typological program in the mid-1740s in a twenty-page octavo notebook entitled *Types*, he reflected, "I expect by very ridicule and contempt to be called a man of very fruitful brain and copious fancy, but they are welcome to it. I am not ashamed to own that I believe that the whole universe, heaven and earth, air and seas, and the divine constitution and history of the holy Scriptures, be full of images of divine things, as full as a language is of words."[47] Crucially, here, Edwards was

---

[44]Frei, *Eclipse*, 153.

[45]W. Reginald Ward, *Early Evangelicalism: A Global Intellectual History, 1670–1789* (Cambridge: Cambridge University Press, 2006), 132-33.

[46]Ward, *Early Evangelicalism*, 185.

[47]Jonathan Edwards, *Types, Works of Jonathan Edwards, Volume 11: Typological Writings*, ed. Wallace E. Anderson, Mason I. Lowance Jr., and David H. Watters (New Haven, CT: Yale University Press,

returning to the ancient idea in Augustine and Hugh of St. Victor that the objects of the material world and the events of the temporal world could be read like ciphers in a book. And he rejected the idea that these objects and events were inert, explainable only at the level of simple mechanical causation. Ralph Cudworth had earlier objected to the new science as producing a dead world of "stupid matter" filled with "dead, cadaverous things."[48] Not so for Edwards. He embraced Newtonian science but placed it within a metaphysic in which God was present and active, every moment creating the universe anew. His typological program was an extension of his larger philosophical project, so that the universe was everywhere and always the very language of God.

For Edwards, the clear typological examples in the Scriptures could be taken as a clue to the nature of reality itself and to the manner of God's working more generally. If in the course of sacred history God ordained that certain events would foreshadow later events and find their fulfilment therein, then it seemed logical to think of such figuration in general terms as "a certain sort of language, as it were, in which God is wont to speak to us."[49] Between 1744 and 1749, while a minister in Northampton, he thoroughly traced what he took to be the types of the Messiah in the Old Testament in one of his Miscellanies entries (no. 1069), turning this into a treatise of seventy-three densely written folio sheets.[50] It was a kind of exercise book for learning God's language. He came to believe that "the works of God are but a kind of voice or language of God, to instruct intelligent beings in things pertaining to himself."[51] This idea of typology as a language is central to Edwards's program and he thinks through its implications. A language must be acquired—whether naturally as one is trained up to learn a native tongue, or as a second language learned through education—but it requires much practice and a kind of discernment, good taste, or judgement to become expert in it. So also with learning the language of divine types. If one has not learned the language

---

1993), 11:152. Available in *Works of Jonathan Edwards Online*, Jonathan Edwards Center at Yale University, http://edwards.yale.edu/. Hereafter cited as simply as WJEO, with volume number.

[48]Ralph Cudworth, *The True Intellectual System of the Universe: The First Part; Wherein All the Reason and Philosophy of Atheism Is Confuted*, 2nd ed., 2 vols (London, 1743), 1:138, 147, 148, 155.

[49]Edwards, *Types*, WJEO, 11:150.

[50]Edwards, *Types of the Messiah*, WJEO, 11:155-328. It includes Edwards own two-page table of entries cross-referenced to the text (pp. 325-28)

[51]Edwards, *Images of Divine Things*, WJEO, 11:67 (entry no. 55).

well, then attempts to speak will be pretentious or barbarous. And with divine types, "there is room for persons to be learning more and more of this language and seeing more of that which is declared in it to the end of the world without discovering all."[52] In a way, Edwards was returning to the patristic and medieval mode of reading nature like literature, such as we see in Augustine's *Confessions*, where he described the heavens like "a canopy of skins" and added, "These heavens are your Book, your words in which no note of discord jars."[53] In a similar way, Edwards felt that nature could be *read*, not just observed, classified, and quantified.

Because learning to identify typological meanings is like learning a language, Edwards was able to leave plenty of room for getting it wrong. One must keep practising and it required "much use and acquaintance," but it was possible to get the knack of it. What though were the keys to learning this language? How does one learn what "the heavens declare," beyond the mathematical descriptions and taxonomies of science? Here Edward thought the key was to study Scripture carefully and let it be the guide. Scripture first of all gives us the antitypes—that is, the ultimate spiritual meanings to which all history and all material things point. But also, second, it is the interpreter of nature "in actually making application of the signs and types in the book of nature as representations of those spiritual mysteries in many instances."[54] Thus, Edwards read in Ephesians 5:30-32 that marriage is declared to represent the mystery of Christ and the church, and he says, "It is evident that God hath ordered the state and constitution of the world of mankind as he has to that end, that spiritual things might be represented by them."[55] Edwards generalizes from the example of marriage to the constitution of the world itself as likewise sacramental.

Another example of this method would be Edwards scouring the Bible to try to understand the way light is spoken of. We must picture him in his study in Northampton with a concordance open beside his Bible. He looks up the word *light* and then reads every reference to see if there is any clue to the deeper antitypical meaning of light. He begins to get a hunch that light often symbolizes glory or revelation or holiness and so on. It is like he is learning

---

[52]Edwards, *Types*, WJEO, 11:152.
[53]Augustine, *Confessions*, trans. R. S. Pine-Coffin (Harmondsworth: Penguin, 1961), 13.15.
[54]Edwards, *Images*, WJEO, 11:106 (entry no. 156).
[55]Edwards, *Images*, WJEO, 11:67 (entry no. 56).

a language inductively. He was especially attentive where something was spoken of in Scripture in superlative terms. This was a clue to the fulfilment of the type. So when Christ is described in the Gospel of John as the "true light" that was come into the world (John 1:9), this was a sure indication that *all* light signifies Christ. "The type is only the representation or shadow of the thing, but the antitype is the very substance, and is the true thing."[56] It would not be too far wrong to say that Edwards explored the Scriptures inductively in order to discern the Platonic forms that govern the meaning of the universe. It was a very Protestant way to be a Platonist. So even though the concept of language acquisition allowed some reserve about this or that instance of typological reading, Edwards was still advancing a *realist* epistemology of types. There was an ontological structural relation between the light of dawn on a summer morning or the light of a candle and Christ as the true light. In medieval terms, Edwards was a realist, not a nominalist. He believed in universals but thought these could be found through Bible study rather than pure intuition. In truth, though, Edwards was closer to Abbe Suger's medieval Gothic theory of light than he was to the physico-theologians of the early eighteenth century, who were trying to work out their theology within Isaac Newton's cosmology.

Edwards's manuscript, *Images of Divine Things*, was begun around the time he settled in Northampton in 1727 and was continued until near the end of his life in 1758. It contains 212 entries in a forty-eight-page folio volume. It was here, above all, that Edwards wrote up his finding from his methodic searching of the Scriptures to see if there were consistent patterns to its use of metaphors as clues to the inherent (realist) symbolism of nature. This was his language acquisition notebook, if you like. He began with the easy ones. Death temporal was shadow of death eternal. The stars signified the glorious inhabitants of heaven. But then he differentiated the sun and the moon. The sun was always Christ, and the moon, the church. Once he arrived at these interpretations, they remained fixed. The symbolic meaning of the type was not multiple but singular. The moon was *always* the church, because it was ontologically ordered to be a shadow of this reality. Vegetation as it grows, bears fruit, and flourishes in response to sun, rain, light, and heat from above— this represents spiritual flourishing in dependence on the effusions of the

---

[56]Edwards, *Images*, WJEO, 11:106 (entry no. 156).

Holy Spirit. Storms, the wrath of God; thunder, his majesty; blue sky, his goodness, grace and love. The setting of the sun, the death of Christ; its rising, his resurrection. Color represents the various graces and beauties of God's Spirit. With some insight from Newton's *Opticks* on the refraction phenomenon of light, Edwards added that white, containing all other colours, typified holiness. Ravens, feeding on carrion, devils; hills and mountains, heaven.[57]

That rivers all flow to the ocean spoke of all things tending to one, even to God, and this included history.[58] This will be picked up in Edwards's view of history as "so many lines meeting in one center."[59] On the other hand, the typology of trees works the opposite way, how from one common stock arise many branches: Christ, therefore, the trunk, and the church, the branches. Gravity, another key concept in Newtonian science, also had a deeper typological meaning, since the mutual attraction of bodies represented love in the spiritual world—an idea that would be central to Edwards's wider thought.[60]

More oddly for modern readers, Edwards extended this symbolic mode of perception to history, politics, economics, and technology. The triumph of the Roman armies in battle was a real picture of Christ's ascension. Roman polity and citizenship in the time of Christ was a type of the spiritual polity of the heavenly Jerusalem. Transatlantic trade emanating from America signified the day when the world would be supplied by spiritual treasure from the new world. Complex wheels in machines symbolized God's providence moving events along according to his purposes.[61] Again, it is important to remember that all these connections were for Edwards not pretty emblems or illustrations. This was not inventive fancy, constructing pleasing metaphors that belong only to the mind of the poet. Edwards was aiming for a spiritual perception of underlying truths. He would be the first to say that like learning a language, one might never get these correspondences exactly right, but one was to stay immersed in God's typological language in Scripture and work toward greater and greater fluency.

At one level, Edwards was simply working out in more detail and with more thoroughness, and taking further, what many other evangelicals were

---

[57]Edwards, *Images*, WJEO, 11:51, 52, 54, 58, 64, 67, 70, 72, 77 (entry nos. 1, 4, 13, 27, 28, 50, 58, 61, 64).
[58]Edwards, *Images*, WJEO, 11:77 (entry. no. 77).
[59]Edwards, *History of the Work of Redemption*, WJEO 9:519.
[60]Edwards, *Images*, WJEO, 11:80-81 (entry nos. 78, 79).
[61]Edwards, *Images*, WJEO, 11:82, 87, 101, 188 (entry nos. 81, 91, 178, 214).

doing, such as James Hervey in his popular *Meditations* or Augustus Toplady in his "Sketch of Natural History."[62] Indeed, John Newton spoke in terms remarkably like Edwards when he wrote, "The works of creation may be compared to a fair character in a cypher, of which the Bible is the key. . . . The Lord has established a wonderful analogy between the natural and spiritual world. This is a secret only known to them that fear him."[63] But where John Newton was content to make a few general symbolic connections between nature and God's providence, power, and glory, Edwards was trying to learn a whole language. In conception and scope, it was a grand project.

A PARTIAL ECLIPSE?

In conclusion, we might observe that the path of any eclipse is local, and it is never the entire world that is darkened. There were 251 solar eclipses in the eighteenth century, and none of them were of course worldwide events. Likewise, the "eclipse of biblical narrative" was not universal. Traditional patterns of biblical reading may have been eclipsed for certain elite thinkers, but for many evangelicals, from William Williams in Wales to Jonathan Edwards in New England, the Bible continued to shine brightly, as we have seen. Moreover, it continued to pull readers into its frame and allow them to understand their lives by its illumination. And for thinkers such as Edwards, the reinvigoration and expansion of traditional typology was part of a deeply considered effort to respond to those elements in Enlightenment thought that seemed to be exiling God from the universe.

Was evangelicalism a product of the Enlightenment? One could argue that there was indeed a stylistic change from the baroque to the Augustan in the eighteenth century. The Royal Society, for example, called for simpler style of prose, more compatible with the age of science, so at a stylistic level there would be less scholastic hypotaxis in the sentence structure of evangelical writings (though Edwards could still pile on the clauses and certainly made ample use of the semicolon). There was also a kind of shift from the syllogism to the axiom, the complex to the simple, and the deductive to the inductive. However, this stylistic change was not the really important thing. The turn to nature was much more consequential. What really mattered was the dangerously

---

[62]I explore these figures in Bruce Hindmarsh, *The Spirit of Early Evangelicalism: True Religion in a Modern World* (Oxford: Oxford University Press, 2018), 145-55.

[63]John Newton, *Omicron*, letter 15, in *The Works of the Rev. John Newton*, vol. 1 (London, 1808), 215.

isomorphic dualism that appeared with the rise of science. Early on, the Cambridge Platonist Ralph Cudworth identified a new naturalism as a deep and troubling metaphysic underlying mechanical philosophy. Metaphysical naturalism was emphatically not an aspect of the Enlightenment that evangelicals could accept. Quite the contrary. In the seventeenth century, Cudworth and Henry More opposed this naturalism in what could be described as a baroque manner—developing highly elaborate ideas, including a gnostic emanationist doctrine of a "hylarcic principle" or "cosmoplastick power" intermediate between God and the world. Edwards was certainly doing something vastly different from this in style and substance, but he was equally opposed to every form of naturalism in Enlightenment thought. He opposed Enlightenment naturalism, whether in its science and metaphysics, its historiography, its ethics, its psychology, or, as we have been exploring here, its reading of Scripture. Edwards's project was in crucially important ways anti-Enlightenment.

The devotion of evangelicals worked profoundly to re-enchant the world, and indeed, to re-enchant the Scriptures whenever they were being read like any other book. The indwelling presence of the Holy Spirit in the believer ("the life of God in the soul of man") was a basis for viewing the natural world, along with the social and political world, as one in which God was vitally active. From Charles Wesley's "Come Holy Ghost, All Quickn'ing Fire," to George Whitefield's sermon "On the Indwelling of the Holy Spirit," to John Wesley's sermon on "Salvation by Faith," to Edwards's discourse on "A Divine and Supernatural Light," evangelicals were doing something radical by invoking the Holy Spirit as a present reality in the Enlightenment era. It was for Edwards, more than anyone else, to try to work out the implications of this across nearly every area of eighteenth-century thought. At every juncture he proposed divine intimacy in opposition to divine absence. Typology was one more means for him to do so, joining together, as the ancients had, the two books: the book of Scripture and the book of nature.

David Bebbington made a strong case thirty years ago for the compatibility of early evangelicalism with the Enlightenment. After three decades, I think I am ready to hand David my notes on his lecture. I would just add a small insertion. I would simply suggest inserting the words "some aspects of." Evangelicalism was compatible with *some aspects of* the Enlightenment.

3

Faith, Free Will, and Biblical Reasoning in the Thought of Jonathan Edwards and John Erskine

Jonathan Yeager

JONATHAN EDWARDS IS OFTEN PORTRAYED as America's greatest theologian. His early works, including *A Faithful Narrative of the Surprising Work of God* (1737), *The Distinguishing Marks of a Work of the Spirit of God* (1741), *Some Thoughts Concerning the Present Revival of Religion in New-England* (1742), and *A Treatise Concerning Religious Affections* (1746), had a profound influence on transatlantic revivalism during and after his lifetime, and his later theological treatises *Freedom of the Will* (1754) and *Original Sin* (1758) significantly shaped evangelical Calvinism from the eighteenth century to the present. Edwards, however, did not always write about Calvinism in a way that conformed to classical Reformed thought. At times, he deviated from traditional Reformed biblically inspired language of describing faith during the process of salvation, and whether the human will is free and able to accept God's offer of divine grace. This chapter examines Edwards's Scripture-informed views on faith and free will, comparing him with his friend and most frequent Scottish correspondent, the Reverend John Erskine of Edinburgh. Examining each man's use of reason and theological interpretations of the Bible, the central question asked in this chapter is: Did all early evangelical Calvinists share the same view about saving faith and human volition? As will be demonstrated in the course of this chapter, Edwards and Erskine had much in common, and both were undoubtedly evangelical Calvinists. But the two men deviated substantially when discussing the nature of faith and human volition in the process of salvation, with Edwards taking a holistic, compatibilist, and voluntarist approach to faith and free will, and Erskine positing an intellectual and rational perspective.

JONATHAN EDWARDS'S VIEW OF
FAITH AND FREE WILL

There has been much debate about whether Jonathan Edwards advocated classical Reformed theology when speaking about justification by faith and human free will. At first glance, Edwards's stance on justification by faith appears to be entirely in line with standard, biblically inspired Reformed theology. Using Scripture as the guide, the orthodox Calvinist perspective typically portrays Christ's righteousness as imputed to a believer, so that in a legal sense such a person is in right standing in the eyes of God. Such a perspective of imputed righteousness means that a believer is not actually righteous but is seen as such when that person receives Christ's righteousness. With this understanding, the believer is the same sinner as before this divine act, but because God only sees Christ's righteousness covering that individual, that person is declared in right standing because of the work of Jesus on the cross. Edwards would have agreed with most of these statements. In fact, one of his sermons was aptly entitled, "None Are Saved by Their Own Righteousness."[1] Better known is his 1734 sermon, "Justification by Faith Alone," in which he vigorously defended through the Bible and reason the notion that human works had nothing to do with being justified in God's sight throughout this lengthy discourse. Sounding very much like other Calvinists, Edwards stated that Christ's righteousness was imputed to the elect through faith, placing them in right standing with God. Any talk of believers meriting eternal salvation, Edwards clarified, came only after they were acquitted of sin on account of Christ's sacrifice.[2]

---

[1] *The Works of Jonathan Edwards* (New Haven, CT: Yale University Press, 2009), 14:229-357, hereafter *WJE*.
[2] See *WJE*, 19:143-243.

Edwards also adamantly declared his orthodox Calvinistic leanings in his private notebooks, including the "Blank Bible" and "Notes on Scripture," and in many of his public sermons. In the "Blank Bible" (1730), for instance, he wrote of the "freeness of God's grace," which was not "at all for our righteousness."[3] Earlier, in his "Notes on Scripture" (1722), he jotted down that all humans are guilty of sinning and in a state of condemnation, so that they cannot save themselves. In this predicament, salvation came only by way of "the righteousness of God through Christ received by faith alone."[4] Also in his sermons delivered on passages such as Romans 4:16 (1730), Hebrews 12:22-24 (1740), and John 5:45 (1741), Edwards made it clear to his parishioners in no uncertain terms that there is nothing that humans can do to save themselves; rather, it comes only by God's grace mediated through Christ's work on the cross.[5]

Taking into account his other writings, however, Edwards's position on faith can be said to deviate substantially from classical Calvinism. Scholars studying his view of faith, including George Hunsinger, Gerald McDermott, Thomas Schafer, Anri Morimoto, Michael McClymond, and Lawrence Rast, have all showed that Edwards posited a holistic view of justification by faith that was not unlike Lutheran and even Catholic soteriology on this subject.[6] Edwards argued that a believer actually becomes righteous by receiving Christ's nature, which by consequence merits God's approval. In his "Miscellanies" notebooks, his sermons "God Glorified in Man's Dependence" and

---

[3] WJE, 24:677.

[4] WJE, 15:294.

[5] See Douglas A. Sweeney, *Edwards the Exegete: Biblical Interpretation and Anglo-Protestant Culture on the Edge of the Enlightenment* (New York: Oxford University Press, 2016), 206-9.

[6] See George Hunsinger, "Dispositional Soteriology: Jonathan Edwards on Justification by Faith Alone," *Westminster Theological Journal* 66 (2004): 107-20; Gerald McDermott, "Jonathan Edwards on Justification by Faith—More Protestant or Catholic?," *Pro Ecclesia* 17 (2008): 92-111; Thomas A. Schafer, "Jonathan Edwards and Justification by Faith," *Church History* 20 (1951): 55-67; Anri Morimoto, *Jonathan Edwards and the Catholic Vision of Salvation* (University Park: Pennsylvania State University Press, 1995); Michael McClymond, "Salvation as Divinization: Jonathan Edwards, Gregory Palamas, and the Theological Uses of Neoplatonism," in *Jonathan Edwards: Philosophical Theologian*, edited by Paul Helm and Oliver Crisp (Aldershot: Ashgate, 2003), 139-60; Lawrence R. Rast, "Jonathan Edwards on Justification by Faith," *Concordia Theological Quarterly* 72 (2008): 34-48. Even Sang Hyun Lee, who disagrees with McDermott and others that Edwards advocated a position close to Catholicism with regard to faith, admitted that the American Congregational minister did not adhere to a traditional Reformed model when explaining this doctrine. See Sang Hyun Lee, "Grace and Justification by Faith Alone," in *The Princeton Companion to Jonathan Edwards*, edited by Sang Hyun Lee (Princeton: Princeton University Press, 2005), 130-46.

"Charity and Its Fruits," and in other writings, Edwards employed the Catholic terminology of *infusing* and *inherent* to describe the kind of righteousness that a Christian receives.[7] McDermott describes Edwards's position this way:

> God has decided that at the moment when, by his election, a person trusts in Christ, that person becomes so merged with the person of Christ that the two become one, and Christ's righteousness swallows up the believer's sin. Therefore imputation is not a legal fiction or a cooking of the books, but God's perception of a new fact: the new moral character of the person called Christ who includes what used to be called the sinner alone.[8]

McDermott is quick to point out that like Martin Luther, Edwards did not distinguish between the biblically inspired terms of justification and sanctification. As opposed to the forensic explanation tied to orthodox Reformed thought, whereby a believer is simply declared righteous in a legal sense, Edwards conflated the theological concepts of justification with sanctification, so that a Christian actually becomes righteous by way of their union with Christ, a view that he shared with Luther and medieval Catholics like Thomas Aquinas.[9]

In his published sermon on *A Divine and Supernatural Light* (1734) and from reason derived from Scripture, Edwards described divine grace in terms of degrees. It was a higher degree of illumination than what the natural body normally experienced, a "true sense of the divine and superlative excellency of the things of religion; a real sense of the excellency of God, and Jesus Christ, and of the work of redemption, and the ways and works of God revealed in the gospel." Edwards said that "there is a divine and superlative glory in these things; an excellency that is of a vastly higher kind, and more sublime nature, than in other things; a glory greatly distinguishing them from all that is earthly and temporal. . . . He don't merely rationally believe that God is glorious, but he has a sense of the gloriousness of God in his heart."[10] Edwards gave the example of knowing about honey, as opposed to tasting and experiencing its sweetness. As he noted, there is a vast difference between simply knowing about God and experiencing the excellence of his beauty and goodness.

---

[7] E. Brooks Holifield, "Edwards as a Theologian," in *The Cambridge Companion to Jonathan Edwards*, ed. Stephen J. Stein (Cambridge: Cambridge University Press, 2007), 150.
[8] McDermott, "Jonathan Edwards on Justification by Faith," 97.
[9] McDermott, "Jonathan Edwards on Justification by Faith," 98-100.
[10] *WJE*, 17:413.

Coupled with Edwards's perspective on justification by faith was his bibli-cally informed view of the will, which has also been analyzed extensively by scholars.[11] Prior to the publication of *Freedom of the Will* in 1754, dozens of Harvard theses throughout the seventeenth century were written on the nature of the will. The heart of the matter can be traced all the way back to Augustine's voluntarist approach in the fourth century (which did not distinguish between the will and affections), and the intellectual counterargument provided by the scholastics of the thirteenth century. In his study of these Harvard theses, Norman Fiering claims that virtually everyone at that time believed that humans were free enough to be held responsible for their sins, because they were not coerced or compelled to behave in a certain way, and that the will is located in the higher faculties as part of the rational soul, and not in one's animalistic nature. The center of the discussions in these theses instead was on whether freedom was exclusively an act of the will, or whether the will and intellect worked together in a unified effort to make decisions. According to Fiering, the consensus was that the will and intellect were two separate faculties, even though they collaborated. Fiering argues that Edwards followed the sixteenth-century English Protestant William Ames and the seventeenth-century Dutch Reformed theologian Petrus van Mastricht—through Augustine—in treating the will synonymously with the affections of the heart, and not as an individual's rational decision-making ability.[12]

---

[11]It does not appear that the issue of whether Edwards conformed to, or deviated from, classical Reformed thought when writing about human volition will be settled any time soon. See Norman S. Fiering, "Will and Intellect in the New England Mind," *William and Mary Quarterly* 29 (1972): 515-58; Allen C. Guelzo, "Freedom of the Will," in *The Princeton Companion to Jonathan Edwards*, ed. Sang Hyun Lee, 115-29; Allen C. Guelzo, *Edwards on the Will: A Century of American Theological Debate* (Eugene, OR: Wipf and Stock, 2007 [1989]); Peter Boohong Jung, "Jonathan Edwards and New England Arminianism," PhD diss., University of the Free State, South Africa, 2004; C. Samuel Storms, "Jonathan Edwards on the Freedom of the Will," *Trinity Journal* 3 (1982): 132-69; James Harris, *Of Liberty and Necessity: The Free Will Debate in Eighteenth-Century British Philosophy* (New York: Oxford University Press, 2005); Philip J. Fisk, "Divine Knowledge at Harvard and Yale: From William Ames to Jonathan Edwards," *Jonathan Edwards Studies* 4 (2014): 151-78; Philip J. Fisk, *Jonathan Edwards's Turn from the Classic-Reformed Tradition of Freedom of the Will* (Gottingen: Vandehoeck and Ruprecht, 2016). For an example of some of the more recent vigorous debates on Edwards's view of the will, see Richard A. Muller, "Jonathan Edwards and the Absence of Free Choice: A Parting of Ways in the Reformed Tradition," *Jonathan Edwards Studies* 1 (2011): 3-22; Paul Helm, "Jonathan Edwards and the Parting of the Ways," *Jonathan Edwards Studies* 4 (2014): 42-60; Richard A. Muller, "Jonathan Edwards and Francis Turretin on Necessity, Contingency, and Freedom of Will. In Response to Paul Helm," *Jonathan Edwards Studies* 4 (2014): 266-85; Paul Helm, "Turretin and Edwards Once More," *Jonathan Edwards Studies* 4 (2014): 286-96.

[12]Fiering, "Will and Intellect in the New England Mind," 515-53.

Edwards would have been familiar with these debates while an undergraduate at Yale, but became interested in writing on the will as a way of combating "Arminianism," which he saw as a counter-Calvinistic movement that improperly utilized Scripture, was gaining ground in western Massachusetts in the mid-1730s and strengthening throughout the so-called communion controversy that led to his dismissal from Northampton in 1750. Edwards's "Quaestio" thesis (1723), published sermons on *Justification by Faith Alone* (1723) and *God Glorified in Man's Dependence* (1731), *Treatise Concerning Religious Affections* (1746), and *Farewell Sermon* (1750) were all aimed at countering the growing Arminian trend in New England, which culminated in 1754 with his most focused work on the subject, *Freedom of the Will*.[13]

In this influential book, Edwards claimed that the will is a not a separate faculty from the intellect and power of reasoning. Rather, willing is simply choosing one's strongest desires. In the preface, Edwards defined the will as "that by which the mind chooses anything. The faculty of the will is that faculty or power or principle of mind by which it is capable of choosing: an act of the will is the same as an act of choosing or choice."[14] In describing the will in this way, he cited John Locke and his seminal *Essay Concerning Human Understanding* (1690) as positing a similar definition, even though he rejected the Englishman's distinction between preferring and choosing.[15] Edwards's purpose in writing this treatise was to refute the supposedly Arminian teaching that liberty consisted in a self-determining will that could choose any number of possible options. Edwards denied this possibility, claiming instead that individuals do not have the freedom or liberty to do as they please because they are driven by their strongest desires. In other words, willing is not done arbitrarily or indifferently; humans make

---

[13]Peter Jung rightly assesses that Edwards's interest in free will was a result of the circumstances of New England at the time, particularly the influx of books donated to Yale by Jeremiah Dummer in 1714, the "great apostasy" of Timothy Cutler and others from Yale to the Church of England in 1722, the Hampshire Ministers Association scrutiny towards the teachings of Robert Breck in the mid-1730s, his concern about Arminianism gaining ground in his parish at Northampton during the 1734-1735 revival, his analysis of those who lapsed after supposedly experiencing conversion during the Great Awakening of the early 1740s, and finally in his judgment on the people of Northampton during the time of his dismissal in 1750. See Jung, "Jonathan Edwards and New England Arminianism," 95-121.

[14]*WJE*, 1:137.

[15]Fisk, *Jonathan Edwards's Turn*, 308-9.

decisions based on the most compelling option placed before them. Just as faith was a comprehensive term meant to describe the process of a believer's consent to a union with Christ, Edwards produced a voluntarist definition of the will that was an all-encompassing act, incorporating the use of reason and circumstances, but most importantly desire. He said that the will is "the whole of that which moves, excites or invites the mind to volition, whether that be one thing singly, or many things conjunctly. Many particular things may concur and unite their strength to induce the mind; and when it is so, all together are as it were one complex motive."[16] For Edwards, willing is an action that results in choosing. The choices that humans make are based on their strongest motivations and future assessment of benefits.

Edwards went further by saying that certain motivations are so strong that humans cannot avoid giving in to them. On this point, he differentiated between what he called natural and moral necessity. Natural necessity refers to a person's decisions that are dictated by the forces of nature. He used the example of feeling pain in the body from a wound. Such a sensation occurs by natural necessity, as the body involuntarily reacts to certain feelings.[17] Related to this term is natural inability. By this Edwards meant that humans are restricted by natural laws. Humans have to abide by certain laws of nature when they make choices. So, for example, a young boy might imagine himself sprouting wings and flying like a bird, but he is incapable of actually doing this because of his limited physical characteristics. Edwards put it this way: "We are said to be naturally unable to do a thing, when we can't do it if we will, because what is most commonly called nature don't allow of it, or because of some impeding defect or obstacle that is extrinsic to the will; either in the faculty of understanding, constitution of body, or external objects."[18]

More controversial was Edwards's explanation of moral necessity. According to Edwards, moral necessity can be just as strong of a force as natural necessity. If motives are strong enough, humans cannot morally resist them. Edwards said that moral inability consists "either in the want of inclination; or the strength of a contrary inclination; or the want of sufficient motives in

---

[16] *WJE*, 1:141.
[17] *WJE*, 1:156-57.
[18] *WJE*, 1:159.

view, to induce and excite the act of the will, or the strength of apparent motives to the contrary."[19] He used the example of an alcoholic's inability to
refuse a drink, or, in a positive sense, a woman of honor and chastity unwilling
to succumb to prostitution. In either case, habits and desire work together
as a person chooses options based on their strongest motivations. An alcoholic
man might know that excessive drinking is harmful to his body, but because
of years of abuse might not be able to resist the urge to imbibe. Similarly, a
chaste woman might have been raised in such a way, and formed certain
habits, so that promiscuity is unthinkable to her. Using Edwards's definitions
of natural and moral necessity, one can see that while it is technically possible
for humans not to sin (because no natural laws deter people from wrongdoing),
it is morally impossible to avoid giving in to all evil desires because of the
strength of certain motivations.

By describing the will as such, Edwards thought that he had safeguarded
the Calvinistic emphasis on the sovereignty of God and provided a reasonable
explanation for how humans can be held responsible for their sin. According
to Edwards, God does not make anyone sin. Rather, sin occurs because
humans have a corrupt nature that compels them to make poor choices.
Important to Edwards in this discussion is that God permits sin to accomplish
his purposes but does not force anyone to do anything contrary to their
nature.[20] Edwards described the relationship between human sin and God's
permitting of it in the following way: "Men do *will* sin as sin, and so are the
authors and actors of it: they love it as sin, and for evil ends and purposes.
God don't will sin as sin, or for the sake of anything evil; though it be his
pleasure so to order things, that he permitting, sin will come to pass; for the
sake of the great good that by his disposal shall be the consequence."[21] Edwards
compared God with the sun, in that there is a difference between the sun's
production of light and heat when its beams reach the earth, and the frost
and darkness that is created by its absence. In each case, God and the sun are
not the cause of sin and darkness.[22]

---

[19] *WJE*, 1:159.

[20] Edwards did not go as far as his disciple Samuel Hopkins in saying that God willed evil into
existence in order to create the best possible world. See Samuel Hopkins, *The System of Doctrines,
Contained in Divine Revelation, Explained and Defended* (Boston: Isaiah Thomas and Ebenezer
T. Andrews, 1793), 1:135-41.

[21] *WJE*, 1:408-9.

[22] *WJE*, 1:404

From Edwards's perspective, God maintains his sovereignty because he has absolute and certain foreknowledge of the free actions of moral agents.[23] In his explanation of God's perfect foreknowledge, Edwards referred to Scripture extensively, with countless examples from the Old and New Testaments of characters in the Bible whose moral conduct was divinely foretold. Pharaoh's stubborn refusal to free the Israelites from slavery in the book of Exodus, for instance, was predicted by God as he instructed Moses on how to respond to Egypt's ruler. Edwards offered several other examples, including King Josiah's opposition to idolatry foretold some three hundred years before he was born, Micaiah's prophecy of the sinful acts of King Ahab, the immoral conduct of King Hazael, Cyrus's decree to allow the rebuilding of the temple, Daniel's prophecy of the horrendous acts of Antiochus Epiphanes, Christ's prediction that Peter would deny him, and the future kingdom of God.[24] Edwards's appeal to Scripture was limited in *Freedom of the Will*, however, because as Paul Helm rightly argues, this was primarily a philosophical work that was intended to meet enlightened "Arminian" authors on their own philosophical ground.[25]

Edwards also employed the Bible to show that Jesus Christ was perfectly holy in his earthly ministry and was necessarily flawless from a moral standpoint. He quoted from Isaiah 42:1-4, Isaiah 50:5-9, and Jeremiah 23:5-6 to demonstrate that Christ was blamelessly able to endure all forms of suffering and temptation as a sinless savior who was perfectly righteous. Edwards's point in referring to these passages was that Christ would not have been reliable if the promises about him could have failed. Jesus therefore did not have the free will to sin or not to sin, to be holy or not to be holy. Instead, Christ was so perfectly moral that he was not capable of making sinful choices. Edwards wrote that Christ was "under such a strong inclination or bias to the things that were excellent," that it was "impossible that he should choose the contrary."[26] Like humans, Christ was motivated by his strongest desires. But unlike humans, his moral necessity was perfectly righteous.

---

[23] *WJE*, 1:239.
[24] *WJE*, 1:239-47.
[25] Helm, "Jonathan Edwards and the Parting of the Ways," 44.
[26] *WJE*, 1:291.

JOHN ERSKINE'S VIEW OF FAITH AND FREE WILL

John Erskine had great respect for Edwards as a theologian but did not appreciate the American minister's views on faith and human free will. Erskine's relationship with Edwards commenced with an exchange of letters sometime in the 1740s, probably initiated by the Scottish evangelical around the time of the Cambuslang Revival. This was the largest revival in Scotland, which centered around two communion services held at a small western parish during the summer of 1742, with reports of some thirty thousand to fifty thousand people in attendance. Scottish evangelicals like Erskine consulted Edwards's early works on revivalism, including *A Faithful Narrative of the Surprising Work of God*, *The Distinguishing Marks of a Work of the Spirit of God*, *Some Thoughts Concerning the Present Revival of Religion in New England*, and his *Treatise Concerning Religious Affections*, and then contacted Edwards with questions about the nature of true religion, and whether extraordinary experiences like fainting, weeping, and crying out should be deemed a work of God's Spirit.[27] Erskine was a law student at Edinburgh University at the time of the Cambuslang Revival, but shortly afterward changed the course of his studies to divinity once he had witnessed the remarkable effects that evangelical preaching had on the crowd.

Although growing up in a wealthy household and prodded towards a career as a barrister, Erskine decided to become a minister in the Church of Scotland instead, serving as a clergyman in two small towns before moving in 1758 to Edinburgh, where he remained until his death in 1803. From 1768 until his death, he held the position of co-minister at the prestigious Old Greyfriars Church in Edinburgh with the church historian William Robertson while retaining his family estate in Carnock. The wealth from his land holdings provided him the means to build an impressive library of over four thousand volumes, and to send books gratuitously to an extensive list of

---

[27]On Edwards's influence in Scotland, see Jonathan Yeager, "Jonathan Edwards and His Scottish Contemporaries," in *The History of Scottish Theology, Volume II: The Early Enlightenment to the Mid-Nineteenth Century*, ed. David Fergusson and Mark W. Elliott (Oxford: Oxford University Press, 2019), *Jonathan Edwards and Scotland*, edited by Kenneth P. Minkema, Adriaan C. Neele, and Kelly van Andel (Edinburgh: Dunedin Academic, 2011), Harold P. Simonson, "Jonathan Edwards and His Scottish Connections," *Journal of American Studies* 21 (1987): 353-76, and Christopher W. Mitchell, "Jonathan Edwards's Scottish Connection," in *Jonathan Edwards at Home and Abroad*, ed. David W. Kling and Douglas A. Sweeney (Columbia: University of South Carolina Press, 2003), 222-47.

correspondents in America, England, and the Netherlands that included Jonathan Edwards.[28]

Erskine shared a love of books and learning with Edwards. Living in the remote towns of Northampton and Stockbridge, Massachusetts, Edwards did not have easy access to books. Erskine helped feed Edwards's appetite to read the latest religious and philosophical publications by sending the American minister countless pamphlets, treatises, and sermons. Perhaps one-third of Edwards's personal library can be attributed to Erskine's generosity.[29] For his part, Edwards kept Erskine up to date on his current book projects and used the texts sent to him from Scotland to aid his research for treatises like *Freedom of the Will* and *Original Sin*. After Edwards died in 1758, Erskine convinced Jonathan Edwards Jr. to send several of his father's manuscripts to him in Scotland, where they were edited and published. With Edwards Jr. transcribing the manuscripts and Erskine editing them, this collaboration resulted in such publications as *A History of the Work of Redemption* in 1774, *Practical Sermons* in 1788, *Miscellaneous Observations on Important Theological Subjects* in 1793, and *Remarks on Important Theological Controversies* in 1796. In addition to helping publish these posthumous editions, Erskine used his contacts in the bookselling community to reprint earlier works, including Edwards's *Life of David Brainerd* and collections of his sermons. Largely from his endeavors, all but one of Edwards's books were published in Britain before Erskine died in 1803.[30]

Theologically, Edwards and Erskine had much in common. Both were evangelical Calvinists who wanted to enhance Reformed theology during the Age of Enlightenment. Both opposed "Arminianism" while defending traditional Reformed doctrines such as the sovereignty of God, original sin, predestination of the elect, limited atonement, and irresistible grace. Both also made extensive use of Scripture to substantiate the theological claims that they made in their sermons and treatises.[31] However, they did not agree on the subject of saving

---

[28]On Erskine, see Jonathan Yeager, *Enlightened Evangelicalism: The Life and Thought of John Erskine* (New York: Oxford University Press, 2011).

[29]Christopher Wayne Mitchell, "Jonathan Edwards's Scottish Connection and the Eighteenth-Century Scottish Evangelical Revival, 1735—1750," PhD diss., St. Mary's College, University of St. Andrews, 1997, 233.

[30]On the publication history of Edwards's works, see Jonathan Yeager, *Jonathan Edwards and Transatlantic Print Culture* (New York: Oxford University Press, 2016).

[31]On Edwards's voluminous use of Scripture, see Sweeney, *Edwards the Exegete*, Robert E. Brown, *Jonathan Edwards and the Bible* (Bloomington: Indiana University Press, 2002), and *Jonathan*

faith and human free will. While Edwards advocated a biblically inspired voluntarist and affectional approach to understanding the nature of faith and
human free will, Erskine utilized his understanding of Scripture to refute
volition of any kind as part of God's justifying the elect, instead insisting on a
purely intellectual view of saving faith. What makes Erskine's perspective particularly interesting is that the intellectual view of faith is usually associated
with liberal Christians, such as Edwards's antagonist Charles Chauncy.[32]

The most extensive discussion of faith and free will by Erskine can be
found in an essay titled "The Nature of Christian Faith," published in his 1765
Theological Dissertations. In the preface to this volume, Erskine forewarned
his readers that his sentiments on faith were significantly different than
Jonathan Edwards's.[33] Erskine argued that faith is persuasion or assent that
is based upon testimony and intrinsic evidence. On this point, Erskine
sounded like Charles Chauncy and other antirevivalist and liberal Protestant
ministers who argued that religious beliefs came through reasonable persuasion.[34] As opposed to Edwards's holistic and affectional definition of faith,
Erskine wrote that faith when referenced in Scripture "does not signify choice,
affection, temper, or behavior . . . but merely persuasion or assent, and commonly a persuasion founded on testimony."[35] On this point, he cited Exodus 4:1,
1 Samuel 27:12, Proverbs 26:25, Habakkuk 1:5, John 4:21, and James 2:19 to
show that in these, and other biblical verses, faith is presented in Scripture
as assent and equated with knowledge. According to Erskine, "In these passages knowledge must mean faith, because the distinguishing properties,
attendants, and consequences of faith, are ascribed to it, in them."[36] Addi-
tionally, in verses such as 2 Corinthians 5:11, 1 Thessalonians 5:2, 2 Timothy 1:12,
and I John 2:21, knowledge is depicted as persuasion. Putting together all his
biblical findings, Erskine inferred that knowledge in Scripture, when refer-
encing faith, meant persuasion.

Edwards and Scripture: Biblical Exegesis in British North America, ed. David P. Barshinger and
  Douglas A. Sweeney (New York: Oxford University Press, 2018).

[32]Fiering, "Will and Intellect in the New England Mind," 552-56.

[33]Erskine, *Theological Dissertations* (London: Edward and Charles Dilly, 1765), x.

[34]See Charles Chauncy, *The Only Compulsion Proper to be Made Use of in the Affairs of Conscience
  and Religion* (Boston: J. Edwards, 1739), and his *Seasonable Thoughts on the State of Religion in
  New-England* (1743).

[35]Erskine, *Theological Dissertations*, 139.

[36]Erskine, *Theological Dissertations*, 140-41.

Erskine argued that other ways of describing faith gave too much credit to human ability. He wrote that "other ideas of faith, substituted in the place of persuasion, are better calculated to flatter the pride of man, that his acceptance with God is founded on something worthy and excellent in the frame of his mind, in the choice of his will, and in the bias of his affections."[37] Erskine furthermore stated that "faith has no moral efficacy towards procuring our pardon and acceptance." Here, Erskine pitted himself against Edwards's view that a believer's union with Christ produced a kind of beauty and righteousness that merited God's approval. By contrast, Erskine opined that any volitional definition of faith would open the possibility of human achievement, even if it was presented as a subordinating cooperation with divine grace.

Erskine insisted that saving faith should never be equated with a general assent to Christianity. Like Edwards, Erskine admitted that nonbelievers can have a general understanding of Christianity that is not related to saving faith, what Calvinists often referred to as common grace. The unregenerate can know certain aspects of Christianity, including various doctrines, moral principles, miracles in the Bible, and even the reality of Jesus.[38] Saving faith, however, is different. It is the one fundamental truth revealed to the elect, namely that salvation comes through Jesus Christ's death on the cross and resurrection.[39]

Interestingly, Erskine also appealed to John Locke as advocating a similar opinion, in this case about what faith is. But different from Edwards, he did not cite Locke's *Essay Concerning Human Understanding*, but rather the English philosopher's *Reasonableness of Christianity* (1695) because of its rationalist bent in arguing that authentic Christianity rests on believing the proposition that Jesus was the Messiah and Son of God.[40] Erskine further stated that such a revelation about Jesus is revealed throughout the Bible, informing his readers that "all these Scriptures lead to one conclusion, that the only begotten of the Father was sent by him to this wretched world, to be the propitiation and advocate of sinners: and that a fullness of grace dwells in him, and power is given him over all flesh, that he might give eternal life to those given him of the Father."[41] Only certain people receive this kind of saving knowledge.

---

[37]Erskine, *Theological Dissertations*, 141.
[38]Erskine, *Theological Dissertations*, 177.
[39]Erskine, *Theological Dissertations*, 148.
[40]Erskine, *Theological Dissertations*, 151-52.
[41]Erskine, *Theological Dissertations*, 150.

Erskine was in fact closer to Locke's understanding of faith in his *Reasonableness of Christianity* than Edwards. Not unlike Erskine, Locke had written decades earlier that faith in Christ and in divine revelation constituted truths "above reason," but the mind could nevertheless assent to such propositions about Jesus as the Messiah and humanity's Savior on the basis of evidence that appealed to one's natural senses. Edwards had a much more holistic and expansive view of the way that God interacted with a person. Admittedly, sometimes he spoke about saving faith in such a way that he sounded like he fell in line with Locke and Erskine on this matter. In a "Miscellanies" entry in the early 1730s, Edwards described "that spiritual light that is let into the soul by the Spirit of God, discovering the excellency and glory of divine things." Such divine light, Edwards said, "not only directly evidences the truth of religion to the mind . . . but it sanctifies the reasoning faculty, and assists it to see the clear evidence there is of the truth of religion in rational arguments."[42] But from examining the larger corpus of Edwards's writings, it becomes clear that he had no intention of restricting knowledge of God to any of the five senses. Instead, he argued for a spiritual "sense of the heart" that was divinely given to a believer whereby that person now had a transcendent connection with God that defied reason alone. While Edwards followed Locke in believing that knowledge came from experience, he deviated from the English philosopher by positing a kind of spiritual intuition that was divinely given. Once obtained, this new sense of the heart would provide spiritual experiences that formed the basis of supernatural knowledge of God's essence.[43] So, whereas Erskine and Locke sought to produce an argument for the reasonableness of intellectual assent to godly truths above reason, using the mind and a person's natural senses, Edwards posited that a completely new and affectional sense was necessary in order to form authentic experiences of the Almighty. All three men could be said to approach faith biblically and empirically, but Erskine via Locke differed from Edwards in taking a more rationalistic approach.

Erskine talked about saving faith as presented to the elect in such a convincing manner that they must believe, that is to say, rationally assent to it. According to Erskine, "The spirit takes from the Scriptures, the grand evidence

---

[42]*WJE*, 18:156-57.

[43]Robert E. Brown, *Jonathan Edwards and the Bible* (Bloomington: Indiana University Press, 2002), 82-83.

of faith which he had lodged there, and carries it to the hearts of the elect, and then the light and power of divine truth so apprehends and overcomes the soul, that it can no longer resist."[44] Erskine's use of "heart" and "soul" in this passage should not be misunderstood to mean something other than the mind. For him, saving faith was like a light in the elect's mind that God switched on, and could not be turned off. Erskine utilized the classic biblical definition of faith found in Hebrews 11:1—"Now faith is the substance of things hoped for, the evidence of things not seen"—to substantiate his claim about the overwhelming evidence that God establishes within the minds of those he redeems. He appreciated the way that this verse presented faith as the visualization of something that was previously unseen. Erskine wrote that "faith renders invisible things visible, and absent things present. It gives so lively and realizing a representation of things hoped for, that they seem, as it were, actually existing before us. Our persuasion of them is as undoubted, as if we saw them with our bodily eyes, or had a mathematical demonstration of their reality."[45] He gave the example of Stephen in the book of Acts, who saw heaven open and Jesus at the right hand of God while he was being stoned. Through divine intervention, Stephen gained a glance of a heavenly vision that was not apparent to those around him. The revelation of such an experience is like putting on a pair of glasses and experiencing sights that were previously blurry or could not be perceived, even though they existed in reality. Although a prorevivalist and evangelical, Erskine had more in common with Charles Chauncy and John Locke on the subject of faith than Edwards, by emphasizing through Scripture-informed reasoning God's enlightening effects on the mind, rather than the affections.[46]

Erskine's intellectual spin on faith as knowledge and visual perception directly contrasted what Edwards said in several of his writings. In *A Divine and Supernatural Light*, Edwards wrote that spiritual and divine light does not consist of an impression made upon the imagination. Specifically, from studying the Bible, Edwards claimed that divine illumination was "no impression upon the mind, as though one saw anything with the bodily eyes; 'tis no imagination or idea of an outward light or glory, or any beauty of form of countenance, or a visible luster or brightness of any object. The imagination

---

[44]Erskine, *Theological Dissertations*, 177.
[45]Erskine, *Theological Dissertations*, 142.
[46]Fiering, "Will and Intellect in the New England Mind," 556.

may be strongly impressed with such things; but this is not spiritual light."[47] Also different from Erskine, Edwards said that the natural faculties are active in obtaining this supernatural light.[48] They are not simply passive in the way that Erskine described. In an entry in his "Miscellanies" on conversion, Edwards reasoned from Scripture that "there must be a reception of Christ with the faculties of the soul in order to salvation by him, and that in this reception there is a believing of what we are taught in the gospel concerning him and salvation by him." Importantly, he followed up this statement by further declaring that this reception "must be a consent of the will or an agreeableness between the disposition of the soul and those doctrines."[49]

Even though Erskine claimed to consult Scripture exclusively for the ideas that he put forward in his treatise, he came curiously close to presenting a view of faith that was similar to the Scottish secessionist John Glas.[50] Acting from the conclusions he drew from his study of Scripture, Glas left the Church of Scotland in 1725 to form a separate Presbyterian society. He laid forth his views about church structure and rejection of a national covenant in his *Testimony of the King of Martyrs Concerning His Kingdom* (1729). Within this work, Glas showcased his view of faith, arguing that Scripture presented it as "a persuasion of a thing upon testimony."[51] Sounding very much like Erskine, Glas denied any human volition, instead stating that saving faith was the truth about Jesus Christ's identity as the Savior, passively received by the understanding.[52] Glas's son-in-law Robert Sandeman later expanded upon this definition in his *Letters on Theron and Aspasio* (1757), again saying that faith was passive, and merely an impression upon the mind.[53] Erskine referred to Glas's *Testimony of the King of Martyrs* more than once in his essay on faith, and even acknowledged that some readers might find his views to be similar to that of Robert Sandeman.[54] But he distanced himself from Glas

---

[47] *WJE*, 17:412.

[48] *WJE*, 17:416.

[49] *WJE*, 13:213.

[50] Erskine, *Theological Dissertations*, ix-x.

[51] John Glas, *The Testimony of the King of Martyrs Concerning His Kingdom* (Edinburgh: George Lyson, 1729), 219.

[52] John Howard Smith, *The Perfect Rule of the Christian Religion: A History of Sandemanianism in the Eighteenth Century* (Albany: SUNY Press, 2010), 39.

[53] See David Bebbington's chapter, "Evangelical Theology of Scottish Nonconformity," in the second volume of *The History of Scottish Theology*.

[54] Erskine, *Theological Dissertations*, 151, 167, 178.

and Sandeman by insisting that unlike them, he encouraged the means of grace for conversion.[55]

Even if it is granted that Erskine did not blatantly borrow from the thought of Glas and Sandeman on the subject of faith, there can be no doubt that he had been educated in such a way to appreciate a rationalistic form of Christianity. While an undergraduate student at Edinburgh University, he wrote an essay for John Stevenson's logic class in 1737 that demonstrated his proclivity toward an intellectual view of faith and free will. The title of Erskine's thesis was *De recta rationis usa legitimo, sive de libertate cogitandi* (On the legitimate use of right reason, or on liberty of thinking).[56] Erskine began his essay by stating that the legitimate use of right reason can only take place when the mind is free from preconceived opinions and "vicious emotions." He argued that propositions can be determined to be true or false by weighing the strength or weakness of the evidence, which must be considered without favoring authorities or prejudgments. A child of the Enlightenment *and* an evangelical Christian, the young Erskine wrote that

> God, the almighty and the maker of the universe, who has made nothing in vain, has given us all a mind, by which we can investigate unheard of things and weigh those that are heard. For what reason, then, has God dignified us with an extraordinary and pre-eminent faculty? Certainly not so that we may perceive things through the eyes of others and in a blind impulse greedily seize upon whatever pleases us with some show of authority; but so that we may use it so to speak with a more certain and better light by which we may distinguish the true from the false, and so that everywhere enriched with reason we may walk so to speak in the clear light, we may rely on the evidence of our judgement in all things as much in philosophical as in religious matters, we may think better for ourselves.

Erskine blamed the ignorance of previous generations in believing the "most absurd and ridiculous opinions" to the influence of Aristotle, who lorded over the sciences and oppressed liberty of judgment with "almost dictatorial power." Thanks to the forward thinking of the early Enlightenment thinkers Pierre Gassendi, Francis Bacon, René Descartes, and John Locke, who had

---

[55]Erskine, *Theological Dissertations*, x.
[56]See "Notes from Lectures," John Erskine's Essay for John Stevenson, April 30, 1737, Edinburgh University Library, Dc.4.54. (translated by Robin Sowerby).

"shaken off the Aristotelian yoke," humanity was now progressing in liberty of thinking.

But Erskine cautioned his audience from following the Deists by going too far in the use of reason in religion. They "demand such kind of proofs in order on behalf of the Christian religion as the nature of the matter does not admit," and persistently require "a mathematical demonstration, which in such matters could never be held." Erskine's point was that knowledge of various sciences should be sought from different principles, so that it would be absurd to demand a mathematical demonstration using geometry or arithmetic to determine if Julius Caesar or Pompey existed. The same must be true for determining the reality of Christ and his ministry on earth. For Erskine, the mind could assent to the Christian faith because it was a reasonable religion. So, even if authentic Christianity depended on believing truths "above reason," such truths, if supernaturally enlightened by God, nevertheless complied with a person's natural use of reason.

CONCLUSION

This comparison of Edwards with Erskine on biblically inspired reasoning pertaining to faith and the nature of the will demonstrates that not all eighteenth-century evangelical Calvinists thought alike. Some, like Edwards, could deviate from typical Reformed language to talk about faith in a way that could sound Lutheran and even Thomistic, even as they cited Scripture. Like Edwards, they might also follow the voluntarist tract, from Augustine to sixteenth- and seventeenth-century Protestant divines in arguing for a holistic and affectional view of the will. Other evangelical Calvinists, including Erskine, could take a more rational path in explaining faith and free will, while also citing the Bible to substantiate their claims. At times, they might sound like liberal intellectuals in emphasizing the mind over the affections, but they were firmly in the evangelical camp as evident in their prorevivalist outlook, their sometimes scrupulous use of the Bible, and their belief in God's supernatural power to produce conversion experiences. As bookish Calvinists interested in the latest philosophical and theological arguments that could be used to bolster the Reformed tradition, Edwards and Erskine appealed to John Locke, but noticeably each man found inspiration from different works by the English philosopher. In Edwards's case, he cited Locke's *Essay Concerning Human Understanding* as agreeing with his compatibilist definition of the will as the power to choose one's strongest desires or preferences. Erskine, on the other hand, referred to Locke's *Reasonableness of Christianity* when describing faith, because of its intellectual stance that genuine Christianity rested on the belief that Jesus was the Messiah and Son of God. Studying Edwards and Erskine on the subjects of faith and free will highlights the fact that Calvinists could adhere to competing epistemological—and specifically soteriological—claims while also being evangelicals with a high view of Scripture.

Part Two

The Nineteenth Century

4

"Young People Are Actually Becoming Accurate Bible Theologians"

Children's Bible Culture in Early Nineteenth-Century America

K. Elise Leal

IN 1818, THE PHILADELPHIA SUNDAY and Adult School Union, a voluntary association created two years prior to found Sunday schools in the mid-Atlantic region, issued its second annual report. Recounting the successes of the society's auxiliaries, the report emphasized pupils' interactions with the Bible. A Presbyterian Sunday school in Wilmington, Delaware, for example, described how "the teachers in this society have observed with pleasure, a great love for and delight in the holy Scriptures" amongst students. Other children collected money to purchase their own Bibles, which they "brought to school and exhibited with great exultation."[1] Most significantly, pupils eagerly memorized Scripture. One little girl from the same auxiliary, who supposedly possessed no knowledge of Scripture prior to joining the

---

[1] Sunday and Adult School Union, *The Second Report of the Philadelphia Sunday and Adult School Union, Held at their Annual Meeting, Held in St. Paul's Church, May 25, 1819* (Clark & Raser, 1819), 12; American Sunday School Union, Papers, 1817-1915, Presbyterian Historical Society, Philadelphia (hereafter referred to as ASSU papers).

Sunday school, arrived to class one day able to recite "two entire chapters" of the Bible. Upon being questioned further by her teachers, the girl reportedly exclaimed, "Oh I love my Bible; I read it every night and morning; and my mother says she loves to hear me read the Bible."[2]

The story of this anonymous little lover of Scripture represents just one in a host of similar narratives told about children's devotion to the Bible in the early nineteenth century, accounts that often originated within a Sunday school context. As I have argued elsewhere, this era witnessed a transformational moment in American religious history when Protestant reformers from a wide range of denominations—prompted by the forces of religious disestablishment, republican concerns about virtue, and romanticized reconstructions of childhood—united to create institutions and ministries exclusively for young people on a mass scale. The resulting dissemination of institutions such as Sunday schools established physical and imagined communities of faith exclusively for children and youth that were designed to be, first and foremost, Bible-saturated cultures.[3] Sunday school supporters claimed that Bible instruction was the institution's primary benefit, circulating hundreds of stories such as the one above to substantiate the legitimacy and effectiveness of their efforts at childhood religious formation. When compared alongside other institutional records and accounts written by pupils, this rhetoric about young people's love for Scripture begins to reflect broader nineteenth-century trends of childhood and youth engagement with the evangelical culture of biblicism. Sunday schools popularized a modified strand of biblicism—a children's Bible culture—that not only inculcated evangelical norms into the rising generation but also enabled young people to interact with Scripture as emergent religious agents.

The creation of a children's Bible culture was one outcome of the expansion of evangelical biblicism that occurred in the early United States, a subject that has received immense scholarly analysis in recent decades. David Bebbington was the first to argue, now famously, that biblicism, or "a particular

---

[2]Sunday and Adult School Union, *Second Report*, 13.

[3]K. Elise Leal, "'All Our Children May Be Taught of God': Sunday Schools and the Roles of Childhood and Youth in Creating Evangelical Benevolence," *Church History: Studies in Christianity and Culture* 87, no. 4 (2018): 1056-90. Currently, the authoritative monograph on American Sunday schools is Anne M. Boylan, *Sunday School: The Formation of an American Institution, 1790–1880* (New Haven, CT: Yale University Press, 1988).

regard for the Bible," was one of the distinctive features of Protestant evangelicalism in his 1989 *Evangelicalism in Modern Britain*.[4] Subsequent scholarship traced the impact of biblicism in the American context, exploring how a commitment to "the Bible alone" shaped culture, politics, race relations, gender roles, and social structures.[5] The relationship between Scripture and early American life remains fertile ground for exploration, with recent work including Mark Noll's *In the Beginning Was the Word: The Bible in American Public Life, 1492–1783*. This study charts the complex impact of American efforts to use the Bible as the primary guide to life, "sometimes with liberating or comic effects and sometimes with oppressive or tragic results."[6] Seth Perry's 2018 *Bible Culture and Authority in the Early United States* extends this analysis by asking more practical questions of exactly how this process of cultural formation played out on the ground amongst different constituencies. While nineteenth-century Protestants claimed that religious authority stemmed from "the Bible alone," Perry demonstrates that the influence of Scripture came from the way that readers used the text in various written, oral, and performative ways to create and contest authoritative relationships. He suggests that a more productive approach to understanding the Bible's cultural influence is the theoretical framework of scripturalization, in which historians treat the Bible not as a fixed object but as an "ongoing, dialogical process" in which the "status, nature, and content of scriptural texts change constantly."[7] Scripturalization rituals became an increasingly significant

---

[4]David Bebbington, *Evangelicalism in Modern Britain* (London: Unwin Hyman, 1989), 16. For an assessment of the impact and longevity of Bebbington's work, see Timothy Larsen, "The Reception Given *Evangelicalism in Modern Britain* Since Its Publication in 1989," in *The Advent of Evangelicalism: Exploring Historical Continuities*, ed. Michael A. G. Haykin and Kenneth J. Stewart (Nashville: B&H Academic, 2008), 23-36.

[5]A sample of this scholarship includes Nathan Hatch and Mark A. Noll, eds., *The Bible in America: Essays in Cultural History* (New York: Oxford University Press, 1982); Theophus H. Smith, *Conjuring Culture: Biblical Formations of Black America* (New York: Oxford University Press, 1994); Paul C. Gutjahr, *An American Bible: A History of the Good Book in the United States, 1770–1880* (Stanford, CA: Stanford University Press, 1999); Peter Johannes Thuesen, *In Discordance with the Scriptures: American Protestant Battles over Translating the Bible* (New York: Oxford University Press, 1999); David Lyle Jeffrey, ed., *The King James Bible and the World It Made* (Waco, TX: Baylor University Press, 2011); James P. Byrd, *Sacred Scripture, Sacred War: The Bible and the American Revolution* (New York: Oxford University Press, 2013); Daniel L. Dreisbach and Mark David Hall, eds., *Faith and the Founders of the American Republic* (New York: Oxford University Press, 2014).

[6]Mark A. Noll, *In the Beginning Was the Word: The Bible in American Public Life, 1492–1783* (New York: Oxford University Press, 2016), 1.

[7]Seth Perry, *Bible Culture and Authority in the Early United States* (Princeton: Princeton University Press, 2018), 6.

foundation for intersubjective authoritative relationships as Americans' use of the Bible expanded in frequency and variety in the first half of the nineteenth century. Perry argues that this shift provided the means by which Scripture created and constrained authority in the early national period, while also generating "an ever-developing effect on the scripturalized status of the Bible itself," ensuring that the text would continue to wield cultural influence into the present.[8]

While Perry's work makes a valuable contribution to an already rich field of scholarship by providing a framework for understanding how the Bible was operationalized to shape lived experience in the early national period, his work does not fully answer the question of how these scripturalization practices were transmitted from one generation to another. Here, then, is where an assessment of children's Bible culture assumes heightened importance. As one of the most popular child-centric institutions founded in the nineteenth century, the Sunday school provides an ideal lens for examining strategies for socializing young people into habits of biblical literalism, interpretation, and application. But examining children's Bible culture within Sunday schools does more than provide answers to the question of how scripturalization practices were transferred intergenerationally on the ground. It also helps broaden historical analysis of how biblicism functioned by tracing its role in shaping religious identities across the lifespan, which in turn reframes scholarly assumptions about who should be counted as religious agents within this formative era of the expansion of American evangelicalism. Children and youth—both as human beings and as socially constructed life stages—are often positioned as biological and metaphorical opposites of adults. Whereas young people are typically considered to be passive and submissive dependents, adults are assumed to be independent and assertive agents, making them the only subjects traditionally considered worthy of historical study. Yet as Paula M. Cooney asserts, "To the extent that children are neglected as proper subjects, themselves agents of a sort and persons in their own right, the adults studied remain abstracted from their full historical context." Studying religious experiences strictly from the standpoint of adulthood turns historical subjects into "individuals who use reason to contract relationships without regard to significant historical circumstances,

---

[8]Perry, *Bible Culture and Authority in the Early United States*, 9.

including religious ones, that produced them," resulting in an incomplete analysis of religious formation "lacking in richness."[9]

This chapter, therefore, not only explores how children's Bible culture in Sunday schools helps answer the question of how scripturalization practices were transmitted across generations, but also challenges the adult-child binary that exists within narratives of American religious history. Instead of viewing children as the inferior opposites of adults, this chapter examines Sunday school Bible culture through the lens of what childhood studies scholar Marah Gubar calls a kinship-model analysis, which maintains that "children and adults are fundamentally akin to one another, even if certain differences or deficiencies routinely attend certain parts of the aging process."[10] While childhood and youth are distinctive life stages that entail more obvious forms of economic, physical, and social dependency, adults also exist in a compromised position. Contrary to the assumption that they function as fully autonomous agents, adults usually act to some degree in response to other individuals, communities, and cultural norms, meaning that their supposed independence is actually constrained by a dependence on external factors. Adults, do not have a monopoly on agency. Rather, agency is a state of being that is always developing and changing in accordance to life stage. Thus, it is possible for scholars to acknowledge that "children, like adults, have agency, even if aspects of the aging process are likely to limit the form or degree of agency" that subjects have at any given life stage.[11]

---

[9]Paula M. Cooey, "Neither Seen Nor Heard: The Absent Child in the Study of Religion," *Journal of Childhood and Religion* 1, no. 1 (2010), 4-5. Cooey is one example of a scholar who is calling for the integration of children and childhood into the fields of theology and religious studies. For additional examples, see Pamela Couture, *Seeing Children, Seeing God: A Practical Theology of Children and Poverty* (Nashville: Abingdon, 2000); Marcia J. Bunge, *The Child in Christian Thought* (Grand Rapids: Eerdmans, 2001); and Peter B. Pufall and Richard P. Unsworth, eds., *Rethinking Childhood* (New Brunswick, NJ: Rutgers University Press, 2004). In recent decades, the history of childhood has also gained popularity as a subfield, exemplified in the work of scholars such as Steven Mintz, *Huck's Raft: A History of American Childhood* (Cambridge, MA: Belknap, 2004); Karen Sanchez-Eppler, *Dependent States: The Child's Part in Nineteenth-Century American Culture* (Chicago: University of Chicago Press, 2005); and Rodney Hessinger, *Seduced, Abandoned, and Reborn: Visions of Youth in Middle-Class America, 1780-1850* (Philadelphia: University of Pennsylvania Press, 2005), to name a few. However, much of this scholarship does not treat religion as a major category of analysis, meaning that historians lag behind theologians in their attempts to incorporate religion into their studies of childhood.

[10]Marah Gubar, "The Hermeneutics of Recuperation: What a Kinship-Model Approach to Children's Agency Could Do for Children's Literature and Childhood Studies," *Jeunesse: Young People, Texts, Cultures* 8, no. 1 (2016), 299.

[11]Gubar, "The Hermeneutics of Recuperation," 300. For additional perspectives on the same topic, see the first issue of *Journal of the History of Childhood and Youth*, which is devoted almost entirely

Applying this kinship-model understanding of agency to early nineteenth-century Sunday schools reveals that the specific form of biblicism practiced in these institutions was designed, in part, to position young Americans as emergent religious agents within the evangelical community. As a close examination of Sunday school pedagogy and community rituals demonstrates, evangelical efforts to mobilize Scripture to shape the culture of the early republic entailed adaptation of biblicism to different life stages. As a result, Sunday schools socialized young people into the imagined community of evangelical thought and practice by providing standardized interactions with biblicism through which children and youth could formulate religious identities and even assume ownership of the scripturalization process, both personally and communally. While this ownership did not constitute autonomy and was always performed in relation to adults, scripturalization practices in Sunday schools were also oriented around acclimating young people into the art of biblical interpretation and application in their own right. After a brief overview of the origin and structure of the Sunday school movement, this chapter then explores how young people were trained in the scripturalization process as emergent religious agents via memorization, Bible examination curriculum, and teaching.

The evolution of children's Bible culture within Sunday schools began with the institution's turn toward offering exclusively child-centric religious education. American Sunday schools founded in the last decades of the eighteenth century and the initial decades of the nineteenth century accepted both adult and child pupils. However, the broader shift toward creating ministries and institutions specifically for young people described above prompted Sunday school leaders to begin prioritizing child evangelism. Although some adult populations, particularly African American adults, continued to be drawn to Sunday schools, the institution catered almost exclusively to childhood and adolescent religious formation by the 1820s.[12] Sunday schools spread rapidly thereafter, particularly after the formation of a national society called the American Sunday School Union (ASSU) in 1824. A nonsectarian association, the ASSU promoted a "Bible alone" approach to saving souls and cultivating a virtuous citizenry, aspiring to place a Scripture-saturated

---

to the subject of children's agency, and Kristine Alexander, "Agency and Emotion Work," *Jeunesse* 7, no. 2 (2015): 120-28.

[12] For more on this shift, see Leal, "All Our Children May Be Taught of God," 1076-77.

religious education "within the reach of every individual in our country."[13] Acting on this goal, the society established over seventy thousand new Sunday schools over the course of the century, spreading the institution from the Atlantic to the Pacific.[14] By 1832, over ten percent of White American children attended an ASSU school, and by the 1850s a church without a Sunday school was considered an anomaly.[15]

This shift toward a Bible alone, child-centric approach is exemplified by two ASSU auxiliaries that provide the primary case studies for the remainder of this chapter: the Mason Street Sabbath School and the Brandywine Manufacturers' Sunday School. Founded in 1816, the nonsectarian Mason Street Sabbath School opened with ten teachers plus a superintendent and admitted children ages five and above. Classes were gender segregated, a practice shared by most Sunday schools throughout the antebellum era. The school attracted 336 pupils within its first year.[16] By the 1830s, the Mason Street Sabbath School enrolled between 200 and 250 pupils annually, although the number of active students was generally around 150.[17] Approximately thirty-five teachers staffed the school under the oversight of superintendent Samuel H. Walley, a prominent businessman and politician who created the majority

---

[13] American Sunday School Union, *First Report*, 12, in ASSU papers.

[14] Mark Noll, *A History of Christianity in the United States and Canada* (Grand Rapids: Eerdmans, 2003), 339. The ASSU's efforts were part of a vast network of northeastern voluntary associations led by members of the intellectual elite and merchant middle class, a group that Sam Haselby calls the "national evangelists," competing with the "frontier revivalists" of the West to convert the nation. Haselby argues that the frontier revivalism that emerged in the early national period produced religious movements that were more egalitarian, emotional, and chaotic than nationalist missionary initiatives based in the northeast, which included the Sunday school movement. These frontier groups—such as the Methodists, Mormons, Disciples of Christ, and the Millerites—not only challenged the dominance of the middle-class intellectual reformers who aspired to lead the Christianization of the Republic but also represented a threat to the new American political order. Thus, Haselby argues that the religious conflicts that emerged in the antebellum era were primarily social and geographic in nature, rather than denominational. See Sam Haselby, *The Origins of American Religious Nationalism* (New York: Oxford University Press, 2015).

[15] American Sunday School Union, *The Fourth Report of the American Sunday-School Union: Read at Their Annual Meeting, Held in the City of Philadelphia, on Tuesday Afternoon, May 20, 1828* (Philadelphia: I. Ashmead, 1828), 4, ASSU papers; Boylan, *Sunday Schools*, 162-64.

[16] The Mason Street Sabbath School was originally under the oversight of the Boston Society for the Religious and Moral Instruction of the Poor. For founding information, see Boston Society for the Religious and Moral Instruction of the Poor, *Report of the Boston Society for the Religious and Moral Instruction of the Poor. Presented at Their Annual Meeting, October 8, 1817* (Boston, 1817), 3, Boston Athenaeum. Hereafter referred to as *1817 Report*.

[17] See Samuel H. Walley, Reports of the Superintendent of Mason Street Sabbath School 1835 and 1837, Congregational Library and Archives.

of the school's surviving records during his tenure as superintendent from 1835 to 1842.[18] The Mason Street Sabbath School attracted pupils from the ranks of middle-class and lower-class children, many of whom were immigrants. Female students generally outnumbered male students, and this gender pattern held true for the teachers as well.[19]

Founded a year after the Mason Street Sabbath School, the Brandywine Manufacturers' Sunday School was located near Wilmington, Delaware, and catered to the children of local factory workers and farmers. Because public weekday education developed slowly in Delaware, the Sunday school combined emphasis on evangelism and religious instruction with training in reading, writing, and arithmetic, a practice that continued into the 1850s.[20] The school's founding document promised to admit "children of every denomination who are equally entitled to its benefits."[21] As with many Sunday schools founded in this era, the Brandywine Manufacturers' Sunday School initially admitted adults as well. But in keeping with larger trends across the Sunday school movement, young people composed the majority of pupils. Consequently, the school was entirely child-centric by the 1820s. The Brandywine Manufacturers' Sunday School became an ASSU auxiliary in 1824, primarily for the purpose of obtaining the society's cheap, nonsectarian reading material. The school grew steadily under the leadership of Victorine du Pont, the daughter of one of the founders, French immigrant Eleuthere Irenee du Pont, who ran a gunpowder manufactory in Wilmington.[22]

---

[18]Walley was a member of the Massachusetts State House of Representatives in 1836 and 1840-1846, serving as speaker from 1844 to 1846. In addition to his political and business roles, Walley actively supported benevolence work and was a corporate member of the American Board of Commissioners of Foreign Missions from 1848-1867. Biographical data accessed from http://bioguide .congress.gov/scripts/biodisplay.pl?index=W000087. The earliest record I have been able to find from Walley's term as superintendent is a letter he wrote to Mason Street Sabbath School teachers dating from 1835, housed at the at the Boston Athenaeum. Walley's record book, contained at the Congregational Library and Archives, is dated 1838-1842. His tenure as superintendent may have lasted past this period.

[19]For examples, see Walley, 1835 and 1837 reports.

[20]This practice of combining basic academic education with religious education was common in other rural Sunday schools throughout the country.

[21]Victorine Du Pont, report to the ASSU, 1830, Winterthur Manuscripts, Group 6, Series A, Box 13, in the Brandywine Manufacturers' and Christ Church Sunday School Records Collection, Hagley Museum and Library. By 1856, the nonsectarian Brandywine Manufactures' Sunday School became affiliated with the newly formed Christ Church Episcopal congregation, at which point the lessons became increasingly denominational in focus.

[22]The most thorough study of the school's history is Ruth Linton's master's thesis, "To the Promotion and Improvement of Youth: The Brandywine Manufacturers' Sunday School, 1816-1840"

Widowed at the age of twenty-four, Victorine took up Sunday school teaching to find solace in her grief. She became superintendent in 1827, a post she maintained until her death in 1861. As the administrative head of the school, Victorine oversaw the religious training of the more than two hundred pupils who enrolled in the school annually, with ages ranging from four to seventeen years old. Females pupils outnumbered males, just as women also constituted the majority of the teachers.[23]

The Mason Street and Brandywine Manufacturers Sunday schools exemplified another pattern within the Sunday school movement, in that these particular institutions were for White pupils only. African American Sunday schools also existed in the early republic, but they are harder to track given that thorough records were often not kept of these institutions due to the cultural resistance to Black education, particularly literacy. ASSU emissaries working in the South often hesitated to use the word *school* to describe their efforts to found auxiliaries in that portion of the country, preferring the more ambiguous term *catechesis* to avoid the implication that they were teaching African Americans to read.[24] Nevertheless, as historian Janet Duitsman Cornelius demonstrated, Sunday schools for Black children existed throughout the country, particularly in southern states where African Americans were a majority. Many of these schools were founded by White missionaries affiliated with the Presbyterian, Methodist, and Baptist denominations, although some were also affiliated with the ASSU.[25] The African Methodist Episcopal Church and the African Methodist Episcopal Church Zion also led many of these efforts. Richard Allen's Mother Bethel Church in Philadelphia opened its first Sunday school by 1827.[26] The denomination spread Sunday schools as far west as Ohio by 1829, and by 1842 they had also established Sunday schools as far south as Louisiana and Georgia.[27]

(University of Delaware, 1981) and her article, "The Brandywine Manufacturers' Sunday School: An Adventure in Education in the Early Nineteenth Century," *Delaware History* 20 (1983): 168-84.

[23] Linton, "Promotion and Improvement of Youth," 50, 73-74.

[24] Janet Duitsman Cornelius, *Slave Missions and the Black Church in the Antebellum South* (Columbia: University of South Carolina Press, 1999), 132.

[25] Cornelius, *Slave Missions*, 135-37; Albert J. Raboteau, *Slave Religion: The "Invisible Institution" in the Antebellum South* (New York: Oxford University Press, 1978), 151-63.

[26] Christian Recorder, "Sabbath School Celebration in Bethel Church," January 25, 1862, 14.

[27] John B. McFerrin, *History of Methodism in Tennessee*, vol. 2 (Nashville: Southern Methodist Publishing House, 1874); Daniel Payne, *History of the African American Methodist Episcopal Church* (Nashville: Publishing House of the A.M.E. Sunday School Union, 1891), 222-25; Richard Wright Jr.,

For both Black and White pupils, the world of the Sunday school was infused with Scripture, not just in the theological training the institution provided, but in the communal rituals and material culture that shaped pupils' experiences. Sunday school literature narrated Bible stories and concepts in imaginative, juvenile-friendly language. Songbooks and prayer books provided pupils with a weekly diet of Scripture-laden exhortations and reflections.[28] The Sunday school sermon, usually given by the superintendent or a local pastor, was the centerpiece of the weekly routine. While each of these practices is worthy of closer examination, the rituals surrounding memorization and Bible examination curriculum provide the clearest examples of how children were not only socialized into engaging with the evangelical world of biblicism but how these practices also cultivated the traits of emergent religious agency.

Memorization was central to the Sunday school's scripturalization routine. During the movement's initial phase of growth, Sunday school teachers emphasized the importance of memorization as the key to inculcating scriptural values and thereby awaking faith in the hearts of pupils. Such thinking echoed standard educational philosophy at the time, and it also reflected the popularization of romanticized conceptions of children's intellectual and spiritual malleability.[29] Based on the idea that children's minds were empty receptacles

---

ed., *Encyclopedia of the African Methodist Episcopal Church* (Philadelphia: A.M.E. Book Concern, 1916), 14; Michael Patrick Williams, "The Black Evangelical Ministry in the Border States: Profiles of Elders John Berry Meachum and Noah Davis," in *Black Apostles at Home and Abroad: Afro-Americans and the Christian Mission from Revolution to Reconstruction,* ed. David W. Wills and Richard Newman (Boston: G. K. Hall, 1982), 90; Boylan, *Sunday School,* 28-29; Cornelius, *Slave Missions,* 133.

[28] For contextualization of how the material world of the Sunday school fit within larger changes in the material world of Scripture and religious publishing, see Gutjahr, *An American Bible,* 125-36; Candy Gunther Brown, *The Word in the World: Evangelical Writing, Publishing, and Reading in America, 1789–1880* (Chapel Hill: University of North Carolina Press, 2004); David Paul Nord, *Faith in Reading: Religious Publishing and the Birth of Mass Media in America* (New York: Oxford University Press, 2004); and Perry, *Bible Culture and Authority in the Early United States,* 17-39. For an assessment of how children engaged with Scripture in related institutional contexts, primarily Protestant church services, see E. Brooks Holifield, "Let the Children Come: The Religion of the Protestant Child in Early America," *Church History* 76, no. 4 (2007): 750-77.

[29] For more, see Barbara Finkelstein, "Casting Networks of Good Influence: The Reconstruction of Childhood in the United States, 1790–1870," in *American Childhood: A Research Guide and Historical Handbook,* ed. Joseph M. Hawes and N. Ray Hiner, 111-35 (Westport, CT: Greenwood, 1985); Boylan, *Sunday School,* 133-65; Philip J. Greven, *The Protestant Temperament: Patterns of Child-Rearing, Religious Experience, and the Self in Early America* (Chicago: University of Chicago Press, 1988); Jacqueline S. Reiner, *From Virtue to Character: American Childhood, 1775–1850* (New York: Twayne, 1996); and Mintz, *Huck's Raft.*

that needed to be filled, educators believed that if children "commit the precious truths to their tenacious memories" their hearts would necessarily be changed.[30] Sunday school organizations kept careful records of students' recitation performance and were quick to boast of these activities in their annual reports. The Philadelphia Sunday School Union reported with pride that many of their pupils regularly recalled entire books of the Bible, considering this to be a sign of "great love for and delight in the holy Scriptures."[31] Sunday school teachers considered memorization so key to children's spiritual development that they incentivized it with a rewards system, in which students earned prizes, or premiums, based on the number of verses recited per week. Prizes often reflected the goal of infusing children's lives with Scripture. Bibles were regularly awarded as premiums, along with items such as ornate picture cards displaying Scripture passages or decorative gift books containing biblically inspired stories.

Memorization was the primary teaching tool in African American Sunday schools, but the practice varied according to location. Whereas African American pupils in northern states were free to engage in the scripturalization ritual of memorization by first reading the Bible themselves and thereby select passages to commit to memory, Black children in southern states were usually barred from this type of engagement. When enslaved Americans were given a Sunday school education, teachers were expected to communicate the basics of Christian doctrine without violating antiliteracy laws, restricting their activities to singing, prayer, and oral recitations of select Bible passages and catechetical lessons.[32] In some cases, Sunday school teachers attempted to incorporate literacy instruction into memorization rituals in defiance of the law.[33] For example, over one thousand Black students who attended Episcopal Sunday schools in South Carolina in the 1850s were given access to literacy aids as part of their education, including religious pamphlets, ASSU hymnals, and the Child's Scripture Question Book.[34] Southerners accused Sunday

---

[30]Boston Society for the Moral and Religious Instruction of the Poor, *The Annual Report of the Boston Society for the Religious and Moral Instruction of the Poor. Presented at Their Anniversary, Nov. 8th, 1819* (Boston, 1819), 14, Boston Athenaeum.

[31]Sunday and Adult School Union, *Second Report*, 12, 19, 25.

[32]For just one example of how one Sunday school complied with these laws, see Calvary Church of Charleston, South Carolina, *Public Proceedings Relating to Calvary Church, and the Religious Instruction of Slaves* (Charleston: Miller & Browne, 1850), specific examples on 5, 31, 82-83.

[33]Cornelius, *Slave Missions*, 137-39.

[34]See *Journals of the Conventions of the Diocese of South Carolina* (1855), 46-47, 53, 68-69, 70-71.

school workers of being secret agents of the antislavery movement with increasing frequency throughout the antebellum period, in part due to such efforts to link literacy with the rituals of memorization.[35]

Surviving accounts from Sunday school pupils demonstrate children's complex relationship with these Scripture memorization practices.[36] Children often expressed pride in their memorization skills and the premiums they earned. Ten-year-old Caroline Clarke of New York made memorization of seven Bible verses to recite at Sunday school a standard part of her weekly religious ritual, noting in her diary when she delivered the verses flawlessly, along with her younger sister, Anne.[37] Adult reflections on past Sunday school experiences also reinforce the centrality of this practice. S. Wells Williams, a former student of the First Presbyterian Church Sunday School in Utica, New York, wrote in mid-life that "my first remembrance of the Sunday school was standing up in a row, with many other children" for recitations, writing "it was a point of emulation . . . to repeat the verses of the lesson perfectly."[38] As such comments illustrate, Scripture recitation not only gained students premiums but also enabled them to earn a measure of social standing amongst their peers. Memorization functioned as a way for pupils to mark their place within the child-centric religious community of the Sunday school, while for children such as Caroline, it also seemed to operate as a way of tracking the consistency and validity of her personal religious formation.

The earnestness with which Caroline and Wells memorized their Sunday school lessons reflected the common enthusiasm for the rewards system among most Sunday school pupils, and the students at the Mason Street Sabbath School and the Brandywine Manufacturers' Sunday School were no different. A substantial amount of Walley's record book was devoted to keeping an account of the premiums awarded, testifying to high levels of sustained interest in the system amongst the students. Victorine du Pont kept

---

[35]Boylan, *Sunday School*, 28-29. See also John W. Kuykendall, *Southern Enterprize: The Work of National Evangelical Societies in the Antebellum South* (Westport, CT: Greenwood, 1982), 76-77.

[36]As of now, I have only been able to unearth Sunday school accounts from the perspective of white American children.

[37]Caroline Cowles Clarke Richard, *Village Life in America 1852–1872; Including the Period of the American Civil War as Told in the Diary of a School-Girl* (New York: Henry Holt, 1913), 11, 17.

[38]S. Wells Williams, "Letter to the Superintendent, Teachers, and Scholars of the Sunday School of the First Presbyterian Church, Utica," May 31, 1866, in *A Memorial of the Semi-Centennial Celebration of the Founding of the Sunday School of the First Presbyterian Church, Utica*, 35-36.

similarly careful records of premiums, detailing dozens of pupils who earned prizes for memorization and good behavior throughout her tenure as superintendent. Many of the Brandywine Manufacturers' Sunday School students took pride in consistently achieving high marks for recitations and good behavior. Mary Aikin, the daughter of a blacksmith who began attending the school along with her brothers James, Samuel, and John in 1823, racked up numerous prizes over a multi-year period, including tracts, a psalmbook, a thread case, and a "collar trimmed with Nun's lace." Her brother, James, on the other hand, was not nearly as dedicated. James forfeited a premium at least once a year for various minor offenses. Finally, he managed to win a storybook, perhaps aptly titled *The Prodigal Son*.[39]

James may present a more accurate picture of the rate at which students earned premiums at the Brandywine Manufacturers' Sunday School, not simply because other children were similarly prone to misbehave but because attendance often fluctuated. As in other Sunday schools, inconsistent attendance on the part of some pupils kept them from earning regular premiums. The same was true at the Mason Street Sabbath School. While the school averaged around 150 pupils annually, this number often varied considerably over the course of a year. For example, in 1837 attendance began at 202, but fell to 64 by the end of the year. Walley fretted over the "disadvantages resulting from these constant changes," pointing out that "the impressions which we hope to have made while with us, are more apt to be transient."[40] Yet continued use of the memorization and premium system even in the face of such difficulties testifies to its popularity among the students. By encouraging the premium system, du Pont and Walley demonstrated their awareness that Sunday schools were only viable insofar as they remained responsive not just to the spiritual needs of their students, but to their temporal desires as well. Anne Boylan argues that while this was possibly "a means of manipulating children," it also "represented a capitulation on the part of teachers to children's interests."[41] Memorization remained a central feature of the Sunday school experience throughout the nineteenth-century in part because, simply

---

[39]See Mark Books 1827–1833, Box 2, Acc. 389, in Brandywine Manufacturers' and Christ Church Sunday School Records, Hagley Museum and Library.

[40]Samuel H. Walley, *Report of the Superintendent of Mason Street Sabbath School* (Boston, 1837), 3, Congregational Library and Archives. Hereafter referred to as 1837 Report.

[41]Boylan, *Sunday School*, 157.

put, children wanted it. Students' preferences exercised influence over Sunday school pedagogical practices, giving them a small measure of agency in shaping the institution.

Nevertheless, the memorization and premium system also attracted critique. By mid-century, many educational theorists began arguing that memorization was a faulty pedagogical tool that actually did little to shape a child's intellect, as information could simply be recited without having to demonstrate understanding. Moreover, in the case of the Sunday school, teachers began to fret that the premium system motivated pupils to focus on memorization merely for the sake of earning rewards, thus interfered with the work of evangelism.[42] The ASSU complained in 1827 "that many pupils of Sunday schools are ignorant of the meaning of those passages of Scripture which they commit to memory."[43] Merely dispensing Scripture via memorization in hopes of shaping children's hearts was insufficient. Minds must also be engaged to ensure lasting change.

Attempting to redress the problems with rote memorization, the ASSU began emphasizing the importance of teaching young people how to perform scriptural analysis and application via a new curricular model based on a series of lesson books called the *Union Questions*. Designed to be used in small groups of approximately ten pupils, these lesson books contained sequenced sets of ten to twenty Bible verses that students were required to memorize during the week. Teachers were also given corresponding question books to quiz pupils on the meanings of the verses following recitation. This practice was not simply designed to keep children from overburdening themselves, or their teachers, with reciting dozens or even hundreds of verses. It also trained students in biblical reflection and application. In order to achieve this, the *Union Questions* did not contain prepared answers. Rather, answers to the questions were contained within the assigned verses for that week, requiring both teachers and pupils to achieve mastery of scriptural content in order to move through the curriculum. Boylan argues that the popularization of this pedagogical model marked a significant transition in the history of Protestant religious education. From the Reformation onward the

---

[42]Boylan, *Sunday School*, 135-41.

[43]American Sunday School Union, *The Third Report of the American Sunday-School Union: Read at Their Annual Meeting, Held in the City of Philadelphia, on Tuesday Afternoon, May 22, 1827* (Philadelphia: I. Ashmead, 1827), xxvii, ASSU papers.

indoctrination of children was oriented around memorization and teaching young people to parrot the beliefs of their elders. By downplaying memorization and using materials that required students and teachers to work together to formulate answers, she argues that Sunday schools "necessarily permitted some measure of initiative, even spontaneity" to this scripturalization practice, thereby helping to reshape Protestant approaches to childhood religious formation.[44]

As participants in these pedagogical shifts, the Mason Street Sabbath School and the Brandywine Manufacturers' Sunday School not only utilized the Union Questions but also implemented additional curricular innovations designed to enhance children's engagement with the Bible. Victorine du Pont believed that standardized lesson plans should be adapted to specific Sunday school classes, prompting her to spend many of her weekday hours developing additional questions for her teachers to use based on students' ages, needs, and interests. She also encouraged instructors to internalize the lesson for themselves during the week so they could be fully equipped to explain the Scriptures to their students on Sunday.[45] Walley issued similar pleas, asserting that if teachers diligently studied the lessons each week "a still greater amount of benefit would result to the scholar, and much information, as to the state of mind, would be elicited; and this might direct to cautions of counsels of a more appropriate character than might, perhaps, otherwise be given."[46] In a letter to instructors from 1836, Walley stressed that memorizing the weekly Scriptures made teachers more relatable to students, adding that "where the lesson is rather longer than usual, you can dispense with a few of the verses at your own discretion; but a portion I will always require."[47] Like du Pont, Walley recognized that relationships were the bedrock of the scripturalization process within the Sunday school context.

---

[44]Boylan, *Sunday School,* 139. See also American Sunday School Union, *Union Questions 5* (Philadelphia: American Sunday School Union, 1835), iii-iv.

[45]Linton, "Promotion and Improvement of Youth," 52. Victorine's record books and lesson plans contain countless examples of customization and improvisation, for examples see Recitation and Premium Books 1828-1873, Box 3, Acc. 389, Folder 14, in the Brandywine Manufacturers' and Christ Church Sunday School Records Collection, Hagley Museum and Library.

[46]Walley, *1837 Report,* 11. For examples of how Samuel also customized the Union Questions and incorporated the lesson series material into his superintendent addresses, see Walley, Record Book, 1838-1842.

[47]Italicized as in original, Samuel H. Walley to the teachers at the Mason Street Sabbath School, 1836, found in the back of *The Mason Street Sabbath School Library,* 1832, Boston Athenaeum. For an example of Mason Street Sabbath School curriculum, see *Mason Street Sabbath School, July 1837, How Sin Came into the World,* Congregational Library and Archives.

As a curriculum, the power of the Union Questions rested in part on its ability to be customized to different life stages. By the antebellum era, Sunday school workers became particularly interested in programming for youth, which was a flexible term that encompassed ages ranging anywhere from ten to twenty-five. In the early nineteenth century, this broad category called "youth" was increasingly recognized as a distinct life stage separate from both childhood and adulthood when individuals began developing an independent sense of self with increasing capacity for autonomous thought and action.[48] As the movement developed, Sunday school workers struggled to retain pupils transitioning into this youth life stage. A Boston Sunday school society commented in 1822 that "a mistaken notion prevailed among some of the children, that when they arrive at the age of thirteen or fourteen they are too old to go to a Sabbath school." The society lamented this trend, declaring that "in fact, they ought never to relinquish their connexion . . . with it, but, when qualified to become teachers, should endeavor to pay the debt of gratitude they owe" by passing along the instruction they had received to younger children.[49] Affirming this sentiment, the ASSU once again adapted scripturalization practices to shifting ideas about life stage by creating a specialized version of the Union Questions for students age thirteen and above. Called Bible classes, this curriculum featured more extended and complicated weekly lessons, along with basic pedagogy training. Bible classes were embedded into the Sunday school experience by the 1830s. As a result, the ASSU hoped, Sunday schools could not only enhance their self-purported reputation for providing rigorous Bible training, but also enable adolescent pupils to develop a distinct sense of belonging—even superiority—through a Bible class that would keep them connected to the institution while also motivating them to take increasing ownership of their scriptural knowledge.[50]

---

[48]The modern concept of "adolescence" was still developing in this period, leading to greater flexibility in the ages that could be considered "youth." See Joseph Kett, "Adolescence and Youth in Nineteenth-Century America," *The Journal of Interdisciplinary History* 2, no. 2 (1971): 283-90; Lois Banner, "Religion and Reform in the Early Republic: The Role of Youth," *American Quarterly* 23, no. 5 (1971): 678; and Julia M. Gossard, "Tattletales: Childhood and Authority in Eighteenth-Century France," *The Journal of the History of Childhood and Youth* 10, no. 2 (2017): 169-87.

[49]Boston Society for the Religious and Moral Instruction of the Poor, *Sixth Annual Report of the Boston Society for the Religious and Moral Instruction of the Poor. Presented at Their Anniversary, Nov. 6, 1822* (Boston, 1822), 11-12.

[50]Boylan, *Sunday School,* 109-11.

Bible classes further encouraged youth to become emergent religious agents supervising the process of scriptural analysis and application as teachers of younger classes, which was a role that adolescents could assume upon completing the curriculum. The curriculum thereby placed youth in the dual role of being both student and teacher of the Bible, which offered the added benefit of creating a self-sustaining labor force for the institution while also capitalizing on the national trend of high youth participation in revivalism and organized reform.[51] Serving as a Bible instructor provided many young people with a public outlet for spiritual formation and helped them develop language and behaviors by which they testified to the legitimacy of their affiliation within the evangelical community. Twenty-two-year-old Elizabeth Prentiss described in a letter to her brother how "at Sabbath-school this morning, while talking with my scholars about the Lord Jesus, my heart, which is often so cold and so stupid, seemed to melt within me, with a view of His wonderful, wonderful love for sinners, that I almost believed I had never felt it until then."[52] Michael Floy, who taught morning and evening Sunday school classes in New York as a young adult, believed that his work as a Bible instructor kept him from becoming a "backslider," noting in his diary how he instead developed the virtues of punctuality, seriousness, and morality.[53]

In addition to strengthening individual piety, adolescent teachers felt that the work of dispensing Bible knowledge to the younger souls under their charge added spiritual vitality and meaning to their lives. Eleuthera and Sophie du Pont, two of Victorine's younger sisters who began as pupils in their sister's Sunday school and became teachers in their mid-teens, wrote in letters and diaries of how they labored over their Bible class lessons each week so as to achieve optimal insight for their young pupils. They also relished opportunities to extend their mentorship of students into weekday interactions, such as by starting sewing groups for the female pupils. In a letter to

---

[51]Banner, "Religion and Reform in the Early Republic," 678-79; Mary P. Ryan, "A Woman's Awakening: Evangelical Religion and the Families of Utica, New York, 1800-1840," in *History of Women in the United States,* ed. Nancy Cott (New York: K. G. Saur, 1993), 57-58; Joseph Kett, *Rites of Passage: Adolescence in America 1790 to the Present* (New York: Basic Books, 1977), 64.

[52]Elizabeth Prentiss to George Prentiss, September 12, 1840, in George L. Prentiss, *Life and Letters of Elizabeth Prentiss* (New York: Anson D. F. Randolph, 1882), 35.

[53]Richard Albert Edward Brooks, ed., *The Diary of Michael Floy, Jr. Bowery Village, 1833–1837* (New Haven, CT: Yale University Press, 1941), entries for February 28–March 2, 1834, and November 8, 1833.

Sophie, Eleuthera joyfully described how "there will be at least 30" girls in the sewing circle that she and Victorine started.[54] Joanna Smith, a close friend of the du Pont sisters who taught at a nearby Sunday school, followed the same practice and wrote that "many of my Sunday scholars attended, and I am more and more convinced of the immense advantage to be gained from being associated with these charges during the week. I have then an opportunity of becoming acquainted with their habits and dispositions."[55] Floy also approached his work as Bible instructor with solemnity, describing in his diary how he anxiously studied the verses assigned to his students each week. But he also seemed to enjoy his interactions with students, writing that "the children are very near my heart."[56]

Adolescent teachers were also crucial to the dissemination of a children's Bible culture due to their role as executors of pedagogical innovations that institutional leaders created, including the *Union Questions*. While the ASSU developed this new curricular model, the society recognized that youthful teachers were often the ones who implemented it, commenting that "very much good has been accomplished by the instrumentality of young ladies and gentlemen" across the country in their capacity as Bible teachers.[57] ASSU president Archibald Alexander boasted that, as a result of such work, "many of our intelligent young people are actually becoming accurate Bible theologians."[58] This statement is particularly significant in light of the fact that many of the young people Alexander called "accurate Bible theologians" were women. Perhaps in part because they were denied the opportunity to occupy the role of biblical theologian in spaces such as the church or the academy because of their age and gender, young women eagerly filled this role in Sunday schools, and female teachers almost always outnumbered male teachers.[59]

---

[54]Eleuthera du Pont to Sophie du Pont, February 28, 1828, Winterthur Manuscripts, Group 6, Series C, Box 24, in the Brandywine Manufacturers' and Christ Church Sunday School Records Collection, Hagley Museum and Library.

[55]Joanna Smith to Sophie du Pont, February 4, 1835, as cited in Linton, "Promotion and Improvement of Youth," 53.

[56]Brooks, *The Diary of Michael Floy*, entry for December 3, 1833.

[57]"General Assembly's Narrative," *The American Sunday School Magazine* 1 (1824): 19.

[58]Archibald Alexander, *Suggestions in Vindication of Sunday-Schools, but More Especially for the Improvement of Sunday-School Books, and the Enlargement of the Plan of Instruction* (Philadelphia: American Sunday School Union, 1829), 7.

[59]Boylan, *Sunday School,* 114-15. This trend was also due to the fact that teaching—in both Sunday schools and common schools—was one of the few non-domestic roles available to women, in part because female teachers were deemed to be more naturally suited to the care and nurture

Within this institutional context, young women could claim a role traditionally reserved for parents and pastors—religious education of children—as their own via the practice of Bible instruction. Although not at the apex of formal authority within most Sunday school organizations, young women often represented the face of biblical interpretation and pedagogical innovation from the perspective of the pupils entrusted to their care.[60]

Despite the opportunities for spiritual fulfillment and influence offered to adolescent teachers of both genders, these emerging "Bible theologians" did not function as autonomous agents. Like their pupils, youthful teachers were expected to adhere to the standardized curriculum and engage with the Bible under the constant oversight of adult supervisors. Sunday school scripturalization rituals were designed to indoctrinate young people into prescribed evangelical values with little room for recipients to assume formal authority or originality in their engagement with these rituals. In some cases, superintendents would deviate from these prescriptions with additions to the curriculum, such as when the Mother Bethel Sunday school combined ASSU material with anti-slavery literature, a subject that the ASSU encouraged its teachers to avoid.[61] These decisions, however, were made by adults. Within Sunday schools, religious agency was limited by young people's inherent dependency on their superiors, underscoring the importance of age as a factor in shaping encounters with biblicism.

But these qualifiers are also key to understanding the processes by which Protestant practices of scripturalization were transmitted across generational

---

of children, per the ideology of true evangelical womanhood. According to Mary Kelley, "American classrooms were rapidly becoming a woman's domain" in the early national period, and by 1860 65 to 80 percent of the teachers in urban areas were female. Mary Kelley, *Learning to Stand and Speak: Women, Education, and Public Life in America's Republic* (Chapel Hill: University of North Carolina Press, 2006), 10. For more on women's leadership in reform organizations in the early nineteenth century, see Lori Ginzberg, *Women and the Work of Benevolence: Morality, Politics, and Class in the Nineteenth-Century United States* (New Haven, CT: Yale University Press, 1990); and Anne Boylan, *The Origins of Women's Activism: New York and Boston, 1797–1840* (Chapel Hill: University of North Carolina Press, 2002).

[60] Ann Braude, "Women's History Is American Religious History," in *Re Telling U.S. Religious History*, ed. Thomas A. Tweed (Berkeley: University of California Press, 1997), 91. Perry notes the women were often the primary actors in scripturalization rituals, particularly through their role as readers of Scripture. See Perry, *Bible Culture and Authority in the Early United States*, 20.

[61] See Mother Bethel A.M.E. Church Sunday School Roll Book and Library Catalogue, 1864, Pennsylvania Historical Society. For examples of the ASSU avoiding the subject of slavery, see American Sunday School Union, "Instructions to Missionaries," Minutes of the Committee on Missions, June 25, 1833, ASSU Papers. For a comparison of the ASSU's response to slavery with other organizations with the Benevolent Empire, see Kuykendall, *Southern Enterprize*, 76-80, and Cornelius, *Slave Missions*, 141-45.

lines. The evangelical culture of biblicism was disseminated in relational contexts that socialized young people into various forms of scriptural engagement. In some cases this transmission was from adult to child, in others it was from youth to child. In the latter case, young people were empowered to assume a higher level of responsibility in coaching children in biblical memorization, analysis, and application. In all cases, children were positioned as responders, not simply passive observers. Exploring both the possibilities and limitations of these complex roles and the rituals that undergirded them provides a more expansive view of how Scripture was mobilized in personal and communal ways to shape the lives of even the smallest Americans in the first half of the nineteenth century. Scripture was mapped onto life stage considerations in ways that both reflected and shaped ideas about childhood and youth in this defining period of American history, and many of the same assumptions that gave rise to children's Bible culture continue to shape current evangelical strategies for childhood religious formation. Recognizing the existence and dynamism of children's Bible culture, therefore, not only furthers the scholarly project of interrogating how Scripture was operationalized to shape historical experiences across generational lines but also positions young people as historical actors alongside adults in pursuit of understanding how biblicism functions to shape identities across the lifespan, both in the past and into the present.

5

Missouri, Denmark Vesey, Biblical Proslavery, and a Crisis for *Sola Scriptura*

Mark A. Noll

IN THE EARLY HISTORY OF THE UNITED STATES, the defense of slavery from Scripture gradually gained credibility as the country became more Christian.[1] This fateful transition took place from about 1800 onward as energetic Protestants combined evangelical belief with the democratic and republican ideology of the American Revolution. As Protestants of several varieties embraced the separation of church and state and left behind the assumptions of Christendom, they flourished. Freeing White men to read the Bible for themselves—and thereby inadvertently also encouraging White women, Native Americans, and Black Americans to do the same—significantly broadened and deepened active faith throughout the nation. To be sure, Native Christians and Christians of African descent were proving that religion required democracy as little as Europeans thought it required Christendom. Yet for Christianity among White Americans, democracy was working splendidly. Methodists, limited only by their own energy and persuasiveness, were reaping an unprecedented spiritual harvest. Presbyterians and

---

[1]This chapter draws on material from Mark A. Noll, *In the Beginning Was the Word: The Bible in American Public Life, 1492–1783* (New York: Oxford University Press, 2016); and Mark A. Noll, *The Rise and Decline of America as a Bible Civilization, 1794–1911* (forthcoming, I hope), which provide fuller documentation for a long and complicated history.

Congregationalists, limited only by the creativity of their voluntary initiatives, were mobilizing the land and blanketing it with print. Baptists and groups that called themselves simply "Christians," recognizing no limits beyond the Bible and the rights of private conscience, were making sectarian forms of Protestantism increasingly meaningful for ever greater numbers.

In post-Christendom America—with its republican rejection of tradition as corruption and its democratic scorn for elites—devotion to Scripture came to mean almost everything. So it was that either explicitly for Baptists and other sectarians—or implicitly for Methodists, Presbyterians, and Congregationalists—reasoning from "the Bible only" shaped every aspect of corporate Christian life, and often with positive effects.

Yet an insight from David Bebbington's pathbreaking book, *Evangelicalism in Modern Britain*, underscores the important fact that a common evangelical "devotion to the Bible" has never yielded harmony or cohesion. Bebbington focused on the different theories that British Evangelicals entertained for what it meant for Scripture to be inspired. But his conclusion stands as well for differences in the interpretation of Scripture: "There was agreement among Evangelicals of all generations that the Bible is inspired by God. When it came to determining the implications of inspiration, however, there were notable divergences."[2]

In the full scope of American history, the rise of "the Bible only" affected nothing more powerfully than the use of Scripture to adjudicate the morality of slavery. To be sure, from the first efforts in the late seventeenth century to assess the legitimacy of the institution, through the accumulation of arguments that began in the Revolutionary era, to the all-out cultural warfare that preceded (and outlasted) the shooting war, to contest slavery was to contest Scripture.[3] The years from roughly 1800 to 1830 were distinct, however, because they witnessed *both* unusually sophisticated biblical attacks

---

[2]David W. Bebbington, *Evangelicals in Modern Britain: A History from the 1730s to the 1980s* (London: Unwin Hyman, 1989), 12-13.

[3]Particularly pertinent for this chapter is Larry R. Morrison, "The Religious Defense of American Slavery Before 1830," *Journal of Religious Thought* 37 (1980): 16-29, along with several works focusing on decades after 1830 that are nonetheless essential for this earlier period: William S. Jenkins, *Pro-Slavery Thought in the Old South* (Chapel Hill: University of North Carolina Press, 1935); H. Shelton Smith, *In His Image, But: Racism in Southern Religion, 1780–1910* (Durham: Duke University Press, 1972); Larry E. Tise, *Proslavery: A History of the Defense of Slavery in America, 1701–1840* (Athens: University of Georgia Press, 1988); and John R. McKivigan and Mitchell Snay, eds., *Religion and the Antebellum Debate over Slavery* (Athens: University of Georgia Press, 1998).

on slavery *and* the full-scale emergence of persuasive biblical arguments defending the institution.

This chapter briefly summarizes the situation for the Bible and slavery before 1800 along with important developments in the denominations after that time. It then expands to consider the sophisticated antislavery arguments that were published in the first two decades of the nineteenth century, but also the full-blown proslavery position locked into place after contentious debates over Missouri statehood and consternation following a planned slave rebellion in Charleston, South Carolina. Regarded from a wider angle, the near simultaneous appearance of articulate biblical antislavery and convincing biblical proslavery manifested a crisis for traditional Protestant trust in the Bible as supreme authority, or *sola scriptura*, which emerged for all to see in that era, and which for American Bible-believers has never gone away since that time.

Arguments from the Bible concerning slavery were rare before, in the words of Christopher Brown, "the colonial revolt against British rule touched off a revolution in the public conversation about human bondage."[4] From the late seventeenth century a number of Quakers had enlisted specific biblical texts and broader biblical reasoning to condemn the institution, including George Keith, John Hepburn, Ralph Sandiford, Benjamin Lay, John Woolman, and Anthony Benezet. But slaveowners and their defenders barely noticed.

During the Revolutionary era it was different. In 1772 Lord Mansfield of the Court of King's Bench ruled that James Somerset, a slave brought by his West Indian master to England, must be declared free because no English positive law had ever authorized the institution. Although the decision did not directly affect slavery in the British Caribbean or British participation in the slave trade, it did mark the beginning of intensified opposition to the slave trade by Quakers, Anglican Evangelicals, and British Dissenters of all theological positions. That opposition prompted vigorous defenses of slavery and the slave trade that drew copiously on the Scriptures, which in turn prompted attacks that also enlisted the Bible. And so the battle was joined.

As could be expected, Protestants who championed "the sacred cause of liberty" against British tyranny eagerly merged sanctions from religious

---

[4]Christopher Leslie Brown, *Moral Capital: The Foundations of British Abolitionism* (Chapel Hill: University of North Carolina Press, 2006), 105.

precept and political principle to condemn Black chattel slavery. Almost all such appeals elided appeals to the Declaration of Independence ("all men are created equal") and to the Bible. Yet if defenders of the institution were backfooted for a brief period, several extensive publications using Scripture to support the institution also appeared in this era. Moreover, debates in political circles referenced Scripture only slightly less frequently than controversies among clergymen. Remarkably, in light of the intense biblical scrutiny to come in the decades that followed, almost all of the specific texts, general biblical constructs, and pairings of Scripture with other considerations had already surfaced in these early years.

The story of Methodist, Presbyterian, and Baptist retreat on slaveholding is well-known because of an enduringly important monograph by Donald Mathews and many other subsequent studies.[5] The simple summary is that, in the immediate wake of the Revolution, statements by national Methodist and Presbyterian bodies, along with several from regional Baptist associations, condemned slavery as, in the words of a Baptist pastor from 1798, "contrary to the laws of God and nature."[6] But then the stance softened for a number of material, ecclesiastical, ideological, and demographic reasons, especially the success of the White evangelical denominations in gaining increasing numbers of White adherents in the slave-holding states. Significantly, that

---

[5]Donald G. Mathews, *Slavery and Methodism: A Chapter in American Morality* (Princeton: Princeton University Press, 1965); and for an account treating all denominations, David Brion Davis, *The Problem of Slavery in the Age of Revolution, 1770–1832*, new ed. (New York: Oxford University Press, 1999), 203-12. For Methodists, later treatments include John H. Wigger, *Taking Heaven by Storm: Methodism and the Rise of Popular Christianity in America* (New York: Oxford University Press, 1998), 125-50; Cynthia Lynn Lyerly, *Methodism and the Southern Mind, 1770–1810* (New York: Oxford University Press, 1998), 119-45; Douglas Ambrose, "Of Stations and Relations: Proslavery Christianity in Early National Virginia," in *Religion and the Antebellum Debate over Slavery*, 35-67; Dee E. Andrews, *The Methodists and Revolutionary America, 1760–1800* (Princeton: Princeton University Press, 2000), 122-39; Charles H. Irons, *The Origins of Proslavery Christianity: White and Black Evangelicals in Colonial and Antebellum Virginia* (Chapel Hill: University of North Carolina Press, 2008), 74-76; and John H. Wigger, *American Saint: Francis Asbury and the Methodists* (New York: Oxford University Press, 2009), 122-25. Literature for Presbyterians and Baptists is not as extensive, but see James H. Morehead, "Between Hope and Fear: Presbyterians and the 1818 Statement on Slavery," *Journal of Presbyterian History* 96 (2018): 48-61; and for Baptists, Bruce Gourley, "John Leland: Evolving Views of Slavery, 1789–1839," *Baptist History and Heritage* 40 (2005): 104-16; Monica Najar, *Evangelizing the South: A Social History of Church and State in Early America* (New York: Oxford University Press, 2008); and Thomas S. Kidd and Barry Hankins, *Baptists in America: A History* (New York: Oxford University Press, 2015), 98-116.

[6]Carlos R. Allen Jr., "David Barrow's Circular Letter of 1798," *William and Mary Quarterly* 20 (July 1963): 445.

softening process occurred as Americans threw off the habits of Christendom and resolved to live by the Bible alone.

LANDMARK ANTISLAVERY PUBLICATIONS

It is, however, striking that in the very years when the main Bible-focused churches moved steadily away from emancipationist positions, evangelical authors produced some of the most explicit, most comprehensive Bible-based attacks in all of American history. Moreover, these full-scale scriptural arguments, encompassing both specific texts and elaborated biblical theology, came out of the most energetic and the most intellectual Protestant denominations—Methodists applying their gospel-intensive theology and Presbyterians sustaining some of the instincts of the Reformation. The presence of these works should at least modify what some historians, including myself, have written about the "victory" of proslavery biblical argument in the antebellum era.[7]

During the first two decades of the new century, proslavery uses of Scripture never faded away. The shock of Gabriel's Rebellion, when at the dawn of the century slaves around Richmond, Virginia, conspired to liberate themselves through violence, silenced some Methodists and Baptists who had earlier preached emancipation. Private interchanges involving influential figures like the Baptist Richard Furman kept proslavery texts alive. In 1809 and 1813 Virginia evangelicals published exhortations to "masters and servants" that took for granted the biblical propriety of slavery, but focused on encouraging spiritual responsibilities within the system itself.[8] Bibles and catechisms published for use among the enslaved likewise stressed the obedience verses of the Pauline epistles or simply edited out anything that could be construed as emancipationist.[9]

Similarly, antislavery advocacy also reprised earlier positions. The Black Edwardsean pastor Lemuel Haynes used a Washington's birthday sermon

---

[7] See Elizabeth Fox-Genovese and Eugene D. Genovese, *The Mind of the Master Class: History and Faith in the Southern Slaveholders' Worldview* (New York: Cambridge University Press, 2005), 526; Mark A. Noll, *The Civil War as a Theological Crisis* (Chapel Hill: University of North Carolina Press, 2006), 49-50.

[8] William Gray, ed., Samuel Davies, *The Duty of Masters to Their Servants* (1809); William Meade, ed., *Sermons Addressed to Masters and Servants* (1813). See Irons, *Origins of Proslavery Christianity*, 90.

[9] On the impact of Gabriel's Rebellion on the churches, see Davis, *Slavery in the Age of Revolution*, 210; and Mathews, *Slavery and Methodism*, 31, which points out that Gabriel's conspirators planned to exempt Methodists from their attacks because of the denomination's antislavery stance.

in 1813 to express doubts about the War of 1812. As he emphasized themes of benevolence and the affections, he also chastised President Madison for the hypocrisy of worrying about the liberty of a few impressed sailors while hundreds of thousands of Africans languished in real bondage in Madison's own state of Virginia. In the continuing move of former Federalists to voluntary approaches toward social betterment, John Jay became the first president of the New York Manumission Society, while his sons, William and Peter Augustus, devoted more of their energies to mobilizing Christian opinion against the institution.[10] Not incidentally, the debate over Missouri that began in 1819 accelerated the antislavery activity of the older and younger Jays.

Yet even as older sentiments survived through the administrations of Presidents Jefferson and Madison, a new generation of abolitionists produced the era's most important statements with fresh, creative, and comprehensive biblical arguments pronouncing a divine condemnation on slaveholding and the slave trade. If conclusions about the era had been drawn only from these publications, the false impression might have been communicated that Gabriel's horn had blown, and the judgment day for slavery was at hand.

The Methodist condemnations came from two leading figures who exploited the spiritual dynamic of their movement with unusual force. Freeborn Garrettson (1752–1827) authored the first in 1805.[11] Garrettson, who had been ordained at the Methodists' organizing Christmas Conference in 1784, grew up in a wealthy, slave-owning family, but reported that at his conversion God had told him to free his own slaves. By early in the next century, Garrettson had evangelized effectively in Nova Scotia, his native Maryland, and throughout New York state where he had married into the wealthy Livingstone clan. Although Garrettson retained conventional views about the racial superiority of Whites, he also offered wide-ranging encouragement to many

---

[10] Lemuel Haynes, *Dissimulation Illustrated: A Sermon . . . Being the Anniversary of Gen. Washington's Birth-day* (Rutland, VT: Fay and Davison, 1814); on the Jays, see Jonathan J. Den Hartog, *Patriotism and Piety: Federalist Politics and Religious Struggle in the New American Nation* (Charlottesville: University of Virginia Press, 2015), 190-96; and John R. Van Atta, *Wolf by the Ears: The Missouri Crisis, 1819-1821* (Baltimore: Johns Hopkins University Press, 2015), 86.

[11] See Ian B. Straker, "Black and White and Gray All Over: Freeborn Garrettson and African Methodists," *Methodist History* 37 (1998): 18-27; and George A. Rawlyk, "GARRETTSON, FREEBORN," in *Dictionary of Canadian Biography*, vol. 6, University of Toronto/Université Laval, 2003, www.biographi.ca/en/bio/garrettson_freeborn_6E.html.

African Africans, including Richard Allen in the work that led to the founding of the African Methodist Episcopal (A.M.E.) Church.

The take-off point for Garrettson's substantial pamphlet, which took the form of a dialogue, was when "Professing-Christian" heard "several of my black people" singing hymns and praying. After he "fled to my Bible" in order to learn more about suffering endured by the godly, including his slaves, Garrettson's alter ego, "Do-Justice," encouraged Professing-Christian to explore "the external evidences of religion"—that is, the "good works" that a Christian should pursue.[12] When Professing-Christian sought chapter-and-verse references relevant to the question, Do-Justice went into high gear, citing "a number of passages of Scripture to prove, pointedly, the iniquity of the practice of slave-keeping." The more than thirty specific passages Garrettson quoted, with eighteen of them crammed on to a single page, represented one of the most extensive biblical litanies that any abolitionist ever published. Passages included Jeremiah 22:13 ("Woe unto him that buildeth his house by unrighteousness, and his chambers by wrong; that useth his neighbor's service without wages, and giveth him not for his work"), Proverbs 22:16 ("He that oppresseth the poor to increase his riches, and he that giveth to the rich, shall surely come to want"), and many others that decried the strong who robbed, despoiled, abused, or cheated the weak.[13]

Impressive as such a proof-texting parade might seem, Garrettson put even more energy into rebutting the use of Leviticus 25:44-46 to defend American slavery. This passage had already been frequently cited to justify slavery; it stipulated that Israelites could not enslave fellow Hebrews, but could keep non-Hebrews and their issue in perpetual slavery. For Do-Justice, that passage could simply not hold up "under the gospel dispensation" once Professing-Christian understood "the intricacy of the subject" and that the Hebrews of the Old Testament were "differently circumstanced."

- *God* commanded Israel to settle the Promised Land (not to travel "three thousand miles to capture the poor Africans, without any special command from heaven").

---

[12] Freeborn Garrettson, *Dialogue Between Do-Justice and Professing-Christian. Dedicated to the . . . Abolition Societies, and to all other Benevolent, Humane Philanthropists, in America* (Wilmington: Peter Brynberg, [1805]), 5-7. The pamphlet is dated in 1805 by Straker, "Black and White," and other authorities on Garretson.

[13] Garrettson, *Dialogue*, 25 (prove pointedly), 29 (eighteen on this page).

- God authorized enslavement of Israel's enemies as an alternative to killing them outright.

- But, with reference to the story of Abraham, the Israelites encouraged their slaves to believe in God and then to be circumcised.

- Once circumcised, the slaves could partake of the Passover (Numbers 15:13-16).

- And since they were in God's eyes now counted as part of Israel, they had to be freed from enslavement in the Jubilee Year (every seventh) since the children of Israel were forbidden to enslave their fellow Hebrews.

- Thus, understanding the Old Testament correctly meant understanding how its provision of slavery was only a means to extend the scope of God's mercy.

For Garrettson, as a Bible-only Methodist, it was obvious that both the Scripture's individual texts and its central message of salvation ("the dispensations of God are dispensations of mercy") condemned slavery without equivocation.[14]

The second important Methodist publication came from Daniel Coker (1780–1846), an African American who had also benefited from Garrettson's support as one of Richard Allen's key colleagues in founding the A.M.E.[15] Coker later became a noted missionary to Sierra Leone where he helped establish Methodism in west Africa while also serving in several governmental positions. His more compact pamphlet, published in 1810, deserves special consideration as the first full-scale abolitionist work by an American Black. While also referring to a few individual texts, it mostly recapitulated Garrettson's argument in another imagined dialogue, this one between a Virginia slaveholder and an African Methodist minister. Coker concentrated on Abraham's circumcision of his slaves (Genesis 17:13) to show, as Garrettson had done, that slaves could be incorporated into Israel and, once incorporated, enjoyed all the benefits God bestowed on the chosen people. Thus, he concluded, once Africans came under the hearing of the Christian gospel, they became like Israel's enslaved opponents who were invited into the company

---

[14]Garrettson, *Dialogue*, 11-14.
[15]Will B. Gravely, "African Methodism and the Rise of Black Denominationalism," in *Perspectives on American Methodism: Interpretive Essays*, ed. Russel E. Richey et al. (Nashville: Kingswood, 1993), 109; and H. T. Maclin, "Coker, Daniel," in *Biographical Dictionary of Christian Missions*, ed. Gerald H. Anderson (Grand Rapids: Eerdmans, 1998), 143.

of the circumcised—and so protected against perpetual enslavement. With Garrettson, Coker also emphasized the stark differences between enslavement by the Hebrews and enslavement by Americans: "The Israelites were not sent by a divine mandate, to nations three hundred miles distant, who were neither doing, nor meditating any thing against them, and to whom they had no right whatever, in order to captivate them by fraud or force . . . and then doom the survivors and their posterity to bondage and misery forever."[16]

Significantly for what would come later in controversies over interpreting crucial texts, Coker like Garrettson also deployed a "differently circumstanced" argument when taking up the apostle Paul's injunctions for slaves to obey their masters. Paul issued these commands, wrote Coker, to show that the church supported order under a Roman government looking for any excuse to persecute the Christians. "In such circumstances," according to Coker, had "the apostle proclaimed liberty to the slaves," it would have brought violent retribution "without the prospect of freeing one single individual." "But ours," he added ironically, "is not a heathen, but is called a Christian government."[17]

For Garrettson, with his quiver full of pointed proof-texts, as for both Garrettson and Coker, with carefully developed biblical theology, a Scripture defense of slavery failed for simply disregarding many individual verses. More importantly, the biblical gospel that as Methodists inspired their entire lives, made the enslavement of others for whom Christ died simply unimaginable.

Although Presbyterians enjoyed a higher reputation for intellectual acumen than Methodists, the Bible arguments from Garrettson and Coker were actually more sophisticated than the polemics thundered by the era's two Presbyterian authors. In particular, Garrettson and Coker dealt with the bearing of historical context on biblical interpretation more self-consciously than did their more learned Presbyterian peers. Where later polemics would feature history *versus* the Bible (*either* trust Scripture *or* relativize its teaching by appealing to modern ethical consciousness), Garrettson and Coker insisted on addressing the question with a combination of Scripture *plus* history.

Yet considered as a whole, the Presbyterians gave nothing away in their zeal to open the Scriptures. The works were authored by Alexander McLeod,

---

[16] Daniel Coker (who is identified on the title page as "a descendent of Africa" and "Minister of the African Methodist Episcopal Church in Baltimore"), *A Dialogue Between a Virginian and an African Minister* (Baltimore: Benjamin Edes, 1810), 22.

[17] Coker, *Dialogue*, 23.

an immigrant from Scotland and a minister in the tiny Reformed Presbyterian church, and George Bourne, who after migrating from England and a short period associating with Methodists, became a minister in the main American Presbyterian denomination. In their new homeland, both fiercely contended for an older notion of *sola scriptura* rooted specifically in the polemics of the Reformation.

McLeod (1774–1833), as a Reformed Presbyterian, or Covenanter, upheld an extreme Protestant version of what Joseph Moore has aptly called "the heart of Presbyterian history"—that is, "a structural concern for creating and maintaining godly societies."[18] The Covenanters took their name from the Scottish National Covenant of 1638 that memorialized Scottish opposition to King Charles I and the Solemn League and Covenant of 1643, which in the early years of the English Civil War briefly united England's Parliament and Scotland in opposing Charles I. Both covenants emphasized a bedrock commitment to Scripture for regulating all of life, state as well as church, an emphasis that Reformed Presbyterian immigrants softened but did not abandon.[19]

When in 1802 Alexander McLeod published his lengthy sermon, *Negro Slavery Unjustifiable*, he relied unreservedly on a commitment to *sola scriptura* coming out of the Scottish Reformation, but also its vision of a godly society under the specifically Christian guidance of government. While McLeod's extensive "Discourse" did range widely, at its heart lay his exposition of Exodus 21:16—"He that stealeth a man, and selleth him, or if he be found in his hand, he shall surely be put to death"—but as reinforced by "the eighth precept of the decalogue" (Exodus 20:15, "Thou shalt not steal") and 1 Timothy 1:9-10 ("Knowing this, that that law is not made for a righteous man, but for the lawless and disobedient—for MAN STEALERS—and if there be any other thing that is contrary to sound doctrine").[20]

McLeod was prompted to compose this discourse when he discovered that the congregation to which he was called in Orange County, New York, included slave owners, whom he immediately challenged. At almost the same

---

[18]Joseph Moore, "Epilogue," *Faith and Slavery in the Presbyterian Diaspora*, ed. W. H. Taylor and P. C. Messer (Bethlehem, PA: Lehigh University Press, 2016), 252.

[19]On the biblicism of this Scottish heritage, see Noll, *In the Beginning*, 92-93.

[20]Alexander McLeod, *Negro Slavery Unjustifiable: A Discourse*, 11th ed. (New York: Alexander McLeod, 1863 [orig. 1802]), 6.

time, the Reformed Presbyterians, who were in the process of organizing their denomination, went on record expelling slave owners from their churches.[21]

McLeod's discourse stands as a significant landmark in the history of controversy over slavery because with other Covenanters he was, again quoting Joseph Moore, an "antislavery biblical literalist."[22] In a history of controversy where antislavery tended to focus on the Golden Rule and the spirit of Scripture while proslavery hammered at individual texts, McLeod demonstrated that the debate did not have to break along those lines. As he catalogued numerous evils of enslavement, McLeod did move in many directions: he viewed slavery as opposed to "the natural rights of man," contended that it paved the way for civil tyranny, and cited the Declaration of Independence.[23] But the heart of the treatise came from following his confession that "my text is in the Bible." Accordingly, he returned repeatedly to condemning American slavery as nothing but a product of unjustifiable kidnapping—while also denying the relevance of the curse of Canaan from Genesis 9, showing that the slavery allowed by Leviticus 25:44-46 in no way resembled the American institution, and explaining the Pauline instructions to slaves in the New Testament as subordinated by "the spirit of that religion" (i.e., faith in Christ), which is "righteousness and peace."[24]

Two years after this *Discourse*, McLeod published *Messiah, Governor of the Nation*, an interpretation of the book of Revelation read as instructing governments how they should support institutional Christianity. This work defended the general principle that the *Discourse* had advocated concerning slavery. In its terms, "legislatures and statesmen" were responsible for "exert[ing] themselves in the cause of righteousness." About the need for governments to act against slavery there could be no doubt, because "it is inconsistent with the natural rights of man; it is condemned by the Scriptures; it is at war with your republican institutions; it ruins the minds and the morals of thousands; and it leaves you exposed to the wrath of heaven."[25]

---

[21]For the occasion of this work, see the "Advertisement" prefacing the 1863 edition of the *Discourse*, (iv); and Joseph S. Moore, *Founding Sins: How a Group of Antislavery Radicals Fought to Put Christ in the Constitution* (New York: Oxford University Press, 2016), 93-100.

[22]Moore, *Founding Sins*, 93.

[23]McLeod, *Negro Slavery Unjustifiable*, 8, 18, 21.

[24]McLeod *Negro Slavery Unjustifiable*, 40 (Bible), 6, 11-13, 37-38, 40 (man-stealing), 27-29 (curse), 32-33 (Leviticus), 37 (Paul).

[25]McLeod, *Negro Slavery Unjustifiable*, 41-42. Government support for the churches was the part of the Westminster Confession (XXIII.3) edited out by the American Presbyterians in 1789.

As McLeod added natural rights and republicanism to the Bible, he brought the reasoning of Scotland's Reformation history to bear on the circumstances of his new homeland. The United States may have separated the institutions of church and state, but rulers still needed to follow God's law. Scripture remained foundational and, in McLeod's view, must be followed to the letter.

If McLeod centered his shrapnel attack on the biblical prohibition against man-stealing, George Bourne's *The Book and Slavery Irreconcilable* mustered that prohibition as a single massive cannon blast.[26] Bourne (1780–1845) migrated to the United States in 1804 because as a Dissenter he favored republican government and a voluntary approach to religion. His Reformation stance was not McLeod's attachment to a comprehensive Christendom but the ur-Protestant link between militant *sola scriptura* and militant anti-Catholicism. Historians know Bourne for his antislavery animus but also for his contribution to the anti-Catholic hysteria that would increase in step with growing Catholic immigration. Later in life he edited, wrote, or brought back into print a host of inflammatory publications including *Jesuit Juggling*, an attack on the Catholics' Rheims Bible, and a convent exposé, *Lorette*, that anticipated the even more extreme *Maria Monk*.[27] For Bourne, Catholicism represented spiritual enslavement at its most malignant. He felt just the same about the American system of Black chattel slavery.

Bourne's *The Book and Slavery Irreconcilable* arose from conflicts that dogged his early career as a Presbyterian minister. Upon his arrival in the United States, he had worked briefly as an editor in Baltimore, during which time Bourne wrote the first American biography of John Wesley, but then moved to Virginia where near Harrisonburg he organized a church for recently arrived Scotch-Irish Presbyterians. After thorough examination by the Presbytery of Lexington, he was ordained to the ministry in 1812. Things began smoothly at Bourne's South River Church, in his presbytery, and as a delegate

---

[26]On Bourne, see especially John W. Christie and Dwight L. Dumond, *George Bourne and the Book and Slavery Irreconcilable* (Philadelphia: Presbyterian Historical Society, 1969), with a monographic introduction and a complete reprinting of *The Book and Slavery*; Daniel Yacovone, "Bourne, George," *American National Biography*, https://doi-org.proxy.library.nd.edu/10.1093/anb/9780198606697.article.0800158; and Ryan C. McIlhenny, *To Preach Deliverance to Captives: Freedom and Slavery in the Protestant Mind of George Bourne, 1780–1845* (Baton Rouge: Louisiana State University Press, 2020).

[27]On Bourne's anti-Catholic exertions, see Cassandra L. Yacovazzi, *Escaped Nuns: True Womanhood and the Campaign Against Convents in Antebellum America* (New York: Oxford University Press, 2018), 24 (on the possibility that Bourne was the real author of *Maria Monk*) and 51-55.

to the national General Assembly in 1813 and 1814. But trouble was brewing as Bourne pondered the Presbyterian doctrinal standards he had subscribed to as part of his ordination. The particular issue was Question 142 of the Westminster Larger Catechism, "What are the sins forbidden in the eighth commandment?" (Thou shalt not steal.) The answer began, "the sins forbidden . . . are, theft, robbing, man-stealing, and receiving any thing that is stolen." Bourne's emancipationist convictions fastened on to the basic Question and Answer, but even more on the footnote appended to "man-stealing" in the 1806 edition of the denomination's *Constitution of the Presbyterian Church in the United States of America.*

When in the early years of the English Civil War, Parliament convened an Assembly of Divines to prepare a replacement for the *Book of Common Prayer* and its *Thirty-Nine Articles of Religion*, the Assembly after deliberating several years presented to Parliament the Westminster Confession, two catechisms, and a Directory of Worship.[28] Parliament, in an early instance of the biblicism that would become endemic in the United States, requested that the Assembly provide biblical proof-texts for all of the assertions in all of its documents. Although Parliament never authorized the Westminster standards for England, they were adopted, with the footnoted proof-texts, by Scottish and Irish Presbyterians, and later by American Presbyterians as well. The first meeting in 1789 of the American General Assembly, which reorganized Presbyterians after the War for Independence, amended the Westminster Confession to eliminate the original's assignment of church oversight to government. It did not, however, eliminate the proof-texts that had been earlier supplied for the standards, which editors over the years had adjusted in different printings.

So it was that near Harrisonburg, Virginia, while the United States was engaged in warfare against Great Britain, George Bourne became convinced that, because American Presbyterian officials were violating their ordination vows, he too should go to war. Omitting only the Latin of Hugo Grotius's statement against slavery and beginning with a citation of 1 Timothy 1:10, where the New Testament echoed the Old, the footnote to "man-stealing" in Answer 142 read as follows:

> I Tim. i. 10 (The law is made) for whoremongers, for them that defile themselves with mankind, for men-stealers. (This crime among the Jews exposed the

---

[28]For the centrality of Scripture at Westminster, see Noll, *In the Beginning Was the Word*, 83-89.

perpetrators of it to capital punishment; Exod. 21.16 and the apostle here classes them with sinners of the first rank. The word he uses in its original import, comprehends all who are concerned in bringing any of the human race into slavery, or in detaining them in it. . . . Stealers of men are all those who bring off slaves or freemen, and keep, sell, or buy them. To steal a freeman, says Grotius, is the highest kind of theft. In other instances we only steal human property, but when we steal or retain men in slavery, we seize those who in common with ourselves, are constituted by the original grant, lords of the earth. Gen: 1.28.)[29]

All of the fire that burned in Bourne's veins against the evils of Rome now burst forth against what the Presbyterian standards had so clearly defined as "sinners of the first rank." First he took steps to expel slave-owners from his own church. Then he overturned his presbytery and, with a few colleagues in 1815, the national General Assembly. When at this Assembly Bourne was asked why he had not followed through against slave-owners in Virginia, he replied that opinion in the state was so corrupt no justice could possibly be served there. Disputing over Bourne's charges lasted until the 1818 vote when the General Assembly agreed with the Presbytery of Lexington to defrock Bourne for harming, rather than building up, the church.

Two years before this final decision, Bourne fired his 150-page cannonade that, like McLeod's *Discourse*, featured exposition of the Bible's "man-stealing" texts, Exodus 21:16 and 1 Timothy 1:10.[30] Yet compared to Bourne, McLeod had been only playing games. McLeod had paused to explain that "slavery" in some forms could be justified when a lawbreaker deliberately injured an "innocent fellow creature," but Bourne made no concessions.[31] McLeod had commended the president of the College of New Jersey (Princeton), Samuel Stanhope Smith, for publishing an explanation of how skin color could change over time, while Bourne condemned Smith because in a textbook on moral philosophy Smith had excused the continuation of slavery in America despite defining it as an evil.[32]

---

[29] *The Constitution of the Presbyterian Church in the United States of America, Containing the Confession of Faith, the Catechisms, and the Director of Worship of God. Together with the Plan of Government and Discipline as Amended and Ratified by the General Assembly at Their Sessions in May, 1805* (Philadelphia: Jane Aitken, 1806), 277-78.

[30] George Bourne, *The Book and Slavery Irreconcilable, with Animadversions upon Dr. Smith's Philosophy* (Philadelphia: J. M. Sanderson, 1816).

[31] McLeod, *Negro Slavery Unjustifiable*, 7.

[32] McLeod, *Negro Slavery Unjustifiable*, 26; Bourne, *Book and Slavery*, 143-54.

And where McLeod had begun with Exodus 21:16 but then spent most of his *Discourse* going further afield, Bourne kept his outrage at "man-stealing" front and center throughout his entire work. To be sure, Bourne also cited the Declaration of Independence, along with libertarian assertions from several state constitutions. He added quotations not only from the Bible, but also from a score of authorities such as Charles James Fox, William Wilberforce, and William Paley. He also ran through an even broader array of proof-texts than Freeborn Garrettson had marshalled.

Yet throughout Bourne returned repeatedly to passionate application of the straightforward statements that almost all Americans in this era understood as coming from Moses and the apostle Paul. On the key Exodus and 1 Timothy passages, he quoted from at least fifteen commentaries that agreed in reading these texts as condemning enslavement. One of his sharpest statements came early in the book's second chapter ("The Law of God and Man") when after quoting the key verse from Exodus, and piling on additional quotations about protecting escaped slaves from Deuteronomy 24:7, Deuteronomy 23:15-16, 1 Samuel 30:10-16, Isaiah 16:3, and Obadiah 14-15, he let fly:

> These Scriptures proclaim that *slave-holding* is an abomination in the sight of God: for it justifies the slave in absconding from his Tyrant, and enjoins upon every man to facilitate his escape, and to secure his freedom. Does this injunction comport with a Christian's advertising as a fugitive criminal, a man who has merely fled from his cruel captivity, or with his aiding to trace and seize him who had thus burst from "durance vile"? It is a reiteration of the theft: yet he professes to be influenced by the Gospel! [And with this footnote] "Well may we blush when we hear a man boasting of his rights as an American, and of his citizenship among the Saints, with a whip in one hand, a chain in the other, and before him, a Negro flayed from the head to the loins!"[33]

The Book and Slavery Irreconcilable delivered a bravura performance. Surely, if American Presbyterians honored the Scriptures—if they gave any credence at all to their own doctrinal standards—they would have to renounce slavery as a great evil and excommunicate all those who participated in the system as lawless, disobedient, ungodly sinners. What could be plainer than straightforward obedience to the unambiguous words of Holy Scripture,

---

[33]Bourne, *Book and Slavery*, 27.

interpreted literally? Yet, as we have seen, the church disagreed. Judicially, the General Assembly ruled against Bourne on a technicality—where an earlier General Assembly had ratified the Westminster Larger Catechism, it had not specifically ratified the footnotes for Question and Answer No. 142.[34] Culturally, too many material interests along with the Presbyterians' deep investment in maintaining the orderly, forward movement of their denomination made it impossible to heed Bourne's appeal to scriptural literalism and the manifest bearing of their own doctrinal standards.

A near absence of recorded responses to the substantial works by Garrettson, Coker, McLeod, and Bourne suggests that they were voices crying in the wilderness. Enslaved and free Blacks in Charleston who formed an A.M.E. congregation shortly after Richard Allen founded the denomination certainly knew about Coker, as Allen's fellow-bishop, and perhaps even of his dialogue.[35] William Lloyd Garrison made a life-changing discovery of Bourne's *The Book and Slavery* after it had it languished for more than a decade with few convinced readers; when Garrison founded his passionately antislavery *Liberator* in 1831, he recruited Bourne as one of the main writers for the journal.[36] For his part, Bourne until he died in 1845 continued to publish regularly against both slavery as man-stealing and Catholicism as destroying families.

Yet before, during, and after the War of 1812, and despite the signal efforts of the authors examined here, contention over the Scriptures' judgment on slavery remained mostly beneath the surface. The denominations drifted. The Word of God as exegeted by a notable corps of dedicated abolitionists fell on stony ground. Biblical argumentation seemed to be making less and less of a difference.

Then came Missouri—and Denmark Vesey.

1819–1822

In February 1818 residents of the Missouri Territory petitioned Congress to be admitted as a state.[37] Their petition languished because of uncertainties

---

[34]Christie and Dumond, *George Bourne*, 18, 26, 52.

[35]For references to Coker in connection with Denmark Vesey, see Egerton and Paquette (full citation below at n46), 19, 702.

[36]On the Bourne-Garrison connections, see Christie and Dumond, *George Bourne*, vi, 83-98.

[37]Superb background for this section is found in Robert Pierce Forbes, *The Missouri Compromise and its Aftermath* (Chapel Hill: University of North Carolina Press, 2007); and Forbes, "Slavery and the Evangelical Enlightenment," in *Religion and the Antebellum Debate over Slavery*, 68-106.

about slavery in the trans-Mississippi Louisiana Territory until a year later Representative James Tallmadge of New York offered an amendment to the enabling legislation. It proposed that the slaveholders already present in Missouri be allowed to retain their slaves, but with provisions for their future emancipation and a prohibition on the importation of additional slaves. This proposal unleashed a storm of congressional controversy that included lightning flashes of Christian concern. Tallmadge himself contrasted the generosity of White southerners in supporting "moral institutions for Bible and Missionary Societies" with southern states "legislating to secure the ignorance and stupidity of their slaves."[38] His fellow New York Representative, John Taylor, used a biblical analogy to suggest that if Congress missed the present opportunity to check the expansion of slavery with one simple piece of legislation, "shall we not expose ourselves to the same kind of censure which was pronounced by the Saviour of Mankind upon the Scribes and Pharisees."[39] Representative Arthur Livermore of New Hampshire used charged language to condemn "the sin of holding both the bodies and souls of our fellow men in chains."[40] And in two impassioned speeches, Senator Rufus King of New York, the Federalists' presidential candidate in 1816 and a founding manager of the American Bible Society, laid out an extensive constitutional argument against slavery in any new state. King did note evils attending the American system, like the breaking up of families, but also said he would not address moral questions that "in this place, would call up feelings, the influence of which would disturb, if not defeat, the impartial [i.e., constitutional] consideration of the subject."[41] (Printed copies of King's speeches would wend their way southward to play a part in the next, more intense controversy over slavery that followed hard on the heels of agitation over Missouri.)

The Tallmadge proposal died, but the controversy did not. It boiled over once again as soon as the new Sixteenth Congress convened in December

---

[38] *Papers Relative to the Restrictions on Slavery: Speeches of Mr. King in the Senate and of Messers. Taylor and Talmadge . . . in the House of Representatives* (Philadelphia: Hall and Atkinson, 1819), 28.

[39] *Annals of Congress, 15th Congress—Second Session* (Nov. 1818–Feb. 1819) (Washington: Gales and Seaton, 1855), 1174.

[40] *Annals of Congress, 15th Congress—Second Session*, 1191.

[41] Rufus King, *Substance of Two Speeches delivered in the Senate of the United States on the Subject of the Missouri Bill* (Philadelphia: Clark and Raser, 1819), 5.

1819. The relatively noncontroversial admittance of Alabama as the eleventh slave state now balanced the eleven states that had either outlawed slavery or legislated its future demise. The extensive and heated debate that ensued included a long speech on January 26, 1820 by Senator William Smith of South Carolina who directly attacked assertions that "slavery was forbidden by God, in his Holy Bible." To the contrary, replied the Senator, who then proceeded to quote Leviticus 25:44-46 as delivering "the divine words of the Lord himself to his holy servant, Moses, as a law to his holy people." Moreover, since "Christ himself gave a sanction to slavery," there could be no doubt but that "Scriptures teach us that slavery was universally indulged among the holy fathers." Less than a week later, Senator James Barbour of Virginia reinforced his colleague's conclusions by invoking "Providence"—"the same mighty power that planted the greater and the lesser luminary in the heavens, permits on earth the bondsman and the free."[42] Missouri was the lever that pushed the Bible-defense of slavery out of the ecclesiastical shadows into the glare of congressional scrutiny.

Even as the Scriptures were being cited in Congress, others in the public sphere joined in. Especially noteworthy was a lengthy series of articles in Virginia's leading newspaper, the *Richmond Enquirer*, that appeared just as the Congress took up the Missouri question hammer and tongs. The series included a lengthy reprint on December 3, 1819, of a rejoinder to the *Edinburgh Review*, which had attacked slave-holding; it was filled with references to the Curse of Canaan, Abraham as a slaveholder, the stipulations of Leviticus 25, the New Testament commands for slaves to obey their masters, and Jesus' silence on the subject—in other words, almost all of the texts that had already surfaced to defend slavery and that would continue to be reiterated to the time of the Thirteenth Amendment and beyond. The editor, Thomas Ritchie—friend of Jefferson and ardent foe of restricting slavery anywhere—followed up in early January with two shorter, but still substantial articles by "An American," asserting once again that slavery "was expressly sanctioned by the old, and recognized without censure by the new, testament," and "was sanctioned in the bible, in defiance of the precepts from the new dispensation . . . zealots." Then appeared in early February a massive two-part article, "Scriptural Researches,"

---

[42]*Annals of Congress, 16th Congress—First Session* (Dec. 1819–May 1820) (Washington: Gales and Seaton, 1855), 269-70 (Smith, 26 Jan.); 335 (Barbour, 1 Feb.).

that began with accounts in Genesis providing *"proof positive* that the father of the faithful [Abraham] was a slaveholder," before going on to a full exposition of all Mosaic legislation, including Leviticus 25:44-46.[43] In piecemeal fashion, the *Richmond Enquirer* had published the most comprehensive effort of its kind since the appearance three decades earlier of Raymond Harris's work.

A month after these "Scriptural Researches" appeared in Richmond, Henry Clay maneuvered a compromise through Congress: Missouri would enter as a slave state, Maine to balance Missouri was hived off from Massachusetts and became the twelfth free state, and slavery would be prohibited in the Louisiana Territory north of 36 degrees 30 minutes. With the impassioned airing of arguments that would reverberate for the next four decades, Thomas Jefferson's description of this debate as "a fire bell in the night" accurately described the course of the nation. With Senator Smith's fiery address to Congress and the *Enquirer's* provision of material to be read at leisure, the Missouri controversy also marked, in Robert Forbes's authoritative words, "a turning point in the development of the biblical defense of slavery."[44]

Twenty-seven months after the compromise of March 1820, during which time the American Bible Society distributed close to 110,000 Bibles and Testaments, news of a threatened slave insurrection in Charleston galvanized South Carolina's White citizens into a panic of investigation, judgment, retribution, and aggressive proslavery apologetics.[45] At the center of the insurrection and its far-reaching aftermath lay an open Bible.[46]

The leader of the planned uprising was said to be Denmark Vesey, a Charleston carpenter who had enjoyed almost a quarter century as a freedman. The Black South Carolinians, both slave and free, who joined Vesey were inspired by what they had heard of the antislavery speeches made in Congress during the Missouri debate.[47] Some of them had also listened to the ardent sermons of a maverick Methodist, Lorenzo Dow, who over several months

---

[43]*Richmond Enquirer*, 3 Dec. 1819, 2; 1 Jan. 1820, 3; 8 Jan. 1820, 3; 10 Feb. 1820, 3; 12 Feb. 1820, 3.

[44]Forbes, *Missouri Compromise*, 100 (Jefferson), 149.

[45]Henry Otis Dwight, *The Centennial History of the American Bible Society*, 2 vols. (New York: Macmillan, 1916), 2:577.

[46]I follow Douglas R. Egerton and Robert L. Paquette in their extraordinarily comprehensive edition of primary source documents in treating "the Vesey plot [as] one of the most sophisticated acts of collective slave resistance in the history of the United States"; Egerton and Paquette, *The Denmark Vesey Affair: A Documentary History* (Gainesville: University Press of Florida, 2017), xv.

[47]Egerton and Paquette, *Denmark Vesey*, 37, 214n4, 221, 450, 491.

in 1820 and 1821 preached to Charleston's slaves without permission; his preaching elsewhere, and presumably in Charleston as well, included strong attacks on slavery embellished with vivid apocalyptic imagery.[48] Some of the freed and enslaved Africans who attended Dow were also members of "the African Church," a congregation in fellowship with Richard Allen's Bethel Church in Philadelphia and the African Methodist Episcopal (A.M.E.) denomination that Allen had created with Daniel Coker.[49] In the judicial proceedings that followed exposure of the plot, witnesses both Black and White identified the African Church, along with the A.M.E.'s influence from Philadelphia, as fomenting sedition. Shortly after the Charleston church was formed, Denmark Vesey transferred his allegiance from a local Presbyterian church to the new congregation where he became a class leader.

Vesey's use of Scripture to enlist recruits highlights one of the most significant developments in the American history of the Bible. At the inquest convened almost immediately after White authorities discovered the plot, several witnesses stressed the major role of Scripture in what was planned: "he studies the Bible a great deal and tries to prove from it that slavery and bondage is against the Bible." And, "at this meeting Vesey said . . . we ought to rise up and fight against the whites for our liberties; he was the first to rise up and speak, and he *read to us from the Bible, how the children of Israel were delivered out of Egypt from bondage.*"[50] Other witnesses testified that one of Vesey's associates read from the Apocryphal book of Tobit for the same purpose.[51] Like the exodus story, Tobit tells of faithfulness under duress, in this case an Israelite living in Nineveh after the ten tribes of Israel had been taken captive by Assyria and suffering for remaining true to Jehovah. (Since the American Bible Society did not publish English Bibles with the Apocrypha, Charleston's Blacks probably used a Catholic Bible for this reading or a Bible published in Britain, where until the late 1820s almost all printings included the Apocrypha.)[52] Evidence

---

[48]Egerton and Paquette, *Denmark Vesey*, 18-19. On Dow's preaching, see Nathan O. Hatch, *The Democratization of American Christianity* (New Haven: Yale University Press, 1989), 102, 185-86.

[49]Egerton and Paquette, *Denmark Vesey*, 21-25.

[50]Egerton and Paquette, *Denmark Vesey*, 166, 181, also 295 for another testimony after Vesey's reference to the exodus.

[51]Egerton and Paquette, *Denmark Vesey*, 212, 286.

[52]The ABS printed Spanish-language Bibles with the Apocrypha for distribution in Catholic Latin America until a controversy over the British and Foreign Bible Society's dissemination of the Apocrypha moved the ABS to end even those printings; Dwight, *Centennial History*, 100-1.

at the inquest also suggested that Vesey expounded other Old Testament texts that pronounced prophetic judgments on evil nations at the coming "day of the Lord" (Isaiah 19; Zechariah 14:1-3). With the possibility that themes from the works of Alexander McLeod or George Bourne had seeped into Charleston, he may also have quoted the denunciation of "man-stealing" from Exodus 21:16.[53]

Although some uncertainty attends the exact wording of Vesey's biblical expositions, and even the specific texts he expounded, their general character is clear beyond doubt. Vesey's immersion in Scripture was as deep as of those who would open Scripture to denounce the insurrection. But the message he took from the Bible reflected an interpretive approach—a general hermeneutic—very different from mainstream White procedures. Not historical Protestant differences with Catholicism, not the Enlightenment-inflected standards of linguistically precise exegesis, and not the argument by proof-text that had become second nature to the Protestant churches—rather, Vesey and his associates obviously read Scripture for its narratives of redemption that they then construed as a grand story of liberation.[54]

Methodist gospel preaching, as communicated especially by early leaders of the A.M.E., and themes of equality surviving from Revolutionary rhetoric did link the Bible of Denmark Vesey to the Bible of White South Carolina. Yet even from his very brief transit through the American firmament, it was possible to glimpse a biblicism every bit as powerful as, but strongly contrasting, the era's more influential White versions. In the immediate aftermath of the Vesey conspiracy, however, the most obvious result was a sharper statement of biblical conclusions already deeply engrained and reflecting conventions of White interpretive practice.

The conspiracy was discovered on June 14 and 15, 1822. Vesey and five of his associates were hung on July 2; the execution of twenty-two slaves followed on July 26. On September 23, the founder and sitting president of the Charleston Bible Society and two-time Federalist candidate for president, Charles Cotesworth Pinckney, dispatched a lengthy address on behalf of the Society to Governor Thomas Bennett, requesting a day of public Thanksgiving. Generous quotation from Scripture and repeated thanks for the protection

---

[53]On these specific texts, see Egerton and Paquette, *Denmark Vesey*, 323.

[54]For Vesey's place in the history of such a Grand Narrative, see John Coffey, *Exodus and Liberation: Deliverance Politics from John Calvin to Martin Luther King Jr.* (New York: Oxford University Press, 2014), 162, 167, 219.

of divine providence filled this address. Within months similar views were published by three well-known Charlestonians: Richard Furman, speaking for the South Carolina Baptist Convention as its president; one of the city's leading Episcopal ministers, Frederick Dalcho; and Edwin Holland, a young lawyer who had previously edited the *Charleston Times*. Together, in the same way that the insurrectionists anticipated certain later emphases from Black Bible readers, establishment Charleston set out a full-blown proslavery biblicism that over the next four decades became increasingly influential throughout the entire nation. Three of its propositions would be crucial for bringing many northerners at least part way to White southern opinion; two spoke more directly to the South.

The Bible sanctioned slavery, full stop. Speaking for South Carolina's Baptists, Richard Furman began his exposition of Scripture by again quoting Leviticus 25:44-46, which William Jenkins rightly labeled the biblical "rock of Gibraltar. . . . used in all of the Biblical defenses from the earliest to the last."[55] To the Mosaic instructions about perpetual enslavement of non-Hebrews, the Episcopalian Rev. Dalcho added a long discussion of the Curse of Canaan from Genesis 9: "perhaps we shall find that the negroes, the descendants of Ham, lost their freedom through the abominable wickedness of their progenitor."[56] On the New Testament, Dalcho's negative ("slavery is not incompatible with the principles and profession of Christianity") became the Bible Society's positive (the apostles regulated the master-slaver relationship "explicitly and reinforced by eternal sanctions").[57] Reference to Abraham's ownership of slaves and to the apostle Paul returning the slave Onesimus to Philemon completed this case. The Baptist Furman acknowledged that "the benevolent Wilberforce" had accurately pointed out the evils of the slave trade, while the Episcopalian Dalcho conceded "the evil which attends" slave-keeping. But Dalcho had no hesitation in agreeing with Furman that "the

---

[55]*Rev. Dr. Richard Furman's Exposition of the Views of the Baptists, Relative to the Colored Population of the United States, in a Communication to the Governor of South-Carolina* (Charleston: A. E. Miller, 1823), 8. Jenkins, *Pro-Slavery Thought*, 202.

[56]A South Carolinian [Frederick Dalcho], *Practical Considerations founded on the Scriptures, Relative to the Slave Population of South-Carolina* (Charleston: E. E. Miller, 1823), 8. Dalcho expatiated at length on Ham and Canaan as the progenitors of Africans (8-20) because he felt Furman for the Baptists had slighted the passage.

[57]Dalcho, *Practical Considerations*, 20; "The Charleston Bible Society Asks Governor Bennet for a Day of Thanksgiving," in Egerton and Paquette, *Denmark Vesey*, 674.

right of holding slaves is clearly established in the Holy Scriptures both by precept and example."[58]

The use of Scripture to attack slavery abused, vitiated, and perverted the Bible. So certain did the Bible's sanction appear to these apologists that they could come to only one conclusion about anyone who thought that Scripture opposed the institution. While the Bible Society ascribed such views merely to "a misconstruction, or Perversion of the Scriptures," the lawyer Edwin Holland held nothing back: "[T]hose . . . who are acquainted with the rise and progress of that nefarious plot, know how blasphemously the word of God was tortured, in order to sanction the unholy butchery that was contemplated. . . . Religion was stripped of her pure and spotless robe, and panoplied like a fury, was made to fight under the banners of the most frightful Conspiracy that imagination can conceive."[59]

Trust in providence, reliance on Scripture as the Word of God, and the defense of slavery constituted a seamless whole. The White Charleston statements moved away from proof-texting when they interpreted their rescue from the planned massacre as "a providential, gracious interposition." Like believers of all sorts, they did nothing unusual in praising God for their deliverance. Yet because that praise was combined with a biblical defense of slavery—and because they also looked so fixedly on Scripture as given "to make [Man] wise unto salvation"—their religion drew together a set of powerful convictions into a single whole.[60] God's Word, God's care, God's salvation in Christ, and God's provision of slavery could never be construed as separable entities, but only as one.

Furman, speaking of divine providence, repeated the word *interposition* three times in as many paragraphs in describing the city's deliverance. The lawyer Holland also employed the word when he praised "the activity and intelligence of a wise and efficient police, strengthened and enlightened as they were by the protecting interposition of a beneficent Providence."[61] As historians know, the same word would not long thereafter express White

---

[58]Furman, *Views of the Baptists*, 11; Dalcho, *Practical Considerations*, 6; Furman, *Views of the Baptists*, 7.

[59]"Bible Society," 674; [Edwin Holland], *A Refutation of the Calumnies Circulated against the Southern & Western States, respecting the institution and existence of Slavery among them* (Charleston: A. E. Miller, 1822), 12.

[60]Furman, *Views of the Baptists*, 4; "Bible Society," 674 (quotation 2 Timothy 3:15).

[61]Furman, *Views of the Baptists*, 4-5; Holland, *Refutation*, 13.

South Carolina's defiance of a "tariff of abominations" passed by Congress and enforced by President Andrew Jackson. But the same word had already appeared in yet another context in more than half the American hymnbooks published from the 1790s. It came from a hymn by the English minister, Robert Robinson, "Come, thou fount of every blessing": "Jesus sought me when a stranger, / Wandering from the fold of God; / He to rescue me from danger, / *Interposed* his precious blood." Without pushing the linguistic coincidence too far, "interposition" in these three highly charged, but strikingly different, domains, still testifies to the blurring of worlds that so pervasively characterized the public history of Scripture in the early United States.[62]

While a perverted Bible invited slave rebellion, the Bible properly understood encouraged model slave deportment. Robert Forbes has pointed out that the White responses to the Vesey conspiracy were directed expressly at southern readers who once again questioned the value of religious instruction for slaves.[63] As had been the case in early colonial history, once again church leaders were asserting that the Bible—rightly understood!—made slaves into better slaves. Furman and Dalcho both condemned the African Church for promoting perverse readings of Scripture; both also stressed that Blacks associated with the traditional churches took no part in the planned outrage. Dalcho even went out of his way to claim that Black Episcopalians never indulged in extemporaneous worship but instead kept themselves strictly to words from the Book of Common Prayer. The Bible Society lobbied Governor Bennet with the same message: "one of the best securities we have to the domestic Peace and Safety of the State, is to be found in the sentiments and correspondent dispositions of the religious Negroes; which they derive from the Bible."[64] Good exposition, in other words, made good servants.

Organized northern philanthropy imperiled an entire way of life by inciting Blacks to violence. A second message primarily for fellow White southerners defended their slave-based civilization. In the very years when the ABS was leading the way with bold new attempts to evangelize and reform the nation, Charleston Whites felt threatened, as the lawyer Holland fumed, "by the swarm of Missionaries, white and *black*, that are perpetually visiting us, who with the Sacred Volume of God in one hand . . . scatter, at the same time,

---

[62]On the "blurring of worlds" in this era, see Hatch, *Democratization*, 34.

[63]Forbes, *Missouri Compromise*, 149-51.

[64]Furman, *Views of the Baptists*, 17; Dalcho, *Practical Considerations*, 33-35; "Bible Society," 675.

with the other, the fire-brands of discord and destruction, and *secretly* dis-
perse among our Negro Population, the seeds of discontent and sedition."
When these incendiaries distributed "among our Negroes . . . *religious magazines, newspaper paragraphs* and *insulated texts of Scripture,* they threw such
a delusive light upon their condition as was calculated to bewilder and de-
ceive, and finally, to precipitate them into ruin." Dalcho repeated the charge,
but in frankly materialistic terms, when he denounced schemes to send
manumitted slaves to Africa. Don't they realize, he complained in italicized
type, "*our servants are our money. . . .* Manumission would produce nothing
but evil"?[65]

The message coming out of White Charleston in the wake of the failed
Vesey insurrection spoke loudly. Rescued by providence, menaced by phil-
anthropic wolves in the religious clothing of sheep, and yet everywhere upheld
by Scripture, the White South would repel its enemies and survive as a blessed
civilization under God.

A CRISIS FOR *SOLA SCRIPTURA*

The near conjunction of debate over Missouri and panic over Denmark Vesey
hardened the trajectory of American disputing on the Bible and slavery. The
Revolution-inspired impetus against the institution had passed. Within a
decade the publication of David Walker's *Appeal*, the founding of William
Lloyd Garrison's *The Liberator*, the Nat Turner rebellion, and the creation of
the American Antislavery Society would further confirm that trajectory. But
these later developments only extended the furrows dug by the simultaneous
appearance of powerful antislavery works based on both literal and theological
deployment of Scripture, the main denominations' retreat from earlier scriptural condemnations, and confident assertions by leading White spokesmen
of scriptural approval for the slave system.

With the increasing salience of the Bible in so many spheres of early United
States history, many Americans—both Black and White, female and male—
were finding in Scripture a source of life, an inspiration for personal righteousness, and a rock in times of tumult. Even as trust in elites, historical
precedents, and official learning continued to decline, confidence in Scripture
reached new heights. Yet questions that could only have arisen in a civilization

---

[65]Holland, *Refutation*, 11-12; Dalcho, *Practical Considerations*, 6.

fulfilling the aspirations of Protestants to live by *sola scriptura* now remained to trouble that same civilization:

- How could responsible citizen-believers choose between conflicting proof-texts?

- How could they choose between contradictory theological or ideological convictions expressed alike in biblical language and supported by biblical exposition?

- If Scripture was God's coherent Word, how did God's revelation given in Jesus Christ (New Testament) affect interpretation of God's revelation to Israel (Old Testament)?

- Could foundational loyalty to Scripture be confirmed by how individual texts were interpreted? (In other words, could a person's profession of belief in the Bible be credited if that person willfully misinterpreted scriptural passages whose meaning was transparently clear to me?)

- How did assumptions about God's providential care for the United States shape interpretations of Scripture, and vice versa?

- Why did biblical teachings align so easily with so many different convictions about the economy, society, politics, gender, and race?

- And when so many Americas debated the Bible and slavery so obsessively, who besides African Americans would be interested in biblical revelation concerning race?

In the early decades of the nineteenth century, Scripture became America's book. As such, discerning its meaning for the nation became more important—but also, as Missouri pushed the questions of slavery center stage, increasingly fraught. The American history of the Bible always included much more than dilemmas concerning race and slavery, but also never less.

6

Josephine Butler's Mystic Vision and Her Love for the Jesus of the Gospels

Mary Riso

WHEN I FIRST READ Josephine Butler's *Personal Reminiscences of a Great Crusade*,[1] I immediately became interested in her inner life and spirituality. I discovered that her writings are full of her thoughts and insights about her personal relationship with God; these comments are always connected to scriptural references that show a deep understanding. She is generous in sharing what God taught her through his Word. The biblical references that she chose fall into certain categories: the compassion and love of Jesus, the justice and refuge of God, and what it means to "take up one's cross" and engage in spiritual battle for the sake of God's work. In 1869, Josephine wrote an introduction to a series of essays, *Women's Work and Women's Culture*. She gives her view about the words of Jesus in relationship to the rest of the Bible. "My appeal is to Christ, and to Him alone,

---

[1] Josephine E. Butler, *Personal Reminiscences of a Great Crusade* (London: Horace Marshall & Son, 1896). What Josephine Butler (1828–1906) called her "Great Crusade" was a campaign to repeal the Contagious Diseases Acts (passed in 1866, 1868, and 1869)—acts which placed full responsibility for sexual sin on women while intentionally protecting the men involved. The legislation allowed police officers to arrest prostitutes in certain ports and army towns and subject them to compulsory checks for venereal disease. It made the hiring of prostitutes easier and safer for men while humiliating and imprisoning the women. Josephine Butler's work on behalf of women eventually expanded beyond Great Britain to France, Belgium, Switzerland, France, America, and India.

not to any Church, or traditions, or Councils, or catechisms, nor yet even to an Apostle . . . His teaching was for all time; much of Paul's was for a given time."[2] This may seem to suggest that she emphasized the Gospels at the expense of the Epistles. However, Josephine Butler wrote thousands of pages, comprising books, letters, articles, pamphlets, and speeches. It is hard to believe that this view remained with her throughout her life because it is not consistent with the vast number of biblical references that appear in her work.[3] Nonetheless, the incarnate Jesus is without question at the center of her theology and her lived faith. They had an intimate and tender relationship; she valued "venturing straight into the presence of Christ for the answer to every question"[4] and encouraged others to do the same. The centrality of Jesus for Josephine Butler is also true in two specific ways. First, on a personal level, she saw Christ as her liberator from sin; she had a spiritual experience in which she was betrothed to Jesus "in judgement and in righteousness"; and, due to the suffering involved in her work, she felt that she shared with him the way of the cross. Second, she invited the women that she met into Jesus' presence, and regarded his treatment of women as indescribably beautiful.

In his biography of his grandmother, Arthur Stanley George Butler defined a mystic as "one of a sect professing to have direct intercourse with God who revealed secrets to them." "Mrs. Butler was not a member of a sect; and she did not 'profess' to have anything. But she was undoubtedly a mystic; and she had this great gift of communion with God."[5] It was this communion with God—Josephine's definition of prayer—that formed the roots of her inner life. Towards the end of her life she said, "Thankfully, I will receive any word of help in a book; but I find the only vital, lasting, all-powerful help is such that He gives *direct*."[6] Josephine wrote several biographies: a pamphlet about Saint Agnes, biographies of her beloved sister, Harriet Meuricroffe, and her husband George Butler, and a life of French pastor, Jean Frederic Oberlin. Her most comprehensive biography is of the medieval mystic and

---

[2]Josephine E. Butler, *Women's Work and Women's Culture: A Series of Essays* (London: MacMillan, 1869), lii.

[3]For a general account of Butler and the Bible, see Timothy Larsen, *A People of One Book: The Bible and the Victorians* (Oxford: Oxford University Press, 2011), 219-46.

[4]Butler, *Women's Work and Women's Culture*, lvi.

[5]A. S. G. Butler, *Portrait of Josephine Butler* (London: Faber & Faber, 1954), 173.

[6]Letter from JB to her friend Miss Forsaith (1904) in Butler, *Portrait of Josephine Butler*, 176.

reformer Saint Catherine of Siena.[7] Josephine shared with Catherine a similar spirituality, experienced from their earliest years: "We have, in common with the saint whose life we have followed, an ever-free access to the Father by prayer: That path of prayer which she firmly and unwearingly trod is open to every one of us."[8] From those roots sprang three other branches of her spirituality: suffering, prophecy, and individuality. Josephine believed these to be essential to the work of God. These four features, particularly the belief in direct communication and union with the divine, her self-identity as betrothed to Christ, the radical calling from God, and the focus on suffering shared with Jesus and others, suggest that Josephine's spirituality was mystical in nature.[9]

PRAYER

"Now the things which I believe I had learned direct from God."[10]

"And it came to pass, that, while they communed together and reasoned, Jesus himself drew near, and went with them."

LUKE 24:15

Around 1900, when Josephine was seventy-two, she recalled a pivotal experience that occurred in 1845 when she was seventeen:

> The world appeared to me to be out of joint. A strange intuition was given to me, whereby I saw as in a vision before I had seen any of them with my bodily eyes, some of the saddest miseries of the earth, the injustices, the inequalities, the cruelties practiced by man on man, by man on woman. . . . Looking back

---

[7] A very helpful consideration of Josephine Butler's "Christian mysticism" may be found in Lisa Severine Nolland, "Josephine Butler and the Repeal of the Contagious Diseases Acts (1883/1886): Motivations and Larger Vision of a Victorian Feminist Christian," PhD diss., Trinity College, Bristol, 2001, https://research-information.bristol.ac.uk/files/34495472/364980.pdf, 250-55.

[8] Josephine Butler, *Catherine of Siena: A Biography* (London: Dyer, 1878), 336.

[9] An emphasis on Josephine Butler's spiritual life may be found in a little-known biography: Nancy Boyd, *Three Victorian Women Who Changed Their World* (Oxford: Oxford University Press, 1982). A. N. Wilson's chapter on Butler in *Eminent Victorians* (New York: W.W. Norton, 1989) also offers an appreciation of Butler's inner life. Jane Jordan's biography *Josephine Butler* focuses on the subject's outer life and remarkable accomplishments (London: John Murray, 2001).

[10] Josephine E. Butler, *Recollections of George Butler* (Bristol: J. W. Arrowsmith, 1896), 98. In addition to a biography of her husband, *Recollections* serves as an autobiography of Josephine Butler.

it seems to me the end must have been defeat and death had not the Saviour imparted to the child wrestler something of the virtue of His own midnight agony, when in Gethsemane His sweat dropped like great drops of blood to the ground.[11]

This experience encompassed the central features of Josephine's prayer life, a pattern that would be repeated throughout her life: an acute, intuitive awareness of both good and evil; an experience of God that was connected to a vision; her acknowledged need for God as the only answer to her questions, turning to him in solitude, listening, and waiting; and a vivid image of Jesus in the Gospels. Prayer meant believing in the unseen and listening.

Intuition is defined as "direct perception of truth, fact, etc., independent of any reasoning process; immediate apprehension." Josephine had an awareness of both good and evil that drove her to God, and that was not addressed in any human way. Several factors contributed to her "intuition" that the "world was out of joint." Despite a loving family, beautiful surroundings, and ample resources, Josephine lived in a harsh world. In her youth she came upon the body of a man in the woods who had hung himself. Her brother John went away to sea and died there. Josephine grew up in a home where her father's passionate commitment to social issues surrounding injustice was connected to real events. In this way she was exposed to the sin of slavery, and especially the plight of female slaves. "I remember how these things combined to break my young heart,"[12] she said. As her father studied the Bible every Sunday afternoon, she discovered that one of his favorite passages was: "Is not this the fast that I have chosen? to loose the bands of wickedness, to undo the heavy burdens, and to let the oppressed go free, and that ye break every yoke?" (Isaiah 58:6). Josephine always felt that she had inherited her father's "love of justice." However, her sensitivity to the world around her seems to have preceded these experiences.

Several phrases in Josephine's description of her early "travail of soul" suggest that her horror of injustice and awareness of suffering transcended any particular event. She states, "It was my lot from my earliest years to be haunted by the problems which more or less present themselves to every

---

[11]George W. Johnson and Lucy A. Johnson, eds., *Josephine E. Butler: An Autobiographical Memoir* (Bristol: J. W. Arrowsmith, 1909), 15-16.

[12]Johnson and Johnson, *Autobiographical Memoir*, 14.

thoughtful mind. Year after year this haunting became more tyrannous."[13] "It was my lot," "I was haunted," "I had a strange intuition," "I saw as in a vision." Josephine notes that her husband helped her with the extraordinary burdens not only of her calling but of her nature; it was his gift to help "to restore for me the balance of a mind too heavily weighted with sad thoughts of life's perplexing problems."[14]

The experience of crying out to God which, Josephine suggested, lasted years (she states that the conflict was renewed when "there dawned upon me the realities of those earthly miseries which I had realized only in a measure by intuition; but later still came the outward and active conflict, with, thanks be to God, the light and hope and guidance which He never denies to them who ask and seek and knock . . .") is worth looking at closely.[15] It is clear that before the "outward and active conflict" in which she became engaged, there was an internal experience. This was not just the beginning of her calling and of the features of her prayer life; it presents a description of her which is evangelical, in accordance with David Bebbington's Quadrilateral.[16] This is where the cross of Christ, the Word of God, the call to action, and the recognition of her sin and need for God converged.

> What is our goodness to God? None of us are good. Think of all the people mentioned in the Gospels who sought after Christ. What was it that brought them to his feet? It was not their goodness but their great needs, wants and desires, their sicknesses, their deep heart griefs, and the griefs and miseries of those dear to them. Our only claim in coming to him is that we need him and want him. There is no other.[17]

She took her stand with "the sinful woman of the city" and referred to God as her liberator: "Looking my Liberator in the face, can my friends wonder that I have taken my place, (I took it long ago)—oh! with what infinite contentment!—by the side of her, 'the woman of the city which was a sinner,' of whom He, her Liberator and mine, said, as He can also say of me, '*this*

---

[13]Johnson and Johnson, *Autobiographical Memoir*, 15.

[14]Butler, *Recollections of George Butler*, 102.

[15]Johnson and Johnson, eds., *Autobiographical Memoir*, 16.

[16]The essential features of evangelicalism are defined by David Bebbington in his Quadrilateral: conversionism, activism, biblicism, crucicentrism. D. W. Bebbington, *Evangelicalism in Modern Britain: A History from the 1730s to the 1980s* (London: Unwin and Hyman, 1989), 2-17.

[17]Excerpt from *The Storm Bell* (1899), a periodical in which JB published from 1898 to 1900, in Johnson and Johnson, eds., *Autobiographical Memoir*, 254-55.

woman hath not ceased to kiss my feet.'"[18] Forty-one years later she proclaimed: "I have not an atom of faith in any reform . . . which has not at its roots a real repentance before God."[19] Not only would Josephine take her stand as a sinner before God, she would stand with the "sinful women" of the cities in need of God's love and protection. And she would have a glimpse into the devastating effects of sin and the need for those who had sinned against these women of the city to repent. Her prayers confirmed a recognition of her deep need for God.

Josephine's 1845 spiritual crisis reveals a central element of her prayer life: intimacy with Jesus, the primacy of his words and actions for her inner life and calling to bring the love and justice of God. Here, there are three references to Jesus: in the garden of Gethsemane, with the woman "of the city" who did not cease to kiss his feet, and as the one who answers those who seek, ask, and knock. Josephine had a second spiritual crisis, sometime between 1852 and 1854. When she lived in Oxford with her husband, George, and their first two children, she was reminded to go directly to God, and to listen for his voice. Josephine was disappointed in the learned men of Oxford. As her awareness of "a whole world of sorrows, griefs, injustices, and crimes, which must not be spoken of—no, not even in whispers"—grew: "Now the things which I believed I had learned direct from God. I never sat at the feet of any man; I never sought light or guidance even from any saint, man or woman, though I dearly loved some such whom I had known, and learned much from their example; nor on churches and creeds had I ever leaned."[20] The reality of the Son of God was Josephine's help and refuge. She wrote of how she and George read together the words of life and "were able to bring many earthly notions and theories to the test of what the Holy One and the Just said and did" and how they described the sayings and actions of Jesus as "revolutionary."[21]

In hearing from God through prayerful listening, the scriptural passages most often represented in her writing are the words of Jesus: "In the midst of the present confusion which it seems to me there is among writers, Christian

---

[18]Johnson and Johnson, eds., *Autobiographical Memoir*, 16.

[19]Josephine Butler, "A Woman's Appeal to the Electors" (1886), in Johnson and Johnson, eds., *Autobiographical Memoir*, 185.

[20]Butler, *Recollections of George Butler*, 98-99.

[21]Butler, *Recollections of George Butler*, in Johnson and Johnson, eds., *Autobiographical Memoir*, 35.

and materialist, with respect to the social direction of certain principles of Christianity, my appeal is to Christ, and to Him alone, not to any Church, or traditions, or Councils, or catechisms, nor yet even to an Apostle."[22] In addressing the women she got to know, Josephine delighted in the ways that Jesus spoke to and treated women. She wrote in an 1893 letter, "You remember how sweet and lovely Jesus always was to women, and how He helped their woman diseases, and how respectful He was to them . . . And he was born of a woman—a woman only."[23] In reviewing Jesus' dealings with women: "Search throughout the Gospel history, and observe His conduct in regard to women, and it will be found that the word liberation expresses, above all others, the act which changed the whole life and character and position of the women he dealt with, and which ought to have changed the character of men's treatment of women from that time forward."[24] When she was asked to speak of Jesus to a group of "women of humble rank" in Genoa in 1880, she described him as "the great Emancipator, the friend of womanhood, and of the poor and the weak; the only absolutely Just One, the Saviour of all."[25] Freedom from sexual enslavement was the centerpiece of Josephine's crusade against injustice, and the Jesus of the Gospels was the one who brought freedom and justice.

Josephine's encounter with God in 1845 included what she herself called a vision ("I saw as in a vision before I had seen any of them with my bodily eyes, some of the saddest miseries of the earth"). Her trust in visionary experiences—an intuition of the real although invisible activity of God—was consistent throughout her life and was closely connected to moments of intimate communion with God. Her openness to the unseen varied in its expression from an exceptionally vivid and blessed imagination, to knowledge of a healing of an illness, to glimpses of facts of which she had no prior experience—sometimes involving suffering, sometimes hope, things that were coming in the future consistent with God's will and character, or experiences bringing reassurance through God's presence.

Josephine had an intuition of her calling many years before. A travelling circus had come to Oxford, and a young woman told Josephine and George

---

[22]Butler, *Women's Work and Women's Culture*, xlviii.
[23]Butler, *Portrait of Josephine Butler*, 58.
[24]Butler, *Women's Work and Women's Culture*, lix.
[25]Butler, *Personal Reminiscences of a Great Crusade*, 219-20.

of her longing to leave such a life and serve God. However, she was trapped. Josephine recalled:

> It was a Sunday evening in hot summer weather. I had been sitting for some time at my open window to breathe more freely the sultry air, and it seemed to me that I heard a wailing cry somewhere among the trees in the twilight which was deepening into night. It was a woman's cry—a woman aspiring to heaven and dragged back to hell—and my heart was pierced with pain. I longed to leap from the window and flee with her to some place of refuge. It passed. I cannot explain the nature of the impression, which remains with me to this day; but beyond that twilight and even in the midst of that pitiful cry, there seemed to dawn a ray of light, and to sound a note not wholly of despair. The light was far off, yet coming near; and the slight summer breeze in those tall trees had in them a whisper of the future.[26]

"Before my mind's eye," "as in a vision," "there seemed to dawn": this is the language of Josephine Butler. She was not afraid to state as truth something that she could not fully explain.

Josephine's visions were often inspired by anguish over the suffering of an innocent young girl, an awareness of her calling and the magnitude of the problem. However, the awareness of the darkness was not separated from the light of Christ. In 1897 she wrote an article on the "Joy of God" for the publication *Wings*: "Jesus spoke much of His joy in His last wonderful conversation with His disciples 'that my joy may be in you and your joy may be full' (John xv,11). His joy is His Father's joy . . . It is not possible that the joy of God can be interrupted by the works of the devil, by his apparent present victories . . . and I shouted for joy and victory!"[27] An awareness of sorrow and hardship went hand in hand with hope, based in Scripture. Her visionary experiences were almost always accompanied by a response from God.

Josephine wrote of a personal experience that she had in Geneva in 1886, related not to her work on behalf of women, but to when her husband was critically ill with rheumatic fever. She was beginning to despair because not only was her husband very sick and perhaps dying but she herself was weak and sick. Who would care for him if she couldn't? A light shone into the darkness of her despair:

---

[26]Butler, *Recollections of George Butler*, 97-98.
[27]"Joy of God," in *Wings* (1897), Johnson and Johnson, eds., *Josephine E. Butler*, 234-35.

The promises in the Scriptures with which I had been familiar all my life came to me as if I had heard them for the first time. I fell on my knees, and kept silence to hear what the Lord would say to me; for my own part, I had nothing to say. My trouble was too heavy for speech. "The prayer of faith shall save the sick." "Call on Me in the time of trouble, and I will deliver Thee." "Is this true?," I exclaimed. Yes, I knew it was true. It seemed to become a very simple matter, and grace was given to me, in my pain and weakness, to say only, "Lord, I believe." The burden was removed.[28]

From that day George Butler's condition improved greatly and he lived for four more years. In the last year of George Butler's illness, Josephine had another experience that was a combination of dream and vision. She relates in a letter written to her sister, Harriet Meuricroffre, from Cannes:

Just as I was falling asleep I had such a pleasant sensation. I thought I was lying flat, with a restful feeling, on a smooth, still sea—a boundless ocean with no limit or shore on any side. It was strong, and held me up, and there was light and sunshine all around me. And then I dreamed I heard a voice say: "Such is the Grace of God. Like this ocean are His love, His power, His goodwill—boundless, endless. He is never weary of blessing." I took it to mean that I was to rest in God, and expect all good things from Him.[29]

In prayer, Josephine received from God. Like Catherine of Siena, who constantly spoke of "that which the natural eye hath not seen" (1 Corinthians 12:9), Josephine was convinced that invisible realities could be known. In a series of 1897 articles in *Wings* published under the title "Prophets and Prophetesses," Josephine spoke of the necessity of solitude and listening:

It is in the solitude of the soul, alone with God, that His thoughts are revealed. It is in great humility, in separation from the spirit of the world . . . It required much courage to be alone with God, to elect to retire for a time, and even for long times, and to listen to His voice only . . . the keen searchlight of His presence reveals the innermost recesses of the soul . . . In the clearer light of eternity all things assume their right proportion.[30]

---

[28]Butler, *Recollections of George Butler*, 434-35.
[29]Letter from JB to her sister Harriet Meuricroffe from Cannes (April 28, 1889), in Butler, *Recollections of George Butler*, 456.
[30]From a series of articles, "Prophets and Prophetesses," (1897) in *Wings*, in Johnson and Johnson, eds., *Autobiographical Memoir*, 235-43.

In a letter to her friend, Miss Forsaith, in 1904, Josephine wrote about prayer. She emphasized the importance of listening and silence: "It is as if the Lord came to my room and sat down beside me. I am awed. I don't begin to speak at once; I wait for Him to begin. O! it is so sweet when all prayer becomes *communion* with a Friend."[31] The three main features of Josephine's prayer life—listening in silence and solitude; openness to the unseen; and a particularly close and tender relationship with Jesus—were reminiscent of the medieval mystics, and brought her into the presence of God.

SUFFERING

"To produce a movement of a vital, spiritual nature, someone must suffer, someone must go through sore travail of soul, before a living movement, outwardly visible, can be born."[32]

"Now is your hour, and the power of darkness."[33]

LUKE 22:53

The second feature of Josephine Butler's inner life is suffering. In about 1887, Henry Holland Scott, Regius Professor of Divinity at the University of Oxford and Canon of Christ Church, glimpsed Josephine in London on the eve of the repeal of the Contagious Diseases Act:

> A face looked at me out of a hurrying hansom, which arrested and frightened me. It was framed on pure and noble and beautiful lines: but it was smitten, and bitten into, by some East wind, which blighted it into grey sadness. It had seen that which took all colour and joy out of it. I felt as the children who saw Dante pass as a shadow through the sunny square: and whispered, "He has been in Hell." The face gave a look (I thought) of recognition before it had

---

[31]Letter from JB to her friend Miss Forsaith (1904) in Butler, *Portrait of Josephine Butler*, 176.

[32]From a message sent by JB on the occasion of the thirtieth anniversary of the Federation meeting at Neuchatel in September 1905. Johnson and Johnson, *Autobiographical Memoir*, 300-302.

[33]Butler, *Recollections of George Butler*, 218-19. From an 1869 journal entry about her call to the work, praying for a hatred of injustice, tyranny, and cruelty, and a divine compassion willing to suffer long for souls.

swiftly gone: and after I had recovered my memory, I knew that it was Josephine Butler. She was passing through her martyrdom.[34]

Josephine herself stated that no words could adequately express the evil she faced in the course of her work. She felt the she had walked through death with the women she met, and with Jesus himself. She knew the way of the cross.

Josephine believed that two things were necessary for a new movement of God. First, the movement must be preceded by prayer. Second, to "produce a movement of a vital, spiritual nature, someone must suffer, someone must go through sore travail of soul, before a living movement, outwardly visible, can be born."[35] Here she gave the example of Christ suffering, and his "travail of soul" in Isaiah 53:11. And she included herself as the one who had suffered for the new movement on behalf of women: this is where she related to Jesus through the cross she had taken up. Josephine also believed that, in imitation of Jesus, she suffered *with* the victims of injustice, the women that she encountered every day. It was this lack of distance, this union that brought Josephine such personal pain: "The hour of our redemption has struck! I say 'our' for we have not only *remembered* those that are in bonds, as being bound with them, but actually *suffered with them* in spirit for so long, long years."[36] David Bebbington has written, "The centrality of Christ crucified is the legacy of the nineteenth century to the twentieth, and to the twenty-first."[37] Surely Josephine Butler contributed to this legacy.

It is in this section that we see again the importance of Jesus and the Gospels to Josephine's biblical theology and personal spirituality. Her calling had to do with the mistreatment of women, specifically of the women she calls "Magdalenes":

Christian people! . . . Every act of our Lord's, emphatically recorded by the Evangelists, has a deep and an everlasting significance. A single act of His towards a single individual was designed to be the type, for all ages, of the acts required of every Christian in every similar case—a seed intended to bring

---

[34]Henry Scott Holland, *A Bundle of Memories* (London: Wells Gardner, Darton, 1915), 287.

[35]From a message sent by JB on the occasion of the thirtieth anniversary of the Federation meeting at Neuchatel in September 1905. Johnson and Johnson, *Autobiographical Memoir*, 300-302.

[36]Letter from Josephine E. Butler to her sister Harriet Meuricroffre, January 29, 1875 [from Turin], in Johnson and Johnson, *An Autobiographical Memoir*, 140.

[37]David W. Bebbington, "The Gospel in the Nineteenth Century," *Vox Evangelica* 13 (1983): 19-28.

forth fruit a thousandfold; on each is plainly written the command, "Go and do likewise."[38]

Then Josephine talks about how the treatment of those in need was an area where the church had not followed the Lord's examples—although she gives examples, starting in the thirteenth century, of certain figures in the Roman Catholic Church, Catherine of Siena among them, who made attempts to fulfill the commands of Jesus.[39] It is impossible to overestimate the centrality of suffering to Josephine Butler's personal faith and spirituality. For her, it had to do with the character of God, with walking with others as a manifestation not only of Christianity but of shared humanity, and with the efficacy of her own suffering for the benefit of others. She believed that it drew her closer to Christ, and she saw the suffering Jesus as the utmost representation of God's love. "It has been said that 'no plummet can fathom the depths of human sin.' But I add that 'no plummet can fathom the deeper depths of Divine Love.' The *Cross* was the measure of both, and having been in hell myself, I am driven to believe that there is *Love* below all—otherwise, how could I endure, how could I *love* a God who could doom any sinner to an eternity of hell?"[40] The cross answered the call of God's justice—but one feels as if this is true not only because of substitutionary atonement but because justice and love are inseparable. Her sacrifice of total commitment to her calling was for the salvation of others—not salvation from their own sin, which could only be accomplished by Christ—but from the destructive effects of the sins of others. Josephine never separated suffering from faith. The way of the cross was very hard at the end, as it was for Jesus, "but we cannot complain. For, as with the Lord, we see Victory so near; and the joy of His presence so great, flowing side by side with the pain. His is so near

---

[38] Josephine E. Butler, "The Lovers of the Lost," *Contemporary Review* 13 (1870): 16-40, in Jordan and Sharp, eds., *Josephine Butler and the Prostitution Campaigns: Diseases of the Body Politic* (London: Routledge, 2003), 95.

[39] An enlightening article about Catherine of Siena's relationship to the Bible is Diana L. Villegas's "Catherine of Siena's Wisdom on Discernment and Her Reception of Scripture," *Acta theologica* 33, suppl. 17 (2013), www.scielo.org.za/scielo.php?script=sci_arttext&pid=S1015-87582013000300012. Jenny Daggers and Diana Neal's collection, *Sex, Gender, and Religion: Josephine Butler Revisited* (New York: Peter Lang, 2006) emphasizes Butler's religious motivations (including her relationship with Roman Catholicism) and her identity as a Christian woman.

[40] Letter from Josephine E. Butler to Miss Forsaith and Harriet Meuricroffe, April, 2, 1905 [from Wooler], Josephine E. Butler Collection, University of Liverpool Library, in Jordan and Sharp, eds., *Josephine Butler and the Prostitution Campaigns*, 300.

personally—as the essence of the Godhead, the Creator of the Universe as well as the beautiful tender Man."[41] Josephine focused, as always, on the Jesus of the Gospels.

Josephine's sensitivity to other's sufferings, to the sufferings of the world, to injustice, was exceptional. It was not an average awareness of suffering, and it required action. Upon receiving her call from God, soon after she began working with women in Liverpool, Josephine stated, "I feel as if I must go out into the streets and cry aloud or my heart will break."[42] She described herself as having been in hell, as being on a cross next to Christ. "I envied the sparrows upon the garden walk because they had not the minds and souls capable of torment like mine."[43] As she grew older, she spoke of the purposes of suffering, and comments on the existence of evil. "It is only through conflict and through trial of our integrity that we can become in the highest sense sons and daughters of God. Christ Himself was 'made perfect through suffering.'" She also spoke of her own hope and enthusiasm given by God in the midst of suffering as she aged.[44] In 1900 she reflected: "Long ago I asked a gift of God—companionship with Christ." She thought she would be Mary sitting at his feet, but, "Today it is the companionship with Him of the penitent malefactor, nailed to a neighbouring cross."[45] This was an answer to prayer—it brought her closer to God—but it was different than what she expected.

In her *Personal Reminiscences of a Great Crusade*, Josephine recalls the experiences of a young girl in Brussels, around 1880:

> She told me with much simplicity that, in the midst of these tortures, she was "all the time strengthened and comforted by the thought that Jesus Himself had been cruelly scourged, and that He could feel for her." Before her capture she had one day seen in a shop window in Brussels an engraving of Christ before Pilate, bound and scourged. Some persons, no doubt may experience a little shock of horror at the idea of any connection in the thoughts of this poor child between the supreme agony of the Son of God and her own torments in the cellar of that house of debauchery.[46]

---

[41] Butler, *Portrait of Josephine Butler*, 216-17.
[42] Butler, *Recollections of George Butler*, 220.
[43] Johnson and Johnson, eds., *Autobiographical Memoir*, 88-89.
[44] From *The Lady of Shunem*, a series of biblical essays. Josephine Butler, *The Lady of Shunem* (London: Horace Marshall & Son, 1894), in Johnson and Johnson, *Autobiographical Memoir*, 211-15.
[45] Johnson and Johnson, *Autobiographical Memoir*, 276-78.
[46] Josephine E. Butler, *Personal Reminiscences of a Great Crusade* (London: H. Marshall, 1896), 229.

She goes on: "I believe, and have had many testimonies to the fact, that He visits spiritually these young souls in their earthly prison, many a time, He alone, His majesty of pity, without any intervention of ours."[47] This image of Jesus visiting people is a frequent one with Josephine. Invisible realities were real to her. Josephine often contrasted the life of the soul/spirit and the life of the flesh, and lamented the emphasis placed on the fleshly life by the men who abuse girls and women.

Josephine was not only acutely conscious of her own spiritual battle—but of her physical frailty at times. She describes how she came into the world prematurely, "weak about the heart," which stayed with her for the rest of her life—her symptoms being "a deadly coldness and a heart pain, making my hands stiffen and turn blue."[48] Josephine's physical frailty was lifelong. Her grandson noted that "she suffered much in the last two years, like the saints whose portion it was to be tormented physically as well as spiritually towards the end."[49] She saw her suffering as a purifying process, as in Matthew 3:12: "Whose fan *is* in his hand, and he will thoroughly purge his floor, and gather his wheat into the garner; but he will burn up the chaff with unquenchable fire."

In an early speech she recalled her spiritual experience upon realizing her call—when she first encountered the state regulation of vice—that she asked God to hold her hand as she descended into the darkness. At first she was overcome but later she learned that "God can give more than power to bear the pain; there is a positive joy in His service, and in any warfare in which He, who conquered sin and death and hell, goes before us, and is our reward."[50] In an 1898 article for *The Storm Bell*, considering the fears of mothers for the spiritual well-being of their sons, Josephine relates to the Gospel account of the Syrophencian woman whose dead son Jesus raised. "It is in the dark that His light shines the brightest. One hour with Him, alone, in the dark, in the gloom of despair and helpless woe, has taught me more than years when I walked in the light of happy and hopeful circumstances. I fear nothing now, for I have been alone *with God in the dark*. Hold on, poor mother. Christ has given us His word of honour. That is enough for you and me."[51]

---

[47]Butler, *Personal Reminiscences of a Great Crusade*, 229.
[48]Butler, *Portrait of Josephine Butler*, 213.
[49]Butler, *Portrait of Josephine Butler*, 214.
[50]Johnson and Johnson, eds., *Autobiographical Memoir*, 88-89.
[51]Johnson and Johnson, eds., *Autobiographical Memoir*, 249, 1898.

PROPHECY[52]

*"But when God has Himself led us into some of His secrets, and
the inner meaning of His providential guidings, we no longer
despond; for we come to know that it is a law in the Kingdom
of Grace that death must precede resurrection."*[53]

*"Woe unto you, scribes and Pharisees, hypocrites! for ye pay
tithe of mint and anise and cummin, and have omitted the
weightier matters of the law, judgment, mercy, and faith."*[54]

MATTHEW 23:23

In 1894 the eighty-year-old G. W. Watts painted Josephine Butler's portrait. Initially taken aback by the image, she wrote to her son, Stanley: "It is rather terrible. It bears the marks of storms and conflicts and sorrow so strongly. The eyes are certainly wonderfully done. You know I have no brightness in my eyes now. He said he wanted to make me looking into Eternity, looking at something no one else sees, because—he says—I look like that."[55] Watts saw her gazing at something—or someone—outside of time.

Josephine described prophecy as "showing forth the mind of God on any matter"[56]—not just knowing the mind of God but showing it to others. Referring to Hebrews 12:1, she described the medieval mystics (such as Catherine of Siena) as "an unbroken chain of witnesses to Divine truth all through the Dark Ages."[57] She knew that women had work to do, and called to them, from Isaiah 52:1-2: "Awake, awake, thou that sittest in the dust, put on thy beautiful garments."[58] In fact, Josephine was convinced that God had a far larger work in view than opposing the Act of Parliament, and he used the situation to deepen faith, to educate, to mature judgement, and perfect

---

[52]For a study of Josephine Butler's calling as prophet (an outcast herself) and her understanding of God's love for the outcast, see Barbara Russell-Jones, "The Voice of the Outcast: Josephine Butler's Biblical Interpretation and Public Theology," PhD diss., University of Birmingham, 2015.

[53]From *Wings* (1895), in Johnson and Johnson, eds., *Autobiographical Memoir*, 215-16.

[54]Josephine Butler, introduction to *Rebecca Jarrett* (London: Morgan and Scott, 1886).

[55]Butler, *Portrait of Josephine Butler*, 187.

[56]Letter to her son Stanley in Butler, *Portrait of Josephine Butler*, 197.

[57]Butler, *Portrait of Josephine Butler*, 171.

[58]Isaiah 52:1 (1900), Johnson and Johnson, eds., *Autobiographical Memoir*, 281.

patience.[59] Toward the end of her life, she focused increasingly on the activity of the Holy Spirit, was convinced that a significant spiritual revival was at hand, and was especially interested in the 1904 Welsh Revival. She always felt that the work to which she had been called was part of a larger plan.

In the early years of her travels within England, to educate people about the unjust and cruel laws concerning prostitutes, she was in some danger from those who opposed her message. Her husband stated that "God will keep you alive and strengthen you, until you have finished the work to which He has called you."[60] When Josephine was speaking in Geneva in 1876, her sister Harriet, who, outside of her husband, was the closest person to her, told her that, from Acts 2:4, "they spake with other tongues, as the Spirit gave them utterance."[61] Dr. Kate Bushnell and Mrs. Elizabeth Anderson in America had dreams about Josephine's work. Before she met or corresponded with Josephine Butler, while praying to God for guidance and searching the Scriptures, Dr. Bushnell came upon the stories of dreams given by the Lord and interpretations. She hoped that she too might receive guidance from the Lord in a dream. She "dreamed that I felt myself tossed on the billows of the Atlantic on my way to England to see Josephine Butler." She wrote to Josephine, who told her of the situation of women in India that desperately needed attention. Dr. Bushnell showed the letter to Mrs. Anderson, who said that when she read W. T. Stead's *Life of Josephine Butler* "the Spirit's voice whispered to me, 'You have not worked, you have not loved, as she has worked and loved.'"[62] Writing to her sister, Josephine recalled that every New Year's she cried out to God, and then later saw God's faithfulness.[63] She was convinced she had a message from God about a specific injustice, and that he had prepared her from childhood to recognize it for what it was.

In 1864 Josephine's daughter, Evangeline (Eva), died at the age of four when she fell over a banister at their home in Cheltenham. As she grieved, Josephine felt that she wanted to be with others who were suffering, to say, "I understand: I too have suffered."[64] This led her in 1866 to visit the Bridewell

---

[59]Butler, *Personal Reminiscences of a Great Crusade*, 209; Johnson and Johnson, eds., *Autobiographical Memoir* 125, 145, 209; Butler, *Catherine of Siena*, 237.

[60]Butler, *Personal Reminiscences of a Great Crusade*, 32-33.

[61]Butler, *Personal Reminiscences of a Great Crusade*, 134.

[62]Johnson and Johnson, eds., *Autobiographical Memoir*, 209-10.

[63]Butler, *Personal Reminiscences of a Great Crusade*, 231.

[64]Johnson and Johnson, eds., *Autobiographical Memoir*, 59.

in Liverpool (her husband had become headmaster of Liverpool College), the women's prison and workhouse; her work on behalf of women began there. The day she entered, she heard a young woman reading from John 14 ("My peace I give unto you").[65] Josephine, as always turning to the face of Jesus, went on: "The tall, dark-haired girl had prepared the way for me, and I said, 'Now let us all kneel, and cry to that same Jesus who spoke those words,' and down on their knees they fell, every one of them."[66] The roots of her prophetic voice were in the words of Jesus, his message of salvation and compassion and his exposure of sin and condemnation of evil. Josephine wrote about the plight of many of the women she encountered, including the account of Rebecca Jarrett, who at the age of sixteen was sold into prostitution by her mother, which opens with these words:

> "Woe unto you, scribes and Pharisees, hypocrites! for ye pay tithe of mint and anise and cummin, and have omitted the weightier matters of the law, judgment, mercy, and faith."—Matthew xxiii. 23.

> "And the Pharisees and scribes murmured, saying, This Man receiveth sinners, and eateth with them."—Luke xv. 2.[67]

Josephine's calling concerned this combination of the justice and love of God. She made it very clear to the women she met that they were loved by Jesus, and she was delighted when women wanted to know more about him. In 1889, when her husband was near death, Josephine wrote to her sister that they considered the early sermons of Jesus in the Gospels, and, "If we could keep our eyes always fastened on that face no anxieties would visit us."[68] Josephine modeled her own view of the "lost" women on that of Jesus. In her message to the Conference of the Federation, held in Paris in 1900, she makes some of her many references to "the Saviour."[69] Jesus is "the Lover of the lost, the Friend of sinners," who in Luke 19:10 "came to seek and to save that which is lost," and "the shepherd who goeth after the sheep that was lost until He finds it" (Luke 15:4).[70] Josephine concentrated on the compassion and power of the savior for all victims of injustice and oppression,

---

[65]Johnson and Johnson, eds., *Autobiographical Memoir*, 220.
[66]Johnson and Johnson, eds., *Autobiographical Memoir*, 60.
[67]Butler, introduction to *Rebecca Jarrett*.
[68]Butler, *Recollections of George Butler*, 457-58.
[69]Johnson and Johnson, eds., *Autobiographical Memoir*, 281-82.
[70]Johnson and Johnson, eds., *Autobiographical Memoir*, 281-82.

not only women.[71] She named the sin of the oppressors and brought them to the good shepherd.

In a pamphlet called "The Hour Before Dawn: An Appeal to Men," Josephine looked back on her anguish over the suffering and injustice in the world—and God's response. She describes her third spiritual crisis in 1869. She received her call. "I staggered on the verge of madness and blasphemy. I asked, 'Does not God care?'" In summary, she cried out to God concerning the injustices, miseries, and sufferings of the world. "I asked of the Lord one thing, that He would take of His heart and show it to me . . . so much of it as a worm of the earth can comprehend and endure." The answer she received was that God had made her "a *partaker* of His own heart's love for the world. . . . Sorrow is with me still, the enduring companion of my life. I do not pretend to be able to explain the secrets of God and the great problems of life with any clearness of speech to satisfy another. But I have found the door of hope."[72] When Josephine first realized that the Contagious Diseases Acts had a foothold in England, she wrote "a brief prayer, beseeching that if I *must* descend into darkness, that divine hand, whose touch is health and strength, would hold mine fast in the darkness."[73] He gave her something to say, just as he had done with Catherine of Siena: "I have a mission for thee to fulfill, and it is my will that thou appear before the public."[74] Both Josephine and Catherine were called to a public ministry, which they reluctantly accepted.

"I would have it clearly understood that concerning the wickedness of the unjust and unequal laws against which we contended, I never had the shadow of a doubt."[75] Thus, the central themes of Josephine's prophetic voice are the naming of sin and the coming of God's justice, and God's love and compassion for all, especially the weak and victims of oppression. Supporting these themes is Josephine's conviction about the impossibility of separating the soul and the body. In considering the Contagious Diseases Act, and the behavior of men who were protected by these laws in the same measure as women were

---

[71]Butler, ed., *Women's Work and Women's Culture*, xi. Josephine Butler made it clear that her anger about injustice was not limited to the plight of women, but to anyone who was the subject of disobedience to God's commands as explained in the Gospels.

[72]Johnson and Johnson, eds., *Autobiographical Memoir*, 153-55.

[73]Johnson and Johnson, eds., *Autobiographical Memoir*, 88.

[74]Butler, *Catherine of Siena*, 68

[75]Butler, *Recollections of George Butler*, 341.

damaged by them, she said, "The end, however, will be the failure of their every effort to separate the moral and the physical laws of the universe, and the confirmation of this truth—that the only cure for the evils which they so much dread is purity of life."[76] Committing a sin of the body has an effect on all of life. Thus, God's laws concerning creation must all be obeyed, or evil will result. Josephine's perspective on life as fully integrated appears in her work with some frequency. In her *Personal Reminiscences of a Great Crusade*, she connects principles with immortality: "We are of those who represent the imperishableness of principles, one of the many assurances of immortality."[77] In a letter that Josephine included in her biography of her husband, a friend describes George thus: he was "an easy combination of the natural man—(in its best sense)—of his old pursuits, literary, artistic, athletic, even sporting,—with the new spiritual life."[78] Josephine never understood those who would separate the soul and body, particularly concerning salvation as in the "saving of souls."[79] Sin was a central part of her theology, but it was not separated from God's corresponding love: the love was deeper than the sin. Another thing that becomes clear in analyzing this passage is that justice and love were inseparable for Josephine. This was a hallmark of her life and work. One could not proclaim justice without that tender care of Jesus for the lost and suffering. The ability to integrate her inner life with her activities made Josephine's work exceptionally powerful.

Josephine returned continually to the centrality of prayer in her calling. She believed that she was in communion with God. In an address to the Ladies National Association giving a survey of the work between 1870 and 1880, Josephine considered the relationship between intimate communion with God and prophecy: "Being in the line of Duty, and realizing my oneness with Omnipotence, I cannot possibly fail of success; for Omnipotent Love is pledged for the accomplishment of that for which I trust."[80]

Josephine's statements concerning her relationship with God mirror Catherine of Siena's. Josephine admired Catherine, seeing in her life the way to draw close to God. Like Josephine, Catherine said that "nothing I have learned

---

[76]Butler, *Personal Reminiscences of a Great Crusade*, 245.
[77]Butler, *Personal Reminiscences of a Great Crusade*, 243.
[78]Butler, *Recollections of George Butler*, 138.
[79]Butler, *Portrait of Josephine Butler*, 58.
[80]Butler, *Personal Reminiscences of a Great Crusade*, 237.

concerning God and our salvation was taught me by man,"[81] and "I have seen the secrets of God."[82] Josephine described Catherine's message as "her writings and discourses are permeated from first to last, with the simple evangelic truth, that Jesus Christ, the Son of God, took upon Himself our nature, and died and rose again for our redemption; that by apprehending this truth, by believing in and loving Him who thus loved us, we are saved, and by love are made conformable to Him."[83]

Josephine always turned to Jesus for the word she received. While sitting with her sister on the border of Lake Geneva 1878, considering how many women were needed for the work to come, and where they would be found, she quotes from Luke 24:15: "And it came to pass, that, while they communed together and reasoned, Jesus himself drew near, and went with them." Then, she writes: "I somewhat dimly recall now that there came before my mind's eye a host of women presenting themselves from different quarters of the globe . . . I recollect there came to me one of those moments of re-assurance and hope, which are sometimes granted during such silence of the soul."[84] She relates this vision to receiving guidance directly from Jesus, just as the disciples did on the road to Emmaus. This is how she came to know the mind of God.

INDIVIDUALITY

"Uniformity is not a beautiful thing."[85]

"Peace I leave with you, my peace I give unto you: not as the world giveth, give I unto you."[86]

JOHN 14:27

---

[81]Butler, *Catherine of Siena*, 47.
[82]Butler, *Catherine of Siena*, 71.
[83]Butler, *Catherine of Siena*, 241.
[84]Johnson and Johnson, *Autobiographical Memoir*, 207.
[85]From an article in *The Storm Bell* (1899), in Johnson and Johnson, *Autobiographical Memoir*, 271.
[86]Josephine refers to this verse several times. In 1866, when JB first visited the Liverpool Bridewell, the verse was spoken by one of the girls there. The verse was "issuing from the heart of despair . . . and reaching to the heart of God." Butler, *Recollections of George Butler*, 184. Then again, in 1896 concerning the spiritual battle in Geneva—"The spirit of war however was there, as well as the Master's benediction: 'My peace I give unto you.'" Johnson and Johnson, *Autobiographical Memoir*, 220.

The final central feature of Josephine's inner life is individuality, which is defined as "the particular character, or aggregate of qualities, that distinguishes one person or thing from others; sole and personal nature." Josephine Butler believed strongly that people should value and strive for individuality, and that anything that hindered it also hindered the closest possible relationship with God. Thus, she found institutions (including the church) and organizations to be potentially dangerous to personal spiritual growth—if they became the focus of one's interest and time, and if one believed they could provide answers to life's questions, consolation, or fulfillment. Only the "unseen God," and Jesus, the "image of the invisible God," could provide what the world could never give. She knew that she was rebelling against the laws of the land, but, as she stated early in 1870, at the beginning of her crusade, "We are rebels for God's holy laws. What have I to do with peace anymore?"[87] Josephine referred to Jesus as her example. To be an individual was to never be subject to an institution, a human being, a cause, or an organization. She said, "The insistence on uniformity crushes out individuality and hinders initiative."[88] Individuality meant having a unique relationship with the creator, and having the courage and initiative to live the life one was called to live as a result of that relationship—giving primacy to a relationship that could not be seen, heard, or felt. Each individual soul was unique; this conviction contributed to the respect and sympathy that Josephine had for each girl and young woman she met.

In an article in *The Storm Bell*, Josephine considered the dangers of organizations and institutions, including her own Federation. "God does not need our poor machinery. He can create other methods of spreading a truth." Referring to the intricate mechanism in the first chapter of Ezekiel (wheels within wheels), she felt that such a machine could only soar like an eagle because of the Spirit within it. If the Spirit left it would have come crashing down. "Wherever the spirit would go, they would go, and the wheels would rise along with them, because the spirit of the living creatures was in the wheels."[89]

Individuality in the context of Josephine's spiritual life was not limited to having a distinctive character; it meant that she was willing to live out God's

---

[87]Johnson and Johnson, eds., *Autobiographical Memoir*, 99.

[88]From *The Storm Bell* (1899), in Johnson and Johnson, eds., *Autobiographical Memoir*, 271.

[89]From *The Storm Bell* (1899), in Johnson and Johnson, eds., *Autobiographical Memoir*, 270-73.

call despite danger, misunderstanding, hatred, or the physical and mental toll that it took. Although he was not familiar with her specific work, the artist G. W. Watts exclaimed upon meeting her: "'What would I not give to be able to look back upon such a life as yours!' He does not flatter in the least, but he seemed troubled. I said I did not take it up willingly, I was *driven* to it by anger against injustice. He replied, 'O yes, I know you were driven into it. You were destined for it. But some people refuse to be driven; and you did not refuse.'"[90] In the decisions that Josephine made, and in her sense of calling, she did not seek the permission of other people. She sought God alone. The one time, before their marriage, she did seek her husband's "advice as to certain lines of conduct or action," George's reply was, "He who has hitherto guided your steps will continue to do so."[91] She received encouragement, help, and prayer from her family, friends, coworkers, and others sympathetic to the cause, but she does not seem to have been in doubt concerning her primary calling. She received that through dialogue with Jesus.

Considering that her husband was an ordained Anglican minister, Josephine appears to have been ambivalent about the church and even at times about any organized religion. However, although she rarely referred in her vast amount of written material to churches, to groups, or to movements in terms of personal connection (except for her own movement, and even that she felt was secondary to one's personal journey with God), her evangelical convictions are evident primarily through actions rather than words (although she does say that her husband was a Christian "in the vital sense").[92] During her 1845 spiritual crisis, she stated, "Two miles from our home was the parish church, to which we trudged dutifully every Sunday, and where an honest man in the pulpit taught us loyally that he probably himself knew about God, but whose words did not even touch the fringe of my soul's deep discontent."[93] Thirty-five years later, in a 1880 letter to her sister, she states, "I do not find in ordinary evangelic teaching anything which meets this mystery of wrong and pain."[94] She rarely mentioned denominations at all (except for the Roman Catholic Church regarding medieval mystics and the good work of the church

---

[90]Letter from JB to her son Stanley (1894) in Butler, *Portrait of Josephine Butler*, 186-87.

[91]Butler, *Recollections of George Butler*, 57.

[92]Butler, *Recollections of George Butler*, 111.

[93]Johnson and Johnson, eds., *Autobiographical Memoir*, 15.

[94]Butler, *Personal Reminiscences of a Great Crusade*, 211.

against injustice and suffering). In her biography of her husband, she recalled that in Dilston, "Dissent prevailed largely in the neighbourhood. But during the time that he acted as the clergyman of the parish the church was well filled. Many Wesleyans came, who had not yet entered its doors, as well as several families of well-to-do and well-instructed Presbyterian farmers—shrewd people, well able to maintain their ground in a theological controversy."[95] A rare reference to "correct Evangelical Protestants" occurs in a letter to Miss Forsaith, where she sighs over "Conferences for the Deepening of Spiritual Life" from which they come away gorged with spiritual "sweetstuff . . . O! the Churches! They are a nightmare to me."[96]

Despite being drawn toward medieval mysticism and regard for the Catholic Church, it is interesting to learn that she found both the atmosphere and the lifestyle of monasteries unappealing in the extreme. What troubled her was not the single-minded devotion to God, the solitude, the silence, or the radical life chosen. Rather it was "the uniformity, the rules, the isolation (as distinct from solitude), and, sometimes, the starkness of the environment and of a theology that she felt focused on sin rather than liberty."[97] Her high regard for Catherine of Siena was not the result of a longing for a monastic life; rather it is outlined in her biography's conclusion, where she emphasizes Catherine's love of gospel truth and Jesus and her desire to bring the love of God to others. Surely her life was a role model for Josephine, and listening prayer and social action characterized both their lives.

Josephine had certain views that were hers alone, and others that were her message for the world. However, she did believe that it is important for "men and women to say with courage and humility what they believe, and to witness with fidelity to what God and life has taught them. There is too much of an unconfessed timidity among the boldest of us."[98]

While her proclamation that women and girls were treated unjustly and cruelly was not a matter of opinion, her beliefs about certain things concerning the Bible were. As has been noted, one of the convictions that she had was that the words of Jesus took precedence over other words of the Bible. The precedence given to Jesus over other biblical writers is, she says, her own

---

[95]Butler, *Recollections of George Butler*, 40.
[96]Letter from JB to Miss Forsaith in Butler, *Portrait of Josephine Butler*, 210.
[97]Johnson and Johnson, eds., *Autobiographical Memoir*, 270-73.
[98]Butler, ed., *Women's Work and Women's Culture*, lii.

opinion. However, she also stated that we must not be timid in stating our personal discernment, which she believed to be God-given. This suggests that Josephine considered certain portions of Scripture to be limited by cultural context. However, as mentioned in the opening pages of this chapter, her overall use of Scripture is not consistent with diminishing any portion of the Bible. Rather, her use of the Bible suggests that she had an exceptional love for and intimacy with Jesus. Josephine knew the Bible extremely well; it was read in her home from childhood, and she and her husband and growing family read it together daily. The Bible was George's "constant companion."[99] Josephine loved the sound of her husband's voice reading Scripture, and she recalled in a letter to her sister that in his last illness, when he could not sleep, they would read the Bible together and pray. "What a precious memory for me will be these 'after-midnight teas' and these wonderful moments of communion—heaven's gate being opened when the world's is shut."[100] However, the Bible was not placed before God himself. In a letter to her friend, Miss Forsaith, Josephine made an interesting statement: "He has been showing me that beyond His promises, and beyond Scripture itself, He is God, and that in His Character is our great eternal hope and confidence."[101] This points to God as the author of the Bible, wholly "Other," and that even beyond his Word it is he in whom she placed her hope.

Josephine was convinced that praying for the dead was entirely consistent with God's revelation: "I see nothing in the Bible against our praying for the dead—or rather for the living. They are in a fuller life than we are; so I ask God to give him more joy [her husband], and to restore us to each other."[102] In 1903 she wrote to her son concerning science as an aid to faith: "The Bible is dearer to me than ever; but its value has been enhanced by the great light that is advancing . . . discoveries in the spiritual world are keeping pace with those in the natural world. . . . God is equally the creator of Nature and of all that is spiritual. . . . All your discoveries in so-called inanimate nature point to ME. I am in all things."[103] One of her conclusions is potentially problematic from a traditional, evangelical point of view. Towards the end of her life, as

---

[99]Butler, *Recollections of George Butler*, 356.
[100]Butler, *Recollections of George Butler*, 433.
[101]Butler, *Portrait of Josephine Butler*, 179.
[102]Butler, *Portrait of Josephine Butler*, 215.
[103]Butler, *Portrait of Josephine Butler*, 208-9.

part of her message for the thirtieth anniversary of the Federation, Josephine stated that Christianity was "inclusive and not exclusive," and

> many have given life-long labour to casting out the evil of tyranny, oppression, and injustice; and of these, whatever their formula of belief may be, the Judge of all will say Well done. There are many outside the Christian pale in whom the Spirit of Christ is working came to believe that the God of love . . . none of the great human family are forgotten by Him who redeemed them, by the eternal Father whose name is LOVE . . . the eternal Father will bless the apparently rejected son . . . many have been turned into rebels whose hearts are not really estranged form the true God.[104]

The Bible passages that she used as references are Luke 9:50, "Forbid him not"; John 10:16, "I have other sheep who are not of this fold"; and Genesis 27:38, "Hast thou but one blessing, O my father?" It was her anguish over the suffering of others and her conviction about the love of God that caused her to consider a belief in universal salvation toward the end of her life. This was in keeping with her theology of suffering, which assumed a shared experience with those whom one loved and for whom one had sacrificed. It was also this conviction about "shared suffering" that drew her closer to Christ of the cross, and that led her initially to seek out others who suffered after the death of her daughter.

The four central features of Josephine Butler's inner life (prayer, suffering, prophecy, individuality) are beautifully summarized one to two years before her death, in several letters written to her friend, Miss Forsaith:

> For me, all my life—and more lately—I have found the only teaching to be that of the Spirit of God . . . as we get nearer to God, all prayer resolves itself into *communion*. By union with the Divine, and concentration on something that you will, you create an atmosphere, a circle, round you, unseen but real. . . . I don't know that I have ever recorded what I have recorded in that—to show how a long *incubation* and a painful one is often required for a person whom God appoints to sow a little mustard seed of truth, which is to grow to a large tree. . . . One day he brought to my heart and to my soul's listening ear (after much sorrowful repenting and confessing) these words, "I will betroth thee to Me for ever, in judgement and in righteousness, in loving tenderness and mercies. I will betroth thee to Me in faithfulness."[105]

---

[104]Johnson and Johnson, eds., *Autobiographical Memoir*, 307-308.
[105]Letters from JB to Miss Forsaith (1904–1905) in Butler, *Portrait of Josephine Butler*, 175-80.

Josephine expressed her individuality most strongly through her unwavering conviction that Jesus is real and accessible; that an intimate relationship is possible; and that fruitful conversation with God and outward action result from an intimate knowledge of the Scriptures, and from listening to God in solitude and silence. Josephine did not believe that this special relationship was reserved for her alone. She believed that anyone could enter into God's presence and hear from him. She believed that all human beings could be in union with the divine. She encouraged everyone to go directly to Jesus of the Gospels with every need. Toward the end of her life, Josephine Butler wrote and spoke increasingly of the importance of a unique, individual journey with Jesus Christ as central to doing God's will in this world. She wrote about God's justice and love, as revealed consistently in the Scriptures, and about individual calling to be part of his plan.

BIBLIOGRAPHY

Primary Sources

Butler, A. S. G. *Portrait of Josephine Butler*. London: Faber & Faber, 1954.

Butler, Josephine. *Catherine of Siena: A Biography*. London: Dyer, 1878.

———. *The Constitution Violated: An Essay by the Author of the Memoir of John Grey of Dilston*. Edinburgh: Edmonston and Douglas, 1871.

———. *The Hour Before Dawn: An Appeal to Men*. London: Trübner, 1876.

———. *The Lady of Shunem*. London: Horace Marshall & Son, 1894.

———. *The Life of Jean Frederic Oberlin: Pastor of la Ban de la Roche*. London: The Religious Tract Society, 1886.

———. *Memoir of John Grey of Dilston*. Edinburgh: Edmonston and Douglas, 1869.

———. *Personal Reminiscences of a Great Crusade*. London: H. Marshall, 1896.

———. *Rebecca Jarrett*. London: Morgan and Scott, 1886.

———. *Recollections of George Butler*. Bristol: J. W. Arrowsmith, 1896.

———, ed. *Women's Work and Women's Culture: A Series of Essays*. London: MacMillan, 1869.

Catherine of Siena. *The Dialogue of Saint Catherine of Siena*. Translated by Algar Thorold. London: Kegan Paul, Trench, Trubner, 1907.

Holland, Henry Scott. *A Bundle of Memories*. London: Wells Gardner, Darton, 1915.

Johnson, George W., and Lucy A. Johnson, eds. *Josephine E. Butler: An Autobiographical Memoir*. Bristol: J. W. Arrowsmith, 1909.

Jordan, Jane, and Ingrid Sharp, eds. *Josephine Butler and the Prostitution Campaigns: Diseases of the Body Politic*. Vol. 1. London: Routledge, 2003.

Secondary Sources

Bebbington, David. *Evangelicalism in Modern Britain: A History from the 1730s to the 1980s*. London: Unwin Hyman, 1989.

Bebbington, David W. "The Gospel in the Nineteenth Century." *Vox Evangelica* 13 (1983): 19-28.

Boyd, Nancy. *Three Victorian Women Who Changed Their World*. Oxford: Oxford University Press, 1982.

de Groot, Christiana, and Marion Ann Taylor, eds. *Recovering Nineteenth Century Women Interpreters of the Bible*. Atlanta: Society of Biblical Literature, 2007.

Jordan, Jane. *Josephine Butler*. London: John Murray, 2001.

Larsen, Timothy. *A People of One Book: The Bible and the* Victorians. Oxford: Oxford University Press, 2011.

Neal, Diana. *Sex, Gender, and Religion: Josephine Butler Revisited*. New York: Peter Lang, 2006.

Nolland, Lisa Severine. "Josephine Butler and the Repeal of the Contagious Diseases Acts (1883/1886): Motivations and Larger Vision of a Victorian Feminist Christian." PhD diss., Trinity College, Bristol, 2001.

Russell-Jones, Amanda Barbara. "The Voice of the Outcast: Josephine Butler's Biblical Interpretation and Public Theology." PhD diss., University of Birmingham, 2015.

Villegas, Diana L. "Catherine of Siena's Wisdom on Discernment and Her Reception of Scripture." *Acta Theologica* 33, suppl. 17 (2013). www.scielo.org.za/scielo.php?script=sci_arttext&pid=S1015-87582013000300012.

Wilson, A. N. *Eminent Victorians*. New York: W. W. Norton, 1989.

Part Three

The Twentieth Century

7

The Bible Crisis of British Evangelicalism in the 1920s

David Bebbington

IN THE WAKE OF THE FIRST WAR, the evangelicals of the United States suffered a fundamentalist crisis. Voices had long been heard contending that the landmarks of the faith were being abandoned by more progressive thinkers. From 1910 to 1915 booklets called *The Fundamentals* had been delivered to Protestant ministers throughout the land identifying basics that must be preserved and heresies that must be avoided. The war itself deepened anxieties, induced theological conservatives to identify errors as made in Germany and provoked militancy. There was sense among many premillennialists, holiness teachers, revivalists and upholders of orthodoxy that the culture was slipping from its evangelical moorings. At the root of the catastrophe, they believed, was disrespect for the Bible. The teaching of Scripture, the true foundation of American civilization, was being flouted. The outcome was a series of controversies, especially among Baptists and Presbyterians, that rocked the evangelical world during the 1920s, leading to virtual schism between conservatives and liberals.[1] It has been noticed less often that there was a similar Bible crisis among British evangelicals. *The Fundamentals* were

---

[1]George M. Marsden, *Fundamentalism and American Culture: The Shaping of Twentieth-Century Evangelicalism: 1870-1925* (New York: Oxford University Press, 1980). Marsden's classic case has been modified, but not overturned, by Michael S. Hamilton, "The Interdenominational Evangelicalism of D. L. Moody and the Problem of Fundamentalism," in *American Evangelicalism: George Marsden and the State of American Religious History*, ed. Darren Dochuk, Thomas S. Kidd, and Kurt W. Peterson (Notre Dame, IN: University of Notre Dame Press, 2014), 230-80.

circulated to British as well as to American ministers and after the war there was deep-seated suspicion of widespread disloyalty to Scripture. In 1923 an organization called the Bible League summoned leaders of Protestant evangelical societies supported by the Christian public "to publicly identify themselves with those who stand for the Divine authority, truth, and integrity of the whole Bible." The League wanted its appeal to divide professing Christian bodies into two categories, what it called "*Modernist Societies and the Societies based on the Old Faith*."[2] Modernists were those who had given up belief in the Bible; those adhering to the Old Faith were, like the League itself, steadfast fundamentalists. This article is designed to illuminate which sections of the evangelical world in Britain endorsed the Bible League's analysis. Who believed that the Bible was so much under threat as to demand polarization over the issue?

The Bible League had been formed in 1892, according to its object, "to promote the reverent study of the Holy Scriptures, and to resist the varied attacks made upon their inspiration, infallibility and sole sufficiency as the Word of God."[3] It arose in a decade when the scholars of the various Nonconformist denominations generally accepted that the higher criticism sweeping in from German sources had to be received respectfully rather than dismissed perfunctorily, as it had been in the past.[4] The publication in 1892 by John Clifford, one of the most progressive leaders among the Baptists, of a book on *The Inspiration and Authority of the Bible* showing sympathy for critical views spurred a group of traditionalists to form the Bible League.[5] They believed that the newer understanding of the Scriptures, allowing human speculation about the date and validity of the biblical text, undermined the evangelical faith. Although initially the League was few in numbers, its leaders gradually recruited new adherents and in the aftermath of the First World War they decided to make a stand. On June 11, 1920, a meeting in the Cannon Street Hotel in London passed a resolution urging missionary societies to ensure that their agents were loyal to the Bible. Declaring its

---

[2]*Life of Faith* (hereafter LF), April 18, 1923, 449-50.

[3]Letterhead, R. Wright Hay to Rev. C. E. Wilson and Rev. W. Y. Fullerton, July 21, 1920, Rev. R. Wright Hay File, Box H62, Baptist Missionary Society Archives, Angus Library, Regent's Park College, Oxford (hereafter BMSA).

[4]Willis B. Glover, *Evangelical Nonconformists and Higher Criticism in the Nineteenth Century* (London: Independent Press, 1954).

[5]*Christian* (hereafter C), May 12, 1892, 7; July 14, 1892, 8.

"deep concern as to the bearing of Destructive Criticism of the Bible on Missionary Work," the meeting condemned any missionaries who "deny or doubt that every writing of the Old and New Testaments is God-breathed."[6] A number of missionary societies responded by affirming that their candidates' committees refused to approve any who expressed doubts about the full inspiration of the Scriptures. Over the next three years the Bible League pressed other missionary organizations to do the same and extended its campaign to non-missionary agencies, whether societies or churches. By April 1923 it could list 162 bodies as supporting its appeal to endorse the divine authority of the Bible.

The two dynamic figures in the Bible League who launched this campaign were Robert Wright Hay, the secretary, and Prebendary H. E. Fox, the president. Wright Hay, who had served with the Baptist Missionary Society in India from 1884 to 1901 and so took a particular interest in missionary affairs, had then been assistant minister of Talbot Tabernacle, Notting Hill, one of the churches that associated itself with the appeal, before becoming secretary of the League in 1912.[7] He had been a close friend of R. C. Morgan, the editor of the *Christian*, an evangelical weekly devoted to revivalism, and so was near the centre of the circle of keen evangelicals who leaned to undenominationalism.[8] Crucially, Wright Hay was also a premillennialist in his belief about the future, which, as we shall see, was an important characteristic of many supporters of the Bible League appeal.[9] Prebendary Fox had been born in south India in 1848, the son of Church Missionary Society [CMS] parents, and in turn gave two sons and three daughters to the service of the Society. He was president of the Prophecy Investigation Society, the chief institutional vehicle for premillennialism up to the First World War, and, with private means and the training of a lawyer at Lincoln's Inn, he was a man of outspoken opinions.[10] His "singularly incisive Protestant pen" had caused reservations about his suitability when, in 1895, he had been appointed Clerical Secretary

---

[6]*Bible League Quarterly* (hereafter *BLQ*), April–June 1922, 70.

[7]*Baptist Handbook*, 1920, 178.

[8]George E. Morgan, *A Veteran in Revival: R. C. Morgan: His Life and Times* (London: Pickering & Inglis, 1909), 157-58.

[9]*Advent Witness*, December 1921, 282.

[10]Eugene Stock, *History of the Church Missionary Society*, 4 vols. (London: Church Missionary Society, 1899–1916), 4:442. *Who's Who 1921*, 946. *Record*, May 20, 1926, 321-22. *C*, May 20, 1926, 5.

of the CMS.[11] Although he proved an effective public advocate of the Society until his retirement in 1910, while still in office he made no bones about his stance on Scripture. In 1905 he published *Our Lord and his Bible* contending, like other conservative Evangelical Anglicans of his day, that Jesus' citations of the Old Testament as authoritative overthrew the legitimacy of higher criticism.[12] In retirement Fox followed up this volume with another, *Rationalism or the Gospel?* (1912), which suggested that missions would be hamstrung by the adoption of critical opinion.[13] It was no doubt this case which led to his taking up the presidency of the Bible League around the start of the First World War. The polemical temperament of Prebendary Fox, with its desire to separate sheep from goats, lay behind the Bible League's campaign of the early 1920s.

During the immediately preceding years a number of episodes had warned of stormy days to come. In 1912–1913 Wesleyan Methodism suffered an early fundamentalist dispute. George Jackson, nominated in 1912 for a chair at Didsbury College, Manchester, delivered a lecture in the same year vindicating respect for biblical criticism so that young people would not be alienated from the faith. Published in expanded form as *The Preacher and the Modern Mind* (1912), the lecture caused an attempt by traditionalists to exclude Jackson from his appointment. His judicious self-defence, however, led to the overwhelming rejection of a charge of doctrinal unsoundness and Jackson was confirmed in office. Higher criticism seemed to have made headway in Methodism.[14] In 1917 a group of liberal evangelicals around Guy Rogers, Vicar of West Ham, urged (alongside other recommendations) that the CMS should no longer require its candidates to avow anything further than the formularies of the Church of England on the subject of biblical inspiration. Controversy broke out, resolved by a subcommittee's concordat, which declared in 1918 that doctrinal definitions more suited to those of mature years should not be required, but that a candidate's treatment of Scripture should be in harmony with that of Christ. For the time being the

---

[11]Eugene Stock, *My Recollections* (London: James Nisbet, 1909), 367.

[12]*BLQ* (July–September 1926), 89.

[13]Martin Wellings, *Evangelicals Embattled: Responses of Evangelicals in the Church of England to Ritualism, Darwinism and Theological Liberalism, 1890–1930* (Carlisle: Paternoster, 2003), 283.

[14]D. W. Bebbington, "The Persecution of George Jackson: A British Fundamentalist Controversy," in *Persecution and Toleration*, ed. W. J. Sheils (Oxford: Basil Blackwell, 1984), 421-33.

formula allowed conservatives to continue working with liberals in the CMS, but the incident confirmed to stalwarts like Prebendary Fox that unacceptable views had crept into the Society, the bastion of Evangelical Anglicans.[15] Likewise a section of the Baptists became dismayed in the following year when a proposal to federate the Free Churches generated a doctrinal basis which stated that the Bible merely contained the word of God rather than being identical with it.[16] And the publication in 1919 of a collective commentary on the Bible edited by A. S. Peake, the outstanding scholar among the Primitive Methodists, caused further alarm by its avowal in the first sentence that it explained "the generally accepted results of Biblical Criticism."[17] Across a range of denominations the Bible seemed to conservatives to be under threat.

The range of groups mobilized against the challenges to biblical authority is evident from the organizations listed on the Bible League appeal of 1923. Although their membership commonly overlapped, they can usefully be investigated in turn. One prominent category was the military element. The Soldiers' Christian Association was listed with Colonel D. F. Douglas-Jones as its chairman. Douglas-Jones was himself on the executive of the Bible League, resigning with Fox and another military colleague from the World's Evangelical Alliance in 1917 because they considered it to be insufficiently evangelical.[18] He was a frequent correspondent of the evangelical press, in 1926 protesting in the *Life of Faith*, for example, against a liberal evangelical's claim to have seen new light, as had the Reformation. "What new light?," he burst out. "Our blessed Saviour is the 'light of the world.'"[19] Alongside his organization was the Army Scripture Readers' and Soldiers' Friend Society with Colonel S. D. Cleeve as secretary and the Aldershot Mission Hall and Soldiers' Home, catering for the largest of the army's bases in England, with

---

[15]Gordon Hewitt, *The Problems of Success: A History of the Church Missionary Society, 1910–1942* (London: SCM, 1971), 463-65.

[16]David Bebbington, "Baptists and Fundamentalism in Inter-War Britain," in *Evangelicalism and Fundamentalism in the United Kingdom during the Twentieth Century*, ed. David Bebbington and David Ceri Jones (Oxford: Oxford University Press, 2013), 96.

[17]John T. Wilkinson, *Arthur Samuel Peake: A Biography* (London: Epworth, 1971), 128; Timothy Larsen, "A. S. Peake, the Free Churches, and Modern Biblical Criticism," *Bulletin of the John Rylands University Library of Manchester* 86, no. 3 (2004): 23-53.

[18]Andrew Atherstone, "Evangelicalism and Fundamentalism in the Inter-War Church of England," in Bebbington and Jones, *Evangelicalism and Fundamentalism*, 72.

[19]*LF*, February 3, 1926, 126.

a lady superintendent but with six officers also supporting its listing among those calling for unreserved allegiance to the Bible. Several organizations that were not specifically military also had army officers as their named officials. There was the Open Air Mission with a captain as president and the Scripture Text Carriers with another captain as honorary president. In addition, the Manchester City Mission had a major as its secretary and the Central Asian Mission had a colonel as chairman of its committee. As a coda to this point, three police organizations were listed: the International Christian Police Association (perhaps surprisingly, with a female president at its head), the Christian Police Trust Corporation, and the Convalescent Police Seaside Home at Hove in Sussex. The evangelical ranks included a significant number of military officers and policemen, and it may well be that they were predisposed to do battle for the Bible.

Another section of opinion that strongly inclined to conservatism over Scripture consisted of the members of the many Protestant organizations that existed to resist Catholicism, whether the Church of Rome or the Anglo-Catholics within the Church of England. The Anglo-Catholics were becoming increasingly bold during the 1920s, holding ostentatious congresses where elaborate ritual was deliberately flaunted. In 1927 and 1928 a Revised Prayer Book was to be voted down in the House of Commons because it leant unduly towards accepting Anglo-Catholic demands.[20] Long-held fears of the ambitions of Rome flourished among Protestants. "We know," wrote a correspondent of the *Life of Faith* in 1924, "that the aim of the Vatican is world-power—to capture the Church of England means to capture the British empire."[21] A set of bodies was active in stoking the fires of anti-Catholicism. The National Church League, a moderate body which concentrated on educational work and formal protests against Catholic developments in the established church, was not among the institutions supporting the appeal, but a series of more militant organizations gave it their backing. The Church Association, the National Protestant League, the Protestant Alliance, the Protestant Reformation Society, and the Women's Protestant Union all endorsed the appeal. So did the Protestant Truth Society, whose Kensit Memorial College had Arthur Carter, a former secretary of the Bible League, as

---

[20]John Maiden, *National Religion and the Prayer Book Controversy, 1927–1928* (Woodbridge, Suffolk: Boydell, 2009).
[21]*LF*, January 16, 1924, 83.

its biblical lecturer.[22] Another group supporting the appeal was the Society for Irish Church Missions, whose evangelistic work in Ireland entailed constant confrontation with Roman Catholics. Much of the Protestant underworld, as the Catholic convert Ronald Knox called it, was roused in favor of Bible defense.

Close to the anti-Catholic groupings because of their joint loyalty to the Reformation were a number of Calvinist bodies. One, the Calvinistic Protestant Union, showed explicitly by its title its allegiance to both causes. In this category falls the only whole denomination to back the appeal, the Free Church of Scotland. Concentrated chiefly in the Highlands of Scotland, it was self-consciously conservative in its theological position, adhering closely to the foundation text of Calvinism, the Westminster Confession.[23] In England agencies of the Strict Baptists, who in the nineteenth century had separated from the mainstream Baptists because of a similar desire to retain a strongly confessional form of Calvinist belief, decided to support the Bible League's appeal. The Strict and Particular Baptist Society, the Strict Baptist Mission and the South Indian Strict Baptist Missionary Society were all named as well. So was the Aged Pilgrims' Friend Society, which existed to give charitable aid to elderly Strict Baptists. Sovereign Grace Advent Testimony, which combined expectation of an imminent second coming with traditional Strict Baptist doctrines, had explained when it was formed in 1920 the rationale for its stance. "We adhere," its first members wrote, "to the principle of receiving the Word of God in its *literal sense*, whereby we have been taught the *Doctrines of Grace*. Thus also we receive *Prophetic Truth*."[24] Its twin convictions were both based on a firm adherence to a high view of Scripture. Its chairman and secretary were therefore natural signatories of the appeal.

The devotion of this section of the Strict Baptists to Advent Testimony was a sign of the popularity during the 1920s of premillennial teaching. This belief that Christ would return very soon, and certainly before the period of a thousand years of peace and prosperity on earth that postmillennialists were expecting, had received a boost from the First World War. In the war's apocalyptic atmosphere, the sense that disasters could be rectified only by

---

[22]*LF*, July 2, 1924, 772.
[23]G. N. M. Collins, *The Heritage of Our Fathers: The Free Church of Scotland: Her Origins and Testimony* (Edinburgh: Knox, 1974).
[24]*LF*, April 22, 1920, 18.

the divine intervention of the second coming attracted fresh support. Many evangelicals, however, remained postmillennialists, hoping that post-war reconstruction would be a step towards the realization of the kingdom of God where Christ would reign on earth. G. E. Morgan, who served as consulting editor of the *Christian*, denounced the point of view of such "a rosy Christian idealist" in its pages in February 1919. "This," he contended, "is not what God reveals to us in His Word. He tells us plainly, not that the development of the Kingdom will bring the King, but that the King himself must come to establish the Kingdom; and that He, not man, is to make the Kingdom fit for men to live in."[25] Such premillennialism was rapidly spreading. Its chief vehicle was the Advent Testimony and Preparation Movement, founded in 1917 under F. B. Meyer, a Baptist minister who was one of the most popular Christian writers of the day. Meyer signed the Bible League appeal on behalf of Advent Testimony. Many of its adherents were dispensationalists, holding the elaborate scheme of biblical interpretation propagated by J. N. Darby in the nineteenth century. All of them, according to H. C. Tiarks, vicar of Holy Trinity, Kilburn, at one of its meetings in 1920, accepted the "Lord's actual personal return" and that "He would instantaneously and miraculously remove believers from their present sphere of waiting to His actual presence."[26] The doctrine of the rapture, that was to say, united them. Again such detailed beliefs could be generated only by close study of the text of Scripture. Students of prophecy were another recruiting ground for the Bible League.

The considerable number of evangelicals who made the evangelisation of the Jewish people a priority formed a further constituency. The expectation of the conversion of the Jews and their restoration to the land of Palestine was at this time usually associated with the broader premillennial hope. The signs of the return of the Jews to their own land, according to a correspondent of the *Christian* in 1920, were abounding in their day. That pointed to the fulfilment of the prophecies connected with the premillennial advent of the Messiah.[27] Evangelicals generally deplored another sign of the times, the rise of anti-Semitism, because of their attachment to mission to the Jews. Thus the *Christian* commented in 1926 that "the spirit of Jew-hate" was

---

[25]G. E. Morgan "The Call of the Time: 1: To the Nation," C, February 13, 1919, 22.
[26]C, August 5, 1920, 14.
[27]C, February 5, 1920, 14 (Alfred Porcelli).

contemptible because it was un-Christian.[28] The Bible taught that the Jews held a continuing honorable place in the divine counsels. Accordingly the British Society for the Propagation of the Gospel among the Jews endorsed the Bible League appeal. The Society's chairman, the clergyman J. B. Barraclough, was to succeed H. E. Fox as president of the Bible League.[29] Likewise the Hebrew Christian Testimony to Israel backed the appeal, and so did the Southern Morocco Mission. When the signatory of behalf of the latter mission, D. J. Findlay, the pastor of St George's Cross Tabernacle in Glasgow, visited its stations, he found a work that concentrated on the Jewish population of Tangier and Marrakesh.[30] So mission to the Jewish people, though a niche concern among evangelicals, was a further factor encouraging conservative attitudes to the Bible in the 1920s.

A cause that gathered far wider support in the evangelical world was the holiness movement. Its chief expression by the interwar period was the Keswick Convention together with its network of subordinate conventions. Keswick had sprung up in 1875 to promote the message that holiness was to be discovered not by earnest struggle, as received opinion held, but by personal trust. Seekers of a deeper spiritual experience spent a week in the summer at the Lake District inland resort listening to addresses that urged personal surrender as the path to sanctification. The movement had captured the allegiance of the bulk of Evangelical Anglicans by the opening of the twentieth century and drew in a number of Scottish Presbyterians and English Nonconformists too. The convention's teaching rested once more on close biblical exegesis, and so it was assumed until 1920 that it upheld the full authority of Scripture. Then, however, one eminent speaker gave an address that verged on pantheism, another seemed to toy with higher criticism, and John Battersby Harford, the son of the founder of Keswick, defended the principles of biblical criticism in print.[31] Wright Hay pointed out that Harford had described the book of Exodus as containing legend, questioned its accuracy, and minimized the miraculous.[32] During 1921 critics challenged the

---

[28] *C*, June 17, 1926, 3.

[29] *C*, October 27, 1926, 1218.

[30] Alexander Gammie, *Pastor D. J. Findlay: A Unique Personality* (London: Pickering & Inglis, 1949), 71-72.

[31] Charles Price and Ian Randall, *Transforming Keswick* (Carlisle: OM, 2000), 65-66.

[32] *C*, March 24, 1921, 27.

teaching of other Keswick speakers. But the convention managed to avoid losing the confidence of most of its supporters and eventually cleared itself of the taint of Modernism.[33] So its adherents provided more backers for the Bible League. Prebendary Hanmer Webb-Peploe, a veteran Keswicker, was on the list of supporters of the League's appeal, both as chairman of the Scripture Gift Mission and as president of the Society for the Visitation of the Sick. Charles Inwood, almost the only Keswick speaker from Methodism, was alongside him as Home Director of the Ceylon and India General Mission. The Japan Evangelistic Band, which itself held Keswick-style conventions, was also represented on the League appeal.[34] The holiness movement reinforced the campaign to defend the Bible.

A further organization on the Bible League list was the Pentecostal Missionary Union for Great Britain and Ireland. The inclusion of this body, the missionary arm of early British Pentecostalism, is remarkable. Pentecostals were a recent arrival on the evangelical scene and still highly suspect in most quarters. In response to a number of queries about missions conducted in 1922 by the evangelist George Jeffreys, which included healings and tongues, the *Life of Faith* discussed the gifts with a skeptical eye. There was no need to decide the much debated question of the reappearance of miraculous gifts in this dispensation, the article concluded, because it was clear "how unscriptural, and, indeed, how utterly subversive of genuine spirituality, are the corybantic exhibitions associated with particular types of present-day 'Pentecostalism.'"[35] So the listing of the Pentecostal Missionary Union is surprising. The identity of its president, Cecil Polhill, probably ensured its acceptance. Polhill was a Cambridge graduate, one of the celebrated Cambridge Seven who had responded to the missionary call in 1885 and had gone out with the China Inland Mission. In 1908 he became an exceptional upperclass convert to Pentecostalism, founding the Missionary Union in the following year. He defended a series of meetings held in London by Jeffreys, which he organized himself, in a letter to the *Life of Faith*, claiming it was an ordinary mission but not hiding his belief in the signs following of Mark 16.[36] It was hard to exclude an organization led by Polhill from a list of those

---

[33]Price and Randall, *Transforming Keswick*, 67-69.
[34]*LF*, August 11, 1920, 816.
[35]*LF*, June 14, 1922, 732.
[36]*LF*, February 1, 1922, 123 (Cecil Polhill).

believing the Bible. In addition, the appeal was supported by the Bedford Gospel Mission under Pastor W. Glassby, a correspondent of T. H. Mundell, the Pentecostal Union's honorary secretary.[37] Polhill came from Bedford, and, though he did not attend the Pentecostal meeting there at the end of his life, he may well have prompted Glassby to subscribe to the list.[38] This item in the appeal is a very early instance of the acceptance of Pentecostals by a wider evangelical coalition.

A larger sector endorsing the Bible League appeal consisted of faith missionary societies. Faith missions were undenominational bodies more recent in foundation than the denominational bodies like the Baptist and Church Missionary Societies. Their key principle was that their missionaries went out in faith that the Lord would supply their needs, without the elaborate support structures of the older agencies. The first of them, the China Inland Mission, created by J. Hudson Taylor in 1865, was missing from the list of Bible League supporters, no doubt because its home director at the time, the Anglican clergyman Stuart Holden, was a moderate figure who disliked divisive measures.[39] Some other faith missions, however, had close ties to the Bible League. The Regions Beyond Missionary Union, for example, which had developed from agencies founded by the influential premillennialist Henry Grattan Guinness in the 1870s, had its secretary sign the Bible League appeal. The theological tutor at Guinness's Missionary Training Institute at Harley House in East London, G. D. Hooper, had held a Bible League meeting at his Luton Baptist chapel as early as 1896, the year of his appointment.[40] A catalogue of similar missionary organizations gave their support to the League's efforts in 1923. The Worldwide Evangelization Crusade and the Evangelical Union of South America were among the larger bodies that responded, but there were also the Inland South America Missionary Union, the Russian Missionary Society, the India Christian Mission, the Poona Village Mission, the Kurku Mission serving India, the South Africa General Mission, the Qua Iboe Mission in Africa, the New Hebrides Mission for the South

---

[37]Allan H. Anderson, *To the Ends of the Earth: Pentecostalism and the Transformation of World Christianity* (New York: Oxford University Press, 2013), 266n14.

[38]Timothy B. Walsh, *To Meet and Satisfy a Very Hungry People: The Origins and Fortunes of English Pentecostalism, 1907–1925* (Milton Keynes: Paternoster, 2012), 221n197.

[39]John Stuart Holden, *A Book of Remembrance* (London: Hodder & Stoughton, 1935), 33-36.

[40]*C*, February 13, 1896, 26; July 2, 1896, 12.

Seas, the Mission to Lepers, and the Living Waters Missionary Union. Their faith principle made their agents diligent searchers of the Scriptures for divine promises. Hence, the support of these bodies for a declaration of full confidence in the Bible was to be expected.

A number of interdenominational home mission organizations also gave their backing to the League. They included the Evangelization Society, the One-by-One Band, and the Out-and-Out Mission. The City of London Young Men's Christian Association and the Christian Alliance of Women and Girls served more specialized constituencies. Prominent among these home mission bodies was the London City Mission, an extensive evangelistic agency operating in the capital since 1835. Its signatory, the secretary W. P. Cartwright, had shown his allegiance to premillennial teaching two years before by addressing the Advent Preparation and Testimony Movement on the certainty and nearness of the Lord's return.[41] The Hull, Manchester, and Newcastle City Missions, together with the Brighton and Hove and Enfield Town Missions, likewise supported the appeal. So did several Bible colleges that supplied agents to home as well as foreign missions. Just as in the United States, Bible colleges formed a backbone of support for the conservative cause in these years. The Bible Training School for Christian Workers, recently founded at Porth in South Wales by R. B. Jones, a conservative Baptist minister whom we shall meet again shortly, was one such institution on the Bible League list. So was Ridgeland Bible College in Wimbledon, whose chairman was the Anglican clergyman E. L. Langston, another premillennial champion. All Nations Bible College in Upper Norwood, which, as its title implies, prepared candidates for overseas work, had opened earlier in 1923 under F. B. Meyer as principal with a doctrinal basis stating that Scripture was inspired, trustworthy, and authoritative.[42] The Bristol Missionary Training College, the Redcliffe House for Missionary Students and Mount Hermon Missionary Training College on Streatham Common, all led by women, equally backed the League appeal. Keen evangelists, whether at home or abroad, required a reliable Bible.

The most obvious regional support for the appeal came from south Wales. The leading figure was Rhys Bevan Jones, the Baptist minister of Tabernacle, Porth, whose church adhered to the League's document together with his

---

[41]C, November 24, 1921, 26.
[42]LF, February 21, 1923, 202.

monthly magazine *Yr Efengylydd* (The Evangelist), the Yr Efengylydd Home Mission, and the Bible School already mentioned. Jones was a staunch premillennialist, writing in 1919 what was claimed to be the first book in Welsh on the subject,[43] and equally zealous for Keswick teaching. His first address during a Bible Convention held in Streatham in 1923 was "The Call to Holiness."[44] When, in 1921, the Bible League had issued its first call for missionary societies to declare their allegiance to Scripture, Jones wrote to the Baptist Missionary Society [BMS] calling on it to take a stand.[45] The society's home secretary, W. Y. Fullerton, resented the demand but wrote an emollient reply to Jones. "With signs of spiritual declension and apostasy multiplying," Jones responded, "something more explicit and frank than vague generalisations are [*sic*] urgently demanded."[46] When no firmer statement could be extracted, the Tabernacle resolved to cease sending money to the BMS.[47] It is not surprising that his agencies supported the League appeal of 1923. In the same year Jones addressed a World's Fundamentals Association conference at Fort Worth, Texas.[48] He was the leader of a circle of outright fundamentalists in south Wales. There the legacy of the Welsh Revival of 1904–1905 remained potent, but memories of that time of spiritual fervor contrasted with perceptions of contemporary religious decay. Lack of trust in the Bible was diagnosed as the explanation and alignment with the Bible League was the outcome.

One of the most significant organizations listed on the League's appeal was the Bible Churchmen's Missionary Society [BCMS] because, unlike nearly all the other missionary agencies, it was a denominational body. It was an exclusively Evangelical Anglican society, the result of a split in the CMS. The concordat in that Society between liberals and conservatives which had been reached in 1918 broke down three years later following an address at a CMS summer school in Llandudno when a speaker criticized the conservative standpoint on the Old Testament.[49] At the March 1922 meeting of the CMS

[43]*C*, March 6, 1919, 19.

[44]*LF*, May 23, 1923, 598.

[45]R. B. Jones and Price Lewis to Officers and Committee of the Baptist Missionary Society, December 5, 1921, Tabernacle Church, Porth, File, Box H62, BMSA.

[46]Jones and Lewis to W. Y. Fullerton, January 24, 1923, Tabernacle Church, Porth, File, Box H62, BMSA.

[47]Jones to Fullerton, October 24, 1922, BMSA.

[48]*Bible Call* (hereafter *BC*), November 1923, 160.

[49]G. W. Bromiley, *Daniel Henry Charles Bartlett, M. A., D. D.: A Memoir* (Burnham-on-Sea: Dr. Bartlett's Executors, 1959), 26.

general committee, Daniel Bartlett, the leader of the conservative Fellowship of Evangelical Churchmen (FEC), called for an affirmation that "the authority of Holy Scripture as the Word of God necessarily involves the trustworthiness of its historical records and the validity of its teachings."[50] A decision was deferred to the following July, when, after much negotiation, an amendment was carried, which, in the eyes of the FEC, watered down the resolution. The outcome was unsatisfactory to many conservatives. Members of the Fellowship duly voted to form a separate Bible Churchmen's Missionary Society, which was launched in October 1922. By March 1923 seventy-eight clergy had resigned from the CMS to join the new body, and others were contemplating the same step.[51] The BCMS became a permanent organization with its own mission fields, college, and structure of support. The issue that had given rise to the new Society was exactly the same as the one raised by the Bible League, the trustworthiness of Scripture. Although no British denomination split over that question in the 1920s, the issue was sufficiently divisive to cause actual schism in a leading evangelical missionary society.

Something similar was threatened among the Baptists. The Baptist Bible Union, another organization appearing on the Bible League document, aspired to present a conservative understanding of Scripture as forcefully as the FEC among Evangelical Anglicans. Founded in 1919 to oppose the Free Church federation proposals, it became the focus of opposition to successive instances of lack of sympathy for traditional views of biblical authority. Its driving force, James Mountain of Tunbridge Wells in Kent, was a Baptist by conviction, for he had changed his allegiance in 1893 by being baptized as a believer immediately before he was due to become president of the Countess of Huntingdon's Connexion, a small paedobaptist denomination.[52] His prime loyalty, however, was to the Keswick Convention, where for many years he had organized the music, and he censured speakers there whom he judged to sit loose to scriptural authority.[53] By 1923 he was eighty years old,[54] but he set about pursuing those he believed to be in error with remorseless perseverance.

---

[50]Bromiley, *Bartlett*, 28.

[51]Hewitt, *Problems of Success*, 471.

[52]James Mountain, *My Baptism and What Led to It*, 2nd ed. (London: Baptist Union, 1905).

[53][James Mountain], *The Keswick Convention and the Dangers Which Threaten It* (1920). Mountain, *What Keswick Needs: A Reply to 'What Keswick Stands For'* (1921). Mountain, *Rev. F. C. Spurr and Keswick* (1921).

[54]*BC*, July–September 1928, 33.

In the same month as the Bible League appeal, T. R. Glover, a Cambridge classical scholar who was celebrated for his broad-minded book *The Jesus of History* (1917), was elected vice-president of the Baptist Union with succession to the presidency. Mountain saw this event as a sign that far more than a handful of Baptists were tainted with Modernism.[55] As a result, in September 1923 he turned the Baptist Bible Union into the Bible Baptist Union, a body churches could join corporately, and withdrew from the Baptist Union. "If the apostasy should continue to spread," he wrote, "in that case many excellent people expect a large secession from all Denominations."[56] The attempt at organized separatism, however, collapsed within less than a year, the outfit first reverting to being the Baptist Bible Union and soon becoming inter-denominational.[57] Mountain, though a good publicist, was a poor leader, and nobody replaced him as a champion of Baptist Fundamentalism. A few individual congregations, represented on the Bible League appeal by J. R. Huntley's Widcombe Baptist Church, Bath, and W. M. Robertson's Toxteth Tabernacle, Liverpool, did secede from the Baptist Union, but the threat of schism on a significant scale in the Baptist denomination at home rapidly faded.

There was, however, a parallel campaign against the BMS. A Bible Missionary Trust was another of the bodies listed by the Bible League. It had existed since January 1923, originally under the title "Missionary Trust Fund," as an alternative destination for donations that otherwise would have gone to the BMS.[58] The Society had fallen into disfavor with some conservatives for reasons similar to the CMS. A former missionary working with the Calvinistic Methodists in northeast India, Watkin Roberts, published a booklet with a preface by Prebendary Fox called *The Ravages of Higher Criticism in the Mission Field* denouncing the views of George Howells, a senior BMS missionary, on the Bible.[59] Wright Hay, secretary of the Bible League, followed it up with another booklet attacking Howells and the Society.[60] Erstwhile BMS supporters like R. B. Jones were troubled that the Society refused to give outright support to the Bible League's repeated

---

[55]*BC*, June 1923, 81.
[56]*BC*, October 1923, 152.
[57]*BC*, June 1924, cover; January 1925, cover.
[58]*BC*, January 1923, 8.
[59]W. R. Roberts, *The Ravages of Higher Criticism in the Mission Field* (London: Bible League, 1922).
[60]R. Wright Hay, *The Baptist Missionary Society and Destructive Criticism of the Bible* (London: Bible League, 1923).

requests to endorse the veracity and authority of the Scriptures. "We in our little church," wrote the missionary secretary of Hebron Baptist Chapel, Brynmawr, to the Society, "stand for the full inspiration of the Bible and feel the least deviation from that is not only dangerous, but most dishonouring to our dear Lord and Master Jesus Christ."[61] The Bible Missionary Trust was a focus for such discontent. Its chairman, W. J. Ervine, an elder of the former church of the great preacher C. H. Spurgeon at the Metropolitan Tabernacle, was in March 1923 in charge of a "Bible Convention to uphold the Fundamentals of the Faith and to deepen the Spiritual Life";[62] its secretary was Watkin Roberts, who also signed the League appeal as honorary secretary of the small Thado-Kookie Pioneer Mission working in Manipur; and its treasurer was John A. Bolton, a prosperous children's wear manufacturer who had once intended missionary work, who signed on behalf of Leicester Crusaders' Hall Bible Testimony.[63] Despite such dedicated supporters, the Trust proved remarkably weak. It sponsored only a single missionary couple who actually served under the North-East India General Mission (as the Thado Kookie Mission had become), and it disappeared entirely after 1928.[64] There was therefore an institutional division within missionary support over the Bible among Baptists as well as Evangelical Anglicans, but it turned out to be minor and impermanent.

The polarization of opinion, for or against traditional views of Scripture, which the Bible League sought to achieve therefore enjoyed only limited success. Despite the number of forces ranged behind the League, they made a weak impact and that calls for explanation. It lies primarily in the moderation of many leaders in the conservative evangelical world. Even among the signatories of the League appeal, there were figures who drew back from the fundamentalist temper of vehemence and separatism that was emerging. E. L. Langston, who signed the appeal on behalf of his own congregation at Emmanuel Church, Wimbledon, and the nearby Ridgelands Bible College, though a vocal premillennial spokesman, stood by the CMS, refusing to join

---

[61]Mrs. H. James to W. Y. Fullerton, January 3, 1922, Bible League 1922. BMS Theological Position File, Box H62, BMSA.

[62]BC, June 1922, 44. LF, March 14, 1923, 301.

[63]Ernest E. Kendall, Doing and Daring: The Story of Melbourne Hall Evangelical Free Church, Leicester (Rushden: Stanley L. Hunt, 1955), 124-25.

[64]BC, February 1925, 30. The last reference to it was in BC, July–September 1928, 45, which records that responsibility for it was transferred to Wright Hay.

the BCMS.[65] Likewise Prebendary Webb-Peploe, who signed in two capacities, had urged in the previous month that subscribers should rally to the CMS.[66] His intervention encouraged the editor of the *Life of Faith*, the organ of the Keswick Convention, to call for restraint. "In our struggles for what we conceive to be the truth," he wrote, "we are sometimes tempted to say things calculated to occasion pain and injury. That is not in keeping with the mind of Christ."[67] His fellow editor, Dr. James Thirtle of the *Christian*, which also swayed a large evangelical constituency, took a similar line. Even Benjamin Greenwood, who appeared on the League's document as president of the Nyassa Industrial Mission and was a generous donor to the Baptist Bible Union, was to write in the *Christian* that because we cannot speak with Christ's authority, certainty, and purity, we must restrain our dogmatism.[68] Graham Scroggie, the minister of Charlotte Chapel, Edinburgh, who in 1921 was deeply troubled by potential theological drift in the BMS,[69] came to believe during a visit to North America in 1924 that the bitterness he witnessed around him was damaging the gospel. "Let us clearly understand," he declared in an article on "Fundamentalism," "that the interests of Christ and His Word are not served by raw haste, violent denunciation, presumptuous ignorance, or uncharitableness of spirit."[70] Scroggie, though a firm believer in the premillennial return of Christ and an outstanding speaker at Keswick, refused to make any particular theory of inspiration a test of fellowship. He was one of the leaders who entrenched moderation in the British evangelical psyche.

Nevertheless there was a legacy from the turmoil surrounding the Bible of the 1920s. The Bible League itself endured, continuing to publish its *Bible League Quarterly* down to the present day.[71] The Bible Churchmen's Missionary Society also remains extremely active, since 1992 calling itself Crosslinks.[72] A further development of the 1920s with long-term consequences was the creation of the Fellowship of Independent Evangelical Churches. One of its founders, E. J. Poole-Connor, was a minister who in 1921 chaired a

---

[65]Wilson Cash to E. L. Langston, November 22, 1926, in Hewitt, *Problems of Success*, 72.
[66]H. W. Webb-Peploe and others to editor, *LF*, March 1923, 263.
[67]*LF*, March 14, 1923, 296.
[68]Reproduced in *BC*, January 1926, 13.
[69]W. Graham Scroggie to C. E. Wilson, November 11, 1921, Unmarked File, Box H62, BMSA.
[70]*LF*, July 30, 1924, 895.
[71]See www.bibleleaguetrust.org/the-quarterly/.
[72]See https://en.wikipedia.org/wiki/Crosslinks.

Baptist Bible Union meeting and in 1923 signed the Bible League appeal for
the North Africa Mission.[73] The other was Arthur Carter, former secretary
of the League and minister of Hounslow Undenominational Church, who
after visiting the United States in 1923 to speak at fundamentalist gatherings
published *Modernism: The Peril of Great Britain and America.*[74] In November
1922 they launched a Fellowship of Undenominational and Unattached
Churches and Missions, which from the start upheld the inerrancy of Scripture.[75] It steadily gathered congregations such as the Evangelical Free Church,
Lansdowne Hall, West Norwood, and branches of the Railway Mission, both
of which appear on the League document of 1923. In 2019 the FIEC included
over six hundred churches.[76] The final body emerging from the Bible crisis
was also the most important: the Inter-Varsity Fellowship (IVF) of Christian
Unions. Its strongest student group, the Cambridge Inter-Collegiate Christian
Union, had separated from the Student Christian Movement in 1910 because
it upheld the final authority of Scripture. During the 1920s Douglas Johnson,
an enterprising London medical graduate, organized the creation of fresh
Christian Unions elsewhere and their coordination through the IVF. The
library of CICCU, considered essential in a "hot-bed of criticism," was formed
largely by gifts of books from the Bible League;[77] and in 1926 Johnson contributed an account of biblical witness in the universities to the *Bible League
Quarterly.*[78] The IVF arose too late to respond to the Bible League appeal of
1923, but it emerged from the same milieu. Its growing work among students
during the rest of the twentieth century and beyond was to transform the
churches of Britain.

The response to the Bible League appeal to come out in favor of the divine
authority of the Bible is therefore highly revealing. Military men were especially likely to agree, as were militant Protestants, confessional Calvinists,
upholders of the premillennial advent, and supporters of Jewish missions.
The holiness movement associated with Keswick, the incipient Pentecostal
movement, the large range of faith missionary societies, interdenominational

---

[73]*BC*, March–April 1921, 7.
[74]*LF*, March 7, 1923, 269; August 15, 1923, 969; December 5, 1923, 1447.
[75]*LF*, January 16, 1924, 60.
[76]See https://fiec.org.uk/about-us/history.
[77]Hugh Gough, "A Student's Testimony," *Bible League Quarterly*, July–September 1926, 127.
[78]Douglas Johnson, "Helpers for the War: Biblical Witness in the Universities," *BLQ*, October–
December 1926, 183-87.

home mission agencies and a group in south Wales were all successful recruiting grounds. The newly formed Bible Churchmen's Missionary Society, the smaller Baptist Bible Union, and the even smaller Bible Missionary Trust associated with the Baptists also provided support. Often there were interconnections between these groups, with the leaders of various bodies often sharing premillennial beliefs and Keswick convictions. The crisis left a lasting legacy in the Bible League, the BCMS, the Fellowship of Independent Evangelical Churches and the Inter-Varsity Fellowship. There was therefore a great deal of common ground with the contemporary fundamentalist controversy in North America. The parallel was noted at the time, with the Baptist Bible Union in Britain remarking that it was cheered to see a body with the same name and practically the same basis starting in America.[79] Yet there were differences. Whereas in the United States the Presbyterians were rocked by disputes in the 1920s, their counterparts in Britain, and supremely in Scotland, remained almost entirely unscathed. There was only a single Presbyterian response to the Bible League appeal. Anglicans, who were hardly touched by controversies in the United States, were heavily involved in Britain, an indication of the relative strength of evangelicals in the Church of England. The other great difference was in the spirit of the debates about Scripture. Wild rhetoric such as was common in America was by no means absent in Britain, but it was much less frequently heard. Evangelical leaders of impeccable orthodoxy often refused to join in either denunciation or separatism. Polarization was much less complete than the Bible League desired. Many Bible believers were dubious about higher criticism, but the great majority saw themselves as conservative evangelicals rather than as fundamentalists.

---

[79]*BC*, October 1922, 72.

8

Liberal Evangelicals and the Bible

Timothy Larsen

AFTER MY PHD THESIS WAS PUBLISHED, my next book project was a study of Christabel Pankhurst, a leading suffragette as well as an evangelical author and preacher. I had initially become interested in her story when I was working on the *Biographical Dictionary of Evangelicals*, a project that IVP had approached David Bebbington to edit, but he had graciously convinced them that they should invite me (early career though I was) instead. As I started commissioning for that reference work, I asked another Bebbington PhD student, Linda Wilson, if she would write the entries on a half dozen or so British women. Wilson generously said she would do them all—except for one, Christabel Pankhurst. I therefore decided that I would just write that entry myself. Wilson's instincts had been good, however, as I quickly discovered that there were no scholarly secondary sources to draw upon. This was so emphatically the case that I began to wonder how I had ever even learned that Pankhurst was an evangelical in the first place. It was only much later that I finally figured out that it was because Bebbington, on the basis of his familiarity with the primary sources, had mentioned Pankhurst in passing in his *Evangelicalism in Modern Britain*.

A couple decades on, I have just relived that experience. When Tommy Kidd and I decided that it was time for a collection of studies about biblicism from the Bebbington Quadrilateral, I started to think about what I might be able to contribute. I thought that it would be interesting to explore evangelical identity at a boundary line by focusing on Liberal Evangelicals. The obvious person for such a case study would then be Vernon Faithfull Storr (1869-1940), whom I knew of because of the entry on him in my *Biographical Dictionary of Evangelicals*. But now once again, the secondary literature that I assumed would be there has been lacking. I have been rattled to discover that Storr did not even have an entry in the *Oxford Dictionary of National Biography*. How then had he ended up in my *Biographical Dictionary*? The answer, of course, is the same as before: it was because Bebbington—intimately familiar with the crucial actors and primary sources in all four corners of his quadrilateral—had discussed Storr in *Evangelicalism in Modern Britain*. (Indeed, one of the ways I generated the list of entries for my reference book was simply to go systematically down the index in Bebbington's landmark study.) I am just one of innumerable scholars who have found that research ideas and projects of theirs across the decades have been generated by a prompt from Bebbington's seminal work.

* * *

This chapter is focused upon members of the Church of England, especially clergymen, in the first half of the twentieth century who used "Liberal Evangelical" as a self-descriptor. This has been an oft-overlooked tradition. In 2014, Martin Wellings lamented how "many historians of the twentieth-century Church of England" had "neglected the history and ignored the influence of the liberal evangelicals."[1] Indeed, otherwise well-informed and careful church historians are sometimes not even aware of their existence. Robert Beaken, for instance, in his 2012 study of the archbishop of Canterbury, Cosmo Lang—despite the book being focused on the Church of England at the height of the movement's influence—is so unware of it that when he quotes a letter of Lang's from 1929 in which the archbishop referred to "the Liberal Evangelical movement," Beaken is so sure that no such thing could have existed that he inserted into the block quote: "[sic, Lang probably meant the Liberal and Evangelical movements]."[2] Quite to the contrary, a book analyzing the state of the Church of England which had been published in the

---

[1]Martin Wellings, "The Anglican Evangelical Group Movement," in *Evangelicalism and the Church of England in the Twentieth Century: Reform, Resistance and Renewal*, ed. Andrew Atherstone and John Maiden (Woodbridge: Boydell, 2014), 68-88 (here 68).

[2]Robert Beaken, *Cosmo Lang: Archbishop in War and Crisis* (London: I. B. Tauris, 2012), 170-71.

year before Lang wrote that letter had suggested that the Liberal Evangelicals were "the most important party in the Church."[3]

Liberal Evangelicals in the Church of England were given institutional expression with the Anglican Evangelical Group Movement (AEGM), an organization that was launched in 1923. The AEGM, however, was the next phase of a private fellowship of evangelical Anglican clergymen that was first conceived in 1905 and which referred to itself as the Group Brotherhood.[4] Not everyone in the Group Brotherhood fit the mold of a Liberal Evangelical. W. H. Griffith Thomas, for instance, was an active member in its early years before he moved to Canada,[5] though there are no indications of liberal tendencies in his theology at that time and his mature identity was that of a conservative Evangelical who was more apt to cooperate with fundamentalists than Modernists. Still, from its very creation in 1923, the AEGM unequivocally stood for Liberal Evangelicalism. Keith W. Clements has perceptively observed: "It seems to be a peculiarly Anglican way of producing theology, for a collections of essays to emerge from a circle of 'minds' which have been meeting for some time, perhaps over several years, to discuss questions of common interest and concern."[6] Celebrated examples include the Broad Church volume, *Essays and Reviews* (1860), and the liberal Anglo-Catholic one, *Lux Mundi* (1889). Thus, in the same year that the AEGM was founded, this group of like-minded clergymen also produced their own manifesto volume, *Liberal Evangelicalism: An Interpretation* (1923).[7] In the following year, when the AEGM wished to identify its ethos, it averred: "The recent volume of essays on 'Liberal Evangelicalism' best embodies its spirit."[8] A sequel volume published in 1925 was titled, *The Inner Life: Essays in Liberal Evangelicalism*.[9] Eventually, the *Bulletin* of the AEGM was even renamed the *Liberal*

---

[3]Wellings, "Anglican Evangelical Group Movement," 68.

[4]The official history is A. Eric Smith, *Another Anglican Angle: Liberal Evangelicalism: The Anglican Evangelical Group Movement, 1906-1967* (Oxford: Amate, 1991).

[5]L. Hickin, "Liberal Evangelicals in the Church of England," *Church Quarterly Review* 169 (1968), 46.

[6]Keith W. Clements, *Lovers of Discord: Twentieth-Century Theological Controversies in England* (London: SPCK, 1988), 52.

[7]Members of the Church of England, *Liberal Evangelicalism: An Interpretation*, ed. T. Guy Rogers (London: Hodder and Stougton, 1923).

[8]Anglican Evangelical Group Movement Pamphlets Nos. 1-27 (London: Hodder and Stoughton, 1924). From the inside cover of each pamphlet, "Anglican Evangelical Group Movement."

[9]T. Guy Rogers, ed., *The Inner Life: Essays in Liberal Evangelicalism* (London: Hodder and Stoughton, 1925).

Evangelical. Vernon Storr would also use the term in the very titles of some of his books: *Spiritual Liberty: A Study of Liberal Evangelicalism* (1934) and *Freedom and Tradition: A Study of Liberal Evangelicalism* (1940).[10]

What then did these Liberal Evangelicals stand for? As is often the case with movements, the question that is easier to answer is what they stood against: for one, they knew that they were not Anglo-Catholics. There really does seem to be a sense in which some clergymen were swept into the orbit of the AEGM simply because they were clear on that point. Indeed, a prompt for the launching of the AEGM was the need for an alternative force to organize in order to combat the influence of the Anglo-Catholics on the question of Prayer Book Revision.[11] A 1926 news item on the AEGM in *The Times* was titled, "Evangelical Group Movement. Limits of Latitude."[12] The basic point, drawing from its recent, public pronouncements, being that the AEGM drew the limit of toleration at allowing any greater room for expressions of Anglo-Catholicism in the Church of England. Over time, Liberal Evangelicals would pride themselves in having a less intolerant approach than the staunch Evangelicals of the previous generation to ritual and other high church emphases. In contrast to high, low, and broad churchmen, the AEGM claimed to represent "central" churchmanship. In other words, it aspired to be the natural home for people who primarily knew themselves simply to be Anglicans. This appeal did have some substantial success. It was estimated in 1935 that around 10 percent of clergymen in the Church of England were members of the AEGM—and presumably many more identified with what it stood for without taking the trouble and expense to join it.[13] Moreover, Randall Davidson, who was Archbishop of Canterbury until November 1928, seemed to view Liberal Evangelicals as the safest churchmen to promote and empower. Over the course of the few decades in which the AEGM flourished, at least thirty-six of its members were elevated to the episcopacy.[14] Indeed,

---

[10]Vernon F. Storr, *Spiritual Liberty: A Study of Liberal Evangelicalism* (London: Student Christian Movement, 1934); Vernon F. Storr, *Freedom and Tradition: A Study of Liberal Evangelicalism* (London: Nisbet, 1940).

[11]For the wider context, see John Maiden, *National Religion and the Prayer Book Controversy, 1927–1928* (Woodbridge: Boydell, 2009).

[12]"Evangelical Group Movement. Limits of Latitude." *The Times*, January 14, 1926, 14.

[13]Ian M. Randall, *Evangelical Experiences: A Study in the Spirituality of English Evangelicalism, 1918–1938* (Carlile: Paternoster, 1999), 47.

[14]Smith, *Another Anglican Angle*, 83-84.

Storr himself was Davidson's Examining Chaplain, as well as a close, trusted advisor of his on ecclesiastical matters.[15] (Despite being asked repeatedly, Storr steadfastly refused to accept a bishopric.) This aspiring to centrality, however, never blurred the fact that everyone in the AEGM considered Anglo-Catholicism to be the Other. Storr resigned as a canon of Winchester because his soul revolted against that cathedral's more Catholic forms of worship. When he later became a canon of Westminster, he zealously guarded its Protestant ways. In what Freud no doubt would have seen as a classic example of the narcissism of small differences, Storr vigilantly ensured that the abbey remained lily-white and would never succumb to the temptation to use violet-colored linen during Lent.[16]

And Canon Storr was unquestionably the most important figure in the AEGM. He was its animating spirit and indomitable organizer; he was its chief leader, spokesperson, and public face. Although the Group Brotherhood had existed for seventeen years by then—and Storr had been a member for just six months—at the inauguration of the AEGM he was immediately elected Vice-Chairman.[17] He was then given the title Honorary Organising Secretary, which, in today's terms, really meant something like Executive Director: Storr was in charge of making the AEGM run and its initiatives happen. The title of that office not seeming commiserate with his true importance to the organization, in 1929 the AEGM created a new position of president better to reflect Storr's preeminence. Although officially an election to this new highest office was for a five-year term, as he invariably was re-elected, Storr functionally became president of the AEGM for life. He died on October 25, 1940. It is striking that all sources agree that the AEGM's period of major influence lasted from its founding until "roughly up to the Second World War"—in other words, the same period when Storr was active in it.[18] The official history of the AEGM states that it was led "above all, over a period of nearly twenty years, by one man."[19] A retrospective article published in 1968 to mark the disbanding of the AEGM declared unequivocally: "Storr's outstanding abilities

---

[15]Randall, *Evangelical Experiences*, 67.

[16]G. H. Harris, *Vernon Faithfull Storr: A Memoir* (London: SPCK, 1943), 27-31.

[17]From a Correspondent, "Evangelical Group," *The Times*, June 22, 1923, 17.

[18]Smith, *Another Anglican Angle*, 76. See also, Hickin, "Liberal Evangelicals," 43-54 (esp. 43); Wellings, "Anglican Evangelical Group Movement," 75.

[19]Smith, *Another Anglican Angle*, 24.

soon gave him a commanding position in the Movement; in fact he may be regarded as the Movement's virtual leader for the next seventeen years, until his death in 1940. The decline of the Movement after 1940 is very largely due to the fact that there was no leader of his calibre to take his place."[20]

More pejoratively, the man who succeeded Randall Davidson as archbishop of Canterbury, Cosmo Lang, referred to the AEGM dismissively as "Storr's stunt."[21] His biographer declares that by the time Storr became a canon of Westminster the Liberal Evangelical movement was "the prime concern of his life."[22] Wellings has also observed that Storr was "the leading theologian of Liberal Evangelicalism in the years between the World Wars."[23] As we move toward examining Storr's thought and writings, it is important to keep in mind that he was the preeminent voice for the Liberal Evangelical theological position. His books sometimes bore the official seal of the movement. For instance, *The Light of the Bible* (1938) declared at the very start that it was issued "with the approval of the Anglican Evangelical Group Movement."[24] This is particularly the case with *My Faith* (1927). The title is meant to be appropriated by the reader, who is invited to read this account of Christianity and adopt it as his or her own, to say to themselves, *This is my faith too*. Here is a portion of the preface: "This small book has been written at the request of the Committee of the Anglican Evangelical Group Movement. It has been subjected to criticism by members of the Movement, and may therefore be said to represent in a general way the outlook of Liberal Evangelicalism. . . . The volume is intended to be a simple statement of the Christian Faith, as a Liberal Evangelical views it."[25]

The "liberal" part of the AEGM's hybrid identity was intended to convey that its proponents believed that traditional evangelicalism needed to change to come into line with modern thought. Everyone in the movement pointed to accepting biblical criticism and its implications as the primary area in which such an adjustment was required. Storr's writings have this theme as

---

[20]Hickin, "Liberal Evangelicals," 50.

[21]Smith, *Another Anglican Angle*, 34.

[22]Harris, *Vernon Faithfull Storr*, 38.

[23]Martin Wellings, *Evangelicals Embattled: Responses of Evangelicals in the Church of England to Ritualism, Darwinism and Theological Liberalism, 1890–1930* (Carlisle: Paternoster, 2003), 40.

[24]Vernon F. Storr, *The Light of the Bible* (London: Hodder and Stoughton, 1938). (From a page at the very front inserted before the table of contents.)

[25]Vernon F. Storr, *My Faith* (London: SPCK, 1936), v.

a particular preoccupation. He published multiple books across his career specifically on the nature of the Bible and its interpretation. Moreover, this emphasis was there from the very beginning. He was not ordained until 1900, but already in 1892—when he was just twenty-two years old—Storr wrote a letter to the evangelical newspaper, the *Record*, to weigh in on the liberal side in an ongoing exchange about "The Bible and Modern Criticism." In it, he asserted flatly that "religion does not depend on historical records," and advocated for a faith that was not focused on "how God dealt with the world in bygone ages," but rather on the present and the future.[26] To take just two examples from his books, *The Inspiration of the Bible* was published in 1908, and twenty years later, Storr was still tilling the same ground with *The Bible and the Modern Mind* (1928).[27]

Storr seems to have had a personal antipathy toward machines. In an overheated moment, he even suggested that the rise of machines was pushing humanity toward damnation: "machinery increasingly controls our living. The result is that men are in danger of losing their souls."[28] If Storr wanted to condemn a doctrinal position or religious practice, he dismissed it as a "mechanical" view. This trope runs throughout his corpus and was applied to innumerable issues. In line with classic evangelical thought, Roman Catholic and Anglo-Catholic ways were rejected on these grounds. In *My Faith*, Storr presented the Liberal Evangelical view of each of the various rites and sacraments of the church with this critique in mind. He is wary of auricular confession, for instance, on the grounds that the recipient might "come to regard his confession as a kind of mechanical way of obtaining pardon."[29] Confirmation is a good practice, of course, but only if rightly understood: "we must not make the mistake of thinking that God's grace or help passes through the bishop's fingers as the electric current passes along a wire."[30] Storr also objected to the reserved sacrament on the same grounds.[31] He even read the Old Testament through this lens: the burden of the prophet

---

[26]Letter by V. F. Storr, *Record*, January 29, 1892, 128-29. (Martin Wellings discovered this source, and I am grateful to him for sharing a transcript of this letter with me.)

[27]Vernon F. Storr, *The Inspiration of the Bible*, 3rd ed. (Winchester: Warren & Son, 1925); Vernon F. Storr, *The Bible and the Modern Mind* (London: SPCK, 1928).

[28]Storr, *Spiritual Liberty*, 13.

[29]Storr, *My Faith*, 129.

[30]Storr, *My Faith*, 110.

[31]Smith, *Another Anglican Angle*, 37.

Amos was to denounce the "official machinery of the State Church."[32] Every aspect of true religion has the potential to be corrupted in this way. Real prayer, for instance, is not to be confused with its mechanical imitation. Even grace itself "has too frequently been conceived as something semi-material and external, a stream of force which passes into the soul as an electric current passes into the body."[33] The exception that proves the rule was Storr's account of the punishment of sin. He did not like the idea of God directly punishing people as it seemed to undercut his emphasis on God's love. He therefore developed a view in which the negative consequences resulting from sins are not the direct acts of a personal God but only, as it were, the mechanical outworks of "the laws of the universe."[34]

Storr's theology of punishment can serve as a bridge to his use of the mechanized metaphor in order to criticize views held within the evangelical camp. Even some fellow Liberal Evangelicals regretted the way that Storr so thoroughly ruled out the substitutionary theory of the atonement. It is indicative of how deeply Storr felt the difficulties raised against it that he chose to title his book on the nature of the atonement, *The Problem of the Cross*. Substitutionary atonement, in Storr's way of thinking, is "too formal and mechanical."[35] Storr's rage against the machine was often directed at traditional evangelical views of the Bible. He rejected utterly the notion that the Bible was inerrant or marked by verbal or plenary inspiration. Indeed, Storr sometimes went so far as to teach that the Bible *qua* Bible is not inspired at all: it was only the authors who were inspired—not what they wrote—and they only imperfectly, fallibly, and to varying degrees. The conservative position was dismissed over and over again throughout his career as "a mechanical theory of inspiration."[36] To believe that God dictated the Scriptures is to make the human author "simply a machine."[37] And again: "The Bible was written by men, not automata."[38] As Wellings has observed, Liberal

---

[32]Storr, *Light of the Bible*, 76.

[33]Storr, *Spiritual Liberty*, 114.

[34]Vernon F. Storr, *The Problem of the Cross* (London: Student Christian Movement, 1924), 86.

[35]Storr, *Problem*, 99.

[36]Vernon F. Storr, *The Development of English Theology in the Nineteenth Century, 1800–1860* (London: Longmans, Green, 1913), 170.

[37]V. F. Storr, *The Bible: What It Is and What It Is Not*, AEGM Pamphlets No. 10 (London: Hodder and Stoughton, 1924), 4.

[38]Storr, *Light of the Bible*, 21.

Evangelicals developed the bad habit of attributing to conservatives views that they did not hold.[39] Although you would not realize this from reading Storr's rhetoric, few if any conservative evangelicals held to a dictation theory. Moreover, there was no warrant for Storr's claim that verbal inspiration included a belief that the biblical authors "had for the time being no will or mind or personality of their own."[40] Storr could not have helped but know that even the most conservative of evangelical biblical commentaries standardly made observations about what the text revealed regarding the distinctive personality of the human author.

Because Storr did not believe the Bible was marked by verbal or plenary inspiration, he was at great pains to wean evangelicals away from focusing upon the details of Scripture. Almighty God was in the grand sweep of Scripture, but the devil was in the details. Storr especially stressed this point regarding the Hebrew prophets. Evangelicals had been misled by thinking in terms of predictive prophecy that had been or would be minutely fulfilled. The right way was to stick to the big picture, to the "large, bold outlines," to the Bible's "large, salient characteristics."[41] While a believer in inerrancy might be embarrassed by a prophecy that did not seem to have been fulfilled, Storr had gone so far the other way that at times he seems almost embarrassed by the admitted fact that some prophecies were fulfilled, even in detail. He would concede this, while warning readers not to be led astray by it into expecting such results with other prophetic passages. Moreover, Storr read the whole Bible this way. His recommended approach to the writings of St. Paul, for instance, was essentially that one should stick to the big themes and not become bogged down in the apostle's specific assertions. It would not be an overstatement to say that a main purpose of Storr's teaching ministry across the decades was to attempt to bury forever a traditional approach to Scripture. His rejection of a plenary view of inspiration could be markedly visceral. Using biblical language for bondage, Storr could speak of the conservative view as a "yoke" and shedding it as a "deliverance."[42]

---

[39]Wellings, *Evangelicals Embattled*, 166.

[40]Storr, *Inspiration of the Bible*, 5.

[41]Vernon F. Storr, *The Missionary Genius of the Bible* (London: Hodder and Stoughton, 1924), 12, 19.

[42]Storr, *Spiritual Liberty*, 13; Storr, *Bible and the Modern Mind*, 14.

As was so common in his generation, Storr filled the void left by removing such yokes with a belief in progressive revelation. One can dismiss earlier parts of the Bible as wrong in the confidence that we know this because of what is revealed later on. This perspective is presented so well in an article in the *Sheffield Daily Telegraph* titled, "The Teaching of the Bible. Evangelical View," that it is worth quoting at length:

> Canon Vernon Storr, of Westminster, President of the Anglican Evangelical Group Movement . . . is a representative of the attitude of the younger Evangelicals towards Bible teaching. . . Under the influence of his teaching it seems natural that the thought forms with which we are familiar in the Bible have been outgrown. . . . The doctrine of progressive revelation enables us to see as an organic whole the Old and New Testaments, removing the difficulty which has been felt about the approval given in the Old Testament to lower ethical standards, which the Christian conscience condemns.[43]

In the section "Progressive and Gradual Revelation" in his book *The Inspiration of the Bible*, Storr almost made it sound like a panacea for all the old Bible problems: "The solution of the difficulty is easy in the light of this notion of a gradual development."[44] No wonder that he could enthuse about "the splendour of this conception of a progressive revelation."[45] Moreover, progress continues beyond the Bible. Storr believed that we can see that St. Paul was wrong because of advances that have been made since his time. Related to this was Storr's zeal for the theory of evolution. For him, it was not merely that Darwinism was compatible with the Christian faith; rather it explicated the very nature of Christianity and the ways of God: "How the doctrine of evolution has helped us here . . . God's action none the less divine because it is gradual and continuous. Evolution is God at work. He is always creating."[46] Thomas A. Langford has observed that English theology in general in the formative period of Storr's development, 1900–1920, took evolution and progress as central themes.[47] Storr

---

[43]Oxoniensis, "The Teaching of the Bible. Evangelical View," *Sheffield Daily Telegraph*, December 19, 1929, 5.

[44]Storr, *Inspiration of the Bible*, 21.

[45]V. F. Storr, "The Bible and Its Value," in T. Guy Rogers, ed., *Members of the Church of England; Liberal Evangelicalism: An Interpretation* (London: Hodder and Stougton, 1923), 87.

[46]Vernon F. Storr, *The Old Testament Lessons of the New Lectionary: Sermon Outlines* (London: SPCK, 1925), 32-33.

[47]Thomas A. Langford, *In Search of Foundations: English Theology, 1900–1920* (Nashville: Abingdon, 1969), 12.

asserted that we need not take past theological formulations as binding because they can be relativized by the fact that they were part of a dominant cultural perspective of their day. Anselm's view of the atonement, for instance, was shaped by the assumptions of feudalism.[48] He was unable to follow this insight through, however, to wonder whether history had really come to a full stop in his own generation or if the dominance of optimistic, progressive assumptions in his day might also limit the utility of his theology for subsequent generations.

Storr's belief in spiritual progress beyond the apostles meant that—unlike evangelicals of past generations—he did not accept the Bible as the final authority in matters of faith and practice. What then did he put in its place? To begin, a doctrine of the ongoing work of the Spirit: "If we can believe in the guidance of the Spirit of Truth the golden age lies in the future."[49] That, however, was in some ways just to give a theological rationale for why we can assume progress. In other words, that was more a reassuring conviction rather than an answer to the question, What is the church's final authority in matters of faith and doctrine? When John Henry Newman formulated his theory of the development of doctrine, he recognized that authority cannot be located merely in the past, not even in the church fathers. Newman therefore needed the living church to serve that function in the present and into the future. When the *Lux Mundi* Anglo-Catholics conceded that the Bible was sometimes wrong, they also leaned on the authority of the church by way of compensation.[50] Storr's evangelicalism meant that his road did not lie that way. His solution was to identify the true authority as the mind of Christ. He proclaimed this unwaveringly in the most emphatic of terms: "the very heart of Liberal Evangelicalism is its assertion that the Mind of Christ must be our final standard."[51] Storr was aware that some people found this position to be too nebulous to be of practical use, but he was so pleased with the claim himself that he did not seem to feel the force of that critique. Too often he argued in circles. On the one hand, the Bible provides the needed grounding and specificity: "What other test can be

---

[48]Storr, *Problem of the Cross*, 13.

[49]Vernon F. Storr, *Freedom and Tradition: A Study of Liberal Evangelicalism* (London: Nisbet, 1940), 87.

[50]Peter Hinchliff, *God and History: Aspects of British Theology, 1875-1914* (Oxford: Clarendon, 1992), 37, 114.

[51]Storr, *Spiritual Liberty*, 65.

found except the New Testament, which shows us the mind of Christ and His Apostles?"[52] That would be a lucid observation were it not that the whole point of introducing the mind of Christ is to establish an authority that allows one to reject the teaching of the Bible. So, perhaps the real standard is the words of Christ as recorded in the Bible. Storr would put weight on that claim, but then, when confronted with critical objections that the historical Jesus probably did not say some of the things attributed to him, he will argue that this does not matter as the biblical author who put those words into Christ's mouth was inspired—once again negating the whole point of stressing the words of Jesus.[53] In the end, the Mind of Christ was also just another expression of Storr's optimistic assumption that believers were steadily gaining more truth as they progressed through time: "We cannot prescribe in advance what Christ may have to say to the world through the Spirit . . . [the believer's] final authority is the Christ of the future, rather than the Christ of the past."[54]

For this examination of evangelical identity at a boundary line, it is natural to wonder what aspects of historic Christianity Storr was and was not willing to shed as he travelled lightly into the future. On the orthodox side, despite it being the view of some Modernists in his day,[55] Storr clearly rejected adoptionism: Jesus was God become man, not man become God. The Unitarians were wrong.[56] Not unrelatedly, Storr always affirmed unequivocally that Christ was sinless. Beyond that, there was a lot of shedding or revising that he was ready to do. He rejected the Chalcedonian definition, disliking its two-natures account of the person of Christ.[57] Storr's general approach to the question of miracles was to try to eliminate the very category on the assumption that it would be better if the dichotomy between natural and supernatural could be set aside.[58] As a matter of policy,[59] where he saw an

---

[52]Storr, *My Faith*, 83.

[53]Storr, *Freedom and Tradition*, 101; Storr, *Missionary Genius*, 137.

[54]Storr, *Spiritual Liberty*, 69-70.

[55]Alan M. G. Stephenson, *The Rise and Decline of English Modernism* (London: SPCK, 1984), 8.

[56]V. F. Storr, *The Person of Christ*, AEGM Pamphlets No. 3 (London: Hodder and Stoughton, 1924), 9-14.

[57]Storr, *Person of Christ*, 3.

[58]This too was part of a wider trend; see Arthur Michael Ramsey, *From Gore to Temple: The Development of Anglican Theology Between Lux Mundi and the Second World War, 1889–1939* (London: Longmans, 1960), 19.

[59]Storr, "The Bible and Its Value," 85: "if a natural explanation of a reported strange event can be found, that explanation must be accepted."

opening Storr sought to naturalize biblical events that previous generations of Christians had typically viewed as miracles: manna was just the juice of the tamrisk tree; Hezekiah's sign of the retreating shadow was only the work of refraction in certain atmospheric conditions; and so on. Even the healing miracles of God incarnate are glossed in a naturalizing way when Jesus is described as "the first Christian medical missionary."[60] Isaiah's prophetic vision of the lion lying down with the lamb is just an intuition of the coming of our civilized times in which roaming predators have been largely eliminated, and livestock are safe.[61]

This leads on to the two main miracles of the creeds that were being denied in their traditional sense by some Modernists: the virgin birth and the bodily resurrection of Jesus Christ. On the evangelical side, Storr continued to affirm the literal truth of both of those doctrines. On the liberal side, however, he rejected the notion that these were essential teachings of the Christian faith. He wanted clergymen in good standing to be able to deny them frankly and freely. More than that, Storr's progressive revelation scheme made him particularly anxious about, as it is now put, being on the wrong side of history. This is the theme of his *The Development of English Theology in the Nineteenth Century, 1800–1860* (1913). Despite it being by far Storr's most scholarly book, it was written explicitly as a cautionary tale: "The lesson for ourselves is plain."[62] That lesson is that theology must ever be on the move and therefore you must vigilantly avoid putting yourself in the futile position of fighting against the future. A favorite slogan of Storr's was that the heterodox of one generation becomes the orthodox of the next. He seemed to have feared the fate of having future generations look back on him as someone who had been dogmatic about an idea that was destined to be abandoned in the march of time. While conservative evangelicals were apt to take their stand on Jesus Christ the same yesterday, today, and forever, Storr averred: "We cannot prescribe in advance what Christ may have to say to the world through the Spirit. . . . [The Liberal Evangelical's] final authority is the Christ of the future."[63] The key was to be nimble in one's beliefs: "The Liberal Evangelical

---

[60]Storr, *Missionary Genius*, 117.

[61]Vernon F. Storr, *The Prophets of the Old Testament and their Message: Lessons for Schools and Bible Classes* (London: SPCK, 1933), 21.

[62]Storr, *Development*, 2.

[63]Storr, *Spiritual Liberty*, 69-70.

tries to keep his eye on the future which he feels will be full of surprises. He does not want to be taken unawares. He wants to sit sufficiently loose to his beliefs to be ready for change."[64] The president of the AEGM was on the side of whatever the next generation would decide: "A good defence can be made of the truth of the stories of the Virgin Birth and the Empty Tomb. Time alone can show whether they will remain as constituent parts of the accepted Christian tradition."[65] Storr continually insisted that every generation must decide anew whether past doctrinal formulations are dead dogmas or living truths.

A weakness of Storr's theological vision, therefore, was that he never acknowledged that his generation and future generations might have their own blind spots and temptations which the witness of the church across time could help them guard against. His principle was that "the present must always be the critic of the past,"[66] but he does not even contemplate the possibility that the present might need a critic as well. Storr insisted that if there "is a 'noble army of martyrs'; there is also a noble army of heretics; or at any rate of pioneer, prophetic souls, who under the illumination of the Spirit saw the new truth and gave expression to it in their generation, often at the cost of persecution."[67] Fair enough, but he never addressed the fact that there has also been an ignoble army of heretics who have led people into delusions and confusions and dead ends and errors of all sorts, and therefore the pertinent question is how to discern which is which in one's own time.

His biographer observed that Storr was "a born teacher."[68] One downside to this was that he had the teacher's habit of repeating himself. Storr's books frequently recycle material from his prior publications. Even when he was not reusing earlier prose verbatim, he had decided early in his ministry not only what points he most wanted to make, but even the illustrations he would use to make them, and then went on to repeat this material in publication after publication down the decades. Storr's goal seems to have been to find a simple example that would establish his point in a way that was nonthreatening

---

[64]Storr, *Freedom and Tradition*, 159-60.
[65]Storr, *Spiritual Liberty*, 51. Langford, *In Search of Foundations*, 267: "In a sense, the entire question of authority was removed by the solvent of belief in progress—what should be would be, as the guiding hand of providence worked its will."
[66]Storr, *Development*, 119.
[67]Storr, *Freedom and Tradition*, 162.
[68]Harris, *Vernon Faithfull Storr*, 43.

to those who had imbibed conservative assumptions. Alas, this often meant that the illustration he offered was eminently assailable, and thus one is left reading the same unconvincing reasoning repeated in book after book. For instance, a standard point Storr made was that the different parts of the Bible are not all equally inspired. In a late publication, he made explicit the real motivation for why it was important to make that point: "if we place all the parts of the Bible on the same level of inspiration, we are bound to accept all its statements, however, incredible as true."[69] Rather than tackle that underlying issue upfront, however, Storr just again and again observed that you know as a Bible reader that you wish to revisit more often emotionally charged places in the Scriptures such as the Gospel of John and the Psalms rather than more monotonous ones such as Leviticus and Chronicles. The problem with that argument is that a work of literature could be perfect in every way, and that would still be true. You might not wish one word of *Pride and Prejudice* to be altered and yet, of course, if you were going to choose to read excerpts you would not pick a passage that focused on giving necessary background information but rather one of heightened drama, mischievous wit, poetic lyricism, or piercing insight. Likewise, Storr's favorite way to prove that the Old Testament contains bad morality was to denounce Jael's assassination of Sisera. Repeatedly he asserted: "It was an act which violated all the laws of desert hospitality."[70] Well, it is not clear why Christians today should find something immoral because it defied the customs of an ancient culture. Then there was Storr's standard proof that the Bible contains errors. Here it is from his AEGM pamphlet, *Inspiration*: "In Genesis VI Noah is told to take into the ark two of every living thing; in VII he is told to take seven of the clean creatures and two of the unclean. These are statements which cannot be reconciled."[71] One critical theory is indeed that these two passages have been woven together from separate sources that are inconsistent. It is absurd, however, to maintain that they cannot be reconciled. In another publication, after giving this very animals-in-the-ark example, just two pages later Storr condemns proof-texting by observing, "A writer may say something at one time, which he later qualifies by saying something different."[72] It is

---

[69]Storr, *Freedom and Tradition*, 61.

[70]Storr, *Light*, 28.

[71]V. F. Storr, *Inspiration*, AEGM Pamphlets No. 11 (London: Hodder and Stoughton, 1924), 5.

[72]Storr, *The Bible*, 7, 9.

perfectly possible to reconcile those two passages on the theory that the author first set out the general rule that there needed to be two of every animal before qualifying it in regards to the specific case of the clean animals which needed more.

And while we are on the subject of proof-texting, it is unsurprisingly the case that Storr frequently condemned it as a habit that needed to be rooted out. Nevertheless, what really annoyed him was when people used a text to make a point that he rejected. Thus Storr was a chronic proof-texter himself, but he could not see what he was doing because he really did not think of proof-texting as taking a verse out of context so much as using it to bolster an erroneous claim. When he was using a passage to make a point he agreed with he would even go so far as to defy openly his own ostensible rule: "the passage has a meaning independently of its context."[73] A recurring proof-text for the fallibility of the Bible was 2 Corinthians 4:7: "we have this treasure in earthen vessels."[74] A beloved one for progressive revelation was John 4:28: "first the blade, then the ear, after that the full corn in the ear."[75] By far his favorite proof-text for that insight, however, was the account in Exodus 3 of the divine self-revelation to Moses in which the Almighty proclaims: "I AM THAT I AM." Here is one of numerous places where Storr expounded on that passage:

> The key to the whole development of the religion of Israel, and the core of its thought of God, are to be found in the revelation given to Moses at the burning bush (Exodus iii.) . . . Now "I am" is perhaps better translated "I will be" or "I will become." What underlies the divine name is the thought of a nature or character of God so rich and comprehensive that it could be only gradually unfolded. It is as if God said, "Trust Me, and you will learn what I will be to you." The name suggests progressive revelation . . .[76]

It is a rare Storr publication that does not include that proof-text somewhere. Storr was so pleased with it that it even made him insist, in contrast to his often-skeptical approach to the Pentateuch, that the burning bush incident was an historical event in the life of the historical Moses. And when he really had the bit between his teeth, Storr went so far as to assert that this text was

---

[73]Storr, *Light*, 108.
[74]For instance, V. F. Storr, "The Bible and Its Value," 84.
[75]Storr, *My Faith*, 51.
[76]Storr, *Missionary Genius*, 21–22.

so wonderful that it was itself proof of the historicity of the narrative: "Moses must have been a real figure. See him learning at the Burning Bush about the God of progressive revelation."[77]

Still, Storr was not just chipping around the edges, conceding an accounting error on Noah's ark here and a tedious genealogy there. He was quite ready to jettison core teaching of both Testaments. Moreover, it was not only the miracles of the Old Testament that had to go. To wit, 1 Samuel 15:2-3 records Samuel as prophesying a divine command to slaughter the Amalekites. That is indeed a troubling text. Storr's way to resolve the unsettled response it evokes in many modern readers was remarkably straightforward: "God never gave any such order. Samuel thought He did; but that is a very different matter."[78] The canon of Westminster was so enamored of the magic wand of progressive revelation that the unease that his own critical pronouncements might induce in some believers does not even seem to occur to him. He does not wonder how Samuel should then be distinguished from a false prophet, nor how ordinary Bible readers are to know the false prophecies from the true when reading their way through the Old Testament. Furthermore, Storr's surgery was so invasive that it is not even merely a matter of the New Testament provided the corrective to the Old. The progressive scheme in the Bible arguably reaches its final point with the apostle Paul, yet the president of the AEGM is no less willing to reject his teaching as false. Storr, as we have seen, was utterly sure that the substitutionary view of the atonement was wrong. He admitted that Paul taught it, but then went on to explain that Christians have been led astray on this point by accepting the apostle's teaching as true. To cap off this approach to the whole of the biblical witness, Storr explained that the reason why St. Paul himself had been led astray on this point was because he mistakenly thought that the Old Testament was true.[79]

This then raises the question: What was the difference, if any, between Storr and the AEGM, on the one hand, and the ecclesiastical Modernists, on the other? The answer is that there was no difference when it came to their approach to Scripture. Moreover, there was no difference on issues of doctrine and theological method in general between mainstream Modernists in the

---

[77]Storr, *Bible and the Modern Mind,* 45.
[78]Storr, *My Faith,* 51.
[79]Storr, *Problem,* 35, 41-42, 115-16, 139.

Church of England and the Liberal Evangelicals. The equivalent of the AEGM for Modernists was the Modern Churchmen's Union (MCU). Numerous key Liberal Evangelicals were also members of the MCU, including Storr himself, who rose in it to be a Vice-President.[80] In his publications, Storr frequently leaned on the works of other leading Modernists to commend his own views. For example, Hastings Rashdall has been described as "perhaps the greatest and most erudite exponent of English Modernism,"[81] and he is the theologian that Storr most draws upon to articulate his doctrine of the atonement. On the question of authority in Christian thought, Storr relied on the prominent Modernist, W. R. Inge.[82] On the theme of the Scriptures, he particularly endorsed *The Modern Use of the Bible* (1924), by a prominent leader on the Modernist side in the religious controversies in America, Harry Emerson Fosdick.[83] Or to come at it from the other direction, figures that are standardly just referred to as Broad Church or liberal leaders, Storr tended to relabel as Liberal Evangelicals. He does this, for instance, with Thomas Arnold.[84] Storr even identified the thought of the father of theological liberalism, Friedrich Schleiermacher, as representative of "the general attitude of the Liberal Evangelical."[85] E. W. Barnes's *The Rise of Christianity* (1947) scandalized even many mainstream Modernists with its thoroughgoing rejection of orthodox views on key Christian convictions. The in-house history of English Modernists goes to great lengths to quarantine Barnes as untypical of the movement and to disavow his "notorious," "infamous" book.[86] It is therefore striking that Barnes had not only been a member of the AEGM, but had even contributed a chapter to *Liberal Evangelicalism* and written for its pamphlet series, and was seen as a spokesperson for the "New Evangelical Party."[87]

It was commonly said—sometimes as a compliment—that there was no difference between the Liberal Evangelicals and the Modernists. Storr's response to this assertion included the observation that the MCU contained

---

[80]Harris, *Vernon Faithfull Storr*, 50.

[81]Stephenson, *Rise and Decline*, 59.

[82]Storr, *Spiritual Liberty*, 61.

[83]Storr, *Bible and the Modern Mind*, 35.

[84]Storr, *Freedom and Tradition*, 60.

[85]Storr, *Freedom and Tradition*, 169.

[86]Stephenson, *Rise and Decline*, 11, 168.

[87]"Future of the Church of England. Dr. Barnes on the Rise of New Evangelical Party," *The Times*, January 28, 1926, 16.

liberal Anglo-Catholics, but the AEGM did not. Otherwise, Storr conceded, the "question is not altogether easy to answer, because in broad aim and ideal the two Movements stand for the same thing."[88] Reading various stray comments of his, it seems Storr's real view was that Modernism was a more rarified, intellectual movement. The president of the AEGM saw Liberal Evangelicalism as combining Modernism's theological method, outlook, and conclusions with the pastoral and populist instincts and reach of the evangelical movement. There was a saying that there was no such thing as a Modernist kitchen maid. Storr's vision for Liberal Evangelicalism was that it would be the kind of Anglican identity that could also have a following below stairs.

Storr also held to other evangelical distinctives. In contrast to some Modernists who had shed a traditional view of sin as "the anachronistic survival of animal traits,"[89] Storr emphasized in his preaching God's abhorrence of sin. Even finding a way to criticize the spirit of the age, the canon of Westminster protested the fact that "to-day there is a widespread tendency to whittle away the meaning of the word 'sin.'"[90] Showing marked continuity with conservative evangelicals of the previous generation on this point, when Storr catalogued Britain's "modern national sins" the number one item on his list was drunkenness.[91] Furthermore, the solution to the grave problem of sin was the costly cross of Christ. In *My Faith*, the chapter on the atonement is tellingly titled, "The Cross." Storr was explicitly in line with the Bebbington Quadrilateral on crucicentrism: "The Cross is central in the creed of the Liberal Evangelical."[92] And again: "No fact is more central in Christianity than the fact of the Cross."[93] Storr's writings were peppered with phrases such as "a Cross stands at the centre of life" and "a Cross stands in God's heart."[94] His solidarity with conservative evangelicalism is strongest at this point: "Liberal Evangelicalism has a very definite theology and a definite Gospel to preach. It is the old Gospel of redemption through the Cross and

---

[88]Storr, *Freedom and Tradition*, 111.
[89]Ramsey, *From Gore to Temple*, 157.
[90]Storr, *Problem*, 165. This point is also made in Wellings, *Evangelicals Embattled*, 257.
[91]Storr, *Prophets*, 15.
[92]Storr, *Freedom and Tradition*, 172.
[93]Storr, *Problem*, 9.
[94]Vernon F. Storr, *The Old Testament Lessons of the New Lectionary: Sermon Outlines* (London: SPCK, 1925), 42, 116.

sanctification through the Holy Spirit. It is fundamentally of the same texture as the older Evangelicalism."[95]

Relatedly, reflecting the Bebbington Quadrilateral's activism, Storr was emphatic that all believers are called to evangelize. He was particularly passionate about the necessity of foreign missions: "The heathen have a right to know about Christ, and it is our duty to tell them. . . . Are we refusing to obey our Lord's last command to go and preach the Gospel in all the world?"[96] Storr had a passion for world evangelization: "Christ says . . . I can consecrate this rising life in India, China, Africa. They are mine."[97] A published sermon of Storr's ends with a direct appeal in the classic evangelistic manner: "There are only two roads out of the valley of decision. Which road are you and I going to take?"[98] Conversionism, crucicentrism, and activism are all apparent in the life and thought of this canon of Westminster.

It is the one other marker in the Bebbington Quadrilateral, biblicism, that is largely lacking. There are times when Storr will proclaim the New Testament as an authoritative standard, especially when he has in mind explaining why Anglo-Catholic practices are unwarranted. More often, however, the Bible is noticeable by its absence in his discussions of both evangelicalism and authority. Storr's own definition of evangelicalism listed both its "predominant features" and its main articles of faith, but the Scriptures did not make either list.[99] Storr once pointedly observed that the Christian faith is defined in the Apostles' Creed, "but it says not one word about the Bible."[100] He claimed that one needed to have a construal of the faith that allowed it to keep standing even if and when the Bible should fall.[101] At times, Storr seems to have deliberately sought to replace Scripture with some other authority in certain common theological phrases. Where a conservative evangelical might have spoken of interpreting something in the light of Scripture, Storr's version was "in the light of our moral consciousness."[102] Most pointedly, he defied

---

[95]Storr, *Spiritual Liberty*, 119.
[96]Storr, *Prophets*, 38-39.
[97]Storr, *Missionary Genius*, 191.
[98]V. F. Storr, "The Valley of Decision," in *Lenten Sermons by Representative Preachers*, ed. Frederick J. North (New York: Doubleday, Doran, 1928), 179-90 (187).
[99]Storr, *Freedom and Tradition*, 18-27. This point is also made in Randall, *Evangelical Experiences*, 62.
[100]Storr, *Inspiration of the Bible*, 12.
[101]Storr, *Development*, 163.
[102]Storr, *Problem*, 103.

the Reformers' conviction that the Scriptures are the regulative principle: "Liberal Evangelicalism finds its ultimate ground of authority in the Mind and Spirit of Christ. Here is its regulative principle."[103]

As a young man, Storr himself had tried the traditional views of Scripture and some other doctrines and found them wanting. Could a viable Anglican faith be reconstructed on a different basis? He delayed his ordination until he had first worked through this time of uncertainty and unsettlement.[104] Having come out the other side with a confident, broader faith, Storr's ministry had foremost in mind people trying to make that same journey. He frequently described his target audience: "thousands to-day are perplexed over this very matter. Brought up in an older, traditional view of the Bible, they are dimly aware that such a view is untenable in the light of modern knowledge."[105] Storr believed that conservative views were indefensible and when that realization dawned on believers, they would be in danger of giving up on the faith altogether. In a speech in 1928, he warned that without a new view of the Bible "shipwreck was likely to be made of life and faith" for many.[106] People in such peril often found Storr's way the way forward. The perplexed in faith frequently sought him out and found him to be a steadying counselor. Longing to break the cycle of believers needing to unlearn false views, Storr also spoke of the importance of teaching children right from the start to understand that there are difficulties in the Bible.[107]

Especially in the first half of his ministry, Storr sanguinely assumed that adopting a critical view of the Bible would have negligible impact on people's ability to continue to receive spiritual comfort and edification from the Scriptures. Indeed, he often spoke as if biblical criticism was a gain in this area, promising, for instance, that people "will find that modern study of the Bible has made the Book live as it never lived before."[108] Storr was raised in a culture in which reading the Bible was assumed as a given.[109] His goal was to teach people a way to read it that was less vexing. He was very aware that many

---

[103]Storr, Freedom and Tradition, 172.

[104]Harris, Vernon Faithfull Storr, 9.

[105]Storr, Bible and the Modern Mind, 5.

[106]"Religion and Modern Thought. Coventry Conference Discussion," Midland Daily Telegraph, May 9, 1928, 4.

[107]Storr, Prophets, 76.

[108]Storr, Inspiration of the Bible, 4.

[109]Timothy Larsen, A People of One Book: The Bible and the Victorians (Oxford: Oxford University Press, 2011).

Christians were not reading the Bible regularly at all anymore, but he assumed that was just because they had been taught a traditional view of Scripture that had scared them away by the perplexities it generated. He did his best by his lights to help the cause by being an active member of the Bible Reading Fellowship.[110] Nevertheless, Storr never seemed to grasp that his doctrine of Scripture undercut ordinary people's motivation to read the Bible in a comprehensive way. Why should someone rise early in the morning to read a passage that is admittedly uninspired, offensive, and erroneous? Storr did not even defend the canon, conceding that some parts of the Bible are less edifying than portions of other documents that are not identified as Scripture.[111] In the AEGM publication, *The Inner Life*, M. I. Rogers candidly suggested that the best way to continue to inculcate the habit of the devotional reading of the Scriptures would be to create "An Expurgated Bible."[112] Drawing on the psychological relief that he found in abandoning the conservative view, Storr's own attempted solution was to imagine that critical insights were themselves devotional ones. The payoff for reading Isaiah 35, for instance, was given as follows: "It illustrates this important point that the *details* of the pictures must not always be pressed."[113] His default insight to be gained from all the passages deemed problematic was: "The humanness of the Bible will come home to us in this way very vividly."[114] In other words, the truth that we extract from some parts of the Bible is simply that the Bible is not always truthful. This is, to evoke a biblical analogy that Storr himself used for an opposite-facing purpose, to ask for bread and be given a stone. When the revised lectionary was introduced in 1924, Storr agreed to provide a model sermon from its Old Testament reading for every Sunday of the year. He deserves full marks for taking on this much-needed task. Nevertheless, one of these sermons is titled, "Progressive Revelation," and rather than harvesting anything spiritually beneficial from the text it simply models how to reject a text.[115] Again, for someone who had once held the conservative view and then abandoned it, that might have felt like a spiritually comforting sermon. What it did not offer, however, was a rationale for why those who

---

[110]Harris, *Vernon Faithfull Storr*, 76.

[111]Storr, *Bible and the Modern Mind*, 11.

[112]M. I. Rogers, "The Devotional Use of the Bible," in *The Inner Life: Essays in Liberal Evangelicalism*, ed. T. Guy Rogers (London: Hodder and Stoughton, 1925), 237-65 (here 258).

[113]Storr, *Prophets*, 82.

[114]Storr, *Bible and the Modern Mind*, 57.

[115]Storr, *The Old Testament Lessons of the New Lectionary*, 92.

had been raised with the critical view from the start should bother to continue to read such passages as part of their devotional life.

Storr only belatedly grasped the extent to which, for many evangelicals, his commended, critical view of the Bible was actually more vexing, perplexing, and unsettling than the one he had shed. He was breezily dismissive of such concerns for most of his ministry, but by his final years he started to take them more seriously and to try to bend his rhetoric to accommodate them. In 1938, Storr off-handedly conceded in regards to the Bible, "That will always rightly remain its chief characteristic, that it is the 'Word of God.'"[116] The scare quotes around "Word of God" betray that he is really echoing other people's terminology. In 1913, he had identified as the very view that needed to be abandoned "the belief in the Bible as the authoritative word of God."[117] I suppose those two statements are technically reconcilable if one can imagine the Word of God *not* being authoritative. Even that explanation will not do, however, as the mid-life Storr agreed that the Bible was still authoritative, just not because of a supposed divine origin: "It is authoritative because of the religious and spiritual appeal which it makes to our minds and wills and consciences."[118] If, however, being the Word of God is the Bible's "chief characteristic," why did Storr write an entire pamphlet titled, *The Bible: What It Is and What It Is Not* and never mention that fact? Under the section, "What the Bible is," he lists two points: *It is a national literature* and *It is a selected literature*.[119] If that seems to have been written merely as a corrective to the conservative perspective, less tendentious was his definition in his chapter, "The Bible and Its Value," in *Liberal Evangelicalism*: "The Bible is the record of God's self-revelation to mankind."[120] Once again, if being the Word of God is the Bible's chief characteristic, this manifesto statement on the nature of the Scriptures and their value neglected to mention it altogether.

This chapter has taken the obvious alternative to Liberal Evangelicalism to be conservative evangelicalism. That, however, was not the binary that Storr preferred. He liked to imagine the difference in chronological terms: he was rejecting "the older Evangelicalism" and championing today's

---

[116]Vernon F. Storr, ed., *The English Bible: Essays by Various Writers* (London: Methuen, 1938), vii.
[117]Storr, *Development*, 69.
[118]Storr, *Spiritual Liberty*, 53-54.
[119]Storr, *The Bible*, 9-12.
[120]Storr, "The Bible and Its Value," 80.

Evangelicalism.[121] As he saw it, the goal of his writings was to contrast "the new Evangelicalism with the old."[122] Storr put himself forward as "a representative of the attitude of the younger Evangelicals towards Bible teaching, and to life generally."[123] Even in the last year of his life—by which time he was seventy-one years old—Storr was still confidently presenting himself as a spokesperson for the views of "our younger people."[124] By contrast, in his mind, conservative evangelicals were *ipso facto* "the older-fashioned folk."[125] The irony, of course, was that, towards the end of his life, the general perception was increasingly becoming the reverse. Modernism was seen as moribund and old-fashioned. The new, exciting figures were orthodox critics of Modernism such as Karl Barth and C. S. Lewis.[126] Liberal Evangelicalism and the AEGM were increasingly seen as a quaint survival from the twenties—the ecclesiastical equivalent of dancing the Charleston.[127] The reality was that the Young Turks in the Evangelical movement were conservatives. They found their leader in John Stott. Assuming the mantel of speaking for the younger generation, Stott refounded the Eclectic Society, a gathering of Evangelical Anglican clergymen which stipulated that members had to be under the age of forty.[128] The Liberal Evangelicals have been largely forgotten because the winners wrote them out of the narrative of the movement.[129] Moreover, the winners were so successful that the word *evangelical* came to be shorthand for conservative evangelicalism. As Storr sagely observed in 1940: "It is impossible to say what the historian of the future will select as of real importance in the age in which we are living."[130] In my *Biographical Dictionary of Evangelicals*, the very next entry after Vernon Storr is John Stott. That was not the kind of progress which the Liberal Evangelicals had envisioned.

---

[121]Storr, *Spiritual Liberty*, 33.

[122]Storr, *Development*, 73.

[123]Oxoniensis, "The Teaching of the Bible. Evangelical View," 5.

[124]Storr, *Freedom and Tradition*, 175.

[125]Storr, *Spiritual Liberty*, 120.

[126]Stephenson, *Rise and Decline*, 181.

[127]Ramsey, *From Gore to Temple*, 155-56.

[128]Andrew Atherstone, "The Keele Congress of 1967: A Paradigm Shift in Anglican Evangelical Attitudes," *Journal of Anglican Studies* 9, no. 2 (2011), 175-97 (182).

[129]Wellings, *Evangelicals Embattled*, 2.

[130]Storr, *Freedom and Tradition*, 154.

9

"The Only Way to Stop a Mob"

Francis Grimké's Biblical Case for Lynching Resistance

Malcolm Foley

INTRODUCTION: OF GRIMKÉ AND HIS BIBLE

Perhaps the greatest advantage of David Bebbington's evangelicalism Quadrilateral is its versatility. The four characteristics of evangelicalism are not restricted only to those who self-identify with the movement. Rather, a consideration of these tendencies which tend to cohere together leads one to also consider Christian believers who, though they may not self-identify as evangelicals, still fit the mold. Black American Christians in the late-nineteenth and early twentieth century fit such a category.

Black American Christians rarely referred to themselves as evangelicals, and when they did, it was usually a denominational statement, referring to their identity as Baptists or Methodists. Perhaps one of the primary reasons for this may have been the fact that the term had political freight during that period, as it does now. As a response, Mary Beth Mathews deftly argues that "African Americans created their own traditionalist conservative evangelicalism."[1]

---

[1] Mary Beth Swetnam Mathews, *Doctrine and Race: African American Evangelicals and Fundamentalism Between the Wars* (Tuscaloosa: The University of Alabama Press, 2017), 2.

Mathews rather convincingly argues in her book that on many theological points, African American evangelicals, as she names them, and fundamentalists were in complete agreement. When it came to the definition of the gospel, the centrality of the Scriptures, and the divinity of Christ, there was no disagreement. Yet stark rifts appeared when Black Christians advocated and agitated for racial justice. This chapter explains and narrates the nuances of one such rift.

The four characteristics of biblicism, crucicentrism, activism, and conversionism are best understood not as separate characteristics but mutually informing ones. Thus, to consider evangelical activism apart from biblicism is to misunderstand both. But during the course of American history, that relationship has often been negotiated with race at the table. Part of the racialization of evangelicalism included the strict, often unspoken delineation of what was considered to be worthy activism. Such a phenomenon is brought front and center when one encounters the most publicly violent instantiation of White supremacy perhaps in the whole of North American church history: lynching. In a period when hundreds of Black men, women, and teenagers were burned alive, hanged, shot to pieces, or otherwise brutally killed by mobs, many White churches were silent, complicit, or in support of such events—some claimed, for instance, that Black men raped White women, and thus such brutal retribution was understandable, even necessary. What is perhaps most disconcerting about this period is that Black Protestants knew of and were incensed by this silence. Particularly, from roughly 1890 to 1919, Black Christians battled lynching in diverse ways founded in the Scriptures, but their cries fell upon deaf ears. While that may have been the case in the late nineteenth and early twentieth century, it need not be so now.

One pastor whose sermons must be considered when one considers Black Christian lynching resistance must be Francis Grimké. On November 4, 1850, Francis James Grimké was born to the enslaved Nancy Weston and the slaveholder Henry Grimké. Henry, shortly before his death, gave Nancy and her children to his son, E. Montague, with the intention that he would allow the family to continue to be free under Montague's oversight. It became clear, however, that this was not Montague's intention. Initially Montague Grimké allowed Nancy and her sons (Archibald, Francis, and John) to live in the free Black section of Charleston, but when he married, he attempted to enslave the family again, which, in Francis's words, "led to some complications."[2] Even as a young boy, Francis fled such injustice, joining the Confederate Army as a valet, where he served for two years. After the war, he went to Lincoln University, graduating as valedictorian of his class in 1870, and after starting law school at Howard, changed his mind and considered seminary. After graduating from Princeton Theological Seminary, he went directly to his pastorate at 15th Street Presbyterian Church with the approval and recommendation of A. A. Hodge, where he spent the majority of the next fifty years. During that pastorate, he developed friendships and correspondence with both Booker T. Washington and W. E. B. Du Bois as well as other prominent political and religious figures. His lectures, sermons, and addresses were printed and distributed widely, and his honorary Doctor of Divinity from Lincoln University that he received in 1888 was meant to acknowledge that. Over the course of his career, however, the nation shifted, and his tone and content shifted as well. Carter Woodson summarized the phenomenon well in his introduction to Grimké's works:

> During the beginning of his career, Grimké had looked forward to lecturing and addressing White churches and conferences with respect to the needs of the Negro. Prejudice, however, rapidly reduced the number of these contacts except in cases involving the compromise of one's manhood . . . the large majority of the Presbyterian and other clergy never welcomed Dr. Grimké and even avoided him, contending that he was too bitter and that his leadership was doing the Negro much harm.[3]

The era of lynching, particularly, put weight on Grimké's networks: when he spoke forthrightly about lynching's causes and remedies, he and others who dispelled prominent myths went unfortunately unheeded. The fact that the text often referred to as the starting point for histories of lynching, Arthur Raper's *Tragedy of Lynching* (1933), still suggested that African Americans could mitigate lynching by revealing their own character and by working together with White allies reveals that many were unaware of the frustration precipitated by the fact that neither character nor cooperation extinguished the lynching pyre. That frustration became clear in the works of Francis Grimké.

---

[2]Francis James Grimké, *The Works of Francis J. Grimké*, ed. Carter G. Woodson, vol. 1 (Washington, DC: Associated Publishers, 1942), viii.
[3]Grimké, *Works*, 1:xvii.

For a pastor like Grimké who, while he never referred to himself as an evangelical, vocally espoused every point of the Bebbington Quadrilateral, the problem with an American Christianity that allowed lynching to continue was that it was a Christianity that was not evangelical enough. It did not believe its Bible; it did not trust in the cross of its Christ; it did not do the deeds of its Christ; and it did not grasp the extent of the Holy Spirit's work in conversion. In his sermons from 1898 to 1919, when he approached the Scriptures, he did so with application in mind: what did these Scriptures reveal about God, and what guidance did they offer for how God's people ought to conduct themselves? This chapter traces the trajectory of twenty years of Francis Grimké's preaching with a particular focus on the ways in which he marshalled Scripture to resist lynching. Even more specifically, analysis of two sermon series in 1898 and 1899 take up the bulk of this chapter and provide the framework for understanding the two later sermons that exemplify where Grimké ends up after seeing two decades of seemingly unmitigated racial violence. One could not preach the gospel of Jesus Christ apart from the Scriptures, and for Grimké, the preaching of the gospel necessitated resistance to lynching. The shape of that resistance, however, changed as lynching intensified and as time marched on. This story began in the spring of 1898 with a response to the race riots in Wilmington, North Carolina.

1898: VIOLENCE? MAYBE.

Beginning on November 20, 1898, Grimké preached a set of sermons that were eventually circulated as pamphlets because of their addressing of the Negro Problem.[4] Henry James Ferry, in his biography of Grimké, rightfully

---

[4]The dating of this particular sermon series is both extremely important and extremely frustrating, as, unfortunately due to what are most likely publishing errors, three different dates for these sermons have circulated. The table of contents of Carter Woodson's collection of Francis Grimké's works states that this sermon series was given in 1909. Once one turns to the texts themselves, the footnote clearly states that they were delivered in November of 1900. One must then conclude that one of the two is a clear typo. But Henry J. Ferry's dissertation, still the most comprehensive biography of Grimké, has a still different claim: 1898. Howard University's copy of a pamphlet of one of these sermons has no listed date. At least two of the aforementioned dates are wrong, but which? In searching within the texts, one clue seems to tip the scales. Grimké mentioned race riots in Wilmington, North Carolina, "where Negroes were terrorized, driven from their homes, shot down, murdered, their property destroyed" (Grimké, *Works*, 1:246). He prefaced this statement, however, by saying, "And now in the face of the awful, the unspeakable crimes, etc." This prefacing suggests that the Wilmington race riots/mass lynchings would be in the immediate memory of his hearers and such events took place on November 10, 1898. It is entirely reasonable to then argue

places this sermon in an ongoing narrative about Grimké's conversion from accommodation to agitation, but it also needs to be placed in another context: Grimké's particular responses to unsettling racial violence. These four sermons present as general sermons of uplift: the first two argue that the press, the (White) pulpit, and political parties have been profoundly unhelpful in assisting Black people, while the last two sermons focus on where hope can be found, ultimately in God and in prayer. But they are not general. Their placement in time ten days after the Wilmington race riots and a week after Rev. Dr Peyton H. Hoge preached defending that "carnival of death," as Grimké grimly called them, is not coincidental. Rather, these sermmons are essential in understanding Grimké's preaching career as well as his deeper convictions in times of crisis. The sermons themselves and their biblical foundations merit close consideration.

The first of these sermons, circulating under the title "Discouragements: Hostility of the Press, Silence and Cowardice of the Pulpit," had as its central text the same text that Grimké would preach from for the coming month: Psalm 27:14, "Wait on the Lord; be of good courage, and he shall strengthen thine heart." Such a verse could very easily lead the reader/hearer to assume that this would be a politically quietist sermon. The sermon was not.[5]

Grimké began by outlining the despair of Elijah as described in 1 Kings 19. He beautifully summarized the story, leading the congregation to consider the depths of the prophet's despondency as he fled from Jezebel and questioned whether his calling was sure and whether he would live another day. Grimké then backtracked chronologically to Moses in Numbers 11, crying out to God in the midst of a people who continued to murmur and complain in the wilderness. Moses' prayer was that the LORD might kill him, so deep was his despair. David then completes the Biblical examples, with Grimké quoting Psalm 42, in which David speaks of his soul as "cast down." All of these biblical examples are marshalled toward one goal: to describe the emotional life of Black people in America. Grimké explained: "I have touched

---

that, ten days after the events in Wilmington, Grimké preached about them. The other sermons considered throughout this chapter are direct responses to current events and that context is supremely important in order to understand Grimké's responses to lynching. Also, that same sermon refers to experiencing "thirty-three years of freedom" post-Emancipation, easily dating from 1865 to 1898. All clues point to 1898 as an authoritative dating for this sermon series.
[5]Grimké, *Works*, 1:234.

upon this subject this morning because as a people, I am afraid, there is danger, in view of the terrible ordeal through which we are now passing, and have been passing for some time, of losing heart; of coming to feel as Elijah did, It is enough: there is no use of continuing the struggle."

An honest assessment of the situation of Black people in the United States at that time gave ample reason for despair. Grimké outlined the progression of Black disenfranchisement post-Reconstruction saying, "The sentiment everywhere is: This is a white man's government. And that means not only that the whites shall rule, but that the Negro shall have nothing whatever to do with governmental affairs."[6] Not only was there widespread political disenfranchisement, but Black Americans actually justified such disenfranchisement. Such people, Grimké said, were traitors to their race. Added to internal corruption were the external discouragements of northern White apathy, a hostile press, and silent White pulpits. It is imperative at this point to draw Grimké's distinction starkly: his argument was not that the Christian pulpit is silent. It was that the White pulpit was silent. Grimké's frustration with this state of affairs was clear, even as he couched it in rhetoric: "Whether this [silence] is the result of cowardice . . . or whether it is because they see nothing to condemn, think the Negro is receiving just what he deserves; or whether it is the result of indifference, I do not know. I simply note the fact. This much may be said, however, they are not silent on other matters."[7] Many *Well!* things made the list of concerns for White pulpits, including liquor, gambling, desecration of the Sabbath, the Armenian genocide, the lottery, and polygamy in Utah. Yet the affirmation of Black life was absent. Grimké indicted the North and the South, claiming that if they were truly as indebted to their Bible as they claimed, they would decry racial violence. Instead, Grimké hoped that in the future, the White pulpit would be "a living ministry—a ministry endued with power from on high, baptized with the Holy Spirit," suggesting, of course, that their current ministry enjoyed no such baptism.[8]

Francis Grimké saved the most damning indictment for those who defended racial violence. After outlining the words of Peyton H. Hoge, who just a week prior to this first sermon had affirmed White rioters and murderers as "gallant" for mercilessly rampaging through Black communities,

---

[6]Grimké, *Works*, 1:237-38.
[7]Grimké, *Works*, 1:240.
[8]Grimké, *Works*, 1:243.

Grimké launched into judgment: "It is just such whited sepulchers, such hypocrites in the pulpit, that have always stood in the way of progress, and that have brought the religion of Christ into contempt."[9] What followed was an extensive quotation of Jesus' judgment of the Pharisees from Matthew 23, ending with "Ye serpents, ye generations of vipers, how can ye escape the damnation of hell?" Lest he be misinterpreted, he continued: "If this damnation is reserved for any one, or any class of men, it certainly is for men of this stripe,—men who dare to stand up in the pulpit, and in the sacred name of the holy religion of Jesus, commend such brutality, such inhuman conduct."[10] Grimké could not be clearer. The lyncher and his apologist are both hell-bound, and Grimké saw those words not as his own, but as the words of Christ.

The assault on lynching continued the following Sunday, when Grimké attacked the government for its failure to protect Black life. Proceeding from the themes of the same Psalm, Grimké introduced his sermon with an overview of American history up to 1898, with a particular focus on the plight of Black Americans and the numerous times when hopes were raised and subsequently dashed, culminating in the "third chapter in our history," following the chapter of slavery and the chapter of Reconstruction. Grimké saw himself in a chapter of American history punctuated by lynching and disenfranchisement. Yet he remained hopeful, although he was clear that his hope was neither in "national interposition" nor in either of the "great political parties."[11] It is at this point in the sermon, however, when Grimké began to make tantalizing hints toward his view of violence.

After outlining the ways in which the government had failed, Grimké also expressed that there was not "much ground of hope from an appeal to force."[12] But this was not because of a moral opposition to violence. Rather, his discomfort with violence stemmed from the fact that he was sure that Black people would lose such a war. Yet even that fact did not completely stop the conversation. What followed in the sermon was not an account of failed military uprisings, but rather accounts of other historical circumstances in which violence appeared to be necessary to enact change, primarily the French

---

[9]Grimké, *Works*, 1:246.
[10]Grimké, *Works*, 1:247.
[11]Grimké, *Works*, 1:251-52.
[12]Grimké, *Works*, 1:252.

Revolution and the revolt of John Brown, whom Grimké called "that apostle of force." This then led Grimké to a rather cryptic, yet bracing declaration:

> I am not counseling violence: I am not saying that it is a wise thing for the Negro to resort to violence; but I am saying that sometimes violence is the means which God uses to arouse the sleeping conscience, and pierce the rhinoceros hide of indifference. I trust that it may not be necessary, but if it must come, then, I for one say, let it come, and the sooner it comes the better. The Negro will not be responsible for it.[13]

Grimké attempted to have it both ways, so to speak: to denounce preemptive and retributive violence while also not closing the door to it. The richness of this particular statement is made clearer when one considers Grimké's tradition of preaching on racial violence, but it is apparent that for him, while violence was not the ideal, it was often effective. Moreover, if violence particularly against the White mob were the way in which God wished to save Black people, Grimké would affirm it.

But this was not the substance of Grimké's true hope. That was to be found in the final sermon of this particular series, given on December 11 of that year, which circulated under the title, "God and Prayer as Factors in the Struggle." Grimké would argue in this sermon that God and prayer were actually the decisive factors in the struggle for Black freedom. But the question remained of precisely how that was true. Grimké's exegesis of Scripture and his theological tradition took center stage in this sermon.

First, in hearkening back to the central verse of this sermon series, Psalm 27:14, Grimké asserted that "the ground of hope . . . is in the fact that God is."[14] This God, however, was not a generic deity for Grimké. Rather, this was the faithful God of Abraham, Isaac, and Jacob who had freed the Israelites from the oppressive hand of Pharaoh. Grimké relayed the rhapsody of divine attributes, affirming God's eternity, omniscience, omnipotence, justice, and sovereignty. But this hymnic description was not flowery for the sake of rhetoric. Its purpose was to affirm the character of God: that he is righteous. In the midst of hopelessness, Grimké reminded his congregation that "there is a Just One, who never slumbers nor sleeps, and who is not indifferent to what is going on," even though White pulpits might be. Hope was ultimately

---

[13]Grimké, *Works*, 1:254.
[14]Grimké, *Works*, 1:274.

found in the fact that "yes, God is, and because he is, there is hope for the oppressed Negro in this land."[15] God's presence paired with the people's prayer was to be the way forward.

After the litany of praise to a present and just God, Grimké moved to what the response of the Christian church ought to be: prayer. But for what must the church pray? First, it was important for Grimké to outline what the church was not to pray for: self-effacement. The Black Christian was not to pray for their own political submission to oppression. Instead, they were to pray

> that God would help us by his grace to be true men and women; that He would put deep into our souls a divine unrest, a holy ambition to be something, and to make something of ourselves; that He would kindle in our heart of hearts a desire for the things that are true, and just, and pure and lovely and of good report; that he would help us all to come in the unity of the faith and of the knowledge of the Son of God, unto a perfect man, unto the measure of the stature of the fullness of Christ.[16]

Without explicit citation, Grimké quoted directly from Philippians 4 and Ephesians 4 to establish that the prayer was a prayer for boldness in the face of persecution. It was a prayer for moral uplift, but it was also a prayer for holy protest. It was a prayer that ultimately culminated not in the hope for judgment of the oppressor but rather the hope that God would have mercy on the oppressor. When Grimké ended this particular sermon, he summarized his intentions in three points:

> (1). To let the White people know that we are conscious of what our rights are, and that we mean to have them.

> (2). The hope of helping to awaken the sleeping conscience of the American people to the wrongs that we are suffering.

> And (3) to inspire those of our own people, who may be disposed to become despondent, with hope and with renewed determination to keep up the struggle.[17]

The events that would follow in American history would call into question the ultimate effectiveness of these sermons along the lines of those three objectives. Grimké would sound this horn often, but it would fall on many

---

[15]Grimké, *Works*, 1:276.
[16]Grimké, *Works*, 1:282.
[17]Grimké, *Works*, 1:290.

deaf ears. The following year, one of the most gruesome spectacle lynchings in American history took place, and Grimké was once again driven to the pulpit to address the suffering of his people.

1899: RESISTANCE TO SPECTACLE: TWO SERMONS ON LYNCHING'S CAUSES

In April of 1899, Sam Hose requested time off from his employer, Alfred Cranford. Much can be said about that employer-employee relationship, but what is relevant here is that Cranford interpreted such a request as an insult to his sensibilities. The audacity of a Black man making such a request was apparently too much to bear. In an ensuing argument, Cranford aimed a revolver at Hose, and Hose, axe in hand, threw it and killed Cranford. After fleeing, rumors began to spread that Hose also raped Cranford's wife and assaulted her baby. The powder keg of lynching was lit.

The story ended with a mob finding Hose, chaining him to a tree, dousing him in kerosene, and burning him alive. This particular lynching got nationwide attention, including the attention of the Afro-American National Council, which had been founded the previous year as the first nationwide civil rights organization in the US. When this body heard of Hose's lynching, they responded by designating June 2 as a day of prayer and fasting for the "race problem," a problem that would be later defined by Grimké in his own way. But in conjunction with that, another suggestion was made: that the following Lord's day was to be a day of preaching particularly on lynching. That suggestion was not publicized but it was obeyed by Francis Grimké, and on June 4, 1899, he entered his pulpit with Acts 7:57-58 as his text: "Then they cried with a loud voice, and stopped their ears, and ran upon him with one accord, and cast him out of the city, and stoned him."[18] Over the course of the next month, Grimké would deliver three sermons on lynching, systematically dismantling racist and, in Grimké's eyes, un-Christian narratives.

The first of these sermons focused on lynching's causes in the South, which he summarized as race hatred and a widespread lack of civilization among White Southerners. Sprinkling the sermon with stories of Southern street fights, Grimké drew a picture of the South as exceedingly violent and emotionally sensitive. The worst example of this savagery, however, was the fact

---

[18]Grimké, *Works*, 1:291-92.

that the South treated lynching festively. Grimké quoted newspaper accounts of lynching where the writers would make a point of describing the approving faces, "quiet dignity," and "perfect order" of lynching observers. The juxta-position of the calm, sober observer and the smoldering body of a Black man was rhetorically presented in this June 4 sermon in all of its absurdity. Framed in this way, Grimké invited his hearers to consider whether true humanity included sitting approvingly in the presence of brutality.

While the South's violence exemplified its barbarity to Grimké, the par-ticular focus of the violence was a manifestation of its race hatred. Grimké saw and felt that lynching had taken on a racial dimension. Historian Karlos Hill has recently outlined the racialization of lynching: "by the mid to late 1880s, lynching was a racialized phenomenon in which Blacks were the primary targets of white lynch mob violence."[19] It must be remembered that in the history of lynching, this is the decade in which lynching shifts from a variegated phenomenon that could be understood as an act of popular justice, or as Michael Pfeifer has said, "rough justice" to a racialized phenomenon largely reducible to domestic terror.[20] Grimké, though he did not have access to national statistics, sensed this phenomenon, as did Ida B. Wells before him. This sense that lynching was a racialized phenomenon was largely made plausible by the fact that Grimké saw that anti-Black racism was a deeply entrenched and resilient phenomenon. In describing race hatred as one of the causes of lynching, he preached:

> I know we hear a great deal of the love of the Southern whites for the Negro, and if we are to believe what some of our colored leaders say, the Southern white man is really the best friend that the Negro has. That the Southern white man . . . feels kindly towards him may be true, it is true in a sense, i.e. provided he keeps in his place.[21]

In this quote, one finds that Grimké operated with a plausibility structure different from many of his peers. Grimké agreed with earlier anti-lynching advocates, of which Ida B. Wells is representative and exemplary, that the

---

[19]Karlos K. Hill, *Beyond the Rope: The Impact of Lynching on Black Culture and Memory* (New York: Cambridge University Press, 2016), 37.

[20]For more on this particular argument and the ways in which lynching was routinized into the criminal justice system, see Michael J. Pfeifer, *Rough Justice: Lynching and American Society, 1874–1947* (Urbana: University of Illinois Press, 2006).

[21]Grimké, *Works*, 1:298.

ones inciting the mobs were the ones writing the reports. Thus, Southern apologists were generally not to be trusted at face value because their reasoning could easily be understood to be self-justification. Instead, Grimké looked to the effects of their actions, finding that legislative power had been mobilized to deny Black equality in many ways: outlawing intermarriage, segregating train cars, segregating waiting rooms, segregating churches, and exclusion from the ballot box being many of the ways named in this particular sermon.[22] This weaponization of legislation against Black communities, compounded with unjust sentencing of Black people convicted of crimes when compared to White people convicted of similar crimes and the frequency of lynching, painted a dismal view of the American South, and the description of northern silence painted a dismal view of the nation as a whole.

Notably, however, there was only one scriptural citation in the whole sermon besides the theme text, and it is a mashup of John 15:13 and Romans 5:8, quoted as though they are back to back: "Greater love hath no man than this, that a man lay down his life for his friend, but God commendeth his love to us, in that while we were sinners, Christ died for us." Rhetorically, Grimké produced this Biblical mashup in order to affirm Black patriotism and to bring attention to the apparent absurdity of Black people dying for a country that did not accept or fight for them. For Grimké, it was a situation that shed light on the absurdity of Christ dying for sinners, and within this single example, the reader of the written sermon and hearer of the spoken one were drawn into a world of thought and experience where Biblical narratives found nineteenth and twentieth century parallels. The Bible, then, was not merely a historical account of the past people of God. It was also an account of the current lives of the people of God. While Black people struggled under the yoke of the uncivilized and racially prejudiced South, there were many who claimed that their struggle was their own fault. The prevalence of this particular view merited a sermon on its own.

The second sermon focused on the most common accusation that accompanied lynchings, the oft-mentioned "usual crime": that Black men were rapists, thus lynching was necessary. Using the same argumentation that Ida B. Wells used in the previous decade, Grimké debunked that myth with sociological data. Grimké explicitly discussed the alleged crimes and, specifically,

---

[22]Grimké, *Works*, 1:299.

the narratives that surrounded assertions of Black criminality, knowing and naming the fact that the oft-repeated remedy to lynching was "for the Negro to behave himself, to stop committing such terrible crimes."[23] Because this was the most commonly touted reasoning for the violence (namely that Black people, specifically men, are sexually insatiable beasts and therefore ought to behave themselves so that they won't get brutally executed) and also probably because his other sermons on character could be construed to be making the same argument, it is fitting that Grimké would devote a sermon to this topic.

He proceeded upon the path of articulating Black criminality carefully. First, he acknowledged that Black criminals do exist, and they do exist in an "unusually large percentage." What he denied was the link between that statistical fact and the anthropological claim that "the Negro is by nature more criminally inclined than other races."[24] As a matter of fact, the opposite impulse is apparently present. Among "the better elements of the race," Grimké argued that there was a feeling of pride that was wounded when others commit crimes, stemming from a desire to see other members of the race succeed and conduct themselves well.[25] Through these words, Grimké hoped to in some way combat the essentialization of racial categories, arguing that there are African Americans, like White people or any other group of people, who commit crimes. The sins of those individuals ought not be placed upon their neighbors purely because they share a skin hue. Instead, Grimké argued, Black people, as a collective, hated crime just as much as anyone else. From here, he addressed the primary accusation from White communities: the Black man is lynched because he is a brute.

Such a picture is thrust into harsh color when one considers that the common accusation used to incite lynching is that of raping a White woman. Grimké began by affirming an account of "true womanhood": "I know of nothing more sacred than the virtue of a woman, whether she be white or Black. Every possible safeguard ought to be thrown around her. All that the law can do to render her person sacred should be done."[26] Elsewhere, Grimké would preach about the role of the woman in society, specifically as moral

---

[23]Grimké, *Works*, 1:303.
[24]Grimké, *Works*, 1:304.
[25]Grimké, *Works*, 1:304.
[26]Grimké, *Works*, 1:305.

protector of the family. As such, crimes against women were not merely crimes against individuals but crimes against God, men, home, society, and civilization. But as offensive as the image of Black men running rampant and sexually assaulting White women was, the lives at stake depended on whether or not that image was true. So Grimké also took it upon himself to undermine the validity of the claim that Black men regularly rape White women.

If one looked at any of the records of lynching, one would find that lynching for rape covered a minority of cases.[27] Instead, it was clear that those who claimed that "the Negro was only lynched for rape" did so for shock value in order to construct a view that could perpetuate extreme violence. The anecdote that Grimké referenced to illustrate this point was a chilling one. When one is alone in one's house and someone breaks in, the assumption tends to be that they are breaking in for robbery. But, Grimké argued, especially in this period, the assumption is that a Black man is breaking in to rape (and therefore, lethal force is completely admissible), while a White man is probably breaking in to rob. Through this example, Grimké sought to impress upon his audience the importance of recognizing the root of socially constructed norms as well as to give them resources to argue against said norms. There was no logical reason why, on the basis of skin color, anyone could determine intention. But Grimké discerned many such instances, hoping to use those examples to dispel narratives about the hypersexuality of Black men. Using examples that Ida B. Wells had used years before, he also looked to the period of the Civil War and Reconstruction. Why, he asked, did we not see these kinds of accusations during a time when the men were away from home and women and children were left at the mercy of slaves? Why, he asked, did we not see these accusations when numerous Northern women came to the South to teach newly freed slaves?[28] For Grimké, the answer was that the accusations were rooted in sensationalism more than in actual crimes. As much as the South may have claimed that they only lynched for rape, any cursory investigation proved that to be false. Like Wells, Grimké narrated cases where sexual relations between a White woman and a Black man were consensual, cases where a man was accused of rape because a White woman saw him and just assumed that he was going to rape her, and cases where

---

[27]Ida B. Wells's investigation yielded 30 percent, that is, 30 percent of the lynchings investigated took place because of an accusation of rape.
[28]Grimké, *Works*, 1:305–7.

Black men were not given fair trials, but rather are assumed to be guilty. Similar to Wells' tactic of exposing the truth of lynching, Grimké presented cases to his congregation that directly contradicted the stories they may have heard from the Southern press. But shining a light on the situation was neither the only nor the primary answer for Grimké. Renarrating the interaction between race and gender was not the remedy for lynching. For Grimké, the answer had to be Christianity in some way. The Negro Problem, as instantiated in the phenomenon of lynching, was one that could not be ignored or simply dealt with by economic or political means. It is the remedy offered by the Scriptures and by the Christian Church that he discusses in the third, longest, and last sermon.

THE SCRIPTURAL SOLUTION FOR LYNCHING: SAM HOSE SERMON

The third sermon merits close attention, especially for a volume that intends to focus particularly on the use of the Bible in historical perspective. In this particular sermon, Grimké offered his remedies for lynching, and his reasoning is grounded in the Bible. In the first two sermons, biblical exegesis was less helpful, as they were largely works of cultural exegesis and diagnosis. When Grimké turned his gaze to the remedy, the Scriptures took center stage. Grimké's stated remedy was fourfold. First, the level of civilization in the South needed to be raised. Second, either the White man needed to modify his view of the Black person, or the Black person needed to modify his view of himself, that is, "must be willing to give up his ideas and accept the white man's ideas as to what he shall be and do, or as to what his social, civil, and political status shall be."[29] Third, hate in the White man needed to be eliminated. Last, the general plane on which Black people lived needed to be elevated. The first, third, and fourth points are rather self-explanatory, based on the first sermon in this series which he preached. Point two, however, was a question: who needs to change? Whose view is right? Here was the Southern White man's view according to Grimké: "That the Negro belongs to an inferior race, an inferiority not based upon circumstances, but inherent, in born; in other words, that God created him inferior, and that in virtue of that inferiority, it is his duty to treat him

---

[29]Grimké, *Works*, 1:318.

as an inferior."[30] The rules then were not the same in White-White inter-action as they were in White-Black interaction. There was one place where Grimké ran to refute that statement: the Scriptures.

Rather fervently, Grimké said, "As we are living in a land where there are 135,000 ministers, 187,000 churches, and over 26,000,000 communicants in these churches; a land where there are 1,305,000 Sabbath school teachers . . . 50,000 societies of Christian Endeavor and upwards of 3,500,000 members of such societies, we may assume that the Bible will have some weight in determining the matter." What followed was a repetition of the major narra-tives in Genesis 1, 2, 7, 8, 9, and 10. The question was how to affirm the equality of all human beings. In rather short order, Grimké appealed to three scriptural affirmations: first, that creation placed all human beings on the same playing field because of their descending from Adam or, more recently, Noah. Sec-ondly, the moral standard set by "the Ten Commandments, the Sermon on the Mount and 1 Corinthians 13" is a universal standard. According to Grimké, "the Southern white man cannot consistently hold the Negro to the same moral standard as he does himself and at the same time affirm his natural inferiority." Gone unsaid here but emphasized in the work of Ida B. Wells is the profundity of the hypocrisy of this "crying wolf," when Black women were more consistently victimized by White men and yet had little recourse or defense against such assault. No lynch mobs gathered to protect those women. Third, Grimké pointed to the universality of the Gospel. As Grimké would preach, "In the plan of salvation which this Book reveals, and which we receive as the inspired Word of God, no such difference [between White and Black] is recognized. All men of all races stand upon precisely the same footing. All are invited. All are equally welcomed. The conditions imposed are the same for all. The same gospel is to be preached to all."

These scriptural arguments then led Grimké to his climax and conclusion that "it is evident that the Southern White man's view of the Negro is wrong. It is contrary to the Word of God; and it is contrary to the expressed provi-sions and declarations of the Constitution." Now at this point, the accusation of capitulation to civil religion could be raised, but to do so would also ignore the particular relationship that many Black Protestants had with the Scriptures and the American founding documents. The argument from Grimké was

---

[30]Grimké, *Works*, 1:319.

that the Scriptures provided the ground for those documents. Unassailable authority was to be found in the Word. It just so happened that the Constitution, insofar as it literally appeared to signal universal equality, did so in step with the Scriptures.

For Grimké, the weight of these Scriptures necessarily established the equality of Black people, and thus White people had to change their views. For this to happen, they would need to be educated. Their racist assumptions had to be demolished, and in their wake, a Scriptural affirmation of their fellow human beings would have to take its place. In this early portion of his preaching career, Grimké thought that this would be enough. As was hinted in his 1898 sermons, violence was not a live option. Time would erode that resilience.

1906: THE ONLY WAY TO STOP A MOB

On October 7, 1906, Grimké entered the pulpit with 2 Corinthians 11:24-26, Paul's list of sufferings, where he wrote, "Of the Jews five times received I forty stripes save one. Thrice was I beaten with rods, once I was stoned, thrice I suffered shipwreck, a night and a day I have been in the deep; in journeyings often, in perils of rivers, in perils of robbers, in perils from my countrymen, in perils from the Gentiles, in perils in the city, in perils in the wilderness, in perils in the sea, in perils among false brethren."

After explaining each of those sufferings, Grimké called to mind what had just happened two weeks before: the Atlanta race riots, which he recognized as no more than a mass lynching. Newspapers had reported that four White women had been raped, presumably by Black men (in entirely unsubstantiated claims). As a response, White mobs roamed the streets, indiscriminately attacking and killing Black people and destroying Black businesses. As a response, in this sermon, Grimké said what his audience was doubtlessly thinking as they heard this passage of Scripture: this is us!

Grimké affirmed that sentiment, saying, "What was true of the apostle Paul is true today of our race in this country, especially in the southern section of it. We are in constant peril; no one is safe for a moment. We are liable at any time to be shot down, to be brutally murdered."[31] Neither progress, intelligence, character, nor wealth availed in the face of violent White barbarity.

---

[31]Grimké, *Works*, 1:407.

When Grimké encountered the suffering of Paul in his ministry, he saw the suffering of his own people. Importantly, for Grimké, the assailants were White men. Explicitly, White men were to blame for three reasons. First, they only cared about the protection of White women rather than all women. Second, they anarchically took the law into their own hands. Third and finally, the violence that they visited upon the Black community was indiscriminate.[32] It was clear that justice was not the intent, but vengeance. But then this raised other questions: would he repeat the suggestion that he had made seven years before? Was education the way forward? Would these supposed White Christians(?) change their ways if the Scriptures were just presented to them and explained?[33] Grimké's optimism was fading. Thus, his three pieces of advice were to his African American audience: don't be discouraged; be discreet, cautious, and careful; and be prepared to defend yourself if necessary. That final application was relatively new, but in sermons after this date, that application would be constant. In order to affirm human equality, argued Grimké, one had to be willing to defend it. Earlier, his response to lynching had been a thoroughly nonviolent one, except for the ways in which his educational plan was destructive. In this sermon, however, violence became not merely an option, but rather the option.

By 1906, Grimké had had enough. The silence of White pulpits and the acquiescence of the government in the face of the snuffing out of Black life left Grimké with one anti-lynching option. "There is but one way, as I have already said [earlier in this sermon], to deal with a mob; and that is to shoot it to death; to riddle it with bullets or dynamite it. And the Negro will be doing himself and the whole South a service by being prepared to make it as perilous as possible for the mob."[34]

One heard here, from a Christian mouth, echoes of the voices of many Black nationalists over the course of American history. His words were uncompromising: "If the Negro is not prepared to defend himself, he will be without defense. He will die as the fool dieth."[35] Grimké was very careful to

---

[32]Grimké, *Works*, 1:413.

[33]Here, I use the (?) construction found in Ida B. Wells's editorials when referring to Christian ministers or individuals who either took part in or defended lynching. She and other Black Protestants, including Grimké, were uncomfortable with claiming that individuals who engaged in such activities were truly brothers and sisters in Christ.

[34]Grimké, *Works*, 1:417.

[35]Grimké, *Works*, 1:417.

couch this language entirely in the language of self-defense, avoiding the suggestion that he was suggesting retributive or pre-emptive violence. In doing so, he couched his admonition primarily in an affirmation of dignity rather than the mobilization of aggression.

It is supremely important to consider that this is a conclusion that Grimké came to as a result of the mind-shattering brutality, inhumanity, and terroristic influence of lynching. Grimké regularly preached on race throughout his fifty-year ministry in Washington, DC. Yet, with reference to Grimké's resistance to lynching, the tone of his preaching shifted. It was always grounded in his interpretation of Scripture: his affirmation of universal human dignity was founded upon the Word, and from that it followed that the wisest way to obey that principle was to be willing to defend oneself. In the final sermon considered for this chapter, such ideas came to a head in 1919, following the Red Summer in which cities around the country erupted in racial violence, ultimately resulting in the deaths of hundreds of Black folks.

1919: WHAT DO WE HAVE TO BE THANKFUL FOR?

On November 27, 1919, Grimké was called upon, apparently at the request of President Woodrow Wilson, to preach a Thanksgiving service at the Plymouth Congregational Church in DC. The text that day was Psalm 105:1, "Oh, give thanks unto the Lord, call upon His name; make known among the peoples His doings." The political opportunity of this moment was almost unprecedented. Which direction would Grimké go?

Immediately, Grimké began with the low-hanging fruit: victory in World War I. He listed thankfulness for military victory, relatively lower casualties, and the return of the troops. Such statements were relatively uncontroversial. But it is clear that this was merely prologue for what Grimké intended to talk about all along: racial justice. After a moment on national concerns, he turned to the concerns of his Black listeners, whom he knew lived in a world where "lynchings, the crowning glory of American democracy, still go on unchecked," and where "race prejudice has grown and is growing with a rapidity unparalleled before."[36] What then, he asked, is there to be thankful for? The answer is jarring.

The most prominent phenomenon that Grimké is thankful for is that African American communities have become more and more aware of their

---

[36]Grimké, *Works*, 1:602.

rights . . . and that they are more and more willing to assert them. In other words, hope of assistance has almost run dry. As Grimké would say, "Don't let us fool ourselves here; don't let us imagine for a moment that our rights are going to be secured in any other way except mainly through our own exertions, assisted, of course, by our white friends, but principally through our own efforts."[37] One can and must hear Black nationalist impulses here that stem not from an assumption of racial superiority but rather a sense of racial frustration. Grimké has fully discarded the idea that all that needs to take place for lynching and racial violence to end is to depend on the so-called "better class of whites." Such an approach was attempted and found wanting. Thus, Claude McKay's poem was quoted in his sermon approvingly, a poem that perfectly summarized Grimké's call for willingness to defend oneself:

Oh, kinsmen! We must meet the common foe;
Though far outnumbered, let us still be brave,
And for their thousand blows deal one death-blow!
What though before us lies the open grave?
Like men we'll face the murderous cowardly pack,
Pressed to the wall, dying, but—fighting back.[38]

Where then was the Word? Where are the Scriptures in all of this self-defense talk? This was a response that Grimké faced and responded to, even in this sermon. There had recently been a Bible conference in DC that gathered Christians from around the world. After this conference, Grimké wrote an article to the *New York Independent*, which, though it was not published, circulated in tract form. In it, Grimké described his reaction to the conference:

The colored people here, after such a conference, after such a flood of light upon the Word of God from so many eminent preachers and teachers, ought to see the effect of it in lessening race prejudice . . . but it will have no such effect. Race prejudice will be just as strong, just as pronounced and aggressive in the community and in the churches as before . . . The best way to teach people the value of the Bible and of Christianity is not by holding Bible conferences, but by living the truths of the Bible, by exemplifying the spirit of its Founder. The cause of Christianity and of the Bible is not to be helped by verbal eulogies, but by eloquent examples of Christly living . . . We need everywhere,

[37]Grimké, *Works*, 1:606.
[38]Grimké, *Works*, 1:607–8.

not Bible conferences that will pass over in silence a sin like race prejudice, but Bible conferences that will lift up a standard for the people; that will cry aloud and spare not.[39]

To resist racial violence was not accidental to the Christian faith. It struck at its very substance. Similarly, it was not accidental to scriptural revelation. Rather, the battle against race prejudice was essentially mandated by the Scriptures, and to gloss over such a fact was to do the Scriptures a significant injustice. Grimké no longer worried or cared about the opinions of particularly his White critics who argued that "Grimké used to be a very nice fellow, but he seems in these late years to have gotten soured for some reason."[40] That reason was clear: Black people continued to be discriminated against and brutally and publicly murdered. Education was lauded once more as a path forward for Whites, but that suggestion carried a different weight at this point in Grimké's career. It was not to be understood apart from the suggestion that Black people be willing to defend their God-given dignity by whatever means necessary. In summary, for Grimké, it was necessary that the gospel of Jesus Christ be preached, truly believed, and actively defended. The time of patient suffering and of patient waiting for civil authorities had passed.

CONCLUSION

For Grimké, as for many African American Christians who could fit into the "evangelical" category, biblicism, activism, crucicentrism, and conversionism were not merely identity markers. They were necessities of the Christian life. There was no ethical foundation or understanding of human worth without the Scriptures. There was no salvation apart from the cross. These expressions necessarily manifested themselves in political agitation against injustice, especially something as grotesque as lynching. Anything less was not only less than evangelical. For Grimké, it was less than Christian. Grimké said as much early in his preaching career. His words in 1898 concerning those who made up mobs and who refused to defend Black life remain relevant:

If I could bring myself to believe by any process of reasoning, that these people were really Christians, it would drive me into infidelity: I would utterly repudiate such a religion. But I know that they are not Christians: I know that the

---

[39]Grimké, *Works*, 1:612.
[40]Grimké, *Works*, 1:614.

religion—I was about to say, which they profess, but rather which they possess,— is not Christianity. It is miserable lie to say that it is. And you know that it is a lie: and I know that it is a lie: and these very people who profess to be Christians know that they are lying; and God, before whose judgment seat they shall one day stand to answer for their cowardly and brutal treatment of a weak and struggling race, or their quiet acquiescence in it, knows that they are lying.[41]

The mob was not a distortion of Christianity. To refuse to resist lynching was not a distortion of Christianity. It was not to be seen as an evangelical peccadillo. Rather, it was an outright denial of the faith. But while Grimké's prophetic voice cried out in the wilderness, it found few sympathetic ears.

---

[41]Grimké, *Works*, 1:268.

10

"As at the Beginning"

Charismatic Renewal and the
Reanimation of Scripture in Britain
and New Zealand in the "Long" 1960s

John Maiden

KEN HARRISON BEGAN AS AN undergraduate at Massey University,
Palmerston North, New Zealand, in 1968–1969—a Methodist who had supplemented this upbringing with Brethren youth camps. Reading his Bible two
years earlier, Harrison had been struck by Christ's words in John 14:12-14
(KJV): "Verily, verily, I say unto you, He that believeth on me, the works that
I do shall he do also; and greater works than these shall he do; because I go
unto my Father." He noted in the margins: "When will I ever see the works
of Jesus?" On April 25, 1969 (ANZAC day, so the date was memorable), Harrison attended a student prayer meeting run by Anglicans. The Evangelical
Union at Massey had since 1965 grown increasingly charismatic through the
influence of the Rev. Ray Muller, the curate of nearby All Saints. Harrison
recalled the person to his left spoke in tongues, and to his right offered an
interpretation. Brethren teachings of tongues as a "deceiving doctrine" came
to mind. He left the house, running to a bus stop. While awaiting transport
home, he claims his Bible "literally fell open" at John 14, and that he heard a
voice saying, "What you saw tonight will produce that." Harrison returned
to the prayer meeting and after midnight experienced baptism in the Spirit.

From this point, the Bible "came alive." The next day he prayed for a student on a bad LSD trip. Again, Harrison had an urging—to command the student, "Come out of him!" The student, he believed, experienced deliverance. This was a surprise to Harrison, who began to examine all references in the Gospels to such accounts.

The next year Harrison became president of the Evangelical Union at Massey. Other family members encountered the Spirit (including his grand-mother, who recalled a similar experience through Pentecostal evangelist Smith Wigglesworth decades earlier). Harrison was soon "put out" of his home Methodist church. On moving to Auckland, he joined the Assemblies of God, the denomination for which he became Superintendent for New Zealand from 2003 to 2011.[1] This is not the place to discuss the problem of how historians should approach accounts of the "supernatural" in oral testimony. Rather, the relevance here of Ken Harrison's Spirit baptism narrative is what it reveals about dynamics common to charismatic renewal in the "long" 1960s. Like Harrison, many who found themselves involved in the movement had been searching, to some degree, for a newly em-powered Christianity in the 1950s and 1960s. The gift of tongues, through the influence of Pentecostals, became an identity marker for charismatics, but also a target for hostility within their Christian traditions. The primary significance of Harrison's account for the purposes of this chapter, though, is what it reveals about interplay between biblical text and lived experience in charismatic spirituality.

David Bebbington's *Evangelicalism in Modern Britain* has rightly situated charismatic renewal as evangelicalism in "expressive" cultural mode, a variety of the movement which had a recent antecedent in the Oxford Group.[2] The intricacies of its relationship with the Bible are not discussed at length in histories of charismatic renewal. The topic is also rarely addressed in thematic histories of Christianity and the Bible; for example, Pentecostals and charis-matics are scarcely mentioned in Goff, Farnsley, and Thuesen's otherwise excellent *The Bible in American Life* (2017). Perhaps such absences are due to an assumption that charismatics had little interest in theology and doctrine. Charismatics themselves spoke of a theological deficiency: Michael Harper,

---

[1] Interview with Ken Harrison, Auckland, August 2019.
[2] David Bebbington, *Evangelicalism in Modern Britain: A History from the 1730s to the 1980s* (London: Routledge, 1989), chap. 7.

the prominent Anglican charismatic, said in 1971 the renewal had "no great theologians. Its teaching is varied and unsystematic."[3] But this, of course, is not the absence of biblicism. The Bible was a vital component of charismatic spirituality, and not only for the many card-carrying evangelicals in the movement. Within Anglicanism, High Church, and Anglo-Catholic believers engaged with Scripture in new ways. In many cases evangelical emphases were embraced without sacramental practices being lost. In the United States, Jean Stone, the high churchwoman who established the Blessed Trinity Society—the first charismatic "service agency"—was soon comfortable enough to describe charismatics as "Evangelical."[4] In New Zealand, the largest charismatic parish, St. Paul's, Auckland, led by Anglo-Catholic Kenneth Prebble, was in 1973 described as having successfully "built the Catholic and Evangelical insights into a new and strong integration."[5] Within the charismatic renewal the usual boundaries between traditions were porous.

Mark Hutchinson has said of the charismatic renewal that it was "both strongly biblicizing and at the same time very much about the application of the Bible as a form of spiritual technology for daily life."[6] The early influence of Pentecostalism on charismatic renewal—of the Full Gospel Businessmen's Fellowship International, of international speakers such as David du Plessis and Derek Prince, of Latter Rain–type independent congregations, and of literature such as *The Cross and the Switchblade,* as well as countless examples of local witness—was such that a pneumatic and experiential hermeneutic was an aspect of charismatic renewal.[7] Frank Macchia has referred to the early Pentecostal approach as one of *"participation in the text."*[8] This was also a feature of charismatic renewal. Derek Prince, for example, a Pentecostal Bible teacher who came to play an important role in

---

[3]Michael Harper, *None Can Guess* (London: Hodder, 1971), 8.

[4]Jean Stone and Harald Bredesen, "The Charismatic Renewal in the Historic Churches," *Trinity* 3, no. 1 (1963), 28-35, at 28.

[5]Auckland, John Kimber Library (hereafter JKL), ANG 016/1/1, John Morton, "What Has Happened," Commission on the Charismatic Renewal, September 1973, 6.

[6]Mark Hutchinson, "The Bible in the Twentieth-Century Anglophone World," in *The Oxford History of Protestant Dissenting Traditions, vol. 5: The Twentieth Century: Themes and Variations in a Global Context* (Oxford: Oxford University Press, 2018), 91-130, at 118.

[7]On this hermeneutic, see French L. Arrington, "The Use of the Bible by Pentecostals," *Pneuma* 16, no. 1 (1994): 101-7.

[8]Frank D. Macchia, *Baptized in the Spirit: a Global Pentecostal Theology* (Grand Rapids: Zondervan, 2006), 52.

the movement, would quote an unnamed Scottish preacher who argued "It's better felt, than telt!"[9]

Charismatic renewal, however, was not simply Pentecostalism in a dog collar, however closely connected the two were. This essay situates charismatic renewal and its approach to the Bible in the specific religious, social, and cultural contexts of the long 1960s, and in relation to the distinctive traditions—including Evangelical (mainline, Brethren, and "outlier" interest groups such as British Israelite) and Anglo-Catholic—which converged together in the movement. A tension evident in the renewal was negotiating a powerful new awareness of the pneumatic with submission to Scripture in particular hermeneutical and Bible reading traditions. Something of this is evident in the words of Jeane Stone and Harald Bredesen: "Certainly the Word of God cannot be judged by or made subservient to our experience, but we must ask ourselves if we have not been content with orthodox theology where the New Testament demands living experience?"[10] This chapter discusses a charismatic *reanimation* of the Bible in its non-Pentecostal environs, and the variations and controversies related to Scripture within the movement. It examines specifically the Anglo-world locations of Britain and New Zealand, and an emergent transnational religious network of mainline charismatics. It addresses the charismatic reanimation of Scripture by looking at contexts, readings, practices, and controversies.

CONTEXTS OF REANIMATION

Both Britain and New Zealand were to be significantly influenced by the charismatic renewal. Indeed, New Zealand, as one American charismatic recognized in 1973, probably had "per capita . . . more Spirit filled people than any other country."[11] Two magazines, often cross-publishing and advertising, and which both began in 1966, served as mouthpieces for mainline charismatic renewal: *Renewal*, published in London by the Fountain Trust, and in Christchurch, *Logos*. The Fountain Trust was headed by Michael Harper, until recently a curate of All Soul's, London. He underwent a profound experience of the Spirit in 1962, and the next year spoke in tongues

---

[9]Derek Prince, "From Jordan to Pentecost," *Foundation Series* (Chichester: Sovereign World, 1986), 242.

[10]Stone and Bredesen, "The Charismatic Renewal," 24.

[11]R. H. Hawn, editorial, Episcopal Charismatic Fellowship Newsletter, August 1973, 1.

through the influence of charismatics visiting from California.[12] Harper entered into regular correspondence with various like-minded mainliners in New Zealand from 1964.[13] There were some important differences between the emerging charismatic movements in the two countries: an influence in New Zealand, in particular, was Latter Rain–type independent Pentecostalism.[14] However, there were underlying similarities based on strong religious, migratory, and (before the UK joined the Common Market in 1973) economic bonds. Mainline charismatics in both countries, for example, benefitted significantly from the transnational ministry of Brethren and ex-Brethren leaders; and to a lesser extent old British Israelite networks underlay charismatic connections. Both countries, too, were powerfully shaped by the inchoate movement in the United States. The magazine *Trinity* circulated in both countries and, notably, the Pentecostals David du Plessis and Derek Prince, and the Episcopalian Dennis Bennett visited both nations in the mid-1960s.

Like various other Christian movements of the period, charismatic renewal was in part a response to existential anxieties. The language of post-war ecumenism, for example, indicated a sense of global crisis. In 1958, the Lambeth Conference had produced the conviction that given the "world's confusion" it was "the urgent duty of the Church to be the channel of God's reconciling power."[15] The charismatic trope of "power," which was foregrounded in its reanimation of Scripture, emerged during and immediately after the Cold War's "years of maximum danger" of 1958–1962, where the science of warfare—the threat of the atomic bomb—was fixed in the public consciousness. It was a reality that began to inform the ministry of many clergy in Britain and New Zealand. Don Battley, later a key New Zealand charismatic leader, moved into Christian ministry having seen the film *On the Beach* (1959), which addressed the threat of radiation on Australia in the event of nuclear conflict in the northern hemisphere. He first considered joining the diplomatic service before deciding that spiritual solutions were

---

[12]See Harper's testimony in *None Can Guess*.

[13]London, Lambeth Palace Library [hereafter LPL], Michael Harper papers [MH], 1964/10, correspondence with Rev. Robert Firebrace from August 1964.

[14]For a summary, see Brett Knowles, *Transforming Pentecostalism: The Changing Face of New Zealand Pentecostalism, 1920–2010* (Lexington: Emeth, 2014), 115-25.

[15]On this see, Sam Brewitt-Taylor, *Christian Radicalism in the Church of England and the Invention of the British Sixties, 1957–1970* (Oxford: Oxford University Press, 2019), 113-15, quote at 114.

required.[16] In Whangaroa, on the North Island, in 1966, one Spirit-filled Methodist felt it necessary to preach on "Guided Missiles or Guided Men," seemingly a charismatic spin on language borrowed from Dr. Martin Luther King Jr's "The Man Who Was a Fool" sermon. ("Our scientific power has outrun our spiritual power. We have guided missiles and misguided men.")[17] In Britain and the Commonwealth, the necessity of spiritual power for a *new* age was for some underlined by the passing of the old order, notably Winston Churchill's death in 1965. One Anglican New Zealand cleric wrote to Michael Harper at this time that an incoming era of Spirit-filled leadership would end "human" leadership.[18] The influence of political and geopolitical contexts on charismatic stirrings should not be underestimated.

Another context was the ways in which conservative Christianity in Britain and New Zealand was moving in an experiential direction. There was a resurgence of interest in healing, both mainline, through groups such as the Order of St. Luke, and Pentecostal, with the growing celebrity of Oral Roberts. The post-war years also saw further interest in psychological well-being—including the relationship between religion and mental health.[19] Experientialism was also evident in Protestant and Catholic revivalism. This was not only evident in conversion experiences (though many converts later moved into charismatic renewal). Revivalistic expectation and intensive experimentation in prayer accompanied the Billy Graham crusades (Britain 1954–1955; New Zealand 1959) and other evangelistic initiatives. The atmosphere was one in of almost tangible desire for spiritual breakthrough. John Stott wrote in the All Soul's parish magazine in March 1960 "there is an awakening desire throughout the Church that God will intervene and manifest His glory and holiness among us."[20] An even stronger emphasis on the work of the Spirit

---

[16]Don Battley, *No Way Back: A Personal History of Charismatic Renewal in the New Zealand Anglican Church* (Auckland: Castle Publishing: 2019), ch 1.

[17]Pasadena, David Allan Hubbard library, David du Plessis collection, Box 14, file 21, Betty and Dave Edmonds, Prayer letter, February 19, 1966. For "The Man Who Was a Fool," see Dr. Martin Luther King Jr., *A Gift of Love: Sermons from Strength to Love and Other Preachings* (Boston: Beacon, 2012).

[18]London, LPL, Michael Harper papers, 1965/20, R. C. Firebrace to Harper, January 28, 1965.

[19]Michael Harper commented on this in 1965, arguing "The experience of the Baptism in the Spirit and speaking tongues is proving in some instances to have a therapeutic value in mental illness." Michael Harper, *As at the Beginning* (London: Hodder and Stoughton, 1965), 110.

[20]Quoted in Alister Chapman, *Godly Ambition: John Stott and the Evangelical Movement* (Oxford: Oxford University Press, 2012), 73.

was evident in the preaching of Congregationalist Martyn Lloyd-Jones. Global reflexes were also at play. In both Britain and New Zealand, accounts of revival in east and central Africa fostered interest in the possibility of the supernatural work of God.[21] At St. Mark's, Gillingham (one of the first mainline congregations to be significantly influenced by charismatic renewal) at the end of the 1950s there was discussion of the revivalism described by Roy Hession, and whether African experiences might be transplanted to the English parish.[22] In this climate, too, there was renewed interest in the "higher" or "deeper" life, for example the "full sanctification" espoused by George Ingram of the Nights of Prayer for Worldwide Revival (who used to urge Michael Harper not to travel "second-class" to heaven). Another aspect of growing experientialism was intimate forms of Christian communitarianism—the kind which the Oxford Group movement had cultivated in previous decades. One example would be Camps Farthest Out, an American organization that had begun to work in Europe and Australasia; another was the Servants of Christ the King, whose small group practices were honed by soldiers during the Second World War.[23]

However, in other ways mid-century conservative Christianities were not inclined towards a fresh experience of the Spirit. In post-war Anglo-Catholicism, for example, it was common to find a sense of spiritual aridity. St. John's College, Auckland, was described as "reflecting the fading anglo-catholicism of much of New Zealand Anglicanism of the time," with spirituality "formal and ritualised." "Where was the adventure of knowing a real God?," one ordinand asked. In the world of student evangelicalism, there seemed to be a characteristic suspicion of experience. Tom Walker, later the Vicar of St. John's, Harborne, Birmingham, recalled a powerful experience of God when he was converted. He ran into a friend's university room shouting, "It's real! At last it's real!" The response was telling: "Well done," he said, "now let's go out and buy you a proper Bible with print large enough to read, and an alarm clock."[24] Walker's understanding of the Spirit's post-conversion work had been influenced by evangelical luminaries Tom Rees, the evangelist, and

---

[21]For New Zealand, see Peter Lineham, "Tongues Must Cease: The Brethren and the Charismatic Movement in New Zealand," *Christian Brethren Review* 34 (1983): 17, 19.
[22]Teddy Saunders and Hugh Samson, *David Watson* (London: Hodder and Stoughton, 1982), 71-72.
[23]Battley, *No Way Back*, ch 2.
[24]Tom Walker, *Renew Us by Your Spirit* (London: Hodder and Stoughton, 1982), 63-64.

W. Graham Scroggie, the leading Keswick figure.[25] Rees was clear in *The Spirit of Life* (1961), "God has nothing better and nothing more to give the believing soul than that which He has already given in His Son Jesus Christ."[26] Keswick, of course, had traditionally been a context for experiential evangelicalism. Under Scroggie, while Keswick maintained the offer of a higher life, since the 1920s its emphasis had been shifting from crisis toward process. In 1956 the Scotsman (who while a minister in Sunderland decades earlier had witnessed and criticized the ministry of Anglican Pentecostal Alexander Boddy) asserted that the search for a baptism in the Spirit was "bringing large numbers into bondage and darkness."[27] While Scroggie did not deny the possibility of tongues, in practice he did not expect to see such gifts in operation—a view which in Ian Randall's words was to "prevail in much evangelical thinking about pneumatology."[28] Increasingly, furthermore, the *modus operandi* of Keswick was the expositional preaching of the Word. Similar trends had been evident in American fundamentalism. The missionary Reuben A. Torrey III found that evangelicals were recoiling from his grandfather's teaching on a crisis experience. In an oral testimony at Wheaton College he recalls, "There were a lot of people who didn't want to settle for supernatural power, they wanted to settle for academic power. Study the Bible enough and you'll be okay."[29] Of course, the desire for something "more" is something of a perennial impulse within evangelicals, but by the mid-1950s, as Amber Thomas has shown in her research on *Christian Life* magazine, there were growing calls for a rediscovery of pneumatic power. The dissatisfaction of Myrddin Lewis, a Baptist minister in Britain, with his ministry led him to look again at signs and wonders, and the answer he found in the Scripture was "an embarrassing one." Evangelicals, he concluded, had "robbed ourselves of spiritual blessing."[30] The widely read A. W. Tozer asserted that evangelical notions of "verbal inspiration" had become "afflicted with *rigor mortis*."[31] "The Spirit withdrew

---

[25]Walker, *Renew Us*, 34-35.

[26]Tom Rees, *The Life of the Spirit* (London: Hodder and Stoughton, 1961), 119.

[27]W. Graham Scroggie, *The Baptism of the Spirit and Speaking with Tongues* (London: Pickering and Inglis, 1956), 14.

[28]Ian Randall, "Graham Scroggie and Evangelical Spirituality," *Scottish Bulletin of Evangelical Theology* 18, no. 1 (2000): 71-86.

[29]Wheaton College, Collection 331, Tape 1, interview with Reuben Archer Torrey III, May 14, 1986.

[30]Myrddin Lewis, "Are we Missing Something?," *Christian Life*, April 1953, 28-29.

[31]A. W. Tozer, "No Revival Without Reformation," in *Keys to the Deeper Life* (Grand Rapids: Zondervan, 1959), 8.

and textualism ruled supreme," he argued, as he urged a reformation of New Testament Christianity.[32]

The testimony of Michael Harper reveals something of this experiential gap in one corner of the conservative evangelical world. The Englishman had undergone a remarkable conversion experience in 1950, when he had felt the "touch of God" after walking "without premonition" into a Communion service at King's College Chapel. After this, however, he had become deeply affected by what he called "the ethos of evangelicalism," describing being "processed" through conferences, missions, and camps and the like. He later reflected on how "the first flush of inspiration, when I really did know the imprint of the Holy Spirit upon my life, was gradually lost."[33] In 1962, while studying Paul's prayers in Ephesians 1 and 3, he was struck by the difference between "head knowledge" and "revelation" and the language of being "filled" with God.[34] This culminated with what approximates most closely to an "advanced" Keswick-style experience. It is interesting to read this against his description of life as a curate at the preaching flagship of the Rev. John Stott. In the period before his experience, Harper's study of the Bible had become "increasingly intellectual," and he had nightmares about preaching at All Soul's, such was the standard of preaching.[35] His encounter with the Spirit can be read as something of a release from a mid-century conservative evangelicalism that offered a biblicism that was shaped by a cerebral textualism, an approach to Scripture which could be restrictive for those seeking more experiential spirituality. Stott, as we have seen, was also seeking some greater manifestation of the Spirit—and indeed he initially allowed the visit of Frank Maguire (whose parish, in the suburbs of Los Angeles, had been affected by Spirit baptisms in the late 1950s) and others. However, once Harper began to speak in tongues, tensions emerged. At the Islington Clerical Conference in 1964, Stott argued that Spirit baptism was the "initiatory Christian experience."[36] Perhaps if Harper had not spoken in tongues, but rather urged a pneumatic renewal of evangelicalism more along the lines evident in Martin Lloyd-Jones's

---

[32]Tozer, "No Revival," 9.

[33]Harper, None Can Guess, 13-14, quote at 14.

[34]Harper, None Can Guess, 20-23.

[35]Harper, None Can Guess, 24-26.

[36]John Stott, The Baptism and Fulness of the Holy Spirit (London: Inter-Varsity Fellowship, 1964), 19.

preaching, divisions could have been limited. Harper left All Soul's the same year to establish the Fountain Trust.

The desire of Harper, and others, for a greater manifestation of spiritual power should be understood in the context of contemporary concerns about the rise of "secular" society. A kind of secular panic, as Sam Brewitt-Taylor has suggested, gripped various church leaders, including the Archbishop of Canterbury from the late 1950s—and the standing of these churchmen meant that their concerns were noticed by the media, whereas sociological prophets of secularisation had largely been ignored.[37] The idea that the churches were complacent and lacking power was a prominent aspect of ecclesiastical discourse. It was evident in two influential North American criticisms of the so-called "church boom," Gibson Winter's *The Suburban Captivity of the Churches* (1961) and Canadian Pierre Berton's *The Comfortable Pew* (1965). In Enniskillen, in the north of Ireland, one Spirit-baptised Presbyterian minister recalled how before his experience, Berton's book "produced, to say the least, an uncomfortable pulpit!"[38] Criticisms of the complacency of the church in a rapidly changing environment were a staple of early charismatic literature. Harper's *Power for the Body of Christ* (1964) asserted, "When the Church of today looks at the New Testament Church it appears shabby and emaciated in comparison"—this despite all its "buildings, liturgies, learning and scholarship, and many professional ministers."[39] A common theme in early charismatic testimonies was a sense of powerlessness. As one churchwoman said in *Logos* magazine in 1966, she had found she couldn't read the New Testament and "reconcile that with the state of the Church today and the powerless lives of other Christians as well as my own life."[40]

The Commission on Charismatic Renewal in the Anglican New Zealand church was informed in 1973: "Set against the secular 'death of God' theology of the 1950s and 1960s, the charismatic renewal certainly marks a massive return to a biblically and creedally orientated theology."[41] Primitivism wasn't the only game in town for those seeking the renewal of Christianity in changing times. The pronouncements of radical liberals were initially far

---

[37]Brewitt-Taylor, *Christian Radicalism.*
[38]William J. Hughes, "The God of All Sufficiency," *Renewal*, December–January 1968–1969, 17-19.
[39]Michael Harper, *Power for the Body of Christ* (London: Fountain Trust, 1964).
[40]Muriel Woodfield, "Testimony," *Logos* 1, no. 2 (1966): 6.
[41]Morton, "What Has Happened," 6.

more influential than the testimonies of charismatics. English bishop John Robinson's publishing sensation *Honest to God* (1963) announced an emergent radical theology to the English-speaking world. The reanimated biblical worldview presented by early charismatics was frequently juxtaposed with that of radical liberalism. Indeed, the very first editorial of *Logos* magazine, titled "This Power Is Dynamite," was one of theological confrontation. "We hear much today about the 'Death of God' Theology and the time is right for Christians to witness with bold assurance that God is very much alive," it argued.[42] The next year, criticism of the demythologising of Christianity was again evident in the magazine, concerning the controversy that resulted in the acquittal of Professor Lloyd Geering, the Principal of Knox Theological Hall, of the charge of heresy (for questioning the resurrection and the immortality of the soul) by the Presbyterian Church of New Zealand.[43] The analysis by an anonymous Presbyterian minister in New Zealand during the Geering trial is significant. The question the trial raised, he argued, was, "What do our people want? Legalistically correct doctrine, or a reductionism by which Christ has been rendered virtually powerless?" Neither, was his answer:

> We seek an outward mental light of the Scriptures, but stop short of their inward application to experience. "You shall know the truth, and the truth shall make you free." We have confused truth and doctrine, but the two are not the same. Watchman Nee, the great Chinese Christian writer, writes: "I know well that our word 'truth' in the Chinese Bible is *chen-li* (roughly, 'reality-doctrine'), but in fact the Greek meaning is *chen* without the *li*—'reality,' and the doctrine can come after us.'"[44]

Early charismatics were often to identify themselves as offering a "third way" between the limitations of conservative textualism and the "de-mythologising" of Christianity.

READINGS OF REANIMATION

"Once a man was known to have spoken in tongues, he had as much chance of getting ahead in the Evangelical world as an avowed Christian would in Nero's army."[45] So argued Jean Stone and Harald Bredesen in *Trinity* in 1963.

---

[42]David W. Edmonds, "Editorial," *Logos* 1, no. 1 (1966): 1.
[43]Robert Firebrace, "The Great Lie," *Logos* 2, no. 3 (1968): 3-5.
[44]Anonymous, "Theologians Topic," *Logos* 2, no. 2 (1967): 23-24.
[45]Stone and Bredesen, "The Charismatic Renewal in the Historic Churches," 28.

Many charismatics, like Ken Harrison, endured criticism. In 1967 Michael Harper wrote Cecil Marshall, a fellow Spirit-baptised evangelical in New Zealand, that Anglican charismatics had experienced "nothing but charming cooperation so far from Bishops—it is the fundamentalist Evangelicals who are fighting us hard at the moment, bless them!"[46] Animosity, was particularly marked over *glossolalia*. This, of course, had been divisive within Holiness circles at the beginning of the century. Brethren opposition had an even longer lineage to early nineteenth century controversy with the Irvingites. That the 1950s were a highpoint for the Open Brethren, both in terms of numbers and influence on wider evangelicalism sometimes contributed to a hostile atmosphere for charismatics. Tellingly, the earliest Fountain Trust pamphlets was authored by David Lillie, who defended tongues against criticisms of the "brothers" in New Zealand and Britain. This was not a purely theological matter. Some attacked tongues as a psychological problem; for others, it was a "primitive" practice. In *Pentecostalism and Speaking in Tongues* (1964), Douglas Webster of the Church Missionary Society argued that the apostle Paul wanted to wean the Church in Corinth off the "temporary abnormality" of supernaturalism. There was a condescending air to his argument. "Among the proletarian millions of South America and others of limited education," he asserted, "this ecstatic way of worship may be regarded as natural and possibly necessary at the first stage. But for more mature and educated Christians to revert to primitive and excitable forms of behaviour and even to induce them seem in every respect to court danger and folly."[47] When charismatics went public with their new spirituality, therefore, it was necessary to make the case that their experiences and practices were orderly (not "primitive"), "sane" (the individual was in control), and biblical. The New Zealand Presbyterian, the Rev. Douglas Watt, in a 1967 edition of *Logos*, asserted, "I have to take my stand beside my fellow townsman Edward Irving (I was born in Annan, Dumfrieshire) and state my belief that the use of tongues in the form of ecstatic utterance or as an expression of communion with God is perfectly Scriptural. Nor should it be looked upon as an emotional extravagance."[48] Harper warned fellow charismatics, "Many a person has sunk in the quicksands of experience which have no foundation in the

---

[46]JKL, ANG178, Series 1/15, Michael Harper to Cecil T. Marshall, May 29, 1967.

[47]Douglas Webster, *Pentecostalism and Speaking in Tongues* (London: Highway, 1964), 34.

[48]Douglas Watt, "Editorial," *Logos* 1, no. 4 (1967): 1-2.

Scriptures."[49] *Logos* advertised the charismatic movement it represented as "in strict accordance with the Scriptures."[50] The appeal to Scripture was strongly evident in early charismatic literature.

In some cases, Spirit baptism narratives involved the believer assiduously searching the Scriptures until they were fully convinced, at which point a pneumatic experience followed; however, almost always to some degree a building of a biblical foundation and understanding was undertaken *after* a supernatural experience and as certain gifts came into operation. The re-reading of Scripture with "fresh eyes" was a constant theme. Margaret Stott, the wife of a New Zealand Anglican clergyman, had "received" in 1958, following a period of interest in divine healing and encounters with Pentecostals. The morning after she spoke in tongues, she had "really doubted the experience. However, I was reassured from Scripture and once reassured I was able to enjoy the peace and the tremendous, but quietly controlled, joy that came with it."[51] In her husband's spiritual autobiography, Jeanne Harper is described as reading Scripture and finding that it "perfectly matched what she was experiencing."[52] As their experience and manifestation of the gifts developed, too, the Scriptures were said to have come alive to validate such happenings. One English vicar reported that Acts and the epistles became new books–"1 Corinthians 12 & 14 now fitted quite rightly *around* chapter 13, and were not omitted altogether, as had so often happened in the past."[53]

Influential upon early charismatic defence of the baptism and the supernatural gifts was the debate between Michael Harper and various leading conservative evangelicals in the mid-1960s. Around the time of leaving All Soul's, Harper corresponded with concerned colleagues. The careful construction of a scriptural case was—naturally for a curate of Stott—a priority for Harper. In late 1964, he wrote Stott that recent studies of the Scripture left him convinced of a baptism in the Spirit subsequent to conversion. Indeed, he was "as certain of it as a basic doctrine as I am of justification by faith."[54] This comparison appalled Stott:

---

[49]Harper, *Power*, 13.
[50]Advert, *Renewal* 1, no. 2 (1966): 11.
[51]Woodfield, "Testimony," 4-5.
[52]Harper, *None Can Guess*, 34.
[53]P. L. C. Smith, "A New Work," *Trinity* 3, no. 2 (1964): 26-27.
[54]LPL, John R. W. Stott Papers [JWRS], 5/22, Michael Harper to John Stott August 9, 1964, 209.

> All I can say is that you really have no proper ground for such certainty. Justification by faith is a doctrine plainly taught in Scripture and believed by all evangelical Christians. Your doctrine of the Spirit, however, is not plainly taught in Scripture, for many of us would say that it is not in Scripture at all, and it has not been believed by the vast majority of evangelicals who have studied Scripture.[55]

"Majorities are not always right," Harper replied. He later added there was a "real danger" that we believed "in the infallibility of evangelicals rather than that of the Bible."[56] Harper, though, also appealed to experience. The "basis for a promise of power" in the New Testament was a doctrine he had seen "worked out in literally hundreds of cases." This jarred the cessationism (or at least cessationism-in-practice) of some conservative evangelicals. Oliver Barclay of the Inter-Varsity Fellowship described Harper's examples of healings and prophecy as "rather pathetic" when placed alongside the other pressing issues for church and world. The IVF man believed that where there had been spiritual growth in the case of individual charismatics, it would have been more "stable and humbling" if it had been arrived at purely by way of fresh engagement with Scripture.[57] Harper subsequently published *Power for the Body of Christ* (1964), a book which Stott urged him not to write, saying he would "live to regret it."[58] In the book, Harper was clear: "We should not allow our experience *(or our lack of experience)* to judge the Scriptures"; but his conclusion included a collection of testimonies to "this transformative experience." "Nature dances and people's eyes shine. Poetical? Yes, but metaphor and the language of poetry is the inadequate best I can use to describe the new creation which we now see," read one such letter.[59] Harper, as mentioned above, was to edit *Renewal* and have a significant influence on *Logos*—indeed, the first two issues of the latter included his testimony. His integration of a conservative evangelical approach, involving systematic engagement with Scripture and the defence of baptism of the Spirit in doctrinal terms, with an experiential

---

[55]LPL, JRWS, 5/22, John Stott to Michael Harper, August 14, 1964, 219.

[56]LPL, JRWS, 5/22, Stott to Harper, August 14, 1964, 219

[57]LPL, JRWS, 5/22, Oliver Barclay to Michael Harper, October 14, 1964, 212-14.

[58]The introduction to the 1969 edition also stated, markedly, "There have been no regrets about writing this book." Harper, *Power*, 8.

[59]Harper, *Power*, 8.

hermeneutic was to have a profound influence on many early charismatics in Britain and New Zealand.

As Edmund Rybarczk puts it, for Pentecostals the "biblical *locus classicus*" is the book of Acts.[60] Overlapping the reading of Scripture with "fresh eyes" was awareness of the normativity of New Testament Christianity. This would prompt the purchase of a new Bible. The Scofield Reference Bible appeared to affirm that supernatural gifts and manifestations had ceased at the end of the apostolic age. On the Massey University campus, some Baptist and Brethren students involved in charismatic prayer meetings replaced their Scofield Bibles. They were hungry for knowledge of Scripture but heeded the warning of Derek Prince that the Bible was inspired, but the writing down side was not.[61] The New Testament was an alive world, not a dry text. "The Acts of the Apostles reads like a thriller. Why should the acts of the modern apostles read like a government white-paper?," read the first editorial of *Renewal*.[62] The wife of a Presbyterian minister in Christchurch testified as to how the Bible had "always meant a good deal" to her but was now "the most exciting book in my possession"—with passages in the Acts and the epistles which "did not seem to have a great deal of bearing on life today" becoming "very significant."[63] An important testimony to the book of Acts as a script for normative Christianity today was *The Cross and the Switchblade*. Published in the year same year as *Honest to God,* it was this story—rather than a book of theology—which was the defining early textbook of the charismatic renewal. "In *The Cross and the Switchblade*," wrote one English evangelical, "we breathe the same atmosphere as exists in the New Testament."[64] When Wilkerson preached at the Royal Albert Hall in 1967, the reports of his ministry read like a New Testament passage, with Jesus "strong enough to free" young people from the worst immoralities.[65] Another New Zealand cleric, an Anglo-Catholic, described being "completely shattered" by the

---

[60]Edmund J. Rybarczyk, "New Churches: Pentecostals and the Bible," in *The New Cambridge History of the Bible, Vol. 4: 1750–Present*, ed. John Riches (Cambridge: Cambridge University Press, 2015), 587-605, at 591.

[61]Interview with Ken Harrison.

[62]"Editorial," *Renewal* 1, no. 1 (1966): 2.

[63]J. M. Honders, "J. M. Honders," *Logos* 1, no. 1 (1966): 5-6.

[64]Gavin Read, "How Did It Become a Bestseller?," *Renewal* 1, no. 6 (December 1966–January 1976): 5-7.

[65]Carol Ackworth, "David Wilkerson at the Albert Hall," *Renewal* 1, no 6 (December 1966-January 1967), 5-7.

book, contrasting the power of Wilkerson's ministry with his own.[66] The gospel could work in New York—Gotham—the archetypal secular city. The Book of Acts had come alive.

Another aspect of charismatic reanimated reading of Scripture—one which proved more contested—was eschatological. On the idea of the "latter rain"—one which had obtained a powerful influence on Pentecostals—some were equivocal. Michael Harper could not "see any certainty" that the church was experiencing the final latter rain outpouring of the Spirit, though he admitted that political events and the nearing completion of the great commission signalled that possibility.[67] Space for discussion of the matter was allowed in *Renewal.* "Now, it is thought," the Methodist Charles Clarke explained, "we are seeing the preliminary showers of the latter rain, which will be a world-wide revival, the purpose of which is to ripen the Harvest and make it ready for the sickle of our returning Lord."[68] In New Zealand the more distinctive Latter Rain eschatology that emerged in North America exercised significant influence on some charismatics, so such views were more evident. The emergence of charismatic renewal coincided with global events which stirred the evangelical imaginary. For Bill Grant, the 1967 war in the Middle East heightened the expectation that the Latter Rain was "even now beginning to fall" and the Second Coming of Christ approaching.[69] Some were convinced the baptism of the Spirit produced fresh eschatological illuminations. Robert Firebrace, who by the 1960s was based in New Zealand but in previous years had been active in British Israelite circles with Bill Grant, asserted in *Logos* "the honest study of Scripture and the contemporary world situation, conducted prayerfully in continuous dependence on the guidance of the Holy Spirit" would leave the charismatic believer "in no doubt whatever that we are living in the last days of this dispensation."[70] For Firebrace, the primary task of the Holy Spirit was in fact not to provide "unusual experiences" but to enable the "normal faculties" to engage with eschatology—moving beyond mere "intellectualism" to "reveal to us the

---

[66]David Balfour, "David Balfour," *Logos* 1, no. 1 (August 1966): 6-7.
[67]Interview, "Michael Harper Views the Church," *Charismatic Contact* (Australia) 4, no. 1 (1975).
[68]Charles Clarke, "Quest," *Renewal* 1, no. 5 (1966): 14-15.
[69]Bill Grant, "The Middle East and the Second Coming," *Renewal* no. 10 (August/September 1967), 35.
[70]Robert Firebrace, "Where Do We Go from Here?," *Logos* 1, no. 4 (1967): 3-4, 25, at 25.

truth that is vital for our time."[71] Firebrace's fascination with the end times led some to see him as a bit of an oddity, but charismatic engagement with Scripture often had a strong eschatological dimension.

PRACTICES OF REANIMATION

The emphasis on the Spirit influenced established practices, often producing different degrees of spontaneous and experientialism in the use of Scripture. Evangelicals, of course, have emphasised the work of the Spirit in illuminating the Bible, but charismatic leaders claimed a new relationship with the text that came with the Spirit's infilling.[72] This was evident in the preaching of the Word, where the Spirit was said to bring a new freedom. Preaching at All Saints, Palmerston North, late in 1965, the Rev. Ray Muller reported using notes rather than a script for the first time with an anointing of the Spirit.[73] His friend Michael Harper spoke of relying less on commentaries and being able to leave the safety of his notes. He does not seem to have been joking when he wrote of wondering, when the Spirit inspired his preparation of notes, the "so-called 'dictation theory' of Scripture 'might not have some truth in it after all.'" Harper was one of those who began to escape the grip of the "three-point sermon." One friend of Harper commented with surprise that following his "experience" his usual three points expanded to "at least seventeen!"[74]

"In paperback and hard cover, Bibles are being carried about, read, marked and digested in a way that few living Anglicans can recall."[75] So read a report for the New Zealand Anglican Commission on the Charismatic Renewal in September 1973. The Bible was integral to everyday charismatic practice. Spirit baptism testimonies invariably mentioned a new pietistic enthusiasm for personal Scripture reading. The United States–based Pentecostal Derek Prince, who visited both Britain and New Zealand for ministry in the 1960s, placed great emphasis on an instantaneous illumination of Scripture which came with the baptism in the Spirit.[76] "Often the Holy Spirit will give us

---

[71]Robert Firebrace, "Lo! He Comes," *Logos* 2, no. 1 (1967): 3-4, 22, at 22.
[72]On the effect of Spirit baptism on the illumination of Scripture, see Prince, "Purposes of Pentecost," *Foundation Series* (Chichester: Sovereign World, 1986), 347.
[73]JKL, ANG 178, Series 1/15, item 15, Ray Muller to Cecil Marshall, December 8, 1965.
[74]Harper, *None Can Guess*, 26.
[75]Morton, "What Has Happened," 3.
[76]Prince, "Purposes of Pentecost," 347.

revelation of the word of God," wrote Arthur Wallis. "We may have read a certain promise in the Bible time and again, but one day it lights up."[77] For the Scotsman Tom Smail, the infilling of the Spirit brought a "new sense of being personally addressed by the word of God in Scripture."[78] A more experiential posture of charismatic Bible reading could produce a reflective and meditative approach to time with God. Campbell McAlpine was one of those to recommend a more Romantic approach to the reading of Scripture, reminding readers that a meditational reading of the Bible had a precedent, for example, in the piety of George Muller.[79] Anne Watson, wife of evangelist and clergyman David, for example, would "listen to the Lord, to hear him speak to her," and sometimes focus on "a word, a phrase, a verse, or an aspect of God's character."[80] Where such practices were adopted, they departed quite significantly from the usual features of the mid-century systematic, evangelical quiet time.

The diffuse character of charismatic renewal—largely in the form of informal prayer and Bible study groups, often interdenominational and sometimes lacking the input of clergy—contributed to a greater emphasis on participation and spontaneous patterns of ministry. Where Anglicans were involved, there could be some tension between a more flexible approach and the established calendar of set readings. At Massey University, this was an issue addressed by giving out the Bible passages to all members of the fellowship group in advance, and then engaging with it devotionally. In prayer meetings there was a diversity of approaches to Scripture. In Auckland, for example, some groups engaged in "disciplined and thoughtful study, with commentaries and alternative translations," while others appeared to use verses "culled almost at random, with a claimed relevance to the present situation."[81] Some, including Michael Harper, and David Harper (no relation) in New Zealand, saw the potential pitfalls of literalism.[82] Certainly, there was a tendency towards the atomization of biblical texts.

---

[77] Arthur Wallis, "When Faith Would Fail," *New Wine*, October 1971, 12-13.

[78] Smail, *Renew*, 72.

[79] Campbell McAlpine, "Spiritual meditation," *Vision*, no. 30 (January–February 1979), 28-30.

[80] Anne Watson, *You Are My God* (London: Hodder and Stoughton, 1983), 94.

[81] Morton, "What Has Happened," 3.

[82] For a later critique, see David Harper, "Charismatic Confession," *Latimer* 78 (1982): 10-13.

There was also the question of the relationship between Scripture and prophecy or interpretation of tongues—how to differentiate between the divine inspiration of Scripture and extrabiblical utterances without downplaying the significance of the latter. It was often noted that prophecies and interpretations were given in the medium of the King James Version—this, along with Old Testament prophetic language of "thus saith the Lord," lent authority to the spontaneous utterances. Harper was one of those to ask that the term "thus saith the Lord" should be avoided, suggesting it implied "inerrancy"—a telling word to use in the British context, which certainly underlines Harper's ongoing "high" emphasis on scriptural authority—and made it difficult for the listeners to "weigh" what had been said in the light of Scripture.[83] As new practices and fashions emerged in prayer meetings, often leaders scrambled to search the Bible to investigate their appropriateness. Harper, for example, in 1968 remarked on the trend of speaking in tongues in concert and without interpretation—a practice he argued ran against Paul's command in 1 Corinthians 14:26 that "*all* things" be done for congregational edification. In New Zealand, Cecil Marshall wrote to a fellow Anglican vicar that he was keen to establish whether practices were "normative in scriptural types." In the case of clapping, for example, he was unsure—the references in his concordance suggested clapping was usually done in "anger, grief or contempt" rather than joy. The new experiential territories which were opened up by baptism in the Spirit required searching the Scriptures anew for validation.[84]

A further area of practice which involved the reanimation of Scripture was singing. An emphasis on the text of Scripture in sung worship has often been a feature of movements for renewal in the church. (As David Bebbington mentions in passing in his discussion of biblicism as a core feature of evangelicalism, Charles Wesley's "Lord, and is Thine anger gone" included twenty-six biblical allusions in its sixty-four lines!) While mainline charismatic leaders seem to have been conscious of the importance of including traditional hymnody in the repertoire to highlight continuity with denominational traditions, there was a tendency toward singing paraphrased biblical texts. (Some have been scathing about this—the New Zealander Mike Riddell perhaps

---

[83]Michael Harper, *Walk in the Spirit*, rev. ed. (Eastbourne: Kingsway 1983), 71-72.
[84]JKL, ANG178, Series 1/15, Marshall to Ray Muller June 10, 1966.

uncharitably argued it had "the twin effects of destroying several great Scriptures through repetition and rendering them totally innocuous through their association with music of a powerfully anaesthetic quality.")[85] A former Brethren couple, Dave and Dale Garratt, who attended Queen Street Assemblies of God, Auckland, a church that became influential in the New Zealand charismatic scene, had an important role in the production, collection and popularisation of these songs. Their "Scripture in Song" album of 1968 was followed by the publication "Songs of Praise" in 1971, with multiple further albums and songbooks following. In the *Scripture in Song* series, of the songs produced up to 1971, 46.55 percent included the verbatim use of Scripture, at 27.58 percent an adapted use. This approach was a particular feature of charismatic renewal in New Zealand, where the influence of Latter Rain Pentecostalism—which had traditionally emphasised the spontaneous singing of a "new song," drawing on the words of Scripture—was particularly apparent. Of all the songs from New Zealand in *Scripture in Song* up to 1987, 66.38 percent included a reference to the Bible, and up to 1971 the majority of these included verbatim references, usually from the King James Version.[86] The Garretts had an important role in the popularization of Scripture songs. In Britain, for example, David Fellingham, a musician who attended an Anglican church in Brighton, was inspired by the Garretts' work to write Scripture songs: his chorus "Alelluia! The Lord Reigns" was picked up by the Garretts while they were visiting Britain and then published by Scripture in Song. Charismatic worship was imbued with Scripture.

CONTROVERSIES OF REANIMATION

The emergence of strains of "Pentecostal" practices and terminology among mainline Christians raised a range of issues to negotiate, and not least in evangelical circles. One matter for discussion was the language of "baptism in the Spirit," and the implications this had for theologies of Christian initiation. Early charismatic understanding of Spirit baptism was shaped by the mediation of Californian mainliners who had been particularly influenced by Pentecostals, including David du Plessis. As a result, tongues, if not understood strictly as the "initial evidence," was overwhelmingly regarded as the normal first outward

---

[85]Quoted in Brett Knowles, "'From the Ends of the Earth We Hear Songs': Music as an Indicator of New Zealand Pentecostal Spirituality and Theology," *Australasian Pentecostal Studies* 5, no. 6 (2002).

[86]Knowles, "From the Ends of the Earth."

sign of the experience. In time, though, this framework, and the terminology which came with it, was challenged. In England, Michael Green wondered whether Spirit baptism language could be abandoned: "Could we not bear to call the rose by some other name?," he asked.[87] Another English Anglican, David Watson, was closer to John Stott's theology, preferring a pneumatology of "fillings." During the 1970s, such voices urging a more flexible understanding of the work of the Spirit became increasingly prominent. The issue of rebaptism, too, proved highly divisive. Some mainliners found creative ways of traversing this thorny ground, with Cecil Marshall, for example, using a service which involved immersion, not technically as rebaptism but as a sign of reaffirmation to "satisfy the personal need of the person."[88] Most controversial, though, in the 1960s was demonology and in particular the practices of Derek Prince and Canadian Pentecostal Maxwell Whyte. The literature of these men, replete with biblical references, was initially publicized by the Fountain Trust, but soon practices such as group exorcism—and in particular the theology that Christians could be possessed—raised concerns. Harper visited New Zealand in 1967, and that year warned Anglican charismatic leaders there against the pitfalls of "slavish following" of Pentecostals and radical demonologies.[89]

Initially the mainline renewal associated with *Renewal* and *Logos* was closely bound with various kinds of restorationism. The primitivism of Brethren and ex-Brethren, such as Arthur Wallis, and various independents was influential. Wallis was a main speaker, along with Campbell MacAlpine and Milton Smith, at the 1964 conference at Massey University which was a launchpad for charismatic renewal. The restorationist message was evident in the special prayer composed for the event:

Bound by tradition,
Chained by her own volition
Her ancient birthright sold
Her early fires cold,
The church, in self-made bondage lies,
Powerless, beneath Time's threat'ning skies.[90]

---

[87]Smail, *Renew*, 136.

[88]JKL, Cecil Marshall papers, ANG 178, 1/5, Cecil Marshall to Geoff Ginever, n. d.

[89]LPL, Michael Harper papers, 1967/32, "Encyclical," 25. See also Michael Harper and Jeanne Harper, "Report from New Zealand," *Renewal* (1967): 20.

[90]"A Prayer Composed for the Conference," *Massey Conference Report: I Will Build My Church* (1964): 1.

Wallis and McAlpine, who were both pragmatic in playing down their eccle-
siology where necessary, became prominent in Fountain Trust circles. There
was also cross-fertilization with another variety of restorationism, the theology
and practice of the Latter Rain. In Britain, the independent Pentecostal Cecil
Cousen, another friend of the Fountain Trust, had been impacted by the
Latter Rain while visiting Canada; however, its influence was most evident
in New Zealand, where independents such as Peter Morrow and Assemblies
of God minister Frank Houston (whose son, Brian, became the main leader
of Hillsong, in Sydney) offered support to mainliners.

This restorationist undertow proved increasingly challenging to charismatic unity. The latent problem of whether to remain in the denominations became public in a fascinating transnational exchange of articles
between Anglican New Zealander Ray Muller and David Lillie, the British
independent. A piece by Muller in *Renewal* stated, "I have no intention of
leaving the Church" and made a sharp distinction between "old-type" Pentecostalism and the move of God in the denominations. Lillie's response
was frank: "If this move be of God, then it must be biblical in character,
and it is surely logical to assume that it has been sent to revive and renew
a Church which is equally biblical in character." He stopped short of suggesting Spirit-baptised believers "ought forthwith to quit" their churches,
but there was a weighty inference in his words. From the beginning of the
1970s, the relationship between denominationalists and independents
became increasingly uneasy.

In New Zealand, the influence of Latter Rain–type restorationism began
to undermine charismatic unity. In 1969, *Logos* took a marked change of
direction. Although various denominational Christians, such as Methodist
Owen Woodfield and Anglican David Balfour remained on the editorial
board, Paul Collins, of the Christian Faith Centre, Sydney, was appointed
editor. Immediately, explicit Latter Rain teaching appeared on its pages. Rob
Wheeler, for example, argued a theology of the feast of tabernacles and asserted, "The manifestation of the matured sons of God is ready to burst upon
the world."[91] The magazine developed links with King's Temple, Seattle, whose
founder E. Charlotte Baker, a Canadian with Latter Rain pedigree, became
its American representative. At the same time, the leading teachers of

---

[91]Rob Wheeler, "The Feast of Tabernacles," *Logos* 3, no. 3 (1969): 2-3, 19, quote at 19.

American restorationism—Bob Mumford, Don Basham, and others—became frequent contributors. In 1970 this shift towards restorationism was completed when Howard J. Carter, the former Baptist and future Australian culture warrior became president of the Logos Foundation, and its magazine was renamed *Restore.*

CONCLUSION

In the "long 1960s," Cold War tensions, rapid political, social and moral change, and the perceived rise of the "secular," charismatic renewal—in an atmosphere of post-war revivalism and experientialism—fostered a search for an empowered, authentic Christianity for a "new age." Charismatic renewal was a biblicizing movement, both within and outside of evangelical circles, offering an alternative both to the "demythologizing" approach of radical liberalism and the textualism of mid-century evangelicalisms. This reanimative biblicism drew strongly on the pneumatic-experiential hermeneutic associated with Pentecostalism. Charismatic engagement with Scripture involved mainline Christians and others reading the Bible with fresh eyes, discovered a "New Testament Christianity," previously hidden (or perhaps dismissed in their Scofield Bibles), which they came to understand as normative. Evangelicals set about explaining and defending their new experience of the Spirit, as in Michael Harper's case, integrated a systematic, conservative evangelical approach to Scripture with their own experience. Reanimation involved transformations of practice, with a tendency towards the use of Scripture in more democratized and spontaneous ways, in both private and public. This, however, produced diverse patterns of ministry and efforts to regulate the expressive mode of the charismatic gathering—including the use of Scripture itself—along Biblical lines. In its reanimative approaches to Scripture, the charismatic turn of the long 1960s changed some aspects of evangelical and nonevangelical engagement with Scripture in far reaching and long-lasting ways.

In the first years of charismatic renewal there were strong bonds between those committed to denominational renewal and those Pentecostals and independent evangelicals oriented more definitely toward restorationism. This was partly based on a shared leaning toward primitivism, but it was also in a large part affective—the bind of a shared pneumatic experience. As the movement sought teaching, however, it began to grapple with eschatological and ecclesiological issues requiring a biblical basis. By the beginning of the 1970s, relationships began to stretch. In New Zealand, three years after *Logos* changed direction, various mainliners, mostly Anglican and Roman Catholic friends of Michael Harper, began Christian Advance Ministries—an organization for renewal in the churches with close links to the Fountain Trust. In Britain, from the mid-1970s, with the rise of the House Church movement, commitment to biblicism in both denominational and nondenominational constituencies weakened charismatic unity.

This chapter raises a final question about definitions. David Bebbington's Quadrilateral remains the most widely accepted model of the historic basic characteristics of evangelicalism. However, for evangelicals of various types— Holiness evangelicals of different hues, Pentecostals, and charismatics— pneumatic experience has often been a core characteristic.[92] That this has not been the case for evangelicals universally, I would suggest, leaves the Quadrilateral robust. However, the efforts in the 1960s to integrate experience and biblicism—and the extent to which other evangelicals opposed this—is an example of a core "pneumaticism," which, in some times and places, deserves to be recognized as a fifth mark of evangelicalism. Without recognising this additional mark of pneumaticism, our characterisation of these evangelicalisms will be incomplete.

---

[92]Indeed, Timothy Larsen's definition of evangelicalism, which consciously builds on Bebbington's, includes the claim that an evangelical is someone "who stresses the work of the Holy Spirit": Timothy Larsen, "Defining and Locating Evangelicalism," in *The Cambridge Companion to Evangelical Theology*, ed. Timothy Larsen and Daniel J. Treier (Cambridge: Cambridge University Press, 2007), 1-14.

Part Four

Into the
Twenty-First
Century

11

The American Patriot's Bible

Evangelicals, the Bible, and American Nationalism

Catherine A. Brekus

"HOLD FAST TO THE BIBLE as the sheet anchor of your liberties."

"We cannot read the history of our rise and development as a nation without reckoning with the place the Bible has occupied in shaping the advances of the Republic."

"The fundamental basis of the nation's laws was given to Moses on the Mount."

These quotations about the Bible—from Ulysses Grant, Franklin Delano Roosevelt, and Harry Truman—are reprinted in *The American Patriot's Bible*, a reproduction of the full text of the New King James Version alongside tidbits of American history. Published in 2009 and edited by Richard G. Lee, the founder of the radio program *There's Hope America* and founding pastor of a Southern Baptist megachurch, *The American Patriot's Bible* is designed to reveal the strong biblical foundation of the United States. As Lee explains in his introduction, the nation's founders had many questions about how to construct a free government and society, but they found answers in the Holy Bible, "the book that bound colonial American society together from Maine to Georgia." Lee quotes Andrew Jackson, "*That book, sir, is the Rock upon which our republic rests*," and adds,

Not only was that the opinion of President Jackson, but also the sentiment of countless Americans. On the whole, Americans are a people who love the Bible and the God of the Bible. There is no book more powerful than the Bible to shape the morals and values of men and nations to be right and noble and just. It has proven itself over and over again in the formation and continuance of the greatest nation in history, the United States of America.[1]

The American Patriot's Bible is a hybrid text: most of it is a reproduction of the New King James Version, but it also includes illustrations of famous Americans, glossy inserts about topics such as "Faith of the Founders," and brief introductions to each book of the Bible, from Genesis to Revelation, highlighting its key themes and its connection to the American story. At the beginning of the book of Genesis, for example, readers see images of the Mayflower, the Constitution, two photos of Civil War soldiers in a silver frame, and a photo of World War II soldiers. The summary of Genesis explains, "Genesis contains the foundational truth that God is the source of and beginning of all things and our only hope for the peace, happiness, and true liberty we all crave." As readers turn the pages of Genesis, they encounter full-page inserts about topics such as "The Right to Bear and Keep Arms" along with enclosed boxes within the text, including one that connects the selling of Joseph to the words of Dick Cheney, "It is easy to take liberty for granted, when you have never had it taken from you." Overall, the effect of these juxtapositions is to weave together the Bible and American history, presenting the story of the nation as biblical. Since Richard Lee disappears as a narrator after a brief introduction, readers are left with the impression that both the Bible and American history are being narrated by God.[2]

The American Patriot's Bible does not represent the way that all evangelical Christians imagine the nation, and indeed, when it was published, some evangelicals were appalled by its exaltation of American nationalism and militarism. A reviewer in *Christianity Today*, an evangelical magazine, described the book as "idolatrous" because of its insistence that "God is uniquely

---

[1]Richard G. Lee, ed., *The American Patriot's Bible* (Nashville: Thomas Nelson, 2009), viii. Cited hereafter as *APB*.

[2]*APB*, 1 (Genesis), 16 (Mason), 44 (Cheney). I am indebted to Courtney Bither for making this point about narration in a seminar paper, "A Jeremiad for a New Age: *The American Patriot's Bible*," which she submitted for my course at Harvard Divinity School in the spring of 2019, "Cities on a Hill: Images of America as a Redeemer Nation."

invested and involved in America."[3] Yet even though *The American Patriot's Bible* represents only one strain of evangelicalism, it is a powerful one, and it has deep connections to the evangelical past. *The American Patriot's Bible* builds on a long evangelical tradition by portraying the United States as a new Israel with a special divine destiny and the Bible as an essentially democratic text. Filled with militaristic imagery, *The American Patriot's Bible* suggests that Christianity and military service are two sides of the same coin, with both requiring sacrifice in the service of God. It portrays true Americans— and true Christians—as mostly White and mostly Protestant, and it warns that if the United States ventures too far away from biblical principles and the leadership of White Protestants, especially White Protestant men, then the republic might lose God's favor. Most of all, *The American Patriot's Bible* suggests that the nation itself is redemptive, specially chosen by God to be a model of Christianity and freedom for the rest of the world.

This chapter, a genealogy of *The American Patriot's Bible*, places it within a longer history of evangelical attitudes toward both the Bible and the nation. It reveals that the roots of its distinctive ideas stretch back to the late eighteenth and nineteenth centuries, when the upheavals caused by the American Revolution, Indian Removal, the Civil War, and Catholic immigration led evangelicals to forge a distinctively Protestant understanding of the identity of the United States. *The American Patriot's Bible* represents a particularly stark example of American Christian nationalism, but it also reflects a long historical trajectory of imagining the United States as a free, White, militant, and Protestant nation that has been destined for a special divine purpose.

A striking feature of *The American Patriot's Bible* is its attention to the parallels between the United States and the biblical Israel. At the beginning of the book of Exodus, for example, readers learn that the flight of the pilgrims from oppression "mirrored a much earlier Exodus, when God led the children of Israel out of the bondage and oppression of Egypt and into a land that He had promised their forefather Abraham."[4]

This language builds on a long tradition of grafting the history of the United States onto Scripture. During the Revolutionary era, a coalition of Protestants— both evangelical and liberal-leaning—helped to construct the new nation on

---

[3]Greg Boyd, "Book Review: *The Patriot's Bible* (Part 1)," *Christianity Today*, May 22, 2009, www .christianitytoday.com/parse/2009/may/book-review-patriots-bible-part-1.html.
[4]*APB*, 60.

the model of the Hebrew Bible. The United States was not founded as an explicitly Christian nation, nor were large numbers of the founders evangelical Christians, but the Bible played a crucial role in the construction and defense of American nationalism. Despite the shortcomings of the *American Patriot's Bible*, it makes an astute observation: "Even those who were not Christian were deeply influenced by the principles of Christianity."[5]

When American colonists proclaimed their independence from England in 1776, patriots instinctively turned to the Hebrew Bible for guidance. The Declaration of Independence announced the revolutionary principles of the new nation—the "unalienable rights" of life, liberty, and the pursuit of happiness—but the biblical story of Israel provided the template for what it meant to *be* a nation. Most White colonists were Protestant, even if some were Protestant in name only, and at a time when the Bible was frequently invoked in public life, they were intimately familiar with the story of the Is-raelites. In the words of Adrian Hastings, "The Bible provided, for the Christian world at least, the original model of the nation. Without it and its Christian interpretation and implementation, it is arguable that nations and nationalism, as we know them, could never have existed."[6] From reading the Hebrew Bible, Protestants learned that God had once singled out a nation to do his will on earth, and he had invested that nation with messianic significance.[7]

Americans did not invent their model of nationhood from the Bible alone; they were also influenced by Greek and Roman ideals and, closer to home, the example of England. According to Hastings, England was the first nation, a distinction that can be explained by its early support for the printing and distribution of the vernacular Bible. Proud of their leading role in the Prot-estant Reformation, the English identified themselves as God's chosen people, a new "British Israel" with a providential identity.[8]

---

[5]*APB*, 309.

[6]Adrian Hastings, *The Construction of Nationhood: Ethnicity, Religion and Nationalism* (Cambridge: Cambridge University Press, 1997), 4. Hastings disagrees with Anthony D. Smith, who argues that there is no "causal link" between Judaism and Christianity and nationalism. Rather, religious beliefs are cultural resources for nationalism. See Anthony D. Smith, *Chosen Peoples: Sacred Sources of National Identity* (New York: Oxford University Press, 2003), 257-58.

[7]According to Hans Kohn, there are "three essential traits of nationalism": "the idea of the chosen people, the consciousness of national history, and the national Messianism." See Hans Kohn, *The Idea of Nationalism: A Study in Its Origins and Background* (New York: MacMillan, 1945), 36.

[8]Hastings, *Construction of Nationhood*, 58. See also Kohn, *Idea of Nationalism*, 155; and Linda Colley, *Britons: Forging the Nation, 1707–1837*, 2nd ed. (New Haven: Yale University Press, 2005).

For most of the eighteenth century, colonial Americans shared this identity, and they were proud to identify themselves as part of an expansive British nation linked together by a constitutional monarchy, free trade, and a shared Protestant faith. They described themselves as "Britons," not "Americans," and they treated the words *British*, *Protestant*, and *free* as virtually synonymous. Political liberty was nothing less than a sacred cause: to be a Briton was to defend "the Protestant interest" against the political as well as religious ambitions of the Catholic Church. During the French and Indian War, for example, colonial Americans insisted that "British Israel," God's favored nation, was called to fight against French Catholic tyranny.[9]

During the mid-1770s, however, as colonists became increasingly angry about their lack of political representation in Parliament, their reading of the Hebrew Bible led them to a different conclusion. They still believed that God wanted his chosen people to be Protestant, militant, virtuous, and free, but they concluded that the true "Israel" was not England but rather the United States, which God had chosen to be the locus of his activity on earth. The "imperial Bible" of the British empire—the "Bible enlisted for King and country"—had become the American Bible.[10]

Looking back from the perspective of the *American Patriot's Bible*, one might expect to find evangelicals at the forefront of sacralizing the American nation. In New England, however, the Protestant ministers who tended to be most zealous about describing the United States as a new Israel were not evangelicals, but liberal-leaning or moderate Calvinists who had been critical of the Great Awakening. For example, Moses Mather, who supported open church membership against the Edwardseans, rejoiced during the Revolution that "our affections are weaned from Great-Britain, by similar means and almost as miraculously as the Israelites from Egypt." In 1775, reflecting on the suffering of the people in Boston, Mather compared them to the captive Israelites in Babylon. In 1783, Ezra Stiles preached an effusive election sermon, "The United States Elevated to Glory and Honor," predicting that "by the

---

[9]For an example, see Thomas Foxcroft, *Grateful Reflexions on the Signal Appearance of Divine Providence for Great Britain and Its Colonies in America* (Boston: S. Kneeland, 1760), 12. On the "Protestant interest," see Thomas S. Kidd, *The Protestant Interest: New England After Puritanism* (New Haven: Yale University Press, 2004).

[10]Mark A. Noll, *In the Beginning Was the Word: The Bible in American Public Life, 1492–1783* (New York: Oxford University Press, 2016), 162.

blessing of God," the United States would "prosper and flourish into a great American Republic; and ascend into high and distinguished honor among the nations of the earth." He lauded George Washington as "this American Joshua . . . raised up by God," and declared that the United States was "God's American Israel." With a robust faith in human reason and ability, both Stiles and Mather believed that the entire nation, not just elect believers, were in a special covenant with God.[11]

Some of the public figures who seemed most invested in giving the nation a biblical past were only nominally Christian. Thomas Paine, a Deist, called for the overthrow of the British monarchy on the grounds that God had wanted Israel to be a "republic," and Benjamin Franklin, also best described as a Deist, thought that the model for the creation of the United States was the book of Exodus. In 1774, when Congress considered creating a new seal for the United States, Franklin suggested that it should be an image of "Moses lifting up his Wand, and dividing the Red Sea, and Pharaoh, in his Chariot overwhelmed with Waters." He wanted the seal to include the motto, "Rebellion to Tyrants is Obedience to God."[12]

In contrast, evangelicals were more conflicted about whether to identify America as the new Israel. The ministers identified with the New Divinity were especially cautious. Though they studied the Hebrew Bible to discover what it said about republican forms of government, their earnest biblicism prevented them from making exaggerated claims about the identity of the United States. The only "new Israel," they believed, was the Reformed church. In a sermon about slavery, Samuel Hopkins explained that even though God had permitted the biblical Hebrews to enslave the Canaanites, "this distinction is now at an end, and all nations are put upon level; and Christ, who has taken down the wall of separation, has taught us to look on all nations as our neighbors brethren."[13] Significantly, *The American Patriot's Bible* does not

---

[11]Moses Mather, *America's Appeal to the Impartial World* (Hartford, 1775), 52, 69, 58-59, quoted in Mark A. Noll, "Moses Mather (Old Calvinist) and the Evolution of Edwardseanism," *Church History* 49, no. 3 (1980): 283. Ezra Stiles, *The United States Elevated to Glory and Honor* (New Haven: Thomas and Samuel Green, 1783), 7, 37.

[12]Thomas Paine, *Common Sense* (Philadelphia: R. Bell, 1776), 15. James P. Byrd, *Sacred Scripture, Sacred War: The Bible and the American Revolution* (New York: Oxford University Press, 2013), 47.

[13]Samuel Hopkins, *A Dialogue, Concerning the Slavery of the Africans*, in *The Works of Samuel Hopkins* (Boston: Doctrinal Book and Tract Society, 1854), 2:564. Mark Valeri argues that Edwardsean ministers "were convinced that God ruled through a moral law that transcended particular

include any quotations from Hopkins, but it highlights the religious language of Paine and Franklin, whose skepticism about Protestantism is not mentioned. The impression one gets from reading *The American Patriot's Bible* is that virtually all Americans in the past were Christians.[14]

After the defeat of the British at Yorktown and the ratification of the Constitution, eighteenth-century evangelicals became less hesitant to identify the United States not only as a favored nation but as God's *most* favored nation, a new Israel. The victory of the United States over the mighty British empire seemed so unlikely that only divine intervention seemed capable of explaining it. In 1783, only three months after the Treaty of Paris ended the Revolutionary War, the Reverend George Duffield exulted that the United States had become the center of God's plan to save the world. A Presbyterian minister in Philadelphia and the third chaplain to the Continental Congress, Duffield had earned a reputation as a patriot in 1776, when he preached a sermon comparing George III to Pharaoh. By the end of the war, gratified by the American victory, he was even more convinced that the new nation enjoyed God's special favor. In a sermon on Isaiah 66:8, "Shall a nation be born at once," he claimed that these words not only referred to the coming of the Messiah (the usual interpretation), but also to the creation of an "American Zion." Like Israel, the colonies had been held captive by a king who tried to coerce them "into absolute vassalage," but the same God who had led the Israelites "by the pillar and the cloud, through their wilderness journey" had led them to freedom. Blessed by God, the United States would lead the entire world to redemption. "The light of divine revelation" would "diffuse its beneficent rays" around the globe; "the outcasts of Israel and the despised of Judah" would be restored; and all the nations on earth would "become the kingdom of our Lord and Saviour, under whose auspicious reign holiness shall universally prevail, and the noise and alarm of war be heard no more."[15]

---

national interests." Mark Valeri, "The New Divinity and the American Revolution," *The William and Mary Quarterly* 46, no. 4 (1989): 769. Melvin B. Endy Jr., argues that historians have exaggerated the extent to which Protestant ministers identified the United States as a favored nation with a millennial destiny. See his "Just War, Holy War, and Millennialism in Revolutionary America," *The William and Mary Quarterly* 42, no. 1 (1985): 3-25.

[14]*APB*, 690 (Franklin), 666 (Paine).

[15]George Duffield, *A Sermon Preached in the Third Presbyterian Church in the City of Philadelphia, on December 11th, 1783, on the Restoration of Peace*, reprinted in *Patriot Preachers of the American Revolution*, ed. Frank Moore (New York: Charles T. Evans, 1862), 349, 365, 360-61.

In some ways, Duffield's sermon harkened back to older descriptions of the coming of the millennium, when Christ would return in glory to usher in a thousand years of peace on earth. What was new, however, was Duffield's insistence that the redemption of the globe hinged on the agency of the United States. Unlike earlier evangelical ministers such as Jonathan Edwards and George Whitfield, who had promised during the Great Awakening that the millennium would come through heartfelt conversion, he linked the return of Christ to America's religious and political virtue. In 1794, David Austin, a Presbyterian, proclaimed that the "empire of Jesus Christ" had begun on July 4, 1776, when "civil and religious liberty" were born in the United States. "It seems no unnatural conclusion from ancient prophecy, and from present appearances, that in order to usher in the dominion of our glorious Immanuel, as predicted to take place, and usually called the *latter-day glory*, TWO GREAT REVOLUTIONS are to take place; the *first* outward and political; the *second* inward and spiritual."[16] Now that the first revolution had been accomplished, American Christians were poised to spread a message of freedom, both religious and political, to the rest of the world.

There was nothing inevitable about the sacralization of the nation: the Quakers, in particular, objected to it.[17] But because of the First Amendment and the gradual disestablishment of state churches, it became increasingly difficult for Protestants to imagine any single denomination as the locus of salvation. In addition, as Nathan Hatch has pointed out, Protestants assumed that religious liberty depended on civil liberty, which only the nation had the power to protect. In his words, "The American republic came for very good reason to seem the primary agent of redemptive history. While a church might espouse Christian freedom, only a nation could preserve civil liberty which was its prerequisite."[18] Rather than being simply a political compact, the nation seemed to have a transcendent purpose.

Because of their strong sense of human sinfulness, evangelicals always emphasized that being God's favored nation was a burden as well as a blessing.

---

[16]David Austin, *The Millennium* (Elizabethtown, NJ: Shepard Kollock, 1794), 390 ("empire of Jesus Christ"), 392 ("civil and religious liberty"), 393-94 ("no unnatural conclusion"). On the distinctiveness of Revolutionary millennialism, see Hatch, *Sacred Cause of Liberty*, 24.

[17]Sarah Crabtree, *Holy Nation: The Transatlantic Quaker Ministry in an Age of Revolution* (Chicago: University of Chicago Press, 2015), 4-5.

[18]Hatch, *Sacred Cause of Liberty*, 155. On the religious importance of the nation, see also John Edwin Smylie, "National Ethos and the Church," *Theology Today* 20 (1963): 313-21.

God had punished Americans for their sins during the Revolutionary years, and he would continue to punish them if they violated his commandments. And yet even when eighteenth-century evangelicals sounded most stern about the need for repentance, they never lost their faith that God had chosen the United States for a special destiny.[19]

God's special interest in the United States is a central theme of *The American Patriot's Bible*, which features many famous Americans, including Abraham Lincoln and Ronald Reagan, praising the nation in language usually reserved for Jesus: the United States is "the last best hope of earth," or "the last best hope of man on earth." The nation itself is portrayed as a site of redemption. Next to a picture of the Statue of Liberty, for example, there is a small reference to Luke 4:18, which describes Jesus repeating the words of Isaiah: "The Spirit of the Lord is upon me, because he has anointed me to preach the gospel to the poor; he has sent me to heal the brokenhearted. To proclaim liberty to the captives and recovery of sight to the blind. To set at liberty those who are oppressed." The implication is not only that Luke—and Jesus—was referring to political freedom, but also that the United States has a salvific identity: like Jesus, the nation offers liberty to the oppressed.[20]

These grandiose descriptions of the nation are combined with warnings about its religious decline, but if *The American Patriot's Bible* is a jeremiad, it is so in Sacvan Bercovitch's sense of the word: it warns of possible destruction, but not quite yet. The mood of the book is triumphant. According to historian Richard Gamble, who wrote a review of *The American Patriot's Bible* shortly after its publication in 2009, a promotional video for the book included an image of Jesus at the Last Supper next to another image of the delegates to the Continental Congress. The caption said, "Founding Fathers," and at the very end of the video, these words appear on the screen: "Sometimes history repeats itself."[21]

If there is one theme that links together the disparate material found in the *American Patriot's Bible*, it is freedom: not only spiritual freedom in heaven, but also political liberty on earth. The God of Israel—and by extension, the

---

[19]On this theme, see Sacvan Bercovitch, *The American Jeremiad* (Madison: University of Wisconsin Press, 1978).

[20]*APB*, 718 (Lincoln), 922 (Reagan), 1168 (Statue of Liberty).

[21]On the affirmation of the jeremiad, see Bercovitch, *American Jeremiad*, 6. Richard Gamble, "God's Country," *American Conservative* (Arlington) 8, no. 12 (2009): 41.

God of the United States—is a God of liberty. Many of the famous Americans quoted in the text emphasize that the Bible is the foundation of American democracy and the secret to American greatness. In Deuteronomy, for example, readers encounter the words of Franklin Delano Roosevelt, who declared in 1939 that religion is "the source of . . . democracy and international good faith." Through quotations such as these, *The American Patriot's Bible* suggest that the Bible, at its heart, is a democratic text that preaches freedom, and the United States is the fulfillment of biblical promises, or, as George W. Bush explains on the pages of Judges, "the brightest beacon for freedom and opportunity in the world."[22]

Freedom in *The American Patriot's Bible* is often defined in relationship to military service: Americans have been called to defend their God-given freedom with their lives. The text is filled with martial imagery and lengthy quotations from presidents and other Americans, including General Douglas MacArthur, about soldiers' duty to sacrifice their lives for their country. Next to the words of 2 Samuel 1:25, "How the mighty have fallen in the midst of battle," readers encounter an excerpt from MacArthur's 1962 speech "Duty— Honor—Country": "However horrible the incidents of war may be, the soldier who is called upon to offer and give his life for his country is the noblest development of mankind." When readers turn to the Gospels, they do not see the figure of Jesus, but several other illustrations: a lighthouse; the official motto of the United States, "In God We Trust"; and, in the foreground, an image that looks like World War II soldiers planting a flag at Iwo Jima.[23] The implication is that American Christians should imitate the four Gospels, which recount the salvific death of Jesus, by being willing to fight and die for the sake of democracy. As Richard Lee explains in the introduction to *The American Patriot's Bible*, "Americans have given their lives on foreign soils so that others might experience freedom."[24]

By identifying Christianity so strongly with war and political liberty, *The American Patriot's Bible* echoes ideas that were forged during the Revolutionary era, when evangelicals helped to transform the Bible into a justification for republican political principles and armed resistance to tyranny. For

---

[22]*APB*, 217 (Roosevelt), 292 (Bush).

[23]*APB*, 341 (MacArthur), 692 (Gospels).

[24]*APB*, "The Seven Principles of the Judeo-Christian Ethic," Principle #6. (These "principles" are reprinted before the copyright page and are not paginated.)

hundreds of years, the Bible had been used to support the divine right of kings, and, as Mark Noll has pointed out, "most English-speaking Protestants outside of the United States" associated republicanism with anarchy.[25] But during the Revolutionary years, evangelicals decided that Christianity was not only compatible with republicanism but dependent on it. Like John Adams, they argued that the Bible should be understood as "the most Republican Book in the world."[26] A republican form of government would guarantee that both civil and religious liberty would be protected.

A coalition of eighteenth-century Protestants, both liberal-leaning and evangelical, defended this argument by drawing on the ideas of the radical Whigs of the English Civil War, who had justified the overthrow and execution of Charles I on the grounds that God had ordained Israel to be a republic, not a monarchy. According to this interpretation, the biblical Israelites had been punished after demanding to be given a king like other nations. Not only had they endured the splintering of Israel into two kingdoms and oppressive taxation, but they had also suffered the loss of Jerusalem.[27]

Evangelicals also joined liberals in offering new, radical readings of biblical texts that seemed to sanction monarchy, including Romans 13:1-2, a favorite Loyalist text: "Let every soul be subject unto the higher powers. For there is no power but of God: the powers that be are ordained of God. Whosoever therefore resisteth the power, resisteth the ordinance of God: and they that resist shall receive to themselves damnation." By comparing Paul's words in Romans to Galatians 5:1—"Stand fast therefore in the liberty wherewith Christ hath made us free, and be not entangled again with the yoke of bondage"— patriotic ministers transformed Paul into an apostle of liberty.[28]

Evangelicals continued to describe the most important liberty as freedom from the "despotic power" of sin, but they also insisted that the Bible, when

---

[25] Mark A. Noll, *America's God: From Jonathan Edwards to Abraham Lincoln* (New York: Oxford University Press, 2002), 54.

[26] Adams quoted in *The Founders on Religion: A Book of Quotations*, ed. James H. Hutson (Princeton: Princeton University Press, 2005), 33.

[27] Samuel Langdon, *Government Corrupted by Vice, and Recovered by Righteousness* (Watertown, MA: Benjamin Edes, 1775), reprinted in *The Pulpit of the American Revolution, or the Political Sermons of the Period 1776*, ed. John Wingate Thornton (Boston: Gould and Lincoln, 1860). See also Harry S. Stout, *The New England Soul: Preaching and Religious Culture in Colonial New England* (New York: Oxford University Press, 1987), 288, 294.

[28] According to historian James Byrd, ministers preached more sermons on Romans 13 than on any other text. Byrd, *Sacred Scripture, Sacred War*, 117, 170. On Paul, see 129.

properly read, endorsed the right to political liberty. "Freedom is the very temper and spirit of the gospel," preached the Reverend John Zubly, a Presbyterian from Georgia.[29] The Reverend Levi Frisbie, an evangelical missionary to the Delaware Indians, expressed his fervent hope that liberty, a "sacred flame," would "extend its happy influence thro' all the Kingdoms of Europe, if not to the most distant quarters of the globe." It was not clear from his oration where Christianity ended and American liberty began—both were "sacred"—but there was no doubt that he saw he Bible as a deeply patriotic text.[30]

In search of biblical verses about liberty, patriots were especially drawn to the book of Exodus, the story of the Israelites' revolt against an oppressive king and their miraculous journey out of slavery. In a militant sermon that portrayed the Revolution as a recapitulation of the crossing of the Red Sea, the Reverend Nicholas Street, a Congregationalist from Connecticut, described King George III as Pharaoh and the colonists as the oppressed Israelites. In case anyone missed the parallels, Street explained that "The British tyrant is only acting over the same wicked and cruel part that Pharaoh King of Egypt acted towards the children of Israel above 3000 years ago."[31] In a prayer book written for soldiers, Abiel Leonard, an evangelical army chaplain, recommended that they pray to the God "who didst preserve the children of Israel from the hand of Pharaoh and his host."[32]

If Exodus offered reassurance that a small band of God's chosen people could triumph over a mighty foe, it also suggested that military service and righteous violence would be crucial to the construction of the new nation. In a sermon preached to commemorate the battle at Lexington and Concord, the Reverend Jacob Cushing urged soldiers to imagine themselves as the instruments of God's judgment. "If this war be just and necessary on our part,"

[29]Jacob Duché, *The Duty of Standing Fast in Our Liberties* (1775), in Frank Moore, *The Patriot Preachers of the American Revolution* (New York, 1860), 77 ("despotic power"). John Joachim Zubly, *The Law of Liberty. A Sermon on American Affairs, preached at the opening of the Provincial Congress of Georgia* (1775), 131, in Moore, *Patriot Preachers*.

[30]Levi Frisbie, *An Oration Delivered in Ipswich* (Boston, 1783), 15-16.

[31]Nicholas Street, *The American States Acting Over the Part of the Children of Israel in the Wilderness* (New Haven: Thomas and Samuel Green, 1777), reprinted in *God's New Israel: Religious Interpretations of American Destiny*, ed. Conrad Cherry (Chapel Hill: University of North Carolina Press, 1998), 70.

[32]Abiel Leonard, *A Prayer, Composed for the Benefit of the Soldiery, in the American Army, to Assist Them in Their Private Devotions* (Cambridge: S. and E. Hall, 1775).

he preached, "as past all doubt it is, then we are engaged in the work of the Lord, which obliges us (under God mighty in battle), to use our swords as instruments of righteousness, and calls us to the shocking, but necessary, important duty of shedding human blood; not only in defense of our property, life and religion, but in obedience to him who hath said, 'cursed be he that keepeth back his sword from blood.'" (He was quoting Jeremiah 48:10, a popular biblical text during the war.)[33]

If the God of these Revolutionary sermons had a gender, that gender was masculine: God was a fierce, implacable warrior who called his chosen people to fight for the sacred cause of liberty. In 1777, on the eve of the battle at Brandywine, the Reverend Joab Trout delivered a rousing sermon urging soldiers to remember that "in the hour of battle . . . God is with you! The eternal God fights for you! He rides on the battle-cloud; he sweeps onward with the march, or the hurricane charge! God, the awful and infinite, fights for you, and will triumph!"[34] When preaching from the New Testament, patriotic ministers acknowledged that Jesus had urged his disciples to love their enemies, to bless those who cursed them, and to turn the other cheek, but they were also attracted to the violent image of Jesus found in the book of Revelation: "And out of his mouth goeth a sharp sword, that with it he should smite the nations: and he shall rule them with a rod of iron: and he treadeth the winepress of the fierceness and wrath of Almighty God." In a sermon on the "dignity and importance of the military character," Eli Forbes was careful to insist that Jesus did not delight in "blood and slaughter," but he also praised him as a "victorious commander" who would ride into battle to defend "his people's rights."[35]

In the space of a generation, evangelicals had joined other patriots to accomplish a remarkable feat. Not only had they helped to construct a new nation on the model of the biblical Israel, but they had also changed the way that ordinary people understood the Bible. The Bible remained the greatest story ever told, the story of salvation through Christ, but it had also become

---

[33]Jacob Cushing, *Divine Judgments upon Tyrants: and Compassion to the Oppressed* (Boston: Powars and Willis, 1778), 23. On the popularity of this text, see Byrd, *Sacred Scripture, Sacred War*, 73.

[34]Joab Trout, *A Revolutionary Relic: A Sermon Preached on the Eve of the Battle of Brandywine, Sept. 10, 1777* (Burlington, 1800).

[35]Eli Forbes, *The Dignity and Importance of the Military Character Illustrated* (Boston: Richard Draper, 1771), Revelation 19:15. On Forbes, see Byrd, *Sacred Scripture, Sacred War*, 160-62.

an icon of American freedom, military power, and nationalism. As Alexis de Tocqueville noted after his visit to the United States in 1831, "The Americans combine the notions of Christianity and of liberty so intimately in their minds that it is impossible to make them conceive the one without the other."[36] Like the Declaration of Independence and the Constitution, the Bible was imagined as one of the founding documents of the United States.

The American Patriot's Bible reflects this history, albeit in an exaggerated form. Images of the Constitution appear on many pages, and within the book of Romans, readers encounter the full text of the Declaration of Independence. Next to a portrait of Benjamin Rush, who argued that without religion, "there can be no virtue," is an abbreviated version of Romans 8:2. Instead of the full verse, "For the law of the Spirit of life in Christ Jesus has made me free from the law of sin and death," the quotation reads, "For the law of the Spirit of life in Christ Jesus has made me free."[37] This small revision leaves the impression that Paul's words refer to political freedom, as if the Declaration of Independence should be understood as the realization of biblical promises. Within the pages of *The American Patriot's Bible*, both the Bible and the United States ultimately stand for the same thing. Freedom.

One might think that because of its focus on liberty, *The American Patriot's Bible* would devote significant attention to the African American, Native American, and female Christians who were inspired by the American Revolution to fight for their political rights. Yet despite a few attempts at inclusiveness, much of *The American Patriot's Bible* lends itself to a White nationalist reading of American history. The majority of Americans profiled are White men, and even though the book acknowledges the reality of racism and sexism, it does so only briefly and superficially, a stance that reflects evangelicals' historical ambivalence over how to imagine the United States. In the early nineteenth century, evangelicals agreed that they wanted to create a Christian nation modeled on the Bible, but they clashed—sometimes vehemently—over the kind of nationalism it sanctioned. As evangelicals grew increasingly powerful and led popular revivals in every region of the country, they discovered that turning the Bible into an icon of American freedom had been the easy part. Figuring out how to define both "America" and "freedom" proved to be far more difficult.

---

[36]Alexis de Tocqueville, *Democracy in America* (New York: Adlard, 1839), 1:305.
[37]*APB*, 1286.

Debates over the fate of Native Americans were particularly fraught. In the elaborate biblical comparison that White Protestants constructed during the Revolution, they were the Israelites, the British were the Egyptians, and Native Americans, the original inhabitants of the land, were the Canaanites. In *The United States Elevated to Glory and Honor*, Ezra Stiles compared American Indians to "Canaanites of the expulsion of Joshua," reminding his listeners that Joshua had been commanded by God to kill the Canaanites and take their land.[38] Timothy Dwight, a chaplain in the Continental Army, wrote an epic poem about the Revolution, *The Conquest of Canaan*, which depicts George Washington as the biblical Joshua waging war against the heathen Canaanites. "For now, all over the fight, the heathens yield," Dwight writes, "and Israel triumphs round the dreadful field." When the panicked "heathen" drop their swords, spears, and shields and run into the forest, Joshua relentlessly pursues them and chases them out of the Promised Land. In a later poem, "Greenfield Hill," Dwight expresses sorrow about the Puritans' destruction of the Pequots—"The tombs of empires fallen! And nations gone!"—but he also suggests that the remaining Indians, deficient in Protestant virtues, will soon vanish.[39]

If Dwight thought the Indians resembled the biblical Canaanites, other White evangelicals speculated that they might be best understood as a different group of people in the Hebrew Bible, the ten lost tribes of Israel. Elias Boudinot, a devout Presbyterian and president of the Second Continental Congress, argued that the United States had a special role to play in the advent of the millennium, but the nation was not, in fact, the New Israel but only a refuge for a remnant of the old. The United States "has been raised up in the course of divine Providence, at a very important crisis, and for no very inconsiderable purpose," he wrote, but only to fulfill God's promises to the Jews. "Who knows but God has raised up these United States, in these latter days, for the very purpose of accomplishing his will in bringing his beloved people to their own land." His interpretation managed to preserve Americans' faith

---

[38]Ezra Stiles, *The United States Elevated to Glory and Honor* (New Haven: Thomas and Samuel Green, 1783), 10.

[39]Timothy Dwight, *The Conquest of Canaan; A Poem, in Eleven Books* (Hartford: Elisha Babcock, 1785), 300. Timothy Dwight, *Greenfield Hill: A Poem in Seven Parts* (New York: Childs and Swaine, 1794), 93. See Bill Templer, "The Political Sacralization of Imperial Genocide: Contextualizing Timothy Dwight's *The Conquest of Canaan*," *Postcolonial Studies* 9, no. 4 (2006): 358-91.

in the nation's cosmic importance while also deflating their claim to be God's chosen people.[40]

Though relatively few in number, Native American evangelicals saw themselves as mediators between two worlds, and with a double allegiance to Christianity and to Indian sovereignty, they struggled to disentangle White nationalism from the Bible. William Apess, a Pequot and Methodist minister, not only repeated the argument that Native Americans were the ten lost tribes of Israel, but even more radically, he also compared the United States to Egypt, the villain of the exodus narrative. After the Mashpee were denied sovereignty over their land, Apess testified, "We regarded ourselves, in some sort, as a tribe of Israelites suffering under the rod of despotic pharaohs; for thus far, our cries and remonstrances had been of no avail. We were compelled to make our bricks without straw." (He was referring to Pharaoh's cruel words in Exodus 5:7, "Ye shall no more give the people straw to make brick, as heretofore: let them go and gather straw for themselves.") Well-versed in the tradition of the jeremiad, Apess warned White Christians that "the great American nation" should "fear the swift judgments of heaven on them for nameless cruelties, extortions, and exterminations inflicted upon the poor natives of the forest."[41]

Other Indians tried to dismantle White nationalism by invoking the universalist message of the New Testament. In 1831 Gallegina Uwati, a Cherokee who changed his name to Elias Boudinot out of admiration for him, delivered an address in a Presbyterian church to refute the claim that "It is the purpose of the Almighty that the Indians should be exterminated." Determined to show his audience that the Cherokee were becoming "civilized," he pointed out that they had invented a written alphabet, organized a government, and perhaps most important, translated the New Testament into Cherokee. Boudinot knew that for many White Christians, Indian removal seemed to be justified by the fate of the biblical Amalekites and Canaanites, but he chose to emphasize the creation narrative in the book of Acts: "Of one blood God

---

[40]Elias Boudinot, *The Second Advent* (Trenton: Fenton and Hutchinson, 1815), 532. Elias Boudinot, *A Star in the West; or, A Humble Attempt to Discover the Long Lost Ten Tribes of Israel, Preparatory to Their Return to Their Beloved City, Jerusalem* (Trenton: Fenton and Hutchinson, 1816), 297.

[41]William Apess, *Indian Nullification* (Boston: Jonathan Howe, 1835), 28. William Apess, *The Increase of the Kingdom of Christ* (New York: G. F. Bunce, 1831), 12. See Rochelle Raineri Zuck, "William Apess, the 'Lost Tribes,' and Indigenous Survivance," *Studies in American Indian Literatures* 25, no. 1 (Spring 2013): 1-26.

created all the nations that dwell on the face of the earth."[42] Since Boudinot had been educated in a Christian school run by the American Board of Commissioners for Foreign Missions, he was hopeful that his appeal to the Bible would be persuasive, but his words had little effect on the hunger for Indian land. Thousands of Cherokees died on the Trail of Tears, and in 1839, Boudinot was assassinated by a group of Cherokees who thought he had been too willing to acculturate.

In the case of Indian removal, White nationalism proved to be more powerful than Christianity. Even though many nineteenth-century evangelicals defended the dignity and humanity of Native Americans, few evangelicals remember this history today. *The American Patriot's Bible* includes a full page celebrating the labors of John Eliot, the seventeenth-century "Apostle to the Indians," but its brief description of native people is derogatory. Readers learn that before Indians' exposure to Christianity, their practices includes "wife beating, polygamy, lying, and stealing."[43] No Native American is mentioned by name.

In contrast to Native Americans, who hardly register as either Americans or patriots in *The American Patriot's Bible*, African Americans are given a larger place. In a glossy, four-page insert on "Christianity and Equal Rights," the text tries to align itself with the cause of racial justice. In several paragraphs about the civil rights movement, readers learn that Martin Luther King Jr. was motivated by a "deep love of God," and that the movement was "rooted in two cherished national treasures—the Bible and the promise of true equality in the American Constitution." This section includes a photograph of Barack Obama, whose 2008 election is described as "a fulfillment at least in part of Dr. King's vision for equal opportunity in America." Elsewhere in the text, Frederick Douglass is quoted four times, placing him on par with Noah Webster, quoted five times.[44]

Yet despite this effort to include a few prominent Black voices, *The American Patriot's Bible* offers a selective reading of African American Christian history that softens its political radicalism. The description of King,

---

[42]Elias Boudinot, *An Address to the Whites Delivered in the First Presbyterian Church on the 26th of May, 1826* (Philadelphia: William F. Geddes, 1826), 2, 4.

[43]*APB*, 1131.

[44]*APB*, I-43 (deep love), I-44 (two cherished national treasures, fulfillment). Douglass is cited on 369, 1061, 1073, 1028; Webster appears on I-24, 118, 1180, 363, 316.

for example, emphasizes his aspiration to live in a "color-blind society" more than his desire to dismantle structural racism. The text quotes the section of his "I Have a Dream" speech that has been most admired by conservatives: "I look to a day when people will not be judged by the color of their skin, but by the content of their character." Rather than reprinting any of Frederick Douglass's anguished criticisms of the hypocrisy of American Christianity, *The American Patriot's Bible* quotes his praise of both the Bible and the Declaration of Independence.[45]

Missing in *The American Patriot's Bible* is a full reckoning with evangelicals' role in defending and perpetuating slavery. In more than 1,500 pages of text, only one passage directly addresses proslavery theology—a passage in the introduction to the book of Philemon. "Paul never suggests that Philemon had committed a sin in owning Onesimus," the text explains:

> Pro-slavery advocates used this fact in defending the moral propriety of slavery before the Civil War. Abolitionists, on the other hand, said that referring to slaves as "brothers" undercut the social distinctions inherent in slavery. Abolitionists were correct when they argued that although Paul did not directly condemn slavery, the spirit of his words embodies the principle of love, which motivates Christian action against the oppression of slavery and its violation of the concept of justice and the dignity and value and equality of every human person.[46]

On one hand, *The American Patriot's Bible* declares that White slaveholding Christians did not read Scripture correctly, but on the other hand, it explicitly rejects the word *sin*, and it refuses a deeper engagement with the legacy of racism. Slavery, it suggests, should not diminish our appreciation for either the message of freedom embedded in the Bible or the essentially Christian character of the nineteenth-century United States.

This reluctance to fully address slavery reflects the bitter debates over the meaning of freedom that took place between the founding of the nation and the Civil War. Even though *The American Patriot's Bible* implies that the emancipatory nature of the Bible is self-evident, this was not readily apparent to all eighteenth- and nineteenth-century evangelicals. On one hand, some denounced slavery as an offense against both God and the founding principles

---

[45] *APB*, I-43 (King), 1061, 1073 (Douglass).
[46] *APB*, 1380.

of the Declaration of Independence. Many Methodists and Baptists, after first condemning the injustice of slavery, decided that there was a distinction between the political freedom of White men and the purely spiritual freedom enjoyed by Black people. Citing Genesis 9, the enigmatic story of Ham, they argued that heaven was open to all races, but God had ordained Africans to be subordinate to White men on earth.[47] Others reasoned that if the United States was like the biblical Israel, then Americans, like the Israelites, should be allowed to practice slavery. When Thornton Stringfellow, a southern Presbyterian, published a scriptural defense of slavery in 1841, he briefly mentioned that Jesus had never expressly forbidden it, but most of his evidence was drawn from the Hebrew Bible. In order to highlight the parallels between Israel and the United States, he repeatedly used the word *constitution*—a word that never appears in the King James Version of the Bible—in reference to Israel's government. Slavery, he testified, "was incorporated into the only National Constitution which ever emanated from God." After examining the many instances of slavery in the Hebrew Bible, he concluded:

> we have shown from the text of the sacred volume, that when God entered into covenant with Abraham, it was with him as a slaveholder; that when he took his posterity by the hand in Egypt, five hundred years afterwards to confirm the promise made to Abraham, it was done with them as slaveholders; that when he gave them a constitution of government, he gave them the right to perpetuate hereditary slavery; and that he did not for the fifteen hundred years of their national existence, express disapprobation towards the institution.[48]

Without explicitly stating it, Stringfellow implied that any national constitution genuinely inspired by God would sanction slavery.

Though proslavery theologians marshalled strong biblical support for their position, the Revolutionary generation had been so successful in turning the Bible into an icon of American liberty and patriotism that many nineteenth-century Christians read it through the lens of the founding principles of the

---

[47]Stephen R. Haynes, *Noah's Curse: The Biblical Justification of American Slavery* (New York: Oxford University Press, 2002). Donald G. Mathews, *Slavery and Methodism: A Chapter in American Morality, 1780–1845* (Princeton: Princeton University Press, 1965), 180.

[48]Thornton Stringfellow, "A Brief Examination of Scripture Testimony in the Institution of Slavery" (1841), in *The Ideology of Slavery: Proslavery Thought in the Antebellum South, 1830–1860*, ed. Drew Gilpin Faust (Baton Rouge: Louisiana State University Press, 1981), 139, 165.

United States. They insisted that even if the letter of the Bible sanctioned slavery, the spirit of the Bible did not. "The Book," as Presbyterian George Bourne described the Bible, was irreconcilable with slavery. Since the core message of both the United States and the Bible was freedom, then by definition slavery could be neither Christian nor American. Bourne mocked Samuel Stanhope Smith, the president of Princeton, for betraying both his religious and political principles by trying to take a moderate position on slavery. "What more preposterous!" he exclaimed. "An American Republican, who boasts of his freedom, *driving slaves!*"[49] When abolitionist John Brown was asked to explain his violent resistance to slavery, he blurred the boundaries between what was American and what was biblical: "I believe in the Golden Rule and the Declaration of Independence," he testified. "I think they both mean the same thing."[50]

No one was more passionate about portraying the Bible as a beacon of freedom than African American Christians, who, like Native American Christians, were particularly drawn to the book of Exodus, which gave them hope that God would one day send a Moses to lead them to freedom. As early as 1774, Phillis Wheatley portrayed enslaved Africans as the captive Israelites and White Americans as the oppressive Egyptians. "In every human Breast," she wrote in a letter to Samson Occum, a Native American minister, "God has implanted a Principle, which we call Love of Freedom; it is impatient of Oppression, and pants for Deliverance; and by the Leave of our Modern Egyptians I will assert, that the same Principle lives in us."[51]

The American Patriot's Bible pays homage to this interpretive tradition by placing the stories of two African American Christians within the book of Exodus. A full-page insert focuses on the Reverend Henry Highland Garnett, who gave a speech to Congress in 1865 celebrating the Emancipation Proclamation, and a large box is devoted to Harriet Powers, an ex-slave who crafted quilts featuring biblical themes. Yet most of the material included in

[49]John W. Christie and Dwight L. Dumond, *George Bourne and the Book and Slavery Irreconcilable* (Philadelphia: Presbyterian Historical Society, 1969), 205. See also Andrew E. Murray, "'The Book and Slavery Irreconcilable,' by George Bourne," *American Presbyterians* 66, no. 4 (Winter 1988): 229-33.

[50]Franklin B. Sanborn, William Channing, and Samuel Orcutt, eds., *Memoirs of John Brown: Written for Rev. Samuel Orcutt's History of Torrington, Ct.* (Concord, 1878), 29.

[51]Letter from Phillis Wheatley to Samson Occom, Feb. 11, 1774, in *Phillis Wheatley: Complete Writings*, ed. Vincent Caretta (New York: Penguin, 2001), 153.

Exodus highlights the experience of White Christians. A full-page insert about George Washington, described as the "American Moses," is followed by other text boxes featuring the words of prominent White men, including quotations from Oliver Wendell Holmes Jr., about service, Noah Webster about moral character, William Cullen Bryant about the sacredness of the Bible, and Wernher von Braun, "The Father of the American Space Program," about "the moral law of God." Another box reprints a 1665 law in the New York Colony that mandated the construction of a church in each parish.[52] Readers are left with the impression that Exodus, a story about slavery and redemption, has as much—or more—to do with the Pilgrims, George Washington, and the space program as with the experience of Black Christians.

This interpretive slant overlooks the crucial role played by antislavery evangelicals, both White and Black, in cementing the transformation of the Bible into a symbol of freedom—this time not only for Whites, as had been true during the Revolution, but also for Black people. Henry Bibb, a former slave and a Methodist, was so certain of the Bible's liberating message that he attributed an almost magical power to the Bible's ability to vanquish slavery on its own. In 1849, when the American Missionary Society announced that it planned to distribute Bibles to all slaves in the South, he gave an impassioned speech testifying that masters "might cut, and scourge, and bruise their slaves; they might consign them to the dank and dismal dungeon; they might brand the initials of their names upon the quivering flesh; but the moment the Bible got among them, they (the slaves) could not be held in bondage any longer." In response, Frederick Douglass scoffed at the idea that the mere presence of the Bible in the slave quarters could eradicate slavery, but Bibb had an unshakeable faith in the Bible's emancipatory power. After acknowledging that slaveholders used Scripture to defend themselves, he declared, "I hold to fighting men with their own weapons, and with the Bible as instrument, the overthrow of Slavery is certain."[53]

Despite his criticism of Bibb, Douglass insisted that "the Bible is peculiarly the companion of liberty," an opinion that was widely shared by Black

---

[52]*APB*, 78 (Garnett), 102 (Powers), 64 (Washington), 73 (Holmes), 81 (Webster), 88 (Bryant), 97 (von Braun), 83 (1665 law).

[53]*Annual Report of the American and Foreign Anti-Slavery Society, Presented at New York, May 8, 1849, with the Resolutions and Addresses* (New York: American & Foreign Anti-Slavery Society, 1849), 8.

Christians.[54] Yet the antislavery figure who appears most frequently in *The American Patriot's Bible* is Abraham Lincoln, who is portrayed as standing virtually alone in his wisdom about the true meaning of the Bible. An insert on "The Civil War" quotes his Second Inaugural: "Both read the same Bible, and pray to the same God; and each invokes His aid against the other. It may seem strange that any men should dare to ask a just God's assistance in wringing their bread from the sweat of other men's faces; but let us judge not that we be not judged. The prayers of both could not be answered; that of neither has been answered fully. The Almighty has His own purposes." Even though Lincoln had a complicated relationship to Christianity, there are dozens of images of him in the text. One illustration depicts him reading the Bible to his son, an image that stands as part of a long visual history of emphasizing Lincoln's devotion to the Bible.[55] After the Emancipation Proclamation in 1863, Lincoln was often depicted with a Bible in his hand, as if he had been guided by its message of liberation. In 1864, for example, William E. Winner painted a portrait of Lincoln with the Emancipation Proclamation in his hand and the Bible resting on the table in front of him. In a later woodcut engraving, *Proclamation of Emancipation*, dated tentatively between 1865 and 1880, a group of African Americans fall to their knees in joyful prayer as several things happen at once: a miraculous hand reveals the Bible, Abraham Lincoln appears with the Emancipation Proclamation in his hand, and a Union soldier riding a white horse hands something to a Black soldier—perhaps a copy of the Proclamation or his freedom papers. The focal point of the engraving is the Bible, whose pages radiate the light of freedom, but Lincoln has set things in motion: he is the reason that the true meaning of the Bible has suddenly become apparent.[56]

It is not surprising that *The American Patriot's Bible* echoes this nineteenth-century view of Lincoln as the Great Emancipator, which remains popular today. But Lincoln's brooding image appears at the beginning of each book of *The American Patriot's Bible* from Joshua to Esther, and he is so ubiquitous

[54]Frederick Douglass, "Bibles for the Slaves," *Liberator* 17, no. 4 (January 28, 1848).
[55]*APB*, I-32 (Second Inaugural, illustration).
[56]William E. Winner, *Abraham Lincoln President of the United States signing the Emancipation Proclamation*, engraved by J. Serz (Philadelphia: John Dainty, [1864?]). Woodcut engraving, artist unknown (Richardson?), *Proclamation of Emancipation*, dated between 1865 and 1880. Library of Congress.

that he seems to personify freedom, patriotism, and Christianity. On the copyright page he is pictured alongside Frederick Douglass (and Ronald Reagan, who rides a white horse), but the text suggests that Lincoln revealed the true meaning of the Bible to Douglass and other slaves, not vice versa. Even though *The American Patriot's Bible* acknowledges the contributions of Black Christians, it suggests that the greatness of the nation is due to God's inspiration of illustrious White leaders.

These leaders include women, but only a few: Harriet Beecher Stowe, Elizabeth Cady Stanton, Susan B. Anthony, Lucretia Mott, Angelina Grimké, Lucy Stone, Deborah Sampson (who enlisted in the Continental Army by pretending to be a man), and Harriet Tubman, one of only two African women depicted in the text. (The other is Harriet Powers, the quilt maker who appears in Exodus.)[57] On one hand, *The American Patriot's Bible* argues that Christianity supports women's rights, and it portrays the passage of the Nineteenth Amendment as a victory for biblical principles. Readers learn that "nearly all of the major leaders of the suffrage movement came from Christian backgrounds," and, despite widespread opposition to women's education, property ownership, and voting, "women's suffrage gained in popularity as more and more people began to realize that there was no biblical support for inequality between the sexes." But on the other hand, *The American Patriot's Bible* seems to be aimed at a male audience, and beyond one page on "Women in the Revolutionary War," a second on "Women in the Civil War," and several paragraphs about the suffrage movement, women are virtually invisible. They earn praise for supporting soldiers in times of war, or in the case of Deborah Sampson, fighting as a soldier herself, but most of the patriotic Americans in this book are men.[58] To be a woman in a Christian nation, according to *The American Patriot's Bible*, is to defer to the leadership of White men.

In 2016, Richard Lee edited another version of the Bible, *The American Woman's Bible*, that seems to have been designed to rectify women's absence from *The American Patriot's Bible*. There are many similarities between the two books, especially in terms of its focus on women's contributions to American war efforts, but *The American Woman's Bible* offers an even sharper delineation of women's duties as Christians and Americans. There are some

---

[57] *APB*, 916 (Stowe), I-41 (Stanton, Anthony), I-43 (Stone, Mott, Grimké), 272 (Sampson), 516 and 426 (Tubman), 102 (Powers).

[58] *APB*, I-41, I-43, 272 (Women in the Revolutionary War), 242 (Women in the Civil War).

areas of overlap: both Bibles, for example, describe individuals under the gender-neutral headings of "Humility" and "Service." But in contrast to the *American Patriot's Bible*, which celebrates men's achievements under headings such as "Defender," "Protector," "Honor," "Leadership," and "Moral Strength," *The American Woman's Bible* praises women under headings that do not appear in the other text, including "Love," "Forgiveness," "Influence," "Kindness," and "Obedience." In a section on "Women of America after September 11, 2001," the text compares women to the Statue of Liberty, who has been a "beacon of hope to the world." "She walks forward over the chains of oppression," the text explains, and "her face is motherly and welcoming." "She has looked on as wars have been fought and a nation has survived. She has remained standing through civil unrest and political upheaval. And she stood tall as our nation was targeted by terrorist enemies. She stood tall."[59] Like Lady Liberty, American Christian women seem to stand virtually outside of history, symbolizing the Christian and American values that men must fight to defend.

The individuals who appear most frequently in *The American Patriot's Bible* share three distinguishing characteristics: not only are they White and male but also Protestant. Though the book celebrates religious liberty, it avoids the topic of religious pluralism. Despite a full page on American support for the Jewish state, only three Jewish Americans are mentioned in the text: Rabbi Morris Jacob Raphall, who in 1860 became the first rabbi to open the House of Representatives with prayer; Irving Berlin, who wrote the song "God Bless America"; and Rabbi Alexander D. Goode, one of the four chaplains who gave up their life jackets in 1943 in order to save soldiers on the *Dorchester*, a transport ship that was struck by a German torpedo.[60] The supersessionism of this Bible is clear: Israel is important as the imagined site of the Second Coming of Christ, but real Jews are almost invisible.

The American Patriot's Bible makes it clear that another of the chaplains on the *Dorchester*, Father John P. Washington, was Catholic, but it mentions only a few other Catholics, including Christopher Columbus, who is described as a "devout Catholic," and John F. Kennedy, who is celebrated for

---

[59]Richard Lee, *American Woman's Bible* (Nashville: Thomas Nelson, 2016), 765 (love), 53 (forgiveness), 122 (influence), 702 (kindness), 82 (obedience), insert before 1387 (Statue of Liberty).
[60]*APB*, 694 (Jewish state), 171 (Raphall), 211 (Berlin), 1229 (Goode).

his statement that the nation's guiding principle is "In God We Trust."[61] There is nothing in *The American Patriot's Bible* that is either explicitly anti-Catholic or anti-Semitic, but by focusing almost exclusively on Protestants, the book suggests that Protestants, more than any other religious group, are "American patriots."

This assumption reflects evangelicals' historic tendency to view themselves as the guardians of the nation. Nineteenth-century evangelicals debated over whether or not God wanted the United States to be governed by Whites, but they were certain that God wanted it to be led by Protestants. According to Daniel Dorchester, a Methodist minister, God had hidden America from discovery until after the Protestant Reformation. "The territory originally comprised within the United States was mysteriously guarded and reserved for another—a prepared people," he wrote in 1890. Based on his reading of the Bible, Dorchester believed that God wanted his favored nation to be free, and to be free was to be Protestant.[62]

As massive waves of Catholic immigrants arrived in the United States during the 1800s, evangelicals insisted that the United States was supposed to be a Protestant nation. Just as they had labelled Native Americans as Amalekites or Canaanites, and Africans as the descendants of Ham, they gave the Catholic Church a biblical identity: it was the "whore of Babylon" or the "Beast" described in the Book of Revelation. According to Lyman Beecher, the Catholic Church was deliberately sending immigrants to the United States to try to destroy both Protestantism and democracy. He speculated that "three-fourths of the foreign emigrants whose accumulating tide is rolling in upon us, are, through the medium of their religion and priesthood, as entirely accessible to the control of the potentates of Europe as if they were an army of soldiers, enlisted and officered, and spreading over the land."[63]

One of the marks of the Church's apostasy, according to evangelicals, was its hostility to the Bible. Evangelicals rejected the Church's claim that God reveals his will through tradition as well as Scripture, and they accused the Catholic hierarchy, led by the pope, of restricting access to the Bible and inventing doctrines that were designed to increase the Church's power and wealth. "Popery is the avowed, unrelenting and incurable enemy of the Holy

---

[61]*APB*, 1229 (Washington), 1076 (Columbus), 1397 (Kennedy).
[62]Daniel Dorchester, *Christianity in the United States* (New York: Hunt and Eaton, 1889), 24.
[63]Lyman Beecher, *A Plea for the West* (1835), 54.

Scriptures," warned George Bourne.[64] Though the Catholic Church sanctioned the Douay-Reims Version of the Bible, evangelicals condemned this version as so filled with errors that it hardly deserved to be called a Bible at all. The King James Version was the anchor of American freedom, and if Catholics refused to recognize it as the only true source of authority, then they could be neither true Americans nor true Christians. Harriet Probasco, a Methodist and nativist, warned that "if the BIBLE should be suppressed and liberty of conscience destroyed, then farewell to political liberty."[65] The Bible, according to Noah Webster, was "the genuine source of correct republican principles."

The American Patriot's Bible frequently quotes Noah Webster, who supported Bible reading in public schools, but the anti-Catholic context of his comments has been erased. Like the abolitionist evangelicals who believed that slaves would fight for their freedom if given the opportunity to read the Bible, many evangelicals hoped that if Catholics read the King James Version, or even if they just heard it read aloud, then they would understand the true meaning of liberty: *sola scriptura* would turn them into faithful Protestants and loyal American citizens. "If they could read the Bible, and might and did," Lyman Beecher wrote in 1835 in *A Plea for the West*, "their darkened intellect would brighten, and their bowed down mind would rise. If they dared to think for themselves, the contrast of Protestant independence with their thralldom, would awaken the desire of equal privileges, and put an end to an arbitrary clerical dominion over trembling superstitious minds."[66]

In practice, however, many Catholic parents refused to allow their children to recite the King James Version aloud in school, and a few Catholic priests even burned copies of it, most famously at Champlain in 1842. Two years later in Philadelphia, a riot broke out in response to rumors that Irish Catholic immigrants had demanded the removal of the Bible from public schools. The riots lasted for three days, with two Catholic churches burned to the ground, more than one hundred people injured, and twenty people killed.[67] A year

---

[64]"The Devil Is Come to You," *The Protestant*, ed. George Bourne (New York: James P. Requa, September 24, 1831), cited in *The Nativist Movement in America: Religious Conflict in the Nineteenth Century*, ed. Katie Oxx (New York: Routledge, 2013), 115.

[65]Harriet Probasco, "Our Vignette," *The American Woman*, September 7, 1844, reprinted in Oxx, ed., *Nativist Movement*, 133. Noah Webster, *History of the United States* (New Haven: Durrie and Peck, 1832), 6.

[66]Beecher, *Plea for the West*, 128.

[67]See the Historical Society of Pennsylvania exhibit at www.philaplace.org/story/316.

later, David M. Reese, a Methodist minister, lamented that "the Holy Bible, including the truth of God therein revealed, is disallowed, disparaged, expurgated and prohibited by the church." If Bible reading were banned in public schools, the republic would not endure. "Our country will be in danger of a return to the barbarism of the dark ages," he warned, "for neither civil nor religious liberty can long survive the extinguishment of the light of revelation." As "the Book of Liberty, the magna charta . . . of human freedom and right," the Bible was crucial "for the perpetuity of our country and her glorious institutions."[68]

In nativist cartoons, the Bible was portrayed as an almost magical object that would protect the nation from Catholic aggression. In an 1855 print from Currier and Ives, "The Propagation Society: More free than welcome," the character of "Young America" points to a Bible in his hand while warning a simian-looking Pope, "You can neither coax nor frighten our boys, Sir! We can take care of our own worldly affairs and are determined to Know Nothing but this book to guide us in spiritual things." (He was referring to the Know Nothings, an anti-Catholic organization.) Despite the sword in the Pope's hand, Brother Jonathan (the precursor of Uncle Sam) looks nonchalant, and Young America, brandishing the Bible in front of him, appears confident that it will protect them. His confidence seems well-placed: a priest in the boat complains, "I cannot bear to see that boy with that horrible book," as if mere presence of the Bible will drive him away.[69]

The American Patriot's Bible does not repeat any of this anti-Catholic language or imagery: its enemies are secularists, not Catholics. In a reversal from nineteenth-century history, the text never decries the papacy, and on the contrary, it explicitly praises Pope John Paul II as a "defender" of human life.[70] Nevertheless, *The American Patriot's Bible* builds on a longer tradition by identifying the Bible almost entirely with Protestants—a position that was used in the nineteenth century to suggest that only Protestants could be trusted to interpret the Bible, and by extension, only Protestants could be trusted to govern the nation. In 1845, when David Reese decried Catholics

---

[68]David M. Reese, "Romanism and Liberty," *Quarterly Review of The American Protestant Association* 2, no. 2 (1845): 128, 134, 141, 144-45.
[69]N. Currier (Firm), *The Propagation Society. More Free than Welcome* (New York: Nathaniel Currier, 1855).
[70]APB, 696.

for their opposition to Bible reading in public schools, he affirmed that the United States was a "land of freedom and equal rights" where all were "welcomed to a participation of every blessing of civil and religious liberty," but he concluded, "*none but* the free can either appreciate or realize our freedom. Hence, they who are wither *unable or unwilling* to throw off their allegiance to any foreign despot, be he *king*, or be he *pope*, are morally disqualified for citizenship in this republic." Only Protestants could be trusted to interpret the Bible, and by extension, only Protestants could be trusted to govern the nation.[71]

The American Patriot's Bible is mostly silent about Islam, but a small reference suggests that Muslims, like secularists, have taken the place of Catholics in the evangelical imagination. A full-page insert about "The Barbary Pirates" appears next to a quotation from Genesis about Ishmael, "his hand shall be against every man, and every man's hand against him," as if the Bible forecast the aggression of the "Muslim pirates" who fought in the Barbary Wars—and perhaps, by extension, the Muslim terrorists who attacked the United States on September 11, 2001. To be clear, *The American Patriot's Bible* never explicitly makes this suggestion, but careful readers might draw this inference.[72]

If it is true that *The American Patriot's Bible* reflects a long history of thinking about the nation, it is equally true that it marks something distinctively new. Not only does it suppress the voices of evangelicals who objected to the idolatry of nationalism, but also, as a material object *The American Patriot's Bible* marks a watering down of the evangelical commitment to *sola scriptura*, the Bible alone. Of course, as historian Seth Perry has recently argued, American Protestants never have actually read the Bible alone, not if this means reading the Bible without any marginal notes, headings, cross references, or supplementary material such as maps.[73] But until the rise of the Christian Right during the 1970s, evangelicals did not publish Bibles that placed American history literally alongside verses of Scripture.

---

[71]Reese, "Romanism and Liberty," 130. In most respects, I agree with Richard Gamble's critical review of *The American Patriot's Bible*, "God's Country," in *American Conservative* (Arlington) 8, no. 12 (2009): 40-42. But I do not share his conviction that "the book goes out of its way to be nonpartisan, ecumenical, and racially inclusive" (40).

[72]*APB*, 18.

[73]Seth Perry, *Bible Culture and Authority in the Early United States* (Princeton: Princeton University Press, 2018).

The turning point seems to have come in 1976 during the nation's Bicentennial, when the American Bible Society began publishing Scripture Portions that drew explicit parallels between the Bible and American history. One Scripture Portion, "Proclaim Liberty Throughout All the Land," printed the first four verses of Isaiah 61 in a bell-shaped pamphlet with a picture of the Liberty Bell on the cover. According to historian John Fea, "ABS volunteers, in conjunction with the Pennsylvania Bible Society, distributed over 60,000 of these portions at Independence National Historical Park during the month of July."[74]

Perhaps influenced by this example, Jerry Falwell produced a patriotic edition of the Bible known as the *I Love America Bible* in 1983. Published by the "I Love America Committee," Falwell's political action committee, the Bible included short biographies of all the presidents, the text of the Constitution, a five-page essay on "The Pulpit and the American Revolution," and a list of the seven biblical principles that "made America great." Although Falwell's additions were limited to prefatory material, and he made no alterations to the actual pages of Scripture, his innovation had the effect of presenting the Bible as a patriotic text. The white, padded cover features a picture of three Revolutionary soldiers in the Continental Army with drum and fife.[75]

Falwell's edition of the Bible reflected the expansion of a distinctly evangelical consumer culture during the 1970s: the *I Love America Bible* was one of many religious products marketed to a growing evangelical market. On a deeper level, however, Falwell's Bible also reflected evangelicals' growing concern about their power to shape American culture and about the authority of the Bible in public life. Falwell's list of the "seven biblical principles that made America great," or a "Judeo and Christian ethic," reflects evangelicals' desire to defend their beliefs against movements for social change. The seven principles are "the dignity of human life," "the traditional monogamous family," "common decency," "the work ethic," "the Abrahamic covenant," "God-centered education," and "divinely ordained establishments," which Falwell defined as "the home," "state or civil government," and "religious institution."

---

[74]*Bible Society Record* 121, no. 5 (1976): 25, quoted in John Fea, *The Bible Cause: A History of the American Bible Society* (New York: Oxford, 2016), 296.

[75]*Holy Bible: Patriot's Edition* (Lynchburg: I Love America Committee and Thomas Nelson Publishers, 1983).

The American Patriot's Bible, published in 2009, is clearly indebted to Falwell's *I Love America Bible*, but because it adds American historical material to the actual pages of Scripture, it represents a more radical development. It makes explicit what Falwell's Bible only implied: namely, that worship of God should include devotion to the nation.

Based on the customer reviews posted on sites such as Amazon and Goodreads, some evangelical readers have been alarmed by the blatant nationalism of *The American Patriot's Bible*—one called it "blasphemous," and another "idolatrous"—but the number of enthusiastic reviews is far greater. At Amazon, where it has garnered 572 reviews, it gets 4.8 stars out of 5; at Goodreads, where it has been rated 150 times, it scores 4.4 out of 5.[76]

One measure of the book's popularity is the number of patriotic Bibles that have been published in its wake. In 2011, Lee collaborated again with Thomas Nelson Publishers to create the *Young American Patriot's Bible*, which interleaves the Bible with biographies of presidents and other famous Americans such as Daniel Webster, Buzz Aldrin, Charles Colson, and Rosa Parks, and in 2016, Lee edited *The American Woman's Bible*. Other patriotic Bibles include the *1599 Geneva Bible: Patriot's Edition* (2010), and several Military Bibles.[77]

The most direct competitor to *The American Patriot's Bible* is *The Founder's Bible*, the product of a collaboration between Brad Cummings, David Barton, Lance Wubbels, and Shiloh Publishers. Published in 2012, the book is an imitation of the *American Patriot's Bible*. From the very first pages, the text identifies the Bible as "the key factor in America's success," and in addition to reprinting the stories of prominent Americans within the pages of Scripture, it features inserts on topics such as "the First Great Awakening" and "What Is the 'Separation of Church and State?'" A crucial difference, however, is that *The Founder's Bible* is marketed to a more theologically conservative audience. For example, it includes a strenuous defense of creationism, and it describes the war with the Barbary Pirates as "Islam's War on America." "Many know of

---

[76]See www.amazon.com/dp/B002NANMDM/ref=dp-kindle-redirect?_encoding=UTF8&btkr= 1#customerReviews, accessed October 20, 2020; and www.goodreads.com/book/show/5439630 -the-nkjv-american-patriot-s-bible, accessed October 30, 2020.

[77]Richard Lee, *Young American Patriot's Bible* (Nashville: Thomas Nelson, 2011). Lee, *American Woman's Bible*. David Barton, Brad Cummings, and Lance Wubbels, *The Founder's Bible: The Origin of the Dream of Freedom* (Newbury Park, CA : Shiloh Road, 2012); *Military Bible* (Nashville: Holman, 2017); *Military Families Bible* (Nashville: Holman, 2016); *The Soldier's Bible* (Nashville: Holman, 2004).

the famous September 11, 2001, attacks levied against America by descendants of Ishmael," the text explains, "but few today know that America's first war after the American Revolution was also against those descendants."[78] Unlike *The American Patriot's Bible*, which encourages readers to draw this conclusion on their own, *The Founder's Bible* openly declares its hostility to Islam.

It is hard to understand why readers of these Bibles seem relatively unconcerned about sacralizing the nation, but perhaps they fear the waning authority of Protestantism in American public life even more. Ever since the Revolutionary era, at least some of the Bible's authority in the United States has come from its association with American freedom and nationalism, and today, some evangelicals seem to hope that if they can tie the Bible even more closely to the nation, they will preserve the Bible's cultural power. *The American Patriot's Bible* reveals that an undercurrent of nostalgia for a time when many dreamed that the United States would become a Protestant, free, mostly White, and militant nation led by men. But in their desire to shore up the authority of the Bible, American evangelicals run the risk of doing the opposite—of exalting the United States over the Bible as the central agent of God's work on earth.

In *Evangelicalism in Modern Britain*, David Bebbington argues that since the 1740s, biblicism has been one of the enduring features of the evangelical movement. *The American Patriot's Bible* confirms his interpretation, but it also suggests that in recent decades, American evangelical biblicism has taken a distinctive turn. In the eighteenth and nineteenth centuries, both British and American evangelicals had a tendency to portray the Bible as the key to national greatness, but in the twentieth century, especially after the rise of the Christian Right, American evangelicals began to move in more extreme nationalistic directions.[79] The "Bebbington Quadrilateral" remains a crucial guide to the distinctive characteristics of the evangelical movement, but in the context of twenty-first-century America, any definition of evangelicalism must reckon with the long and close relationship between evangelical biblicism and White Protestant nationalism.

---

[78]Barton, Cummings, and Wubbels, *Founder's Bible*, ix (key factor), 551-58 (First Great Awakening), (Separation of Church and State), 3-6 (creationism), 19 (Islam's War on America).

[79]David W. Bebbington, *Evangelicalism in Modern Britain: A History from the 1730s to the 1980s* (London: Routledge, 1989), 12-14. David W. Bebbington, "The King James Bible in Britain from the Late Eighteenth Century," in David Lyle Jeffrey, *The King James Bible and the World It Made* (Waco: Baylor University Press, 2011), 59.

12

The Evangelical Christian Mind in History and Global Context

Brian Stanley

THIS CHAPTER FALLS INTO TWO PARTS. The first makes an attempt to survey, interpret, and evaluate David Bebbington's remarkable work as a historian of Christianity, especially evangelical Christianity, in the period from the eighteenth to the twentieth centuries. The second seeks to relate the corpus of his work, and in particular the celebrated "Bebbington Quadrilateral"—especially the marker of biblicism—to a wider global context and the emerging field of study that is now widely described as "world Christianity." It thus raises the broader question of the extent to which recent history suggests that evangelicalism is a phenomenon bounded by the intellectual and social horizons of Western societies, or whether it is in principle transferable to the non-Western world.

THE EVANGELICAL CHRISTIAN MIND IN HISTORY

To attempt to encapsulate the central preoccupation of David Bebbington's extraordinarily wide-ranging scholarly output in one brief phrase might appear a foolhardy enterprise, but I am persuaded that the study of "the evangelical Christian mind in history" at least gets close to summing up the scholarly quest that he has set himself. This is despite the acerbic judgment of his long-time friend and collaborator, Mark Noll, that "The scandal of the evangelical mind is that there is not much of an evangelical mind."[1] Contemporary evangelicalism may indeed have its intellectual deficiencies. There may also be problems in writing about it as if it were a single entity—as Darryl Hart has forcibly maintained, even in relation to American evangelicalism alone.[2] Nonetheless, since about the 1730s, there has been a transnational evangelical movement, whose members have exhibited identifiable, though diverse and changing, patterns of thought. Discerning and analysing those patterns, initially within a British context, but latterly on a wider canvas, has been David Bebbington's lifework. Admittedly, he has never viewed himself as a church historian in the narrow sense. Much of the daily fare of his teaching during his forty-three year career at the University of Stirling has been within the field of modern British political history, rather than in intellectual history or religious history. His PhD research at Cambridge was directed to an analysis of the political horizons and involvement of British Nonconformists between 1886 and 1902, and bore fruit in the publication in 1982 of *The Nonconformist Conscience*, a book that extended the same theme over the longer period of 1870 to 1914.[3] However, *The Nonconformist Conscience* was, as its title suggests, a study, not simply of Nonconformist political activity, but of the distinctive moral conscience or Christian mind that animated and directed such campaigns. As the final two sentences of the first paragraph of the book stated, "Corporate political pressure seemed legitimate and laudable, a way of encouraging Christian standards in all departments of life. It was part of a psychology of optimism that dominated the chapels in the late Victorian and Edwardian years."[4] The targets that late Victorian Nonconformists selected for their campaigns reflected what he described as an "Evangelical biblicism," and exhibited a simple typology of Christian political activism that Bebbington would develop in his subsequent work on a wider cross-section of British evangelicalism: "They condemned only what fell into one of two categories: either disobedience to biblical ethics or what directly opposed the spread of the gospel."[5] Evangelical politics combined biblical principle with missionary pragmatism.

---

[1]Mark Noll, *The Scandal of the Evangelical Mind* (Grand Rapids: Eerdmans, 1994), 3.
[2]D. G. Hart, *Deconstructing Evangelicalism: Conservative Protestantism in the Age of Billy Graham* (Grand Rapids: Baker Academic, 2004).
[3]D. W. Bebbington, *The Nonconformist Conscience: Chapel and Politics, 1870–1914* (London: Allen and Unwin, 1982).
[4]Bebbington, *Nonconformist Conscience*, 1.
[5]Bebbington, *Nonconformist Conscience*, 15.

Christian forays into the political realm that fulminate against the toleration of "sin" in public life do not normally fare well in the newspaper columns,
and British Nonconformist politics in this period were no exception. Nonetheless, the more constructive aspect of Nonconformist politics clearly appealed to Bebbington—the pursuit of "Christian standards in all departments
of life" was integral to what it meant to develop a Christian mind. This is a
theme that is evident in his writing from a very early date. Here, for example,
is a quotation from the opening of his essay on "The Dissenting Idea of a
University," which in 1973, as a graduate student of the tender age of twenty-
three, he submitted to the University of Cambridge for the Hulsean Prize in
Ecclesiastical History:

> Evangelicals put the gospel above all other matters. Conversion alone brought
> men to God. Everything in life must conduce to conversion to biblical religion
> as a thing not just of the head but also of the heart. The principle applied
> directly to education, for the head was nevertheless involved in conversion.
> Evangelicals were drawn into the camp of those who believed that education
> was the handmaid to true religion, the guide of the young towards orthodox
> doctrinal beliefs.[6]

Needless to say, the essay was awarded the prize. To point out that Nonconformists of various stripes had their own ideas of what a university should
be, quite distinct from the better-known ideas of a university advanced in
the Victorian age by John Henry Newman or the formally Anglican but increasing sceptic Mark Pattison, was an original contribution.[7] Of greater
interest for our purposes, however, are the anticipations in the paragraph I
have just quoted of the later quadrilateral—at least two, and arguably three,
of the four points can be found here in embryo—and the insistence that
conversion to evangelical Christianity, or "biblical religion," involved both
heart and head. To study evangelicalism, therefore, the scholar needed, not
only to take full account of the range of cultural and social influences that
shaped sentiment, emotion, and the outward expression of faith ("the heart"),

---

[6]David William Bebbington, "The Dissenting Idea of a University: Oxford and Cambridge in
Nonconformist Thought in the Nineteenth Century" (Hulsean Prize Essay, University of Cambridge, 1973), 5-6.
[7]Cf. John Henry Newman, *The Idea of a University*, ed. I. T. Ker (Oxford: Oxford University Press,
1976); John Sparrow, *Mark Pattison and the Idea of a University* (Cambridge: Cambridge University
Press, 1967).

but also to analyze the components of the evangelical mind ("the head"), the motifs which governed the priorities that evangelicals attached to the educational process. Ever since, David Bebbington's academic career has focused on the continual and complex interplay between heart and head in Christian, and specifically evangelical, history. Even his most recent monograph, devoted to the study of Victorian revival movements, displays the same dual focus. In contrast to conventional historical interpretation, Victorian revivals, in Bebbington's characterization, were not merely passionate effusions of religious emotion and enthusiasm: rather, he insisted, "ideas were thoroughly integrated into them."[8] A religious revival, therefore, has a place in intellectual, as well as religious and social history.

Let us return to the theme of the place of the Christian in the modern university. The vocation, and particular challenge, of being an evangelical Christian student in a history department of a leading secular university was in fact what first brought me into contact with David Bebbington. The early 1970s may prove to have been the high-water mark in the University of Cambridge of the influence of conservative evangelicalism, as represented by the Cambridge Inter-Collegiate Christian Union (CICCU). The CICCU at the time was not simply the largest religious society in the university—its membership of five hundred or more made it one of the largest university societies, being surpassed only by the Cambridge Union, the university's renowned debating society.[9] However, the CICCU in the 1970s remained what it had been ever since its secession in 1910 from the Student Christian Movement (SCM)—a predominantly, though no longer almost exclusively, Anglican body, whose cultural ethos was shaped by those educated in the leading independent (so-called "public") schools, into which evangelical influence had made substantial inroads.[10] Furthermore, the bulk of the membership of the CICCU was drawn from those studying the natural sciences, medicine,

---

[8]David Bebbington, *Victorian Religious Revivals: Culture and Piety in Local and Global Contexts* (Oxford: Oxford University Press, 2012), 270 (my italics).

[9]David Goodhew, "The Rise of the Cambridge Inter-Collegiate Christian Union, 1910–1971," *Journal of Ecclesiastical History* 54, no. 1 (2003): 86. Goodhew gives a membership of "more than 400 in 1971," but my own recollection of being an undergraduate from 1972 to 1975 suggests a total of over five hundred throughout the university. My own college, Emmanuel, had at least eighty students in Bible study groups at this time.

[10]See Alister Chapman, *Godly Ambition: John Stott and the Evangelical Movement* (New York: Oxford University Press, 2012), 15-17, 37-38.

engineering, or law; relatively few evangelicals were to be found studying the pure humanities. This was, of course, the era in which overtly theoretical perspectives, some of them more or less Marxist in nature, first became highly influential in the humanities, with major consequences for the study of the role played by religion in society. Such perspectives presented Christian students of history with intellectual challenges that the central meetings of the CICCU did not greatly help them to meet.

In this context, my own memory turns to a small and informal group of Christian undergraduates studying in the Cambridge History Faculty who sought to develop a distinctively Christian approach to the study of academic history. It was only loosely affiliated to the CICCU. Two Research Fellows of Cambridge colleges provided the primary academic leadership for this student-run group. One was Richard Bauckham of St. John's College, who at that early stage in his career was a historian of Tudor Puritanism, specializing in the study of apocalyptic writing;[11] subsequently that interest was to lead him into a career first as a historical theologian and finally as a New Testament scholar of international repute. The other was David Bebbington, by now a Research Fellow of Fitzwilliam College. Between them, the two prepared for undergraduate use a booklet, which included an annotated bibliography, on History and Christianity. It was eventually, in 1977, printed and distributed among the university Christian Unions by the Universities and Colleges Christian Fellowship. The bibliography formed the basis of the original booklist that appears at the end of Bebbington's *Patterns in History*, first published in 1979 by Inter-Varsity Press, and which has remained in print ever since; Baylor University Press issued a fourth and expanded edition, with updated booklist, in 2018.[12]

Patterns in History is an extremely perceptive analysis of the principal ideological trends that have shaped historical thinking and writing from classical antiquity to the present day, including, in the fourth edition, postmodernism. But it is also a provocative exposition of a distinctively Christian view of the historian's vocation, as is implied by the subtitle "A Christian Perspective on

---

[11]Richard J. Bauckham, *Tudor Apocalypse: Sixteenth Century Apocalypticism, Millenarianism and the English Reformation: From John Bale to John Foxe and Thomas Brightman* (Appleford: Sutton Courtenay, 1978).

[12]David W. Bebbington, *Patterns in History: A Christian Perspective on Historical Thought*, 4th rev. ed. (Waco, TX: Baylor University Press, 2018), xi–xii.

Historical Thought," which first appeared in the second edition published in 1990. The book reveals a profoundly Christian mind grappling with the awkward questions raised by the historical process and the writing of history. Hence the theme I have chosen for this first part of this chapter embraces not simply the study of the Christian mind of individuals or movements in the church's past, but also the mind of the Christian historian as he or she brings both the academic craft of the historian and the faith of a believer to bear on the historical process. The chapter in *Patterns in History* on "The Meaning of History" addresses what is probably the most searching problem that confronts the Christian academic historian, namely how to square the biblical insistence that the course of human history is superintended by a gracious divine providence with the observable and often tragic messiness of historical events, and to do so in a way that is acceptable to a generally unbelieving historical profession. Bebbington's answer, namely, that the Christian historian can and should write in a way that is congruent with a faith in divine providence and mercy, but without normally making that faith explicit, does not solve all the problems, but it exemplifies the honesty and integrity that distinguish all of his writing.[13]

One book written by David Bebbington is quite explicitly a study of an individual Christian mind and the implications of that particular mind for society and politics: *The Mind of Gladstone: Religion, Homer, and Politics*, published by Oxford University Press in 2004. Bebbington's fascination with Gladstone goes back a long way. His PhD research uncovered the reverential devotion with which most late Victorian Nonconformists regarded the Grand Old Man of British politics, in spite of obvious theological divergence and the strains imposed by Gladstone's espousal of Home Rule for Ireland in 1886. The first of Bebbington's numerous communications to the Ecclesiastical History Society, published in *Studies in Church History* in 1975, was titled "Gladstone and the Nonconformists: A Religious Affinity in Politics." What evangelical Nonconformists so admired in the Liberal leader was his earnest conscientiousness in seeking to fashion his politics according to principles of Christian faith. As Lord Rosebery observed after Gladstone's death, "The faith of Mr Gladstone, obvious to all who knew him, pervaded every act and every part of his life."[14] Gladstone, for all his foibles, had a Christian mind.

---

[13]Bebbington, *Patterns in History*, chap. 9.
[14]David Bebbington, "Gladstone and the Nonconformists: a Religious Affinity in Politics," In *Church Society and Politics: Studies in Church History*, ed. D. Baker, vol. 12, 372 (Oxford: Basil Blackwell

It is hard to read *The Mind of Gladstone* without also reading the mind of Bebbington. He manifestly shares the admiration of his Victorian Nonconformists for the statesman. At times the portrait of Gladstone has elements of self-portraiture. The book begins by citing a statement in an 1870 sermon by H. P. Liddon, "GENERALLY SPEAKING, men who write books are unpractical,"[15] a sentiment that Eileen Bebbington would heartily endorse, though we should note that both Liddon and Bebbington regard Gladstone as the exception to the rule. Whether Gladstone was any more adept than Bebbington in wielding a screwdriver must, however, await further research.[16] Gladstone, like David Bebbington, was an inveterate collector of books. His personal library, which formed the basis for what became St. Deniol's Library at Hawarden in Cheshire, amounted to twenty-seven thousand volumes.[17] David's own library he currently estimates at twenty-five thousand volumes, though he is still counting. Gladstone was also a painstaking note taker of all that he read, a quality that anyone who has sat next to Bebbington while he is listening to either an academic paper or a sermon will readily recognize.[18]

There is a more serious point to be made here. By directing scholarship on Gladstonian Liberalism to what it had previously chosen largely to ignore—namely, the political significance of Gladstone's voracious reading in theology and Homeric studies—he was making the case that for historians of Victorian Britain, as for Gladstone himself, "There must be no impassable barrier . . . between religion and thought, or religion and society, or religion and politics."[19] In chapter nine of the book, Bebbington argues that the characteristic amalgam of libertarian principles, conservative communitarianism, and respect for tradition evident in Gladstonian Liberalism can only be understood by reference to ideas of the organic unity of humanity that Gladstone drew both from Homer and from Tractarian incarnational theology.

for the Ecclesiastical History Society, 1975); David W. Bebbington, *William Ewart Gladstone: Faith and Politics in Victorian Britain* (Grand Rapids: Eerdmans, 1993), 224.

[15]David Bebbington, *The Mind of Gladstone: Religion, Homer, and Politics* (Oxford: Oxford University Press, 2004), 1.

[16]See Eileen Bebbington, *A Patterned Life: Faith, History, and David Bebbington* (Eugene, OR: Wipf & Stock, 2014), 8, 10.

[17]Bebbington, *Mind of Gladstone*, 2.

[18]Bebbington, *Mind of Gladstone*, 6.

[19]Bebbington, *Mind of Gladstone*, 306; see also 12.

Gladstone, the one-time evangelical, from the 1830s gradually relocated the centre of his theology from the atonement to the incarnation. That was not a trajectory that Bebbington himself followed, and yet it needs to be stressed that he has always been the sort of evangelical for whom the incarnation is no marginal theme in Christian theology. Reading Paul Tillich as a schoolboy (a statement I have never had reason to apply to anyone else) impressed upon him that sound doctrine and faithful action both flow from the Christian's status of being, as someone who is incorporated by grace in the Trinitarian life of God.[20] Christians and churches are incarnate beings, sharing fully in the earthiness of their particular cultural and historical contexts. Even evangelicals, therefore, with whom Bebbington has always been happy to identify himself, are themselves partakers of the cultural relativities that derive from the nature of Christianity as an incarnational religion. That perception, which has drawn upon him some criticism from Reformed exponents of evangelical theology, takes us to the book for which he is most widely known, *Evangelicalism in Modern Britain*.

A revealing sentence in Eileen Bebbington's biography of her husband observes that one afternoon, shortly after he had published *The Nonconformist Conscience* and settled on Gladstone and evangelicalism as the next two objects of his future research, "we decided that David should write a history of evangelicalism quickly before getting on with a study of Gladstone."[21] This "quick" diversion from the single-minded pursuit of Gladstonian studies has in fact redrawn the whole map of historical interpretation of the evangelical movement, and reoriented his academic career.

Bebbington would be the first to acknowledge that the transformation that scholarship of the history of evangelicalism has undergone in recent decades has not been the work of any single author. In the study of American evangelicalism—a field into which he did not venture until the early 1990s—the path-breaking book was Timothy L. Smith's *Revivalism and Social Reform*, published in 1957.[22] A generation later came the foundational work of George Marsden, Nathan Hatch, and Mark Noll. In Britain the transformation is most obviously dated to 1966, with the publication of a seminal essay by

---

[20]See Bebbington, *Patterned Life*, 26.

[21]Bebbington, *Patterned Life*, 91.

[22]Timothy L. Smith, *Revivalism and Social Reform: American Protestantism on the Eve of the Civil War* (Nashville: Abingdon, 1957).

the Oxford historian John D. Walsh on "The Origins of the Evangelical Revival." Walsh's essay, based on a 1956 Cambridge PhD thesis, uncovered the diverse historical roots of the Revival, and effectively undermined the prevailing assumption that John Wesley was the sole or even primary fountainhead of the movement.[23] Walsh's publications are not many, but he is frequently cited in the early chapters of *Evangelicalism in Modern Britain*. Whereas Walsh pioneered an approach to evangelical origins that established a lineage from the religious societies of early eighteenth-century High Churchmanship, W. R. Ward (1925–2010) of the University of Durham, uncovered the central European origins and transnational nature of the eighteenth-century evangelical revivals.[24] Reg Ward's work has made it impossible to write with any plausibility about early evangelicalism as if it were a purely Anglophone movement. It is noteworthy that Bebbington dedicated his book on Victorian Revivals to the memory of this lifelong and confessedly Primitive Methodist historian.[25]

Despite Bebbington's obvious debt to both John Walsh and Reg Ward, we need to look elsewhere if we are to trace the intellectual genealogy of the central argument of *Evangelicalism in Modern Britain*, which appeared in 1989. In 1962, when David was still a pupil at Nottingham High School, an earlier Baptist graduate student in the University of Cambridge, Haddon Willmer, won the Hulsean Prize for an essay on "Evangelicalism, 1785 to 1835." The essay has never been published, but the list of readers' signatures pasted at the front of the essay in the Manuscripts Room in Cambridge University Library gives some indication of the extent of its intellectual influence: they include Bruce Hindmarsh (three times), Alister McGrath, Boyd Hilton, John Wolffe, Donald Lewis, Peter Lineham, Andrew Atherstone, Gareth Atkins, Brian Stanley, and, of course, David Bebbington. I was surprised on a recent visit to find that David did not sign the library copy of the essay until January

---

[23]J. D. Walsh, "Origins of the Evangelical Revival," in *Essays in Modern English Church History in Memory of Norman Sykes*, ed. G. V. Bennett and J. D. Walsh, 132-62 (London: Adam & Charles Black, 1966); see J. D. Walsh, "The Yorkshire Evangelicals in the Eighteenth Century: With Special Reference to Methodism," PhD diss, University of Cambridge, 1956.

[24]W. R. Ward, *The Protestant Evangelical Awakening* (Cambridge: Cambridge University Press, 1992); *Early Evangelicalism: A Global Intellectual History* (Cambridge: Cambridge University Press, 2006); Andrew Chandler, ed., *Evangelicalism, Piety and Politics: The Selected Writings of W. R. Ward* (Farnham: Ashgate, 2014).

[25]Bebbington, *Victorian Revivals*, frontispiece and vii.

9, 1980, two years after I did, which gave me a momentary flush of intellectual superiority, but it has not surprised me to discover that he had in fact read it years earlier, either privately or having signed an earlier list of readers that the library staff have since removed.[26]

Willmer's essay approached early evangelicalism from the perspective of both social and intellectual history. It described evangelicalism as a "distinctively Eighteenth Century expression of the Gospel," well attuned to eighteenth-century English society, with its aristocratic, rural and stable character.[27] Without ever mentioning the term *Enlightenment*, Willmer characterized the first generation or two of English evangelicals as Newtonians. As typified by Charles Simeon of Cambridge, they combined a focus on "Christ Crucified" as the heart of evangelical religion and preaching with the commendation of sobriety, created order, and social harmony.[28] These values prevailed in the movement until the 1830s, when, as "part of the desire for a religion in a Romantic rather than Augustan mould," a new and more radical style of evangelicalism began to supplant it, exemplified by Edward Irving, and marked by an emphasis on the kingship of Christ, the restoration of supernatural gifts and the hope of the Second Advent.[29]

Haddon Willmer subsequently moved into other areas of historical theology. It was left to David Bebbington, over twenty-five years later, to ruminate upon his embryonic insights into the cultural shift in the evangelical mind. Bebbington has observed that "I did not at that point understand what he meant by the cultural change," but the nature of the Enlightenment/Romantic antithesis gradually became clear to him, initially through his final-year undergraduate studies for the paper (that is course or module) in the Cambridge Historical Tripos on "Theories of the Modern State," and later as he taught the history of political thought at Cambridge and Stirling.[30] The eventual result, in 1989, was a more theoretically sophisticated and exhaustively documented argument about the sequence within British evangelicalism of typically Enlightenment, Romantic, and finally "modern" patterns of

---

[26]Haddon Willmer, "Evangelicalism 1785 to 1835," Hulsean Prize Essay, University of Cambridge, 1962, Cambridge University Library, Manuscripts Room, Hulsean Prize Essay 134.

[27]Willmer, "Evangelicalism," 9-10, 45, 66.

[28]Willmer, "Evangelicalism," 22, 40, 45.

[29]Willmer, "Evangelicalism," 33, 135.

[30]Personal email from David Bebbington, July 31, 2019.

thought (the third of these being well beyond Willmer's time period). Willmer's essay receives due acknowledgment in a footnote in *Evangelicalism in Modern Britain* and more explicitly in the historiographical afterword to the comparative volume on evangelicalism edited by Mark Noll, David Bebbington, and the late George Rawlyk in 1994, but has never received the wider recognition that it deserves.[31]

Bebbington's argument about the transition within evangelicalism from an Enlightenment to a Romantic cultural framework is the conceptual cement that holds *Evangelicalism in Modern Britain* together, and indeed has informed much of his subsequent work. It is a compelling argument about the historical evolution of the British evangelical Christian mind in response to a changing philosophical and cultural climate. The book effectively demolished the prevalent view among scholars of Victorian Britain that evangelicals were simply doers who held little interest for scholars of intellectual history. However, the ingredient of the book that has had even wider circulation is a rather more straightforward set of ideas, namely the "Quadrilateral," or four-fold definition of evangelicalism in terms of conversionism, activism, biblicism, and crucicentrism.[32] The Quadrilateral is a decade older than the book. Its genesis can be traced to a talk on the Nonconformist Conscience that Bebbington delivered, in or about 1979, in Lansdowne Evangelical Free Church in West Norwood, South London, whose pastor, Derek Moore-Crispin, was a friend from Cambridge days. Preparing the talk compelled David to attempt to define the evangelical Christianity that fuelled the Nonconformist conscience. The answer he gave, namely that evangelicals were those who combined biblical orthodoxy with evangelistic zeal, he found unsatisfying. Further reflection led to the formation of the quadrilateral, though it seems likely that the order of the four points was originally different from that given later in the book.[33]

---

[31]D. W. Bebbington, *Evangelicalism in Modern Britain: A History from the 1730s to the 1980s* (London: Unwin Hyman, 1989), 30ln5; Mark A. Noll, David W. Bebbington, and George A. Rawlyk, eds., *Evangelicalism: Comparative Studies of Popular Protestantism in North America, the British Isles, and Beyond, 1700–1990* (New York: Oxford University Press, 1994), 411, 414.

[32]Bebbington, *Evangelicalism in Modern Britain*, 4-17.

[33]Eileen Bebbington, *Patterned Life*, 91, incorrectly situates the church in Cambridge. Eileen lists the four points as originally conceived in the order: the Bible; the cross; conversion; activism. Her account was corrected and supplemented in emails from David Bebbington dated July 31 and August 1, 2019. Derek Moore-Crispin had been president of the Robert Hall Society, the

The Quadrilateral has been extraordinarily influential. In spite of various hesitations expressed by some reviewers,[34] the Bebbington Quadrilateral remains intact as an authoritative catechism, dutifully rehearsed by faithful students in a host of essays and doctoral dissertations. As one would expect, in *Evangelicalism in Modern Britain* the quadrilateral is applied mainly, but not exclusively, to the British context. However, Jonathan Edwards, James Caughey, and Charles Finney all make appearances within the pages that introduce the four-fold definition,[35] and hence the book at least implicitly begins to apply the Quadrilateral more broadly within a transatlantic context. In 1989 Bebbington had scarcely turned his attention to the study of transatlantic evangelicalism; that was the year in which he visited the United States for the first time.[36] As his visits to the US proliferated over the years that followed, the Quadrilateral became a framework for defining and understanding evangelicalism as a transnational religious network that spanned the North Atlantic, and increasingly became diffused throughout the English-speaking world. Whether, or in what way, the Quadrilateral can legitimately be applied within a broader geographical framework still, extending in principle to the entire globe, is the question to which I now turn, in the second half of this chapter.

THE EVANGELICAL CHRISTIAN
MIND IN GLOBAL CONTEXT

Philip Jenkins has popularized the thesis that much of contemporary southern Christianity—indeed, most when we limit our gaze to what is conventionally labelled as Protestantism—is conservative in its theological and ethical perspectives and its unashamed commitment to evangelism.[37] We also know that the North Atlantic world that was so formative in the inception of evangelicalism is now relatively marginal to the narrative of world Christianity.

Baptist student society in Cambridge, a couple of years before Eileen Bebbington, and was still present in Cambridge when David arrived as an undergraduate.

[34]See Timothy Larsen, "The Reception Given to *Evangelicalism in Modern Britain* Since Its Publication in 1989," in *The Emergence of Evangelicalism: Exploring Historical Continuities*, ed. Michael A. G. Haykin and Kenneth J. Stewart (Nottingham: Apollos, 2008), 25-27.

[35]Bebbington, *Evangelicalism in Modern Britain*, 5, 7, 8, 10.

[36]Eileen Bebbington, *Patterned Life*, 81.

[37]Philip Jenkins, *The Next Christendom: The Coming of Global Christianity*, 3rd ed. (New York: Oxford University Press, 2011), 8, 100, 254, 272-73.

Conversely, the forms of popular Christianity that predominate in the Global South are shaped by a very different set of cosmological and intellectual assumptions than those that shaped Enlightenment evangelicalism. In Africa, for example, the face of contemporary Christianity owes less to the North Atlantic nexus than it does to that other, and more heavily populated, eighteenth-century network—the one that crossed the South Atlantic, linking West African indigenous religion, slave communities in the American South and the Caribbean, and then back again in African American missions to the mother continent of Africa.[38]

It might appear, therefore, that we face a choice. Should Bebbington's definition of evangelicalism be modified or expanded to accommodate these contrasting styles of popular Protestant Christianity? Or, should we instead conclude that the label "evangelical" simply does not fit much of the non-Western Christian spectrum? The global explosion of neo-Pentecostalism over the last half-century poses these questions of diversity and difference with peculiar sharpness, but this chapter will suggest that they have in fact been present almost from the earliest years of the evangelical movement. I propose to relate these questions to each of the four points of the Quadrilateral, though I shall devote more space to conversionism and biblicism than to the other two.

First, conversionism. As the offspring of Pietism, evangelicalism called individuals to turn from their sins and make a personal commitment of faith to Christ. One could not be born a Christian by virtue of birth, political affiliation or territorial location within Christendom—the new birth of conversion through the supernatural agency of the Spirit was necessary. On the one hand, most popular Christianity in the global South appears equally conversionist in its ethos as its northern-hemisphere evangelical predecessors, but, crucially, is situated within contexts that cannot, despite the title of Philip Jenkins's influential book,[39] properly be described as constituting a new Christendom. There are important exceptions to these generalizations. President Frederick Chiluba, himself a confessed evangelical, declared Zambia

---

[38]Albert J. Raboteau, *Slave Religion: The "Invisible Institution" in the Antebellum South*, new ed. (Oxford: Oxford University Press, 2004), 329, reminds us that before the 1820s between two and three times more Africans crossed the Atlantic by force than did European settlers of the "New World."

[39]Jenkins, *Next Christendom*.

to be a Christian nation on December 29, 1991, and that designation remains. Opportunities to be conversionist might appear a bit limited in a country that the 2010 census declared to be 95.5 percent Christian, with evangelicals, classical Pentecostals, or neo-Pentecostals forming the majority.[40] There are certainly indications in other regions where evangelicals have for long made up the vast majority of the population, such as the south Pacific islands or the north-east Indian states, that conversionism tends to weaken over time, or rather is transferred to new groups, such as Mormons, who are challenging the evangelical establishment.[41] In contexts where churches (such as the Orthodox) have had for many years to defend their right to exist in dominant Islamic or Hindu environments, the pursuit of conversion is simply too de-stabilising to be tolerated, with the result that Christian identity derives from lineage rather than personal decision.

Once these qualifications have been made, however, there is ample evidence of evangelical conversionism being taken up enthusiastically in non-European settings. Thus an emphasis on the spiritual necessity of conversion was characteristic of African American varieties of popular Christianity as early as the eighteenth century. One of the earliest autobiographical conversion narratives that we have from an African American—that of George Liele (c.1750–c.1828), the Virginia slave who later pioneered Baptist work in Jamaica—conforms in all essential respects to the evangelical archetype of the conversion narrative as analyzed by Bruce Hindmarsh.[42] Liele recounts his crushing sense of being a sinner under divine condemnation, then placing his trust in the merits of the dying savior for the salvation of his soul, and finally his request to his Lord to "give me a work" to do in response to his reception of divine grace.[43] We may presume that Liele's narrative, which refers to events that took place "about two years" before the American War of Independence,

[40]Isabel Apawo Phiri, "President Frederick J. T. Chiluba of Zambia: The Christian Nation and Democracy," *Journal of Religion in Africa* 33, no. 1 (2003): 401-28; Naomi Haynes, *Moving by the Spirit: Pentecostal Social Life on the Zambian Copperbelt* (Oakland: University of California Press, 2018), 28-29.

[41]Brian Stanley, *Christianity in the Twentieth Century: A World History* (Princeton, NJ: Princeton University Press, 2018), 106-7.

[42]See D. Bruce Hindmarsh, *The Evangelical Conversion Narrative: Spiritual Autobiography in Early Modern England* (Oxford: Oxford University Press, 2005).

[43]John Rippon, "An account of several Baptist Churches, consisting chiefly of NEGRO SLAVES, particularly of one at *Kingston*, in JAMAICA, and another at *Savannah* in GEORGIA," *Baptist Annual Register* 1 (1790): 332-33.

faithfully replicates the preaching of Matthew Moore, a White Baptist pastor in Burke county, New Georgia, which was instrumental in his coming to faith. It was also penned years later, in a letter of 1791, but there is no substantial reason to discard this testimony entirely as evidence of how Liele understood his experience at the time, at the age of twenty-three.

We have a similar autobiographical conversion account from Liele's most famous convert, David George, the Virginia-born slave who became a leader of the Black loyalist movement in Nova Scotia and subsequently a prominent architect of evangelical Christianity in Sierra Leone. George's narrative, recounted in 1793 to the English Baptist leaders Samuel Pearce and John Rippon, contains the same characteristic emphasis on an overwhelming consciousness of the heavy burden of his sin, leading to despair over the fate of his soul, and eventually to his casting himself on the mercy of God in Christ for salvation. George was illiterate at the time of his conversion, which imparts a particular experiential inflexion to his account: "I saw myself a mass of sin. I could not read, and had no Scriptures. I did not think of Adam's and Eve's sin, but I was sin. I felt my own plague."[44] As Bruce Hindmarsh has noted, George spoke of Scripture as a subsequent witness, confirming what he already knew through his own experience: "what I have in my heart, I can see again in the Scriptures."[45]

Conversionism, then, was not dependent on literacy. It may be significant that accounts survive from Nova Scotia of objections to the stamping, shouting, and emotional frenzy that characterized George's revival services. It would be a mistake, however, to read such attacks in exclusively racial terms. They derive from Anglican sources and were not directed at George alone—similar criticisms were levelled at responses to the preaching of Henry Alline, the Congregational revivalist from Rhode Island, or William Black, the Methodist evangelist from Yorkshire.[46] African Americans possessed no monopoly on revival "enthusiasm," though there is no doubt that their exuberant style of evangelical expression made many White evangelicals particularly uneasy.

---

[44]John Rippon, "An account of the life of Mr. DAVID GEORGE, from Sierra Leone in Africa, given by himself in conversation with Brother RIPPON of London, and Brother PEARCE of Birmingham," *Baptist Annual Register* 1 (1790): 475.

[45]Rippon, "Account," 476; cited in Hindmarsh, *Evangelical Conversion Narrative*, 331.

[46]Mary Louise Clifford, *From Slavery to Freetown: Black Loyalists after the American Revolution* (Jefferson, NC: McFarland, 1999), 54-55.

However, when transplanted to the Caribbean, the tradition represented by Liele and George proved hard to contain within the boundaries of evangelical orthodoxy. The "Native Baptists" in Jamaica and the "Shouter Baptists" in Trinidad both posed challenges to the Baptist Missionary Society through their preparedness to express their sense of being empowered by the Spirit in ways that bore a disconcerting similarity to the possession cults of West African indigenous religions.[47] As the distinguished historian of African American slave religion, Albert J. Raboteau, puts it, "While the North American slaves danced under the impulse of the Spirit of a "new" God, they danced in ways their fathers in Africa would have recognized."[48]

The autobiographies of Liele and George both lend support to Raboteau's claim that an emphasis on personal conversion was typical of the religious lives of the slaves. Raboteau indeed proposes that conversionism should be added to the three defining qualities of slave religion that the celebrated African American writer W. E. B. Du Bois had drawn up in 1901—the preacher, the music, and the "frenzy" expressed in worship by bodily agitation and shouting out loud in response to the infilling of the Holy Spirit.[49] We can note that Raboteau's resulting quadrilateral has two elements that correspond closely to Bebbington's—the preached word of Scripture and the call to conversion—though his other two points suggest a different profile reminiscent of Pentecostal varieties of faith.

An emphasis on the absolute necessity of personal conversion thus proved more than capable of crossing the color bar between White and Black in revolutionary America, becoming indigenized in African American Christian tradition, and then being transmitted by the Nova Scotian settlers to that seminal nursery of African Christianity, the Freetown settlement in Sierra Leone. Both Liele and George told a story of the individual soul wrestling with the agonized consciousness of their sin before discovering the rest of forgiveness and assurance. Such narratives can be found throughout the range of fields reached by Western

---

[47]Peter D. Brewer, "The Baptist Churches of South Trinidad and Their Missionaries, 1815–1892," MTh thesis, University of Glasgow, 1988, 7-30; Brian Stanley, *The History of the Baptist Missionary Society 1792–1992* (Edinburgh: T&T Clark, 1992), 86, 94-95.

[48]Raboteau, *Slave Religion*, 72.

[49]W. E. B. Du Bois, *The Souls of Black Folk* (Chicago: A.C. McClurg, 1903), cited in Raboteau, *Slave Religion*, 266.

evangelical preaching, but they do not represent the most common form of adherence to Protestant Christianity. In non-Western contexts, where Western missionaries were so few that they struggled to control the terms of either Christian adherence or discourse, what conversion came to mean was often rather different.

This first became obvious in the caste society of India, where the essential identity of religious and social identity loaded the dice more heavily against individual conversion than anywhere else, with the possible exception of the Muslim world. It is hard to overestimate the significance of the people movements towards Christianity that became more common in India from about the 1880s, often in response to famine or other natural crises. The eighteenth-century revivals in Europe and North America had witnessed large crowds gathering to hear evangelical preaching, but the challenge to repentance that ensued involved multiple encounters between individuals and their Maker. The decision in December 1928 by the National Christian Council of India to commission a survey into the people movements was a response to the perplexity of both Indian Protestant leaders and missionaries at processes of conversion in which criteria of the perceived temporal welfare of existent social groupings seemed more prominent than the eternal welfare of the individual soul. The resulting survey, conducted under the direction of the Methodist Episcopal missionary, J. Waskom Pickett, was the first systematic attempt to do what the World Missionary Conference of 1910 had called for, namely to use the modern methods of social scientific analysis to chart and interpret trends on the mission field.[50]

One of Pickett's research assistants in his survey was the American missionary Donald Anderson McGavran, a member of the Disciples of Christ. McGavran's parents were missionaries in India who had been present at the World Missionary Conference in Edinburgh.[51] He himself served from 1923 in Chhattisgarh, a district (now state) that had experienced repeated famines in the 1890s, followed by substantial movements of conversion among the Chamar (leather-working) depressed caste. These movements slowed in the early decades of the century but resumed in the

---

[50]J. Waskom Pickett, *Christian Mass Movements in India: A Study with Recommendations* (New York: Abingdon, 1933).

[51]World Missionary Conference, 1910, *The History and Records of the Conference, Together with the Addresses Delivered at the Evening Meetings* (Edinburgh: Oliphant, Anderson & Ferrier, [1910]), 54.

mid-1930s.[52] McGavran's reports from Chhattisgarh clearly influenced Pickett, but Pickett was equally an acknowledged influence on McGavran, who famously said, "I lit my candle at Pickett's fire."[53]

The seeds of Donald McGavran's theory of church growth can be found in his observation of patterns of group conversion in Chhattisgarh. His maxim that "To Christianize a whole people, the first thing not to do is to snatch individuals out of it into a different society"[54] presented Western evangelicalism with a dual challenge. First, it shifted the focus of evangelistic strategy from the individual—where it had resided ever since the Pietist movements of the eighteenth century—to the group. Pietism had distrusted collective Christian confession as a recipe for the nominalism of state religion, and hence directed its evangelistic challenge to individuals, though those who responded were then urged to join classes or societies for fellowship and united Christian action in mission. Second, the unashamed empiricism of McGavran's social analysis subverted the typically Protestant assumption that authentic Christianity is defined by soundness of belief rather than by adoption of a set of ritual and behavioural practices that seem calculated to lead to the flourishing of a particular social unit. To be sure, McGavran's Homogenous Unit Principle has been attacked on theological grounds, ironically for not being radical enough in its departure from Western individualism. As C. René Padilla trenchantly put it, "Membership in the Body of Christ is not a question of likes or dislikes, but a question of incorporation into a new humanity under the lordship of Christ."[55] Yet, for all his theological inadequacy, McGavran had perceived what has become a commonplace of the anthropology of religion, namely that for the majority of the world's population, "religion" is less a matter of adhering to a set of beliefs that can be judged to be doctrinally correct, and more a question of following the ways of wisdom that appear to carry the best prospect of defending the community against

---

[52]Chad Bauman, *Christian Identity and Dalit Religion in Hindu India, 1868–1947* (Grand Rapids: Eerdmans, 2005), 65, 67.

[53]George G. Hunter III, "Donald A. McGavran 1897–1990: Standing at the Sunrise of Missions," in *Mission Legacies: Biographical Studies of Leaders of the Modern Missionary Movement*, ed. Gerald H. Anderson et al. (Maryknoll, NY: Orbis, 1994), 518.

[54]Donald Anderson McGavran, *The Bridges of God: A Study in the Strategy of Missions* (London: World Dominion, 1955), 10.

[55]C. René Padilla, "The Unity of the Church and the Homogenous Unit Principle," in *Landmark Essays in Mission and World Christianity*, ed. Robert L. Gallagher and Paul Hertig (Maryknoll, NY: Orbis, 2009), 76.

all that threatens it, and enhancing the prosperity of its members. The significance of this contrast between religion as sound doctrine and religion as
a proven way of wisdom for the community is immense, and I shall return
to it at the conclusion of this chapter.

The second point of the quadrilateral—activism—is the least ambiguous
of the four in its application to forms of "evangelical" Christianity in the
Global South. Indeed, southern Christians may appear to be markedly busier
in the cause of the gospel than their counterparts in the North. They are
generally more active, not only in spreading their faith and planting new
churches, but also in the provision of Christian schools, colleges, and increasingly universities, not to speak of a range of welfare ministries. The vigorous
engagement of Pentecostals in the public sphere, including increasingly in
politics, is one of the prominent themes of current scholarship on both African
and Latin American Christianity. Daniel Castelo has argued that we should
understand Pentecostalism as a Christian mystical tradition, quite distinct
from evangelicalism.[56] In fact, as Reg Ward took delight in demonstrating,
early evangelicalism—or at least, Pietism—had a strong mystical undercurrent.[57] Moreover, if we associate mysticism with a contemplative tendency
to withdraw from the world into a life of prayer and spiritual illumination,
then few modern non-Western Pentecostals are mystics in that sense.

Bebbington's third defining characteristic of an evangelical—biblicism—is
given particular emphasis by Philip Jenkins in *The New Faces of Christianity*.[58]
Most southern-hemisphere Christians are indeed Bible believers, seemingly
untroubled by the awkward questions raised by European higher critics or
those sceptical of biblical accounts of miracles. The Friday Masowe apostolics
of Zimbabwe studied by Matthew Engelke, who have effectively dispensed
with the Bible altogether, are clearly unrepresentative of African Christianity
as a whole.[59]

Biblicism might appear to be dependent on literacy, but this is not so. Larry
Hurtado has argued persuasively that one of the distinctive characteristics

---

[56]Daniel Castelo, *Pentecostalism as a Christian Mystical Tradition* (Grand Rapids: Eerdmans, 2017).
[57]Ward, *Early Evangelicalism*, 42-45, 102-7, 142-43.
[58]Philip Jenkins, *The New Faces of Christianity: Believing the Bible in the Global South* (Oxford: Oxford
University Press, 2008).
[59]Matthew Engelke, *A Problem of Presence: Beyond Scripture in an African Church* (Berkeley: University of California Press, 2007).

of Christianity in the Graeco-Roman world in the first three centuries was the central place it gave to teaching and hearing the biblical text, even though most Christian adherents were illiterate and printed Bibles were non-existent.[60] The Orality Movement, an influential network of mainly American evangelical mission theorists formed in 2004, has promoted strategies of evangelism and Christian education intended to obviate the necessity of reliance on the biblical text. Its aim is to enable orally-preferred people to access the Christian message via storytelling or drama rather than via the supposedly Western method of reading and teaching the actual biblical text. The Network appears to be willing to dilute evangelical biblicism for the sake of conversionism, though its defenders would deny this charge. An Edinburgh PhD thesis by Billy Coppedge on the reception of orality methods by the Africa Gospel Church in Uganda suggests, however, that the adherence of non-Western Christians to the materiality of the biblical text and of conventional text-based methods of Christian education may be more tenacious than Western missionary promoters of "inculturation" imagine.[61]

Nonetheless, there is no doubt that the nature of evangelical biblicism does, or at least can, change in cultural contexts in which faith is more about communal affirmation and practice than individual cognitive assent to formal "doctrine." Aminta Arrington's study of the Lisu people of southwest China provides an excellent example. The evangelists of the Lisu had impeccable evangelical credentials. The pioneer of the Lisu mission was J. O. Fraser of the China Inland Mission. His successors, Allyn and Leila Cooke, were graduates of the Bible Institute of Los Angeles, an institution of strong fundamentalist and dispensationalist leanings. The Cookes devoted themselves, not simply, as one would expect, to translation of parts of the New Testament into Lisu, but also to encouraging the use of hymn singing as the most effective vehicle for Christian instruction. In this, they built upon Fraser's own remarkable musical abilities. Today, the Lisu hymnbook is a constant companion of the Bible in the hands of Lisu Christians. Indeed, their devotional life is oriented more to the corporate and even individual singing of hymns than

---

[60]Larry W. Hurtado, *Destroyer of the Gods: Early Christian Distinctiveness in the Roman World* (Waco, TX: Baylor University Press, 2016).

[61]William A. Coppedge, "African Literacies and Western Oralities? Communication Complexities, the Orality Movement, and the Materialities of Christianity in Uganda," PhD diss., University of Edinburgh, 2019.

to the private study of the Bible, which remains very rare, something of a cultural eccentricity. The Lisu Bible is not so much read, as orally performed in public worship, and venerated as an object carried to church in brightly embroidered Bible bags. Bible reading and study now sit on the margins of Christian devotion, and yet Lisu piety remains recognizably evangelical— many of the hymns the Lisu sing are radically indigenized versions of Western evangelical classics.[62]

A similar conclusion emerges from an Edinburgh PhD thesis by Wilson McMahon that studies the reception of evangelical Christianity by the Manobo people of central Mindanao in the Philippines. Evangelized from 1976 by the Overseas Missionary Fellowship (successor to the China Inland Mission) the Manobo have appropriated the conservative evangelical emphasis on the supreme authority of Scripture, but in many cases have redefined that authority. For many Manobo Christians, the Bible is authoritative, it seems, primarily because it is new and modern, a replacement for now discredited sources of traditional wisdom. Its authority is inescapably linked to its textual and material character. Forty-eight percent of those McMahon interviewed confessed to having used the Bible as a talisman, a material object that would ward off malign spiritual forces. Manobo Protestants remain persuaded of the supreme value of reading the Bible, though for some that value is quasi-automatic: simply to read the words at random brings peace and comfort.[63]

If the Bible were to become venerated as a ritual object wholly independently of its capacity to engage the Christian mind, then it would become a Protestant holy relic imbued with sacramental power, and evangelical identity would indeed have been dissolved. Are there contemporary contexts in which the redefinition of biblical authority has gone that far, where we should write, not simply of "the global diffusion of evangelicalism,"[64] but of its dissolution? I suspect the answer is "Probably, yes," though I do not think that they yet form anything like the majority. One of the largest of Brazil's

---

[62]Aminta Arrington, *Hymns of the Everlasting Hills: Practicing Faith in Southwest China* (University Park: Penn State University Press, 2019).

[63]Wilson McMahon, "An Analysis of the Reception and Appropriation of the Bible by Manobo Christians in Central Mindanao, Philippines," PhD diss., University of Edinburgh, 2017), 188-89, 194-99.

[64]See Brian Stanley, *The Global Diffusion of Evangelicalism: The Age of Billy Graham and John Stott* (Nottingham: Inter-Varsity Press, 2013).

neo-Pentecostal churches, the Igreja Universal do Reino de Deus (IURD), requires of its new members at their baptism that they declare their belief in the Bible as the eternal Word of God. Yet the use made of the Bible in worship services is almost entirely performative. Texts—or, more often, loosely recalled biblical narratives—are selected for their utility as preludes to the enactment of miracles of healing or exorcism, and the Bible itself has become a material object to be wielded as a weapon of spiritual warfare with demons. In such contexts, asks Ole Jakob Løland, who are the more biblicist, adherents of the IURD, or Catholic members of Base Ecclesial Communities seeking to discover together what message the Scriptures have to bring to their local situation?[65] It is a pertinent question, which suggests that there are indeed some sectors of the neo-Pentecostal movement that do not merit the label "evangelical."

We turn, finally, to the fourth corner of the Bebbington Quadrilateral: crucicentrism. Evangelicals, of course, are not the only Christian tradition to make the cross central: Counter-Reformation Catholicism did so as well, though the exemplarist and passionist message conveyed by the crucifix is different from that of the empty Protestant cross. The question to pursue may therefore be, not whether the cross remains central in much of contemporary non-Western Christianity, but rather in what way or ways it is central, and how these compare with the consistent emphasis on substitutionary atonement that has been the hallmark of Western evangelicalism. McMahon found that the Manobo of Mindanao are drawn to an essentially exemplarist theory of the atonement, despite their evangelical missionaries teaching a substitutionary atonement. He suggests that in a context in which people live in continual fear of the arbitrary intervention of the spirits in their lives, an understanding of the Cross as the act that supremely expressed the consistent kindness and mercy of God has particular appeal. There may also be some influence from Catholic devotion to the suffering Christ, although Catholic missions scarcely reached the inland territory of the Manobo.[66]

If any generalization can be offered, it would be that in much of the non-European world the accent has frequently shifted from the cross as a juridical

---

[65]Ole Jakob Løland, "The Position of the Biblical Canon in Brazil: From Catholic Rediscovery to neo-Pentecostal Marginalisation," *Studies in World Christianity* 21, no. 2 (2015): 98-118.
[66]McMahon, "Analysis of the Reception," 231-33.

solution to the problem of the individual's sin to the cross as a paradoxical exemplification of the victory of God over the powers of darkness. One example must suffice here. J. H. Lorrain and F. W. Savidge, the pioneering English Baptist missionaries to south Lushai (Mizoram), began their evangelistic preaching in 1903 with the classic evangelical message that Christ offered salvation from the penalty of sin, but found that the Mizos "had no sense of sin and felt no need for such a Saviour." Lorrain and Savidge changed their tune to one that proclaimed Christ as the one who in the name of Pathian (the Mizo high god) had on the cross defeated the power of evil spirits and secured entrance for all into the Mizo paradise—Pialral—and found an almost immediate response in terms of conversions.[67]

Unearthly Powers, a recent book by the Oxford historian and anthropologist Alan Strathern, has propounded a universal theory that divides religion into two essential types, immanentist and transcendentalist.[68] Immanentist religion is experimental and experiential, and deploys ritual to harness the unpredictable power of supernatural forces ("metapersons") to ensure that these work to the protection and flourishing, rather than to the detriment, of human communities. Transcendentalist religion, by contrast, is concerned to transcend the limitations of mundane existence and liberate humans from the fallibility of the human condition. It is concerned to preserve truth and individual morality, and not simply with what works for the community. Its teaching is enshrined in sacred Scriptures, whose exposition is the task of a clerisy of religious specialists. The immanentist variety of religion is primary (it used to be called "primal"), whereas transcendentalism is a subsequent superstructure, parasitic on an immanentist base. It is able to make conversionist headway only by making a claim to be more effective on immanentist terms than the primal immanentism that it seeks to replace. The Reformation, argues Strathern, was a reassertion of transcendentalism, seeking to exalt the otherness of God over the realm of the mundane, and to curb the exploitative wonder-working to which immanentist popular Catholicism was so prone. Conversely, he sees Pentecostalism, and the prosperity gospel in particular, as the latest example of the universal tendency of immanentism to resurface, displacing concerns

---

[67] Stanley, *History of the Baptist Missionary Society*, 272.

[68] Alan Strathern, *Unearthly Powers: Religious and Political Change in World History* (Cambridge: Cambridge University Press, 2019).

for doctrinal orthodoxy with a preoccupation with spiritual power and all that makes for human flourishing.[69]

Strathern's thesis is an appealing one, even if painted on such a broad canvas as to make specialists in the history of one religion or another uneasy (his discussion embraces Buddhism as well as Christianity). His Christian examples are taken more from early modern Catholicism than from Protestant evangelicalism, though the evangelical missions to the Pacific in the nineteenth century do receive some attention. Where do we fit evangelicalism within his schema? On the one hand, it seems to be emphatically transcendentalist, focused on individual salvation, scriptural exposition and defence of the truth. Yet on the other, it has always been more of a populist and lay movement than a clerical one. It has frequently made its appeal to large groups gathered in camp or revival meetings or, in non-European contexts, to entire communities.

Evangelical Christianity has thus tended to oscillate between the transcendentalist and immanentist poles. At the Reformed end of the spectrum it has been most obviously transcendentalist, reining in the excesses of popular religiosity through a learned teaching ministry and strong confessional statements. At the more experiential or charismatic end of the spectrum it has made many compromises with immanentism. It can sometimes pursue spiritual power with a pragmatic single-mindedness that keeps the evangelical clerisy awake at night, yet is deeply appealing to many ordinary people, especially those who live in continual awareness of the unpredictability of the natural world and the spiritual forces that lie behind it. Once transmitted to the non-European world and removed from an Enlightenment framework, evangelicalism has gravitated increasingly towards the immanentist pole. Conversionism remains a near-universal feature, but it now often exhibits the more explicitly corporate dimensions typical of immanentist religion. Biblicism also survives, but in places at least, it now displays varying degrees of approximation to a ritual rather than cognitive understanding of the power of the Scriptures that threatens to take evangelicalism back to a pre-Reformation approach to sacred objects. Crucicentrism also survives, but increasingly clothed in immanentist dress, being reoriented towards issues of spiritual power and contestation. To that extent, there is a plausible case

---

[69]Strathern, *Unearthly Powers*, 87, 88n307, 100-102.

to be made that evangelicalism in the non-Western world exhibits a fifth defining characteristic, namely a consistent emphasis on the tangible power of the Holy Spirit, who communicates the victory of Christ over the spirit world and the powers of darkness to the experience of believers.[70] Of the four points of the quadrilateral, activism has changed least, though inevitably the goals to which activism is directed are affected whenever substantial modifications take place to the meaning attached to conversion, the atoning work of the cross, or the authority of the Bible.

These reflections should not be taken as a criticism of Bebbington's thesis. Rather they should be interpreted as an extension of his claim that evangelical forms of Christianity have frequently proved unwittingly responsive to the cultural environment in which they seek to discharge their mission. Evangelicals affirm the abiding relevance of an atonement-centred gospel as a deposit of faith, but their gospel is more incarnational than they realize: it takes flesh within each of the cultural settings in which it finds a home.

It is all too possible to exaggerate the novelty of the transformations I have outlined, or to imagine that they have to do with a primarily geographical transition from Western to non-Western contexts. In reality they represent intensifications of trends that were present from the early days of the evangelical movement. Those who were converted by the eighteenth-century revivals were often unlettered people whose spiritual experience was touched by the everyday realities of poverty, suffering, the power of evil, and the nearness of death—the same realities that fashion the spirituality of millions of non-Western Christians today. From time to time, even early evangelicalism displayed phenomena reminiscent of aspects of contemporary neo-Pentecostalism. Zinzendorf once healed a brother by the laying on of hands and prayer, though he never did it again.[71] Wesley's followers sometimes experienced visions, healings, revelations by the Spirit, and physical convulsions, though he underplayed their significance.[72] In the 1840s, in the Württemberg village of Möttlingen, the Pietist pastor Johann-Christoph Blumhardt finally succeeded in healing a deeply afflicted woman in his congregation by an act of exorcism. A revival ensued, in which many were healed and delivered

---

[70]This suggestion was made at the Baylor symposium by Dr. John Maiden of the Open University.
[71]Ward, Early Evangelicalism, 104-5.
[72]Henry D. Rack, Reasonable Enthusiast: John Wesley and the Rise of Methodism (Philadelphia: Trinity Press International, 1989), 276.

from the power of the devil. In 1852 Blumhardt took over the former sulphur bath at Bad Boll and made it into a centre for healing and exorcism. After his death in 1880, his son Christoph continued the ministry. In this way Württemberg Pietism retained a very lively sense of the malign powers of Satan. The missionaries of the Bremen Mission—most of whom came from Württemberg, and who for a time were trained in the Basel Mission seminary—then took that perception with them to the Ewe people of the Gold Coast and applied it to the realm of the traditional spirits that confronted them there. "Thus," argues Birgit Meyer, "there is a direct line from nineteenth-century Awakened Pietism to twentieth-century Pentecostalism."[73] Meyer's statement was made with primary reference to German rather than African Pentecostalism, though her clear implication is that the link applies to West Africa as well. Whether the line is quite so direct in the African context is debatable, but her words provide a salutary caution against any temptation to erect a simple antithesis between a supposedly rational Enlightenment evangelicalism and a supposedly irrational modern Pentecostalism.

Head and heart coexist in ambiguous ways in the history and contemporary experience of the evangelical movement, which is why David Bebbington's insistence that scholarship on the history of Christianity—and specifically of evangelicalism—must bring head and heart together is so necessary. For his own superb modeling of that synthesis, exemplifying the Christian mind at work in the field of history, we are all deeply grateful.

---

[73]Birgit Meyer, *Translating the Devil: Religion and Modernity Among the Ewe in Ghana* (Edinburgh: Edinburgh University Press for the International African Institute, 2010), 46; for the links of the Norddeutsche Missionsgesellschaft (Bremen Mission) to Württemberg and the Basel Mission seminary, see 29.

Acknowledgments

Thomas S. Kidd

EVERY LEAF, LINE, AND LETTER had its origins in a conference to honor David Bebbington on the occasion of his retirement from a Personal Chair in History at the University of Stirling and his seventieth birthday.[1] The overwhelming sense of the volume's contributors, both in the chapters here and at that scholarly conference at Baylor University in fall 2019, is that Bebbington's greatness as a scholar is exceeded only by his generosity and kindness as a person. For decades Bebbington has trained a host of formidable doctoral students who have taken positions in multiple countries at colleges, universities, foundations, and more, and have published countless books and articles on evangelicalism and related historical topics. Many other scholars (including me) who were not students of Bebbington have benefitted from innumerable conversations, exhortations, endorsements, and readings he has tirelessly given.

Generosity is one of the defining traits of David Bebbington's life and career. We could no doubt compile thousands of examples of that trait, but one will suffice. (David would likely insist that purely personal reflections would muddy up this book, anyway.) I first met David at a conference on Jonathan Edwards that convened in Miami—an improbable location for discussing Edwards—in the year 2000. I was a graduate student at Notre Dame, and I was unpublished and undistinguished. But I knew who David

---

[1] A festschrift for Bebbington includes a bibliography of his writings (up to that point!): Anthony R. Cross, Peter J. Morden, and Ian M. Randall, eds., *Pathways and Patterns in History: Essays on Baptists, Evangelicals, and the Modern World in Honour of David Bebbington* (London: Spurgeon's College / The Baptist Historical Society, 2015).

was, and I hoped maybe I could introduce myself, since he was on the program. David ended up sitting with me for a long time, letting me tell him about my dissertation-in-progress. He asked his now-familiar probing questions and allowed me to do most of the talking. Every friend, colleague, and student of David's has a similar story about his generosity, grace, and kindness. The Quadrilateral is important, and his books are great, but these traits are what we love about him most.

Contributors

David Bebbington is emeritus professor of history at the University of Stirling in Scotland. An undergraduate at Jesus College, Cambridge (1968–1971), he began his doctoral studies there (1971–1973) before becoming a research fellow of Fitzwilliam College, Cambridge (1973–1976). From 1976 he taught at the University of Stirling, where from 1999 to 2019 he was Professor of History. He has also taught at the University of Alabama, Birmingham, at Regent College, Vancouver, at Notre Dame University, Indiana, at the University of Pretoria, South Africa, and on many occasions as visiting distinguished professor of history at Baylor University, Texas. He has served as president of the Ecclesiastical History Society (2006–2007) and was president of the Scottish Church History Society from 2016 to 2020. In 2016 he was elected a fellow of the Royal Society of Edinburgh.

His principal research interests are in the history of religion, politics, ideas, and society in Britain from the eighteenth to the twentieth century and in the history of the global evangelical movement. His books include *Evangelicalism in Modern Britain: A History from the 1730s to the 1980s* (1989), *Victorian Nonconformity* (1992), *William Ewart Gladstone: Faith and Politics in Victorian Britain* (1993), *Holiness in Nineteenth-Century England* (2000), *The Mind of Gladstone: Religion, Homer and Politics* (2004), *The Dominance of Evangelicalism: The Age of Spurgeon and Moody* (2005), *Victorian Religious Revivals: Culture and Piety in Local and Global Contexts (2012), Baptists through the Centuries: A History of a Global People* (2nd ed., 2018), and *Patterns in History: A Christian Perspective on Historical Thought* (4th ed., 2018).

Kristina Benham is a PhD candidate at Baylor University and a historian of early American religion and politics. She is currently working on a dissertation on the exodus narrative in public debate and national identity from the American

Revolution to the Civil War. She also works as an instructor at Baylor with a plan to find a permanent position teaching and researching in American history.

Catherine Brekus is the Charles Warren Professor of the History of Religion in America at Harvard Divinity School. Her most recent books include *Sarah Osborn's World: The Rise of Evangelical Christianity in Early America* and *Sarah Osborn's Collected Writings*.

Malcolm Foley is a PhD candidate at Baylor University, specializing in the history of Christianity and lynching. He is working on a dissertation about Black Christian responses to lynching in the late nineteenth and early twentieth centuries. He received his MDiv from Yale Divinity School and his BA from Washington University in St. Louis.

Bruce Hindmarsh is the James M. Houston Professor of Spiritual Theology and Professor of the History of Christianity at Regent College in Vancouver. His writings include *John Newton and the English Evangelical Tradition*; *The Evangelical Conversion Narrative*; and *The Spirit of Early Evangelicalism*.

Thomas S. Kidd is the James Vardaman Distinguished Professor of History at Baylor University, and the associate director of Baylor's Institute for Studies of Religion. His recent books include *Who Is an Evangelical? The History of a Movement in Crisis*; and *Benjamin Franklin: The Religious Life of a Founding Father*.

Timothy Larsen is McManis Professor of Christian Thought, Wheaton College, and an Honorary Fellow, School of Divinity, University of Edinburgh. He has been a visiting fellow at Trinity College, Cambridge, All Souls College, Oxford, and Christ Church, Oxford. His books include *Crisis of Doubt: Honest Faith in Nineteenth-Century England*; *A People of One Book: The Bible and the Victorians*; *The Slain God: Anthropologists and the Christian Faith*; and *John Stuart Mill: A Secular Life*.

K. Elise Leal is assistant professor of Early American History at Whitworth University. Her scholarship focuses on religion and culture in eighteenth- and nineteenth-century America, with particular emphasis on gender, childhood, and social reform. She is completing a monograph on Sunday schools and youth religious leadership in the early republic. She received her PhD in history from Baylor University.

John Maiden is senior lecturer in religious studies at The Open University in the United Kingdom. He is author of various studies on evangelical, Pentecostal, and charismatic Christianities, including for *Journal of American*

Studies, Journal of Religious History, Twentieth Century British History, and *Studies in World Christianity* and is currently writing a transnational history of charismatic renewal in the Anglo-World. He is the author of the *National Religion and the Prayer Book Controversy, 1927–1928*; coeditor of *Anglican Evangelicals and the Church of England in the Twentieth Century: Reform, Resistance and Renewal*; and coeditor of the forthcoming *Charismatic Renewal in Europe and the United States since 1950*. His doctoral work was supervised by David W. Bebbington.

Mark A. Noll is Francis A. McAnaney Professor of History Emeritus at the University of Notre Dame. His books include *In the Beginning Was the Word: The Bible in American Public Life, 1492–1783* (2016); *The Civil War as a Theological Crisis* (2006); and the second edition of *A History of Christianity in the United States and Canada* (2019).

Mary Riso is director of education administration for the School of Education and adjunct instructor at Gordon College in Wenham, Massachusetts. She received her PhD in history from the University of Stirling under the supervision of professor David W. Bebbington, her MDiv and ThM from Gordon-Conwell Theological Seminary, and her BA from Georgetown University. Mary is the author of *Heroines: The Lives of Great Literary Characters and What They Have to Teach Us*; and *The Narrative of the Good Death: The Evangelical Deathbed in Victorian England*.

Brian Stanley is professor of world Christianity in the University of Edinburgh. He has published widely on the history of Christian missions and the growth of world Christianity. His two most recent books are *The Global Diffusion of Evangelicalism: The Age of Billy Graham and John Stott*; and *Christianity in the Twentieth Century: A World History*.

Jonathan Yeager is UC Foundation and Guerry Associate Professor of Religion at the University of Tennessee at Chattanooga, where he teaches courses on Christian history and thought. His scholarship includes *Enlightened Evangelicalism: The Life of John Erskine*; *Early Evangelicalism: A Reader*; *Jonathan Edwards and Transatlantic Print Culture*; *The Oxford Handbook of Early Evangelicalism* (forthcoming); and *Understanding and Teaching Religion in American History* (coauthored with Karen Johnson).

General Index

Scripture Index